HIGH PERFORMANCE
CAPRIS
Gold Portfolio
1969-1987

Compiled by
R.M. Clarke

ISBN 1 870642 988

Booklands Books Ltd.
PO Box 146, Cobham, KT11 1LG
Surrey, England
Printed in Hong Kong

BROOKLANDS BOOKS

BROOKLANDS ROAD TEST SERIES

Abarth Gold Portfolio 1950-1971
AC Ace & Aceca 1953-1983
Alfa Romeo Giulietta Gold Portfolio 1954-1965
Alfa Romeo Giulia Berlinas 1962-1976
Alfa Romeo Giulia Coupés 1963-1976
Alfa Romeo Giulia Coupés Gold P. 1963-1976
Alfa Romeo Spider 1966-1990
Alfa Romeo Spider Gold Portfolio 1966-1991
Alfa Romeo Alfasud 1972-1984
Alfa Romeo Alfetta Coupés & Saloons Gold Portfolio 1974-1987
Alfa Romeo Alfetta GTV6 1980-1987
Allard Gold Portfolio 1937-1959
Alvis Gold Portfolio 1919-1967
American Motors Muscle Cars 1966-1970
Armstrong Siddeley Gold Portfolio 1945-1960
Aston Martin Gold Portfolio 1972-1985
Austin Seven 1922-1982
Austin A30 & A35 1951-1962
Austin Healey 100 & 100/6 Gold P. 1952-1959
Austin Healey 3000 Gold Portfolio 1959-1967
Austin Healey Sprite 1958-1971
BMW Six Cyl. Coupés 1969-1975
BMW 1600 Collection No.1 1966-1981
BMW 2002 Gold Portfolio1968-1976
BMW 316, 318, 320 (4 cyl.) Gold P. 1975-1990
BMW 320, 323, 325 (6 cyl.) Gold P .1977-1990
BMW 5 Series Gold Portfolio1981-1987
BMW M Series Performance Portfolio1976-1993
Bristol Cars Gold Portfolio 1946-1992
Buick Automobiles 1947-1960
Buick Muscle Cars 1965-1970
Cadillac Automobiles 1949-1959
Cadillac Automobiles 1960-1969
Chevrolet 1955-1957
Chevrolet Impala & SS 1958-1971
Chevrolet Corvair 1959-1969
Chevy El Camino & SS 1959-1987
Chevy II Nova & SS 1962-1973
Chevelle & SS Muscle Portfolio 1964-1972
Chevrolet Muscle Cars 1966-1971
Chevy Blazer 1969-1981
Chevrolet Corvette Gold Portfolio 1953-1962
Chevrolet Corvette Sting Ray Gold P. 1963-1967
Chevrolet Corvette Gold Portfolio 1968-1977
High Performance Corvettes 1983-1989
Camaro Muscle Portfolio 1967-1973
Chevrolet Camaro Z28 & SS 1966-1973
Chevrolet Camaro & Z28 1973-1981
High Performance Camaros 1982-1988
Chrysler 300 Gold Portfolio 1955-1970
Chrysler Valiant 1960-1962
Citroen Traction Avant Gold Portfolio 1934-1957
Citroen 2CV 1948-1988
Citroen DS & ID 1955-1975
Citroen SM 1970-1975
Cobras & Replicas 1962-1983
Shelby Cobra Gold Portfolio 1962-1969
Cobras & Cobra Replicas Gold P. 1962-1989
Cunningham Automobiles 1951-1955
Daimler SP250 Sports & V-8 250 Saloon Gold Portfolio 1959-1969
Datsun Roadsters 1962-1971
Datsun 240Z 1970-1973
Datsun 280Z & ZX 1975-1983
De Tomaso Collection No. 1 1962-1981
Dodge Charger 1966-1974
Dodge Muscle Cars 1967-1970
Dodge Viper on the Road
Excalibur Collection No. 1 1952-1981
Facel Vega 1954-1964
Ferrari Cars 1946-1956
Ferrari Collection No. 1 1960-1970
Ferrari Dino 1965-1974
Ferrari Dino 308 1974-1979
Ferrari 308 & Mondial 1980-1984
Motor & T&CC Ferrari 1966-1976
Motor & T&CC Ferrari 1976-1984
Fiat Pininfarina 124 & 2000 Spider 1968-1985
Fiat-Bertone X1/9 1973-1988
Ford Consul, Zephyr, Zodiac Mk.I & II 1950-1962
Ford Zephyr, Zodiac, Executive, Mk.III & Mk.IV 1962-1971
Ford Cortina 1600E & GT 1967-1970
High Performance Capris Gold P. 1969-1987
Capri Muscle Portfolio 1974-1987
High Performance Fiestas 1979-1991
High Performance Escorts Mk.I 1968-1974
High Performance Escorts Mk.II 1975-1980
High Performance Escorts 1980-1985
High Performance Escorts 1985-1990
High Performance Sierras & Merkurs Gold Portfolio 1983-1990
Ford Automobiles 1949-1959
Ford Fairlane 1955-1970
Ford Ranchero 1957-1959
Thunderbird 1955-1957
Thunderbird 1958-1963
Thunderbird 1964-1976
Ford Falcon 1960-1970
Ford GT40 Gold Portfolio 1964-1987
Ford Bronco 1966-1977
Ford Bronco 1978-1988
Holden 1948-1962
Honda CRX 1983-1987
Hudson & Railton 1936-1940
Jaguar and SS Gold Portfolio 1931-1951
Jaguar XK120, 140, 150 Gold P. 1948-1960
Jaguar Mk.VII, VIII, IX, X, 420 Gold P.1950-1970
Jaguar 1957-1961
Jaguar Mk.2 1959-1969
Jaguar Cars 1961-1964
Jaguar E-Type Gold Portfolio 1961-1971
Jaguar E-Type 1966-1971
Jaguar E-Type V-12 1971-1975
Jaguar XJ12, XJ5.3, V12 Gold P. 1972-1990
Jaguar XJ6 Series II 1973-1979
Jaguar XJ6 Series III 1979-1986
Jaguar XJS Gold Portfolio 1975-1990
Jeep CJ5 & CJ6 1960-1976
Jeep CJ5 & CJ7 1976-1986
Jensen Cars 1946-1967
Jensen Cars 1967-1979
Jensen Interceptor Gold Portfolio 1966-1986
Jensen Healey 1972-1976
Lagonda Gold Portfolio 1919-1964
Lamborghini Cars 1964-1970
Lamborghini Countach & Urraco 1974-1980
Lamborghini Countach & Jalpa 1980-1985
Lancia Fulvia Gold Portfolio 1963-1976
Lancia Stratos 1972-1985
Land Rover Series I 1948-1958
Land Rover Series II & IIa 1958-1971
Land Rover Series III 1971-1985
Land Rover 90 & 110 1983-1989
Lincoln Gold Portfolio 1949-1960
Lincoln Continental 1961-1969
Lincoln Continental 1969-1976
Lotus & Caterham Seven Gold P. 1957-1989
Lotus Elite 1957-1964
Lotus Elite & Eclat 1974-1982
Lotus Elan Gold Portfolio 1962-1974
Lotus Elan Collection No. 2 1963-1972
Lotus Cortina Gold Portfolio 1963-1970
Lotus Europa Gold Portfolio 1966-1975
Lotus Turbo Esprit 1980-1986
Motor & T&CC on Lotus 1979-1983
Marcos Cars 1960-1988
Maserati 1965-1970
Maserati 1970-1975
Mazda RX-7 Collection No. 1 1978-1981
Mercedes Benz Cars 1949-1954
Mercedes Benz Competition Cars 1950-1957
Mercedes Benz Cars 1954-1957
Mercedes Benz Cars 1957-1961
Mercedes 190 & 300 SL 1954-1963
Mercedes 230/250/280SL 1963-1971
Mercedes Benz SLs & SLCs Gold P. 1971-1989
Mercedes S & 600 1965-1972
Mercedes S Class 1972-1979
Mercury Muscle Cars 1966-1971
Metropolitan 1954-1962
MG Gold Portfolio 1929-1939
MG TC 1945-1949
MG TD 1949-1953
MG TF 1953-1955
MG Cars 1959-1962
MGA & Twin Cam Gold Portfolio 1955-1962
MG Midget 1961-1980
MGB Roadsters 1962-1980
MGB MGC & V8 Gold Portfolio 1962-1980
MGB GT 1965-1980
Mini Cooper Gold Portfolio 1961-1971
Mini Muscle Cars 1961-1979
Mini Moke 1964-1989
Mopar Muscle Cars 1964-1967
Morgan Three-Wheeler Gold Portfolio 1910-1952
Morgan Plus 4 & Four 4 Gold P. 1936-1967
Morgan Cars 1960-1970
Morgan Cars Gold Portfolio 1968-1989
Morris Minor Collection No. 1 1948-1980
Shelby Mustang Muscle Portfolio 1965-1970
Mustang Muscle Cars 1967-1971
High Performance Mustang IIs 1974-1978
High Performance Mustangs 1982-1988
Oldsmobile Automobiles 1955-1963
Oldsmobile Cutlass & 4-4-2 1964-1972
Oldsmobile Muscle Cars 1964-1971
Oldsmobile Toronado 1966-1978
Opel GT 1968-1973
Packard Gold Portfolio 1946-1958
Pantera Gold Portfolio 1970-1989
Panther Gold Portfolio 1972-1990
Plymouth Barracuda 1964-1974
Plymouth Muscle Cars 1966-1971
Pontiac Tempest & GTO 1961-1965
Pontiac Muscle Cars 1966-1972
Pontiac Firebird & Trans-Am 1973-1981
High Performance Firebirds 1982-1988
Pontiac Fiero 1984-1988
Porsche 356 1952-1965
Porsche Cars in the 60's
Porsche Cars 1960-1964
Porsche Cars 1964-1968
Porsche Cars 1968-1972
Porsche Cars 1972-1975
Porsche 911 1965-1969
Porsche 911 1970-1972
Porsche 911 1973-1977
Porsche 911 Carrera 1973-1977
Porsche 911 Turbo 1975-1984
Porsche 911 SC 1978-1983
Porsche 914 Collection No. 1 1969-1983
Porsche 914 Gold Portfolio 1969-1976
Porsche 924 Gold Portfolio 1975-1988
Porsche 928 1977-1989
Porsche 944 1981-1985
Range Rover Gold Portfolio 1970-1992
Reliant Scimitar 1964-1986
Riley Gold Portfolio 1924-1939
Riley 1.5 & 2.5 Litre Gold Portfolio 1945-1955
Rolls Royce Silver Cloud & Bentley 'S' Series Gold Portfolio 1955-1965
Rolls Royce Silver Shadow 1965-1981
Rover P4 1949-1959
Rover P4 1955-1964
Rover 3 & 3.5 Litre Gold Portfolio 1958-1973
Rover 2000 & 2200 1963-1977
Rover 3500 1968-1977
Rover 3500 & Vitesse 1976-1986
Saab Sonett Collection No.1 1966-1974
Saab Turbo 1976-1983
Studebaker Gold Portfolio 1947-1966
Studebaker Hawks & Larks 1956-1963
Avanti 1962-1990
Sunbeam Tiger & Alpine Gold P. 1959-1967
Toyota MR2 1984-1988
Toyota Land Cruiser 1956-1984
Triumph TR2 & TR3 1952-1960
Triumph TR4, TR5, TR250 1961-1968
Triumph TR6 Gold Portfolio 1969-1976
Triumph TR7 & TR8 1975-1982
Triumph Herald 1959-1971
Triumph Vitesse 1962-1971
Triumph Spitfire Gold Portfolio 1962-1980
Triumph 2000, 2.5, 2500 1963-1977
Triumph GT6 1966-1974
Triumph Stag 1970-1980
TVR Gold Portfolio 1959-1990
VW Beetle Gold Portfolio1935-1967
VW Beetle Gold Portfolio1968-1991
VW Beetle Collection No.1 1970-1982
VW Karmann Ghia 1955-1982
VW Bus, Camper, Van 1954-1967
VW Bus, Camper, Van 1968-1979
VW Bus, Camper, Van 1979-1989
VW Scirocco 1974-1981
VW Golf GTI 1976-1986
Volvo PV444 & PV544 1945-1965
Volvo Amazon-120 Gold Portfolio 1956-1970
Volvo 1800 Gold Portfolio 1960-1973

BROOKLANDS ROAD & TRACK SERIES

Road & Track on Alfa Romeo 1949-1963
Road & Track on Alfa Romeo 1964-1970
Road & Track on Alfa Romeo 1971-1976
Road & Track on Alfa Romeo 1977-1989
Road & Track on Aston Martin 1962-1990
Road & Track on Auburn Cord and Duesenburg 1952-1984
Road & Track on Audi & Auto Union 1952-1980
Road & Track on Audi & Auto Union 1980-1986
Road & Track on Austin Healey 1953-1970
Road & Track on BMW Cars 1966-1974
Road & Track on BMW Cars 1975-1978
Road & Track on BMW Cars 1979-1983
Road & Track on Cobra, Shelby & Ford GT40 1962-1992
Road & Track on Corvette 1953-1967
Road & Track on Corvette 1968-1982
Road & Track on Corvette 1982-1986
Road & Track on Corvette 1986-1990
Road & Track on Datsun Z 1970-1983
Road & Track on Ferrari 1975-1981
Road & Track on Ferrari 1981-1984
Road & Track on Ferrari 1984-1988
Road & Track on Fiat Sports Cars 1968-1987
Road & Track on Jaguar 1950-1960
Road & Track on Jaguar 1961-1968
Road & Track on Jaguar 1968-1974
Road & Track on Jaguar 1974-1982
Road & Track on Jaguar 1983-1989
Road & Track on Lamborghini 1964-1985
Road & Track on Lotus 1972-1981
Road & Track on Maserati 1952-1974
Road & Track on Maserati 1975-1983
R& T on Mazda RX7 & MX5 Miata 1986-1991
Road & Track on Mercedes 1952-1962
Road & Track on Mercedes 1963-1970
Road & Track on Mercedes 1971-1979
Road & Track on Mercedes 1980-1987
Road & Track on MG Sports Cars 1949-1961
Road & Track on MG Sports Cars 1962-1980
Road & Track on Mustang 1964-1977
R&T on Nissan 300-ZX & Turbo 1984-1989
Road & Track on Peugeot 1955-1986
Road & Track on Pontiac 1960-1983
Road & Track on Porsche 1951-1967
Road & Track on Porsche 1968-1971
Road & Track on Porsche 1972-1975
Road & Track on Porsche 1975-1978
Road & Track on Porsche 1979-1982
Road & Track on Porsche 1982-1985
Road & Track on Porsche 1985-1988
R&T on Rolls Royce & Bentley 1950-1965
R&T on Rolls Royce & Bentley 1966-1984
Road & Track on Saab 1972-1992
R&T on Toyota Sports & GT Cars 1966-1984
R&T on Triumph Sports Cars 1953-1967
R&T on Triumph Sports Cars 1967-1974
R&T on Triumph Sports Cars 1974-1982
Road & Track on Volkswagen 1951-1968
Road & Track on Volkswagen 1968-1978
Road & Track on Volkswagen 1978-1985
Road & Track on Volvo 1957-1974
Road & Track on Volvo 1975-1985
Road & Track - Henry Manney at Large and Abroad

BROOKLANDS CAR AND DRIVER SERIES

Car and Driver on BMW 1955-1977
Car and Driver on BMW 1977-1985
Car and Driver on Cobra, Shelby & Ford GT40 1963-1984
Car and Driver on Corvette 1956-1967
Car and Driver on Corvette 1968-1977
Car and Driver on Corvette 1978-1982
Car and Driver on Corvette 1983-1988
Cand D on Datsun Z 1600 & 2000 1966-1984
Car and Driver on Ferrari 1955-1962
Car and Driver on Ferrari 1963-1975
Car and Driver on Ferrari 1976-1983
Car and Driver on Mopar 1956-1967
Car and Driver on Mopar 1968-1975
Car and Driver on Mustang 1964-1972
Car and Driver on Pontiac 1961-1975
Car and Driver on Porsche 1955-1962
Car and Driver on Porsche 1963-1970
Car and Driver on Porsche 1970-1976
Car and Driver on Porsche 1977-1981
Car and Driver on Porsche 1982-1986
Car and Driver on Saab 1956-1985
Car and Driver on Volvo 1955-1986

BROOKLANDS PRACTICAL CLASSICS SERIES

PC on Austin A40 Restoration
PC on Land Rover Restoration
PC on Metalworking in Restoration
PC on Midget/Sprite Restoration
PC on Mini Cooper Restoration
PC on MGB Restoration
PC on Morris Minor Restoration
PC on Sunbeam Rapier Restoration
PC on Triumph Herald/Vitesse
PC on Spitfire Restoration
PC on Beetle Restoration
PC on 1930s Car Restoration

BROOKLANDS HOT ROD 'MUSCLECAR & HI-PO ENGINES' SERIES

Chevy 265 & 283
Chevy 302 & 327
Chevy 348 & 409
Chevy 350 & 400
Chevy 396 & 427
Chevy 454 thru 512
Chrysler Hemi
Chrysler 273, 318, 340 & 360
Chrysler 361, 383, 400, 413, 426, 440
Ford 289, 302, Boss 302 & 351W
Ford 351C & Boss 351
Ford Big Block

BROOKLANDS RESTORATION SERIES

Auto Restoration Tips & Techniques
Basic Bodywork Tips & Techniques
Basic Painting Tips & Techniques
Camaro Restoration Tips & Techniques
Chevrolet High Performance Tips & Techniques
Chevy Engine Swapping Tips & Techniques
Chevy GMC Pickup Repair
Chrysler Engine Swapping Tips & Techniques
Custom Painting Tips & Techniques
Engine Swapping Tips & Techniques
Ford Pickup Repair
How to Build a Street Rod
Land Rover Restoration Tips & Techniques
Mustang Restoration Tips & Techniques
Performance Tuning - Chevrolets of the '60s
Performance Tuning - Pontiacs of the '60s

BROOKLANDS MILITARY VEHICLES SERIES

Allied Military Vehicles No.1 1942-1945
Allied Military Vehicles No.2 1941-1946
Complete WW2 Military Jeep Manual
Dodge Military Vehicles No.1 1940-1945
Hail To The Jeep
Land Rovers in Military Service
Off Road Jeeps: Civ. & Mil. 1944-1971
US Military Vehicles 1941-1945
US Army Military Vehicles WW2-TM9-2800
VW Kubelwagen Military Portfolio1940-1975
WW2 Jeep Military Portfolio 1940-1990

2743

BROOKLANDS BOOKS

CONTENTS

BROOKLANDS BOOKS

ACKNOWLEDGEMENTS

We produced our first book on the Capri — Capri Muscle Cars 1969-1983 early in 1984. At that time the Capri had been around for nearly 15 years and we fully expected production to come to an end in the forseeable future — how wrong we were.

New models were available well into 1987. Actually, the building of Capris ended in December 1986 with the manufacture of just over a thousand '280 Specials'. This brought the total number built over 18 years to nearly 1.9 million units.

Capri Muscle Cars went out of print last year and we have been inundated with requests to make it available once more. We decided that the whole of the performance Capri story needed recording and so we have incorporated the original book into this larger Gold Portfolio.

We have purposely refrained from writing a detailed introduction because the job has been done so well for us by Classic and Sportscars in their excellent Profile — The Car You Always Promised Yourself? — which can be found one page 175.

Brooklands Books are a reference series for automobile enthusiasts. They endeavour to make available to owners of interesting cars hard to locate information which will enable them to maintain and restore their vehicles. Fortunately the publishers of the worlds leading motoring journals have supported our aims and generously allowed us to reissue their copyright road tests and other stories.

Our thanks in this instance go to the management of Autocar, Autosport, Car — South Africa, Cars and Car Conversions, Classic and Sportscar, Custom Car, Fast Lane, Modern Motor, Motor, Motor Racing, Motor Sport, Performance Cars, Practical Classics, Road & Track, Road Test, Sports Car World, Thoroughbred and Classic Cars and What Car? for their many kindnesses.

R.M. Clarke

*Fastest Capri yet. With the Zodiac
3-litre V-6 engine beneath the
bonnet, a top speed of 114 m.p.h.
is claimed.*

Fastest British Ford yet

The Capri 3000 GT

THEY PROMISED IT when they announced the rest of the Capri range, and now Ford have unveiled the 3-litre Capri. Perhaps with this one model Ford hope to take some of the market cornered so effectively by the specialists who shoehorn the same V-6 motor into smaller Fords or even build new cars around it, because this should be *the* sporting road going Ford—we haven't tried it yet, so must reserve judgement.

Since the original car was designed around this unit, very few changes have been necessary to accept the considerably higher torque output of 173 lb.ft. against the 2-litre V-4 at 108 lb.ft. The engine is the familiar oversquare V-6 used in the Ford Zodiac, developing a gross 144 b.h.p. and a net 128 b.h.p. at 4,750 r.p.m: Changes to it include a revised sump to clear the steering rack and a consequently modified oil pick-up, and a fabricated exhaust manifold to reduce the losses of the Zodiac system and make sure that 128 b.h.p. is a minimum rather than a mean output in production units.

To get the gear lever in the right place and obviate any need for increasing clearance around the gearbox, Ford have made a new gearbox casting to take the standard Zodiac wide ratios; hopes that these would be closer

in the more sporting car are unfounded and first gear, at least, is dictated by Ford requirements for low-speed crawling at 7 m.p.h. and the ability to tow a 23½ cwt. trailer. Raising the final drive ratio to 3.22:1 makes it difficult to raise first gear on these grounds let alone on any economic considerations. With a maximum speed potential around 116 m.p.h. (computed by power comparison with the 2-litre) it was obviously necessary to raise the final drive considerably with the low revving 3-litre unit, and the new axle comes from the German Capri 2300. It has a two-piece prop-shaft, again like the German cars with the centre joint a constant velocity one, but unlike the 2-litre car which has a Hooke joint.

By a little judicious panel-beating it has proved possible to fit the complete Zodiac gearbox and overdrive, but this is obviously not a mass production possibility, and Ford preferred to use the higher final drive instead.

To keep weight distribution as even as possible, the engine is mounted far back without losing any accessibility to the rear-most plugs; it is carried on a stronger engine cross-member which is fastened to the body-work by a wide-based three-bolt fixing instead of the normal two-bolt system. The rubber mounts are different from those of the Zodiac

—little doughnuts with a steel retaining cap on the top part to stop any lateral shake. Coping with the extra loads from the increased power and also the extra weight—about 1 cwt. over the 1600GT has called for further structural reinforcement; the front side members have been reinforced and the top strut mountings have a reinforcing plate welded on top of the existing bodywork.

A few changes were necessary to the suspension, more to accommodate the power/weight increase than to make it into a sports car; the spring rates have been adjusted to give much the same periodicity as on the 1600GT, laden 78 cycles per minute front and 80 c.p.m. rear, in which condition it is about 3 inches off its bump stops. As on the other GTs, the radius arm bushes are deliberately chosen to take advantage of the conflicting geometry of radius arm and spring length to give a variable rate effect. Apparently, in Italy, there is a minimum ground clearance requirement of 4.7 in. so cars for that country have a slightly different rear spring to raise the exhaust system.

All cars will use the 5J rims whatever the option but the sculptured wheels are extra; standard tyres will be Goodyear 185/70 HR-13, high-speed radials capable of 130 m.p.h.,

with a ribbed pattern rather than the usual G800 block pattern. Ford always allow generous clearance around their wheels, really to give chain clearance, but it does let people put on wide rims without too much difficulty; to accommodate the wider tyre the lip inside the wheel arches has been slightly cut back.

Despite the possibility of having to do about 30% more work from a maximum speed stop than on a 2-litre car, the brakes were quite large enough; at the front they are now fitted with harder linings, the rear shoes are slightly wider at 2¼in. x 9in., and a servo is fitted as standard.

Perhaps the GT label did become rather obscured in its Ford environment, but one GT facet they try to keep to is a 300-mile fuel range, so the new tank is up to 13½-gallons which, on the 23½ m.p.g., achieved frequently on the prototype just makes it. The larger tank obtrudes slightly into the boot space which drops from 8.2 cu.ft. to 7.8 with the standard set of SAE cases.

No Ford write-up would be complete without a reference to NVH (Noise Vibration Harshness); we were particularly impressed with the successful assault on this with the 2-litre engine, less so on the 1600, but further attention has been paid to it on the 3-litre. The new prop-shaft, revised engine mounts, more insulation on the floor and around the facia, and better sealing of direct open air noise paths has resulted in even less NVH.

The interior is the same as for any other GT Capri but, since we last tested one, the seat belt mounts have been moved up on to a strengthened door pillar, grab handles are supplied for front and rear passengers, and the flat area in front of the rear screen has now been made into a parcel shelf with a suitable recess, in response to popular request. Options too remain the same with X (interior), L (exterior) and R packages with the addition of a washer button, still on the floor, which also causes one wipe of the screen in the L pack.

Outward differences to identify the 3-litre will be the power bulge on the bonnet (which is necessary to clear the air cleaner) twin

What goes on beneath the shell.

A neat fit. Special side members and front suspension mounting points have been fitted to carry the large engine, larger capacity radiator, and battery.

exhaust pipes, and the 3000GT badge. Its new tyres will be less obvious.

With such performance as 0-60 m.p.h. in a claimed 9.2s. (and it should do this quite easily), and a 115 m.p.h. maximum with plenty of torque as well, Ford should have the answer to many of the popular imports. PRICE: £989 plus £302 3s. 11d. tax and delivery equals £1,291 3s. 11d.

Brief specification
Engine:

Block material	Cast iron
Head material	Cast iron
Cylinders	V-6
Bore and stroke	93.66mm. (3.687 in.) x 72.41mm. (2.851 in.)
Cubic capacity	2,994 c.c. (182.7 cu. in.)
Main bearings	Four
Valves	Pushrod o.h.v.
Compression ratio	8.9:1
Carburetter	Compound Weber
Fuel pump	Mechanical diaphragm
Oil filter	Full flow replaceable element
Max. power (net)	128 b.h.p. at 4,750 r.p.m.
Max. power (gross)	144 b.h.p. at 4,750 r.p.m.
Max. Torque (net)	173 lb.ft. at 3,000 r.p.m.
Max. Torque (gross)	192 lb.ft. at 3,000 r.p.m.

Transmission:

Clutch	S.d.p. diaphragm sprung 9.5 in. dia.
Internal gearbox ratios	
Top gear	1.00
Third gear	1.412
Second gear	2.214
First gear	3.163
Reverse	3.346
Final drive	Hypoid bevel 3.22:1
M.p.h. per 1,000 r.p.m. in top	20.7
Tyres	Goodyear 185/70 HR-13
Wheels	5J-13

CAPRANG!

Just think about it. Four point seven litres of growling V-8 power socking it to the tarmac.

ALLARDS FIRST STAGES OF V8 CAPRI CONVERSION

THINKING caps on fellas! Just go back in time a little while to that day you got your first real close-up of one of Mr. Ford's new, long-nosed, short-booted Capris.

Remember when someone hoisted aloft the bonnet and laid bare that great cavernous hole, in the middle of which lay either a straight 4 with lots of space down the sides, or a V4 with lots of space at the front? In each case, the rad sits well back in said hole, with a large plate leading from it to the top of the grille, on which one could quite easily eat one's lunch.

Now think carefully and put up your hands all of you who thought: "Cor, wonder what a stinking great V8 would be like bunged in there?" or words to that effect. Well, if some similar thought didn't occur to you then or later, you're not qualified to read this magazine, so please turn back to Enid Blyton and start again. (Noddy needs readers!)

One gentleman to whom this thought did occur one fine morn happened to be a Mr. H. R. Moore, a long-standing Ford and Allard fan.

The Capri suited him well and he had ordered, from the Allard Motor Company (residing and carrying on business at 51, Upper Richmond Road, Putney, SW15) a 1600 GT in fern green, standard package model. He knew that Fords were about to sock it to the showrooms with a 3 litre V6, but thought that the American 4.7 (as fitted to the Mustang) would fill that hole to greater effect.

Allard's, who have lots of goodies hanging around their premises (of which more later) did not have any such mills on their shelves, but cast around for a while, eventually lighting upon a whole batch of them complete with ancillaries for £200 a time. For the benefit of US law enforcement officers, Allards are a gen. crowd and ship them over from the Netherlands, so any Stateside Mustang owners who loose their Vs needn't look over here.

First thing on the Capri was to attack aforementioned rad and panel, and remove same. It was immediately obvious that the Capri crossmember and steering rack were going to present The Problem.

Not only that, but the man who designed the Mustang thing saw fit to make the oil pump an integral casting at the front end — very accessible and all that, but it sticks out at a weird angle and cannot be removed to make things fit any better or to lower the overall height of the engine.

A special sump was therefore a top priority to allow the retention of the pump, get round the cross-member etc, and still allow sufficient slippy black stuff to circulate the mill. The end product is a carefully constructed sump pan of rather tortuous shape, as shown in our pic. The Mustang engine mountings were found to be only one inch out when the motor was offered up to the crossmember, so Allards built up the standard member around the mountings to bridge the gaps. It was also deemed wise to flow extra weld along the standard FoMoCo seam welds.

Talking about engine height again, which we did a few lines ago, it's surprising but true (as again can be seen from our wonderful picky) that the V8 is only fractionally taller than the GT.

Unfortunately, by the time you have screwed the dirty great air cleaner on top of the carb, you are quite a way above the standard bonnet line. This problem has been cured merely by obtaining a glassfibre V6 Capri bonnet,

Nearest and dearest in this shot is, of course, the £200 Mustang motor while the upturned frying pan air cleaner sits atop the 1600 GT unit. The recipient sits in the background.

Crewling on hands and paunch, our photographer got this one of the somewhat tortuous sump shape and re-made cross-member. Experiments may be made with different anti-roll bars later.

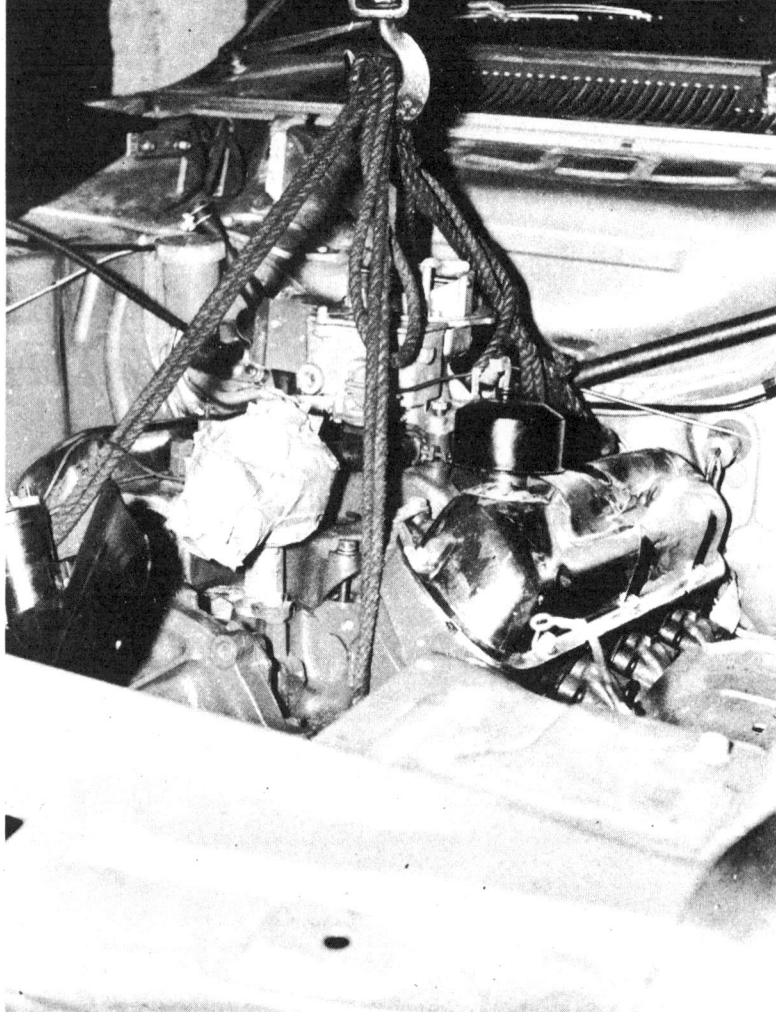

The radiator and part of the horizontal front panel have been removed and the V-8 is lowered in for a trial fitting. The battery shelf is the next to come out.

complete with sexy power bulge, which successfully envelopes the lump. If we may digress a little here — and we shall whether you like it or not — don't be too perturbed if you see a nice Emerald Green Escort circulating the Putney area with a small power bulge off-set to the off-side. At the time of writing, Alan Allard was building up a fuel-injected 1600 GT Escortina to use as his road car, and it looked like aforementioned bulge would be the only answer to the clearance problem.

Anyway, once the Capri's new engine was placed in situ, the next thing was to divert thoughts towards linking it up via items like gearbox and transmission, to the rear wheels.

The length of the Borg-Warner box from the clutch to the bell housing on the V8 is only one inch longer than standard and the tail shaft graunched the gearbox crossmember.

A new gearbox crossmember was built up for extra accommodation and to make subsequent servicing at least a possibility. Much thought had to be given to the choice of back axle. The owner is primarily interested in the Capri as a road car, yet may unleash it

onto a circuit for the occasional Race or Sprint meeting, so a goodly range of ratios was desirable. Something to take the sheer brute brutishness without shattering into a thousand cogs was also The Thing so the final decision went to the German Capri unit. This has a heavier diff casing and ratios up to 3.1 are possible. (Some of those Motorway curves must get pretty tight on a set-up like that!) In fact, present thinking indicates a 3.2 will go in to start off with.

With only minor modding, the original Mustang one-piece prop shaft will mate up to the diff, so no complicated one-off prop will be needed.

Considering the extra mass and all that, it is amazing that the Mustang engine is not all that much heavier than the Ford V6. Compared to the four-pot GT, however, the Stateside unit certainly weighs in to advantage (or disadvantage from the handling point of view). Dry weight of the GT is 260 lbs. and of the V8 is 495 lbs. The gearbox of the V8 adds another 30 lbs. over and above so it is obvious that Something Should Be Done About it in the front suspension, somewhere.

To prevent the car doing a bucking bronco (or Mustang?) and kicking it's rear wheels in the air at the slightest provocation, to say nothing of swopping ends on every bend, uprated front struts are being used along with "the largest discs we can get", to quote Alan Allard, to avoid the instant kamikaze stunt.

In fact the P.16 discs as fitted to the V6 (and the V4? . . . we've run out of catalogues) will be used and assisted by the standard 1600 GT servo.

A weight reduction course is being taken on the front end by using mild steel exhaust manifolds instead of the standard cast iron ones, which is just as well, seeing as the standard efforts wouldn't fit properly. The inlet manifold — a very hefty item of course — is alloy anyway, and that is being retained along with the not-too-special carb, at least for the time being.

Very early on, while the front under-bonnet panel and standard rad were being removed with much gusto, the problem of getting as much cool air as possible to as much radiator as possible was nestling in the back of

Not as nature intended — but who cares? The battery, which previously lived on the right of the engine compartment, is banished to the boot and the Zodiac radiator at foot of pic will have a header tank mounted to the off-side of the mill.

peoples' minds. Now, with the chief headaches sorted out, attention was diverted to keeping those hairy horses simmering without actually coming to the boil.

A commonsense sort of radiator to use may be the Zodiac, thought someone, as they had noticed it was the same height as the Capri rad. In it went, very much forward of the original postition, of course, with lots of increased capacity and a separate header tank mounted up the side of the engine room.

That was all very well, but some crafty panel cutting was then called for to allow sufficient cool air to find its way to the right place. The last job being done on the car, as we finished our Part I visit to Allard's, was the fabrication of a new air duct under the existing grille. This will entail the use of Twin-Cam Escort-style quarter bumpers and should make for a real cool custom front end when the car is complete. Most other aspects of the Capri's outward appearance will be conservative in taste, although the customer is looking forward to using normal Rostyles all round. As and when he takes to the tracks, 8 in.

Minilites on the rear and 7 or 8 in. on the front may be the order of tne day.

Things will remain pretty normal inside the cockpit, which is black needless to say, although a few supplementary instruments may go along the top of the fascia in the same style as the earlier Mk II Cortina GTs. Distinctive, but discrete, badges on a few exterior panels will convey the idea of what lurks beneath the bonnet.

In the vital statistics department, Allard's have come up with some pretty interesting comparison figures for this conversion. The power on tap from the V8 is reputed to be 225 bhp at 4400 rpm (150 net). Put that next to the following:

1600 GT:
92 bhp at 5500 rpm (80 net)
Twin-Cam:
115 bhp at 6000 rpm (100 net)

. . . and like us, you may come to the conclusion that for a small amount of work, this mill is going to produce an awful lot of results!

Alan Allard makes no secret of the fact that on a first-ever car like this, he won't be making any loot. His well-

established and highly rated Escortina conversions are finding a ready market, though, and it is hoped to get the V8 Capri going as a regular conversion along the same lines. Basic price of the car, as converted, will be around £1,700 but a host of competition and custom extras will be available to add on. The cars will be built to individual order, so don't expect to see a row of them standing (or should it be crouching?) outside the Putney premises waiting for buyers.

Any of you lot, who are familiar with American power-plants, will realise that this engine is just considered as a starting point for tuners over there, so some of the cars subsequently ordered from Allards may turn out more akin to ballistic missiles than pretty, road-going four seaters. Just one point worries us about this affair. Allard's mated a Cortina GT mill to an Escort and called it an Escortina. So what's this to be — a Mustapi or a Caprang? Never!

Autotest

FORD CAPRI 3000GT XLR (2,994 c.c.)

AT-A-GLANCE: Effortless performance and considerable refinement at a fair price. Heavier engine results in more understeer. Steering and straight-line stability improved but ride significantly worse. Gearbox ratios not ideal. Larger petrol tank reduces boot space.

MANUFACTURER
Ford Motor Co. Ltd., Warley, Essex

PRICES
Basic	£1,051	0s	0d
Purchase Tax	£321	2s	10d
Seat belts	£14	0s	9d
Total (in G.B.)	£1,386	3s	7d

EXTRAS (inc. P.T.)
*Radio	£34	18s	6d
*Metallic finish	£6	10s	7d

*Fitted to test car

PRICE AS TESTED . . £1,427 12s 8d

PERFORMANCE SUMMARY
Mean maximum speed	113 m.p.h.
Standing start ¼-mile	17.6 sec.
0-60 m.p.h.	10.3 sec.
30-70 m.p.h. through gears	10.6 sec.
Typical fuel consumption	21 m.p.g.
Miles per tankful	290

Above: A powerful engine and good stability make the largest-engined Capri a fine fast tourer for two

FORD announced that there would be a 3-litre version of the Capri when this range of sports coupés was launched in January, but only at the beginning of this month has the car become available. The engine and gearbox are taken from the Ford Zodiac without any significant modification, other than changes necessary to make the marriage. Power output of the 2,994 c.c. vee-6 is 136 bhp(net) at 4,750 rpm, with maximum torque of 181 lb ft at 3,000 rpm. Installed in a car weighing only a little over a ton, this all promises exciting performance.

And performance is the main point of this big-engined Capri. A top speed of 113 mph mean, with a best figure one way of 115 mph, is good for a 3-litre saloon and could most likely be improved with higher overall gearing. Top gear mph per 1,000 rpm of 20.7 means that at maximum speed the vee-6 is turning over at just under 5,500 rpm—over 750 rpm past the claimed peak of the power curve. The car will cruise happily at 100 mph without too much fuss, thanks to a fairly good level of mechanical refinement. A predominant part of what noise there is from under the bonnet is made by the fan, so obviously something other than a fixed pulley coupling would improve this considerably.

From as low a speed as 15 mph in top the acceleration is impressive. The long nose, complete with power bulge, lifts a little as the car pulls away not with the kick you might at first expect, but a strong steady push. Up to 70 mph, the rising engine power just about

Far Left: An engine in proportion to the nose; accessibility is generally very good. Left: Well-planned controls make driving of the Capri relaxed. Below: Room in the back is less limited if the front seats are adjusted for a short driver. Right: Spare wheel lives under the boot carpet

ACCELERATION

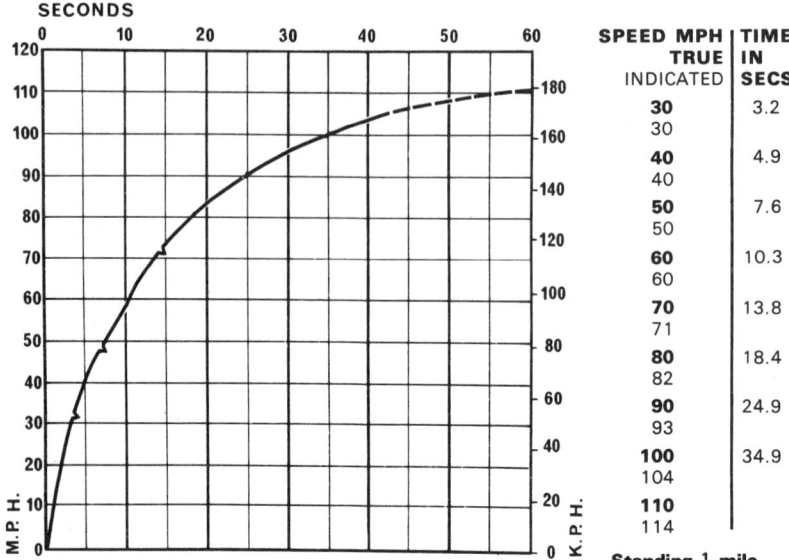

SPEED MPH TRUE / INDICATED	TIME IN SECS
30 / 30	3.2
40 / 40	4.9
50 / 50	7.6
60 / 60	10.3
70 / 71	13.8
80 / 82	18.4
90 / 93	24.9
100 / 104	34.9
110 / 114	

Standing ¼-mile
17.6 sec 79 mph

Standing kilometre
32.3 sec 98 mph
Test distance
1,132 miles
Mileage recorder
1.2 per cent
over-reading

SPEED RANGE, GEAR RATIOS AND TIME IN SECONDS

mph	Top (3.22)	3rd (4.55)	2nd (7.13)	1st (10.19)
10-30	—	5.7	3.5	2.8
20-40	7.5	4.7	3.2	—
30-50	7.2	4.8	3.7	—
40-60	6.9	5.2	—	—
50-70	7.7	6.4	—	—
60-80	8.9	8.6	—	—
70-90	10.3	—	—	—
80-100	16.7	—	—	—.

PERFORMANCE

MAXIMUM SPEEDS

Gear	mph	kph	rpm
Top (mean)	113	182	5,460
(best)	115	185	5,560
3rd	85	137	5,800
2nd	52	84	5,800
1st	38	61	5,800

BRAKES

(from 70 mph in neutral)
Pedal load for 0.5g stops in lb

1	40	6	45
2	40	7	45
3	40	8	45
4	40-45	9	45
5	40	10	45

RESPONSE (from 30 mph in neutral)

Load	g	Distance
20lb	0.25	120ft
30lb	0.40	75ft
40lb	0.60	50ft
50lb	0.78	39ft
60lb	0.90	33ft
65lb	0.98	30.7ft
Handbrake	0.34	89ft

Max. Gradient 1 in 3

CLUTCH

Pedal 28lb and 4.5in.

MOTORWAY CRUISING

Indicated speed at 70 mph	. . . .	71 mph
Engine (rpm at 70 mph)	. . . .	3,380 rpm
(mean piston speed)	. . . .	1,610ft/min
Fuel (mpg at 70 mph)	. . . .	23.3 mpg
Passing (50-70 mph)	. . . .	7.7 sec

COMPARISONS

MAXIMUM SPEED MPH

Reliant Scimitar 3-litre	. . . (£1,692)	121
Gilbern Invader	. . . . . . (£2,402)	115
Ford Capri 3000GT	. . . . **(£1,372)**	**113**
Uren Savage E	. . . . . (£1,725)	107
Sunbeam Rapier H120	. . . (£1,504)	105

0-60 MPH, SEC

Uren Savage E	. . . .	9.2
Reliant Scimitar 3-litre	. . . .	10.0
Ford Capri 3000GT	. . . .	**10.3**
Sunbeam Rapier H120	. . . .	10.3
Gilbern Invader	. . . .	10.7

STANDING ¼-MILE, SEC

Uren Savage E	. . . .	16.8
Reliant Scimitar 3-litre	. . . .	17.1
Ford Capri 3000GT	. . . .	**17.6**
Sunbeam Rapier H120	. . . .	17.7
Gilbern Invader	. . . .	17.8

OVERALL MPG

Reliant Scimitar 3-litre	. . . .	22.1
Sunbeam Rapier H120	. . . .	21.9
Uren Savage E	. . . .	20.7
Gilbern Invader	. . . .	19.6
Ford Capri 3000GT	. . . .	**19.3**

GEARING (with 185-13in. tyres)

Top	. . . .	20.7 mph per 1,000 rpm
3rd	. . . .	14.7 mph per 1,000 rpm
2nd	. . . .	9.0 mph per 1,000 rpm
1st	. . . .	6.6 mph per 1,000 rpm

TEST CONDITIONS:
Weather: Sunny. Wind: 7-13 mph. Temperature: 17 deg. C. (64 deg. F). Barometer: 29.65in. hg. Humidity: 65 per cent. Surfaces: dry concrete and asphalt.

WEIGHT:
Kerb weight 21.2 cwt (2,370lb-1,075kg) (with oil, water and half full fuel tank.) Distribution, per cent F, 56.9; R. 43.1. Laden as tested: 25.5 cwt (2,828lb-1,282kg).

TURNING CIRCLES:
Between kerbs L, 34ft 10in.; R, 34ft 6in. Between walls L, 37ft 2in.; R, 36ft 6in. Steering wheel turns, lock to lock 3.4.

Figures taken at 1,700 miles by our own staff at the Motor Industry Research Association proving ground at Nuneaton and on the Continent.

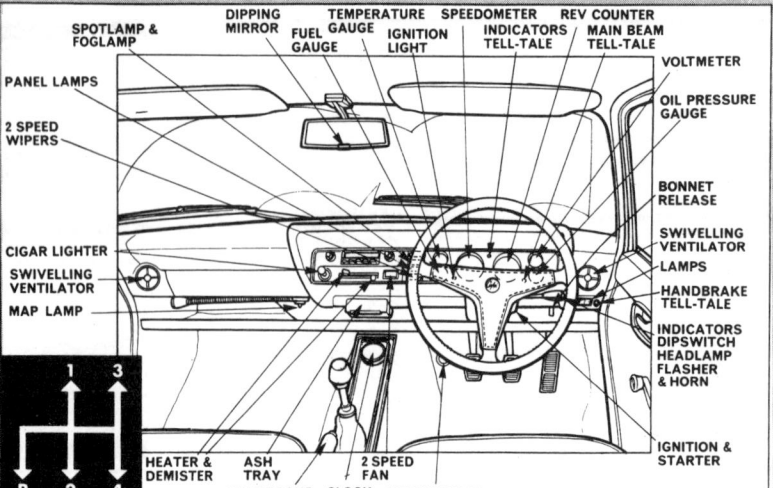

CONSUMPTION

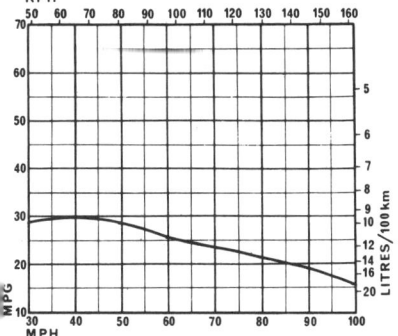

FUEL

(At constant speeds—mpg)

30 mph	. . . .	28.8
40 mph	. . . .	29.8
50 mph	. . . .	28.4
60 mph	. . . .	25.3
70 mph	. . . .	23.3
80 mph	. . . .	21.1
90 mph	. . . .	18.4
100 mph	. . . .	15.4

Typical mpg 21 (13.5 litres/100km)
Calculated (DIN) mpg 21.2 (13.4 litres/100km)
Overall mpg 19.3 (14.7 litres/100km)
Grade of fuel   Premium, 4-star (min. 97 RM)

OIL

Miles per pint (SAE 20W/50) 2,000

SPECIFICATION
FRONT ENGINE, REAR-WHEEL DRIVE

ENGINE
Cylinders . . . 6, in 60-deg vee
Main bearings . 4
Cooling system . Water, pump, fan and thermostat
Bore 93.7mm (3.69in.)
Stroke . . . 72.4mm (2.85in.)
Displacement . . 2,994c.c. (182.7 cu.in.)
Valve gear . . . Overhead, pushrods and rockers
Compression ratio 8.9-to-1 Min. octane rating: 97 RM
Carburettor . . Weber 40 DFA twin choke
Fuel pump . . AC mechanical
Oil filter . . . . Full flow, replaceable element
Max. power . . 136 bhp (net) at 4,750 rpm
Max. torque . . 181 lb.ft. (net) at 3,000 rpm

TRANSMISSION
Clutch . . . . Borg and Beck diaphragm spring 9in. dia.
Gearbox. . . . Four-speed all-synchromesh
Gear ratios . . . Top 1.0; Third 1.41; Second 2.29; First 3.16; Reverse 3.35.
Final drive . . . Hypoid bevel, 3.22-to-1.

CHASSIS and BODY
Construction . . Integral, with steel body

SUSPENSION
Front . . . . . Independent, MacPherson struts, coil springs, telescopic dampers, anti-roll bar
Rear . . . . . Live axle, semi-elliptic springs, radius arms, telescopic dampers

STEERING
Type . . . . . Burman rack and pinion
Wheel dia. . . . 15.5in.

BRAKES
Make and type . Girling disc front, drum rear
Servo . . . . . Girling vacuum
Dimensions . . F 9.63in. dia.; R 9.0in. dia. 1.75in. wide shoes.
Swept area. . . F 189.5 sq.in., R 98.9 sq.in. Total 288.4 sq.in. (232 sq.in./ton laden)

WHEELS
Type . . . . . Standard pressed steel, 5.0in. wide rims (R-pack includes Rostyle wheels).
Tyres—make . . Goodyear
—type . . G800 Grand Prix radial ply tubeless
—size . . 185–70HR13in.

EQUIPMENT
Battery . . . . 12 volt 44 Ah
Alternator . . . Lucas 17 ACR
Headlamps. . . Lucas sealed beam 120/80 watt (total)
Reversing lamp . Standard (with X-pack)
Electric fuses . . 7
Screen wipers . Two-speed, self-parking
Screen washer . Standard, foot-operated
Interior heater . Standard, air-mixing type
Heated backlight Extra
Safety belts . . Extra, anchorages built-in
Interior trim . . Ambla seats pvc headlining
Floor covering . Carpet
Jack-type . . . Screw pillar
Jacking points . 2, under body
Windscreen . . Zone toughened
Underbody
protection . . . Phosphate treatment under paint, plus Tectyl

MAINTENANCE
Fuel tank . . . 14 Imp. gallons (no reserve) (65 litres)
Cooling system . 21.1 pints (including heater)
Engine sump . . 9.9 pints (5.6 litres) SAE 20W/50. Change oil every 6,000 miles. Change filter element every 6,000 miles.
Gearbox. . . . 3.25 pints SAE 80EP. No change needed.
Final drive . . 1.94 pints SAE 90EP. No change needed.
Grease . . . . No points
Tyre pressures . F26psi, R26psi (all conditions)
Max. payload. . 750 lb

PERFORMANCE DATA
Top gear mph per 1,000 rpm 20.7
Mean piston speed at max. power . . . . . . 2,260 ft./min.
Bhp per ton laden 111

STANDARD GARAGE 16ft x 8ft 6in.

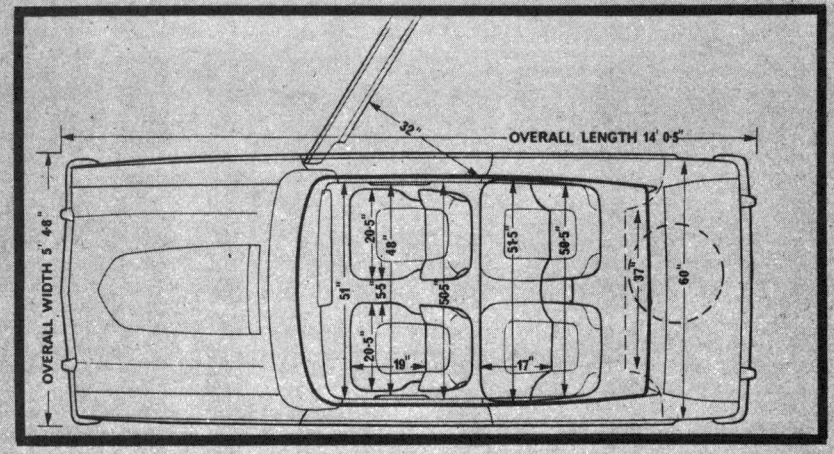

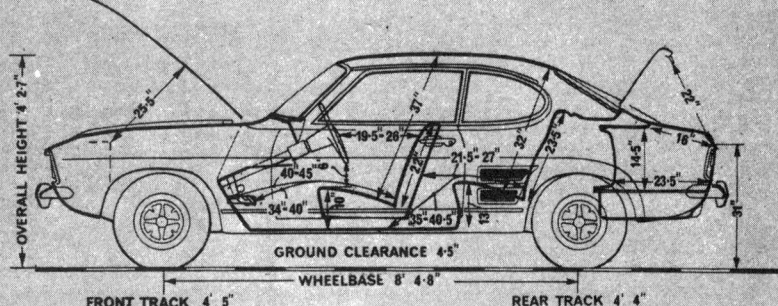

SCALE 0.3in. to 1ft
Cushions uncompressed

Something of a Q-car; only the fatter tyres, the power bulge and the side plaques tell what is under the bonnet

AUTOTEST
FORD CAPRI
3000 XLR . . .

matches the increase in drag, so that the top gear 20-mph time increments are all under 8 sec. The 50–70 mph time of 7.7 sec is appreciably better than most of the 3-litre Capri's competitors.

One cannot really dismiss as unimportant the peculiar set of intermediate ratios in the Mk IV Zodiac gearbox, even allowing for the flexible nature of the engine. For a car with sporting pretensions, second gear is too low, which leaves an annoying gap between second and third. Observing the 5,800 red sector on the accurate rev-counter, first, second and third give 38, 55 and 84 mph maximum respectively. This uneven spacing prevents the car accelerating as well as it could. You notice it not only during acceleration against a stop-watch, but on the road when overtaking.

The gearchange is not as good as on other Fords. There is the same precision, but a rather wider gate with spring-loading towards the third-top plane, Continental fashion; the lever tends to "clonk", and needs quite an effort if you hurry the powerful synchromesh. A trace of clutch drag made engagement of reverse noisy. Clutch pedal load is light.

From a standing start it is possible to provoke wheelspin without axle tramp on a dry surface, 60 mph coming up in 10.3 sec, 80 in 18.4 sec, the standing quarter-mile in 17.6 sec, and 100 in 34.9 sec. Apart from leaving rubber on the concrete all the way to 30 mph, these impressive acceleration times were achieved very easily, with no strain to the car.

Over 20 mpg is easily possible on long journeys, despite fairly hard driving. On a brisk trip to North Wales, 21.5 mpg was achieved. Really hard driving inevitably takes its toll—only 16.0 mpg was returned during a visit to MIRA for performance testing, which reduced our overall to 19.3 mpg. We feel sure

that most owners will better 20 mpg without difficulty.

The vee-6 weighs over 100lb more than the in-line four-cylinder Ford engine, and with what feels like a lot more castor in the steering, the car was much more stable in a straight line than its smaller brothers. A 57 per cent front-biased weight distribution makes the Capri in this form a pronounced understeerer. The steering, however, is fairly precise and by no means unduly low-geared—less than 3½ turns for an under-35ft turning circle. The understeer can be balanced by power, but this, quite naturally, must be used with discretion on slippery surfaces. Traction in the main is surprisingly good. The low-profile Goodyears deserve some of the credit for this. Despite their width, they showed no tendency to aquaplane on very wet surfaces. It is not, however, a car which one feels able to place to an inch and it is at its best touring fast along wide main roads, when its natural stability enables the driver to relax. Comparing it as we did with our long-term 1600 GT Capri staff car, it has almost none of the deadness of steering about the straight-ahead position which we have previously criticized. On the debit side, the steering is a lot heavier by Ford standards, though not too much so in general terms except when parking in confined spaces.

Ride is also considerably harsher than on the smaller-engined car. Any tendency to pitch is well damped but the up-rated springs give a stiffer ride than on the 1600 version. One of the few areas Ford seem to have overlooked in their search for interior silence is around the rear wheel arches. As on Cortinas, one is very conscious of gravel clattering against the bodywork over loose surfaces.

Road noise is generally low, but the new Goodyear 70-series G800 Grand Prix tyres made a very audible hiss over some smooth surfaces. There is noticeable bump-thump on cat's eyes. Wind noise is normally well subdued but door closure is unusually difficult and it took a hefty slam to secure them completely on the test car.

Our standard brake fade test from 70 mph showed up no defects in this respect, though pedal travel increased momentarily after two rapid stops from higher speed; recovery was

very quick. There is servo-assistance which is powerful, requiring only 65lb pedal effort for 0.98g maximum braking, with the rear wheels locked and the front wheels on the point of locking. It is not difficult to lock back wheels with the efficient handbrake, which coped competently with holding the car on the 1-in-3 test slope. Re-starts were no problem for the vee-6 or its clutch.

One aspect of the Capri which is very good is its driving position, which makes one feel masterly and in full command. The steering wheel is neither too high nor too low and all major controls are easy to reach, except the main lighting switch. At times, the foot-operated windscreen washer is too easily squirted unintentionally. Seating is generally quite good, with *just* enough legroom for tall drivers.

In the back there is not a lot of room but enough, and we consider this to be the minimum of what can be classed as a full four-seater. The larger fuel tank (14 gall, compared with the 10.5 gall of the smaller-engined versions) considerably reduces the capacity of what was already quite a small boot.

Some little things were very pleasing, and some others seemed less well planned. The push-to-zero trip control is excellent. The release for the seat-back lock to get into the rear has the opposite way sense from what is natural. Ventilation—an increasingly important feature these days—is effective, though perhaps not so thorough as on the Cortina and Mark IV range; we had to jerk the temperature control on this car to achieve cold air. The note of horns is not in the same class as that aspired to by the car. The oil pick-up problem we have encountered on other sporting installations of this engine seems to have been cured. Restricted rear and three-quarter visibility must be remembered when filtering into merging traffic streams or pulling out to overtake.

Like each of the more powerful Capris we have tried successively, we enjoyed the 3000 GT more than a basic model. As well as the obvious gains in performance, this car is much better on straight line stability and the steering has much more tangible response. The whole car, with the exception of the firm ride, is more refined also. At its price as a high performance GT it represents good value for money. □

Springbok tuning king Basil Green has come up with a Q-car that is likely to set both the boulevarde and the track on fire. David Eastaugh reports on a fiery 260 bhp, 302 cu. in. Capri!

BELOW: Capri V8 at speed. Externally, it is difficult to distinguish from normal Capri, but a drag from the traffic lights soon shows up the 140-plus performance.

SOUTH AFRICA'S V8 CAPRI

EVERY enthusiast cherishes the dream of his own personal super car — that unreal combination of performance, comfort, flexibility and razor edge handling — all at a price which he can afford.

Very occasionally, almost by chance, a great car arrives, which just happens to offer more for less than any of its competitors. A Capri V8 developed in South Africa is the very latest of this rare breed to make the scene.

The Capri V8 prototype has been developed for evaluation tests for Ford by Johannesburg tuning expert, Basil Green. Basil is a leading light in the South African modifications and special equipment field, not to mention his considerable ability in the development engineering side.

After three short months of development, followed by testing to near destruction by Ford Product Engineering men, the verdict was conclusive — the Capri V8 promised to be the fastest and most exciting four-seater car ever put into volume production. Performance figures for the prototype were staggering — top speed is 143 mph at 6500 rpm and

CONTINUED ON PAGE 63

Capri 3000GT - a lazy man's sports car

Slotting the 3 litre V6 into Ford's Capri gives it effortless high performance - and you don't need a fortune to buy it!

When the Ford Capri was announced a year ago, our appetite was whetted by the promise of a 3 litre V6 version. Apart from the model powered by the Cosworth BDA unit (of which surprisingly little has been heard this past twelve months), the 3000GT is the ultimate in the Capri range, a far cry from the standard 1300 yet still following in the Ford tradition of providing extremely good value for money.

It was clear last January that the Ford designers had the V6 version well in mind right from the start of the Capri project. We can recall cars in the past where an original chassis has gradually been provided with bigger and more powerful engines until finally the power has outgrown it. This is certainly not the case with the 3000GT; maybe the chassis is getting a little near the mark with 3 litres under the bonnet, but it definitely copes.

The 3000GT which we drove for some 700 miles during one exhilarating weekend came with the XLR packs to give it the full treatment. With radio and seat belts the price is £1,421, though the price of the basic car is a very commendable £1,291.

Very few modifications have been called for to fit the Zodiac V6 under the bonnet, though an E-Type 'power bulge' is needed to clear the air cleaner. The power unit is mounted well back in the chassis with modifications to the mountings and a strengthened cross member, while the sump has been given a slightly different shape so

as to clear the steering rack and cut out oil surge problems. Accessibility is good all round.

As we know very well from experience with our Zodiac and now an Executive, this V6 unit is a thoroughly good power unit, smooth (apart from a hint of resonance we encountered in the Capri around 3,500 rpm) and with meaty torque. Cold morning starts were achieved at the first touch of the ignition key and the automatic choke worked effectively and unobtrusively.

There is a slight change to the engine, in that fabricated exhaust manifolds are fitted, though no power increase is claimed. The maximum gross output figure is given as 144 bhp, or 136 bhp net, at 4,750 rpm.

The drive is taken through a gearbox using the standard Mk 4 innards, with ratios that are not too happy for the Capri. The 3.44 to 1 final drive of the 2000GT is replaced by a 3.22 to 1 ratio from the German Capri 2300 (which is apparently a heavier duty job).

The smaller engined Capris have a fuel capacity of 10½ gallons, but the 3000GT carries 13½ gallons, which is very necessary but which necessarily cuts further into the carrying capacity of what is already a none-too-generous luggage locker. It seems the intention is to give the 3000GT a range of 300 miles, but in practice this is about 280 miles, and a cautious driver would have been worried on 'our' car by a petrol gauge that settled back at ze. reading when there was

a couple or so gallons still left in the tank.

The only other mechanical change is to the suspension, which has naturally been provided with uprated springs and revised damping.

Outwardly, the 3000GT differs little from its less exotic and slower sisters. The differences consist of the bonnet bulge, side badges just behind the front wheels, twin badges, and the low-profile Goodyear G800 Grand Prix tyres fitted to the 5-inch rim Rostyle wheels. (We would have thought that buyers of this version would have appreciated something more in the external treatment, just to show their friends and others that they have the top-range Capri; after all, ir you've paid the money you might well want others to know.)

The VG engine weighs something like 100 lbs more than the four cylinder unit, and the effect is noticeable in terms of more understeer, though this is by no means pronounced. (The weight ratio between front and rear on the 3000GT is 57:43.)

As for performance, this is, as you would expect, very sporting. Yet driving the car does not give the impression one would expect from the specification. This is partly due to the smoothness of the engine (marred only by a roar which emanates from the fan) and also to the good wind-cheating properties of the body which rates very highly up to at least 90 miles an hour.

Unfortunately, the very low second gear means there is a large gap between that

Specification

Body-chassis: All-steel unitary construction.

Engine: V6, water-cooled. Bore 93.7 mm, stroke 72.4 mm, displacement 2,994 cc. Compression ratio 8.9 to 1. Maximum power 144 bhp (gross), 136 bhp (net) at 4,750 rpm. Push-rod operated overhead valves. Single Weber 40 DFA twin choke carburettor fed by mechanical fuel pump.

Transmission: 9 inch diameter single-dry-plate, diaphragm-spring clutch. Four-speed, all-synchro gearbox with floor shift. Ratios: 3.16 to 1; 2nd 2.29 to 1; 3rd 1.41 to 1; 4th 1.00 to 1; reverse 3.35 to 1. Hypoid bevel final drive 3.22 to 1.

Suspension: Front, independent, McPherson struts, coil springs/telescopic dampers and anti-roll bar. Rear, live axle, semi-elliptic springs, radius arms, telescopic dampers.

Steering: Rack and pinion, 3.4 turns from lock to lock. Turning circle 34 ft 6 in.

Brakes: Front, 9.63 in. discs. Rear, 9.0 in. drums. Total frictional area 288.4 sq in. Power-assisted.

Wheels and tyres: 13 x 5J Rostyle steel wheels (optional) with Goodyear Grand Prix G800 185-70HR13 radial-ply tyres.

Weights and measures: Approx kerb weight 21.2 cwt; length 168.5 in.; width 64.8 in.; height 50.7 in.; wheelbase 100.8 in.; ground clearance 4.5 in.; fuel tank capacity 13.5 gallons.

ratio and third, as shown by the maximum speeds available at 6,000 rpm in each of these gears. No doubt Ford would have liked to uprate second for the 3000GT but were unable to do so on the score of cost; you can't have your cake and eat it, and the 3000GT really does provide performance at what is, by today's standards, a bargain price.

While on the subject of the gearbox, we found the change on this model superior to that on the Zodiac, though inclined to be notchy and somewhat slow compared with the boxes on the smaller Fords. The stubby gear lever is quite heavily spring-loaded towards third and top, and has precise movements. The clutch was pleasantly light.

The Capri 3000GT can be driven in two different ways, either enterprisingly, when some slight deficiencies show up in the handling, or lazily, when it is superb. It simply trickles along effortlessly at the legal 70 mph limit, pulls away in top gear from around 15 mph without signs of strain, and will ultimately get up to nearly 115 mph given a long enough stretch of straight road. If you're feeling in the mood to relax, it is really hardly worth changing out of top gear at all, except in heavy traffic. But for those ill-sorted middle gear ratios, it would be a honey of a sporting beast.

Though the back end of the Capri is a simple design, the wheels are well located and it is possible to feed in a great deal of power on dry surfaces. Only when cornering

fast does it become apparent that this is not a highly sophisticated suspension set-up; for example, the inside wheel spins rather easily.

The Goodyear tyres certainly provide a great deal of adhesion. Indeed they are clearly an important contribution to the car's handling qualities, though inevitably these wide flat treads pick up noise—a hiss on some smooth surfaces and a very audible thumping over cat's eyes. These 'boots' also provide good adhesion in the wet; the steering begins to feel light as cornering speeds increase though there is still something in hand in terms of grip. The balance of the car enables the throttle to be used to keep things tidy, but with this sort of power and torque it is as well for the inexperienced driver to treat rainy weather with some respect.

The brakes always seemed well capable of coping with the performance; they have just the right amount of servo assistance and in our experience were not susceptible to fade. The handbrake was good, too, capable of holding the car on a 1 in 3 gradient.

This, then, is a thoroughly workmanlike machine with a deceptively quick performance. Overall, driving the car on all different types of road—traffic, the twisty stuff and one long motorway journey—we returned a petrol consumption of just over 21 miles per gallon, which we do not consider all that bad. No doubt a lazier approach (which would still be quick) would give a

Performance

Acceleration:

0-30 mph	3.0 sec
0-40 mph	4.8 sec
0-50 mph	7.2 sec
0-60 mph	9.9 sec
0-70 mph	13.1 sec
0-80 mph	17.0 sec
0-90 mph	23.4 sec
0-100 mph	31.8 sec

Speeds in the gears:

1st	39 mph
2nd	55 mph
3rd	85 mph
4th	114 mph

Overall fuel consumption on test: 21.1 mpg.

consumption around 23-25 mpg.

There is little need to describe the interior appointments and controls, since these do not differ from the smaller-engined models equipped with these custom packs. But to recap, the driving position is extremely good, and so is the ventilation system (though not as effective as on other Fords). The lighting switch, to the right of the facia, is not the best-placed of controls, and you have to have the knack before you can find the hole for the ignition key first time.

But these minor irritations apart, the Capri 3000GT is a very desirable machine, well up to the promise suggested when we learned about it a year earlier.

To re-phrase a well-known advertisement, it looks good, feels good, and is good.

Ford Under Pressure

Olaf Fersen tries Michael May's turbo-charged V-6 Capri

SUPERCHARGING car engines was quite popular in the Golden Thirties, but in later years it died a natural death, when the FIA banned blowers from racing circuits and rallies. More recently a different kind of forced-feeding for internal combustion engines took the stage in the USA when turbo-charged Offenhauser four cylinder engines turned the scales at Indianapolis, where they are definitely "in".

Turbo-charging has established itself in the diesel engine field and there is nothing unusual these days. So why not try it on cars ? That is exactly what Michael May, a qualified Swiss engineer thought some while ago. Perhaps there were others pipe-dreaming about the same matter—but May set the ball rolling.

Before he started his career as an independent engineering consultant, May had done a lot of things which now may be regarded as qualifying steps to the turbo-charging experiment: He raced formula Junior cars and became European Champion; he invented a very simple system of fuel injection for which he was granted a

number of patents. Later he joined Daimler-Benz to work in their experimental department on fuel injection and he later did the same at Maranello for Ferrari engines. He designed an interesting radiator fan coupling which he sold to Fichtel and Sachs and he built a tiny fuel injection unit working on the pulsations generated in the crankcase of two-stroke engines. This was by a firm manufacturing forestry saws. He has also had a hand in the development of the turbocharger installations used by Alfa Romeo and BMW for their former Group 5 racing saloon cars.

Last summer the German Ford company approved the May turbo-charger-kit for their V-6 engine and Schwabengarage at Stuttgart, Germany's largest Ford dealers, took over the sale and installation of the kits. Earlier May had applied for official approval by the road traffic authorities and obtained it with certain conditions like mandatory changes to the chassis, braking system, damping and so on.

These chassis improvements are included in the cost of the kit. It is by no means cheap—costing about £325. With this, a German version Capri with 2.3-litre engine costs £1,222 or about the

same as the 80 bhp VW-Porsche. For this money one does not expect to get a car with Porsche roadholding, but in performance the Capri becomes a match for the 911 Porsche.

How it is done

In contrast with the Roots, Cozette, Shorrock or Powerplus blowers, the turbo-charger does not need a mechanical drive. It consists of two tiny turbines running on the same shaft: one driven by the exhaust gases, the other forcing air down the engine's throat. Whereas most pre-war superchargers sucked their charge *through* the carburettor (with the notable exception of the Mercedes SS, SSK and K type motors) May's turbocharger blows *into* the carburettor or carburettors, as the case may be. When the engine is started, or runs at idling speed, there is not sufficient pressure in the exhaust system to make the turbine function. As engine speed rises, so does the volume of exhaust gas, making the turbine turn faster. At about 3,000 rpm a faint whistling noise may be heard, rather like a distant jet plane with its engines turning over at idling speed. Now things start happening. Normally at about 3,000

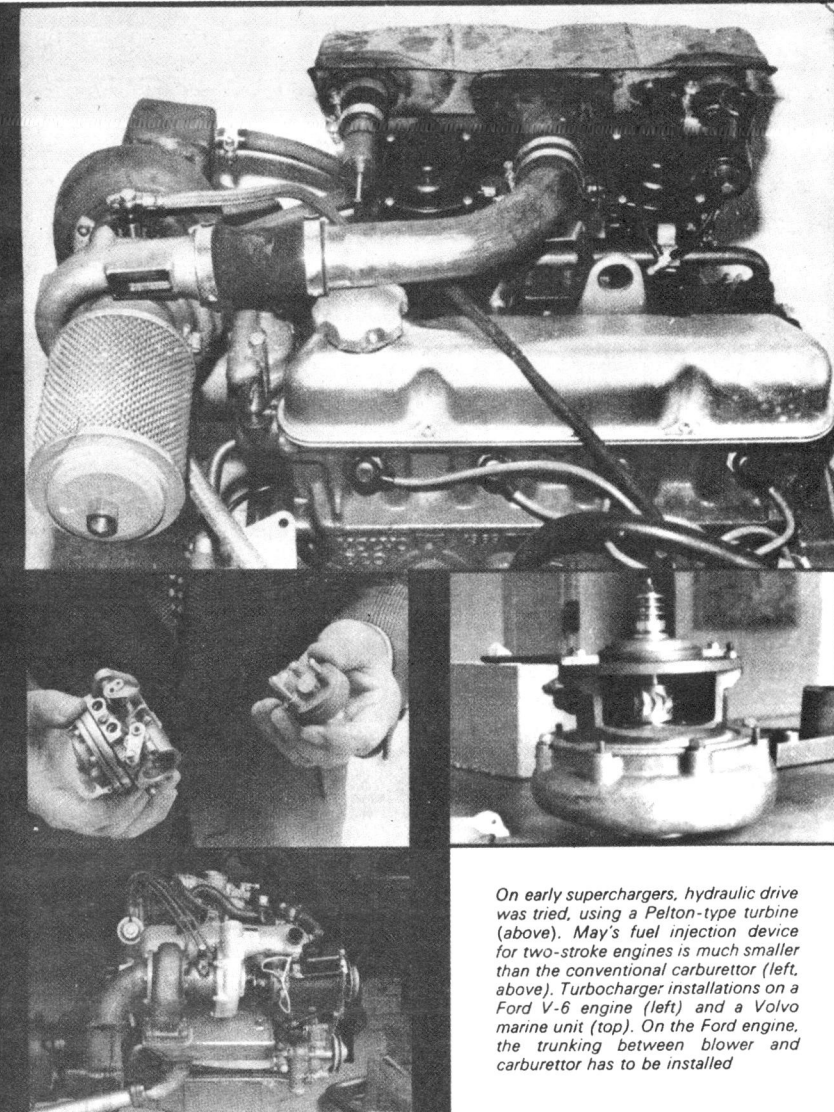

On early superchargers, hydraulic drive was tried, using a Pelton-type turbine (above). May's fuel injection device for two-stroke engines is much smaller than the conventional carburettor (left, above). Turbocharger installations on a Ford V-6 engine (left) and a Volvo marine unit (top). On the Ford engine, the trunking between blower and carburettor has to be installed

pay. Naturally these units were rather expensive.

Exhaust gas from the manifolds is led into a fabricated sheet-steel expansion box on each side of the engine. The turbocharger is mounted on top of the right-hand one and the exhaust pipe from the left side is led round below the gearbox and into the bottom of the right-hand expansion box. The exhaust proper emerges axially from the turbine and the larger-than-standard pipe runs down to the first of two silencers. The expansion boxes damp out any pulsations. The air compressor inhales through a trunk facing forwards and ending in a filter behind the radiator grille. The pressure side is connected to the shell of the former air filter, which has been welded tight at the lid seams. This frying-pan-type canister serves as another expansion box. It sits directly on top of the Solex carburettor. The latter has been sealed and an air pipe to the floatchamber serves the purpose of equalizing pressures. This may sound very simple, but it took May considerable time and lots of experiment to find the best and simplest solution. An electric fuel pump is used, generating a pressure higher than the pressure prevailing in the float chamber.

Wear tests

It seems quite natural to expect some snags with turbocharging a normal production engine without doing any other work on it. To find out about general wear and tear two identical cars were run under equal conditions over an identical mileage. The engines were then dismantled and to May's complete satisfaction the turbocharged unit was found to be in better mechanical condition. The explanation seems to lie with the theory that bearing loads below 3,000 rpm are almost unchanged. They become less at higher revs anyway and at higher mean effective pressures the forces of the rotating crank assembly are at least part-compensated.

The turbo-charged Capri has indeed a split personality. During a brief test run the engine gave the impression of running smoother even than the standard unit and the flexibility proved excellent. When the throttles are opened, the other side of the personality becomes very apparent: Engine speed rises very quickly and there is all the power one could wish for.

The standard 108 bhp Capri is no sluggard, needing a mere 9.8 sec to accelerate from a standstill to 100kph (61 mph). The May-converted car, however, beats it handsomely with an elapsed time of 7.2 sec. Against the 107 mph maximum of the standard product, it has a genuine 120 to offer.

During my visit to the old monastery near Hechingen, where Michael May has installed his workshop and dynamometer and built himself a charming flat, he was working on a B20 Volvo engine for a Swedish customer who wanted a light and powerful engine for his speedboat. On this engine the two Stromberg carburettors were left in place and fed by a turbocharger. At 5,500 rpm an output of almost exactly 150 bhp was achieved.

After sampling the May-Capri and taking a good look at the work going on in the buildings that once had sheltered 16th century monks, supercharging does not look so dead any more. May then had sold about 100 conversion kits and apparently all his customers were quite happy with them. This could well start a trend. □

rpm the torque line starts to ease off gradually. Not so with the turbocharged engine: power and torque increase in a surprising way. This could just go on and on until induction throat diameter becomes the limiting factor. To prevent the conrods vanishing through the side of the block a limiting switch worked by a centrifugal governor cuts the ignition at 5,800 rpm This may sound a bit premature as the Ford V-6 still feels quite happy at about 6,500 rpm. The reason Is that the power output is then well past 180 bhp and that much power could perhaps tie knots in the prop-shaft. There is also another version of the story, having to do with the output Fords are themselves getting from this engine with a very hot camshaft and a hedgehog of carburettors—180 bhp nett!

On the other hand, May may be forgiven for satisfying his own curiosity about the things happening with the governor out of action. The answer was a healthy 240 bhp at 6,000 rpm! Just for curiosity's sake and with an eye on the possibility of pitting a Turbo-Capri against big-bangers on the racing track, a special version of the engine was prepared. This got a Schleicher-ground cam, stronger valve springs and other goodies of this kind. On the brake May got over 300 bhp at 8,000 rpm from this version but some trouble was experienced with head gaskets and the lubrication system. This was in September, but when May motored his Capri round the fast Hockenheim track one month later, it went almost as fast as the hottest Camaros and Falcons and finished fourth after a closely-fought race.

The turbo-kit however, was never intended for racing purposes—although it seems to offer some chances there as well. In the form of Capri plus May-kit the resultant car is a very tractable machine; in fact it runs more smoothly than the standard product at low speeds. Very much increased flexibility reduces the need for changing gear and from about 50 mph upwards it will out-accelerate almost any other car in top.

May uses an Ebersbächer-Bosch turbocharger. Unfortunately the smallest production unit (designed for diesel engines) is too large for the Ford. Ebersbächer, however, had a smaller turbocharger on the drawing board but demanded that May should order 300 of them to make tooling

CR CALLS THE TUNE

THIS MONTH:
The first of a new series on the specialist car builders and tuning firms by CLIVE RICHARDSON, formerly Sports Editor of the BL magazine, High Road.
THIS MONTH: JoMoRo/Mann's Garage Capri 3 litre, Hartwell Imps; cars from Royale

EUROPE'S MOST SUCCESSFUL CAPRI TESTED

WHEN FORD did a Savage on the Capri by dropping in a big lump of 3 litre V6 Zodiac barge engine, the gnomes who know it all were saying that this would be the new Boreham weapon for pulverising Racing and Rallying opposition.

The months went by, nothing happened and rumours began to circulate that the new executive sporty motorway charger had an engine which just wasn't reliable for hard competition. Apart from a sortie with an FWD 3 litre Capri in Rallycross, and Harry Ratcliffe and co. flying around up North in a 2WD version, it seemed as though Boreham weren't interested in disproving the knockers — though admittedly at long last they're prepared for a proper Rallycross attack with FWD versions.

Only one man in Britain had the faith to disregard the cynics. Holman (Les) Blackburn, a director of his family's Mann's Garage, Ford, Rover and Austin dealers at Chiddingfold, Surrey, had set his heart on completing this year's 86 hour Marathon de la Route at the Nurburgring, after three failed attempts with Cooper Ss. This time he decided a big engine in a relatively

small body was the answer to achieving his ambition

So Les's 10-year-old Club Racing Mini, grown over the years from 850 to 1293, had to go, along with father Doug's 1293 Gp 2 Rally Min (driven mainly by Des Silverthorn) and a standard example of the basic model Capri 3000 GT took their place.

That was in April, and by mid-July, after JoMoRo men Jimmy Morgan and Jimmy Rose, that brilliant pair responsible for building the original Bill Shaw Racing Rover, and the Mann's men had had their hands on it, the Capri was in business.

So began what must be an unparalleled record of success involving $11\frac{1}{2}$ thousand Racing and road miles in a total of six days and a record of reliability that must have surprised even the Ford Motor Co. After only a one-hour shakedown session at Goodwood the car was trailed to Spa for the 24 hour Race as a test before the Marathon, with Les and Captain John Moss as drivers. Eighth in class and an average speed of over 100 mph for 24 hours sent them home happy. Then came the Marathon with Lord Cross (the Cobra man) joining Blackburn and

Moss, and convincing success. A first in class and the only British car home, more than fulfilled the Blackburn ambition. The car ran faultlessly for 86 hours and proved the fastest car on the circuit in the wet. Another trip to Nurburgring for the 36 Hours with the German 'Candy' as third driver brought another first in class and fastest lap overall — 13 sec. quicker than the winning Porsche!

The mods built into this remarkable beast are so obviously good that Mann's Garage are to market replica bits under the JoMoRo name.

Most of the magic lies in the suspension department, fully rose jointed front and rear. Designed specially for the 'Ring where penalties for pit stops were huge, the JoMoRo conversion bolts straight on to the standard car, so any replacements needed during the Marathon could be bolted on quickly. That means anybody wanting to do a similar conversion to a Capri needs only a set of AF spanners and a bit of common-sense to do the job.

Up front, besides the rose joints there's a one-sixteenth inch thicker roll bar mounted in alloy clamps and pivots made from PTFE (fibreglass reinforced plastic bought at £5 an inch and hand-turned by Mann's), and track control arms mounted in a similar substance. Front springs proved a problem till some were found that were made for a Corsair that was going across the Sahara or somewhere and were shortened to give a decent ride height. Replicas will be for sale — just as stiff but slightly longer.

The back end is lowered using blocks and flatter springs, with the rear shackles reversed so that the main leaves mount above instead of below. PTFE is used in the eyes. Rad-

ius arms are rose jointed with magnesium retainers. A JoMoRo-designed fully-floating back axle cost £150 to build without the diff. which is a ZF limited slip as used on the German Racing Capris and World Cup Escorts; ratio is the standard 3.22:1. Konic are used all round — the same set for all three Races, just taken up a turn after each one.

Drum brakes are retained at the rear, simply because the VG 95 linings would last the full 86 hour Marathon, whereas discs would have needed a time-consuming pad change. Fronts are standard disc with DS 11 pads and a dual system is connected to the standard servo.

Engine mods were restricted for reliability, though 189 bhp at 6200 rpm gives the Capri a fair bit of poke. Heads are Weslake, modified further by Mann's and the Weslake cam is a road/race compromise. Pistons are just high compression Weslake versions (9.5:1 instead of 8.9:1) and the bottom end is Brabham balanced, running in special Vandervell bearings, with a slightly lightened flywheel. Sump is enlarged to take 14½ pts. of Castrol Competition lube. A larger radiator and 19 row oil cooler keep the temperature down.

Carburation retains the original 4 DFA Weber with enlarged jets, mounted on a Weslake manifold. Exhaust manifolding remains as per Dagenham assembly line branched-type.

Amazingly, clutch and gearbox are standard 'cos there was nothing else available, but they've given no bother. Les is negotiating to have CR sets built to go into the standard casing, for sale.

Seven-inch rim Minilites are shod with Goodyear Rally Specials.

Looks bog standard, but there's 189 Weslake bhp under that pancake filter. Note big radiator. Photos: Spencer Smith.

Les Blackburn's an extraordinarily understanding chap — or mad. He must be to loan me his precious Racer for road use — yes, road use! That's an amazing quality of this car; a superb long distance circuit car, yet still usable on the road. How often can you say that about a Racer nowadays.

Driving DPD 9J was one of those experiences that sometimes you wish would go on for ever and at other times wish had never started: on the smooth open road it was superb, the best set-up big saloon car I've ever driven — at least in the dry. Like all Capris it oversteered like hell, though very controllably unless you stuffed your right foot down too sharply out of a fast bend, when the tail would whip round suddenly. Once I'd got used to the inherent twitchiness and the desire to stuff my boot in hard at the wrong times the Capri felt remarkably safe right up to staggeringly high speeds — except on greasy roads. Then driving it became one long exciting happening, calling for respect as the back end never seemed to stay where it ought to be, even in a straight line. That's all relative though, when you realise that you're doing well into three figues in these conditions, when

most normal saloons would be feeling ragged at the legal limit. Top speed, the way, achieved by Les on the straight at Spa, was 140 mph. Body roll was virtually non-existent, with rock-solid springs and dampers and a thick anti-roll bar.

An amazing thing was the V6's tractability, pulling smoothly from 20 mph in top — though the N 60 plugs wouldn't allow this to become a habit, fluffing above 4000 rpm if the revs weren't kept on the boil. Softer plugs would have made it a superb road engine.

Biggest bugbear was the standard gearbox with that terrific gap between second and third and long, sloppy gearlever travel. Not too much of a drawback on the road, but showing up very badly during performance testing on our pet circuit. Not that performance was lacking — few road-going modified saloons could get near it, though being a long distance machine it was more spectacular when fully wound up on the road when its superb suspension and long-legged engine could be used to the full.

Outstanding memories were the impeccable preparation and outstanding handling. Its achievements adequately praise the quality of the JoMoRo mods, so who better to go to for your Capri bits (and I hear that there may be a few more Capris round the circuits next season). A set of rose jointed suspension bits will set you back about £110 to fit yourself plus a few pounds to set it up when it's bolted on. Contact Les Blackburn at Mann's Garage (042.879 2263) for details. And if you've £2650 to spare, the Capri's for sale, too!

HOW IT WENT: 0-30 2.5 sec, 0-40 4.1 sec, 0-50 6 sec, 0-60 7.2 sec, 0-70 10.2 sec, 0-80 13.1 sec, 0-90 17.0 sec, 0-100 20.5 sec. Maximum speed 140 mph timed during Spa 24 Hour Race.

JUST ROUND the corner from Acorn House, Bob King's Racing Preparations Ltd. design and bolt together those Royale Formula Fords and F 100s which have made their mark on this year's Racing scene — like Ray Allen walking away with the F 100 Championship.

Things are a bit slack in this part of the calendar, so Bob and his band of ace mechanics have put their heads together and filled in time by evolving not one but three completely new circuit cars, to contest Formula Super Vee, Formula Atlantic and Group 6.

Bob has abandoned his old space frame theories for the wedge-shaped Super Vee, replacing them with a brand-new lightweight monocoque structure turning the scales at a mere 70 lb. yet immensely strong.

To get round all the twiddly bits with less chance of going off, Super

Vee Formula does away with the insistence of Formula Vee on standard VW suspenders, so the Royale corners like your actual Formula Racers on wishbone corner pieces. With new-found freedom for the use of Racing tyres production single-seater Super Beetles will probably come out on new Racing boots Firestone are making specially for the Formula, mounted on 6-in. Minilites, with 125 bhp. Bob reckons it should be on a performance par with this season's F3s, being lighter, stronger, and having a lot more low down torque.

John Webb-type Formula Atlantic looks like having plenty of supporters next season so Royale just had to jump onto, or maybe initiate, the band-wagon. Bob's fertile mind worked out a design which is next door to being a full F2 car — but a damned sight cheaper. Maybe it might

turn into a full-house F2 one day? Formula Atlantic or F2, it looks like being a quick tool by any standards. With just a cooking 170bhp BRM Lucas injected TC lump in the space frame's tail, Ray Allen gave this RP8 its first taste of competition at Brands on October 28th, equalling Peter Westbury's 2-year-old F. Libre lap record (with an F2 car) of 91.10 mph (49.00 sec) and smashing Westbury's F2 Race record on the way to a clear win. All very promising.

Shouldn't be long before the pukka BDA mill finds its way between the driveshafts and then the records should really take a hammering.

Royale's Gp 6 car was one of those things that just had to happen, seeing as how the F 100 was an obvious basis for such a beast. And that's just how this FVC F2-engined machine came about.

Performance Road Test

BROADSPEED
BULLIT

PRETTY PUDDLE photographs show off the comprehensive exterior changes. Interior modifications include an excellent pair of Restall bucket-seats.

AS WE commented in a brief paragraph devoted to the Racing Car Show recently, the converted Capri appears to be the modified car for 1971. At the Show both BVRT and Broadspeed displayed sophisticated versions of the 3-litre, though the manner in which they were decorated may have put off the very people who could afford these 120-plus m.p.h. machines. We were unable to borrow the BVRT car, the Lancashire based preparation specialists having no demonstrator: in fact the author has seen a replica of the BVRT show car lurking in the City of London, but that has not helped him to secure such a car for road-test. The subject of this feature is, therefore, the Broadspeed Bullit, the test car being insured for £2,400 and equipped with nearly every optional extra that Broadspeed can provide. However, the performance and handling of "our car" would be much the same as the more basic Bullit models costing £1,825 when based on the 3000GT and £1,995 when the plusher 3000E version of the Capri is used as a starting point. Last year we tried a 1600GT Capri with many of the handling and appearance items which now appear on the Bullit and this "Mini-Bullit" with 110 b.h.p. and roughly the same number of m.p.h. to serve as top speed, is still available at a basic cost of £1,575.

The Bullit name is an adaptation of the film title Bullitt, which is highlighted by a gripping car chase over the massive jumps and inclines of San Francisco city. The stars of the film were the cars, which included a Shelby Mustang that seemed to catch everyone's imagination with its brutal performance blending in so accurately with the somewhat bloody film theme. The winged front and slatted rear window are examples of glassfibre wares which are like those that can be ordered as part of an option pack for the Boss Mustang in the USA. The back slats serve no useful purpose, but they do not seem to restrict the already limited rearward vision unduly, and they do add to the car's individual looks when combined with the Ford black vinyl roof-top.

Before we go into the items which have increased the car's performance, comfort and handling to the point where a new name can be fully justified and an appropriate price tag, perhaps we ought to look at the results. The straight line performance is impressive, the acceleration up to the UK speed limit being as good as, or slightly better than the 4.2-litre Jaguar 'E'-type. Top speed is well down on the Jaguar though, but in practical UK use the Bullit's extraordinarily precise handling and high standard of road adhesion would be hard to beat, unless you have a glassfibre bodied two-seater wearing one of Mr. Chapman's little green badges. Really, where the Bullit scored so heavily with our staff was in its unique blend of handling, braking and power, which complement each other to produce one of the best balanced cars it has been my pleasure to drive. Apart from the initial price, which is not particularly high when compared to the Lotus and Jaguar company in which it can mix without blushing, the snag one pays for turning a simple machine into a formidable device is in fuel and possibly oil consumption. On the latter point we suspect that the engine was deliberately running on wide clearances for maximum performance, for the exhausts produced a fine blue haze whilst idling, though a specific check over a 100 mile period showed no change in

dipstick reading at all. Feather-footing the throttle gave close to 20 m.p.g. and perfectly docile performance whilst the car rumbled its menacing way around town and country. However, the enjoyment of that smooth acceleration curve up to and beyond 100 m.p.h. will return something less than 17 m.p.g., despite the fact that the car feels entirely unstrained until 6,000 r.p.m.—the magic "ton" being approximately 5,000 crankshaft revolutions a minute.

Standard equipment with a Bullit conversion starts off with legally required items such as seat belts (inertia reel variety), four months road tax and number plates. The exciting parts start with a Stage 2 engine conversion giving a claimed 190 gross b.h.p., which corresponds to an installed (DIN) figure of 170 to 175 b.h.p. at 6,500 r.p.m. Modified cylinder-heads using standard parts and compression are included along with a high-lift camshaft, re-choked and jetted carburetter and appropriate inlet manifolding, new gaskets and bearings, plus a clever exhaust system incorporating a crossover, or balance pipe close to the engine down piping. The balance pipe has the effect of giving a small power bonus (approx. 4 b.h.p.) when incorporated into a more efficient twin pipe system and also smooths out the exhaust note so that it never intrudes unduly upon the car's occupants, or those outside. Broadspeed director and founder of the conversion side, Ralph Broad, told us how the firm was established in 1927, to continue as successful BMC dealers and subsequently as competition experts when Broad took over the business from his father during the 1950s. By the early 60s, Broad had switched his allegiance to racing Ford Anglias in Group 5 trim, so that the business subsequently followed on their success with Ford products. Today the concern are Ford Dealers and AVO Dealers as well, operating from £250,000 modern premises at Southam, not far from Banbury. Broad says that the main clientel for the car have come from the professions.

The suspension, steering and braking modifications are successfully aimed at making the ride more pleasant, yet firmly controlled, whilst the crossmember is removed, rebushed and re-installed to give 2½ deg. of castor (the Ford setting is almost without castor in the interests of light steering on a nose-heavy car) and a shade of negative camber. Armstrong Adjustaride 22 telescopic shock absorbers are fitted at the rear. The car sits slightly lower on its haunches and a smaller diameter roll-bar is fitted at the front to cut most of the car's normal understeer down to the point of astonishingly neutral handling for its 43/57% weight distribution.

The braking changes consist of reduced rear drum lining area and DS11 pads, the front to rear brake balance is dramatically altered, with the result that we never managed to lock the wheels, whereas the standard product is certainly capable of this vice, given a panic situation and poor road surface. Summing up the changes the company had made to the Ford, Broad said, "our object is to try and make the car follow the road in the same way as we make it follow the throttle".

The last group of standard Bullit items were all primarily aimed at improving the looks . . . in one way or another. The front of the Capri

has a new lower panel incorporating recessed quartz-iodine driving lamps from Lucas and similarly treated reflective number plate: the air dam is also incorporated, but this £9 foil can be moved from Capri to Capri without bodywork damage. Normally, a pair of Cibie Caprima headlamps, also with quartz-iodine bulbs, would be installed as well but they had most regrettably been removed for our test. A special paint job is also part of the work, using a standard Ford colour as a base for a contrasting pin stripe and black bonnet job which extends around the rear side windows. Finally, the basic price includes those rear window louvres.

Optional extras on our Bullit were a set of five Minilite wheels with 6 in. rims (195 section Goodyear G800 GP tyres were fitted) which cost £120, a pair of fabulously comfortable Restall bucket seats with cloth centre sections at £50; prototype centre console holding stereo-tape deck (£50), clock, oddments compartment and two rocker switches —the console being priced at £20. A sturdy and small diameter leather rim steering wheel looking very functional in all black (£11), the vital and efficient, though noisy when cutting-in, Wood Jeffries fan (£17); dual note air horns which could be switched from one note pattern to the other in a brilliant move which is obviously designed to frighten fellow road users into baffled submission and costs merely £9.45. From Ford there was a sunroof, the rest of the items of extra luxury coming from the selection of a 3000E as a building base.

Broad laid on a very convincing display of the Bullit's abilities before we left the rural Southam air. We were able to watch as the engine pulled from a shade over 1,000 r.p.m. in fourth gear, which is a speed of 20.7 m.p.h. on the production 3.22:1 final drive, to 2,000 r.p.m., at which point the exhaust takes on a more urgent note, pulling the Capri up to 110 m.p.h. and approximately 5,500 r.p.m. in the same gear.

Settling into those superb seats for the first time we found all that we needed was easily operated by the movement conferred by the inertia reel belts. We particularly admired the neat installation of the electric fan warning light alongside the handbrake's similar light. Production instrumentation was retained, the water temperature normally staying within the centre of the dial unless the car was consistently cruised in excess of the standard rev. limit at 5,750 r.p.m. Oil pressure stayed steady at 60 lb. per sq. in., save when the level was low in the sump and the gauge immediately showed its distaste for such a state of affairs by swinging during acceleration and cornering. The steering column lock on the 3-litre is not as badly sited as those on the GT6/Spitfire range, but when it refused to yield to all but a skilled Ford Boreham mechanic I found myself echoing colleague Andrew Marriott's sentiments on these fiddling devices. Surely any car-thief worth his ill-gotten gains can unlock the steering just as quickly as they can admit their unlovely presence to any other part of a car?

Starting hot or cold never gave a moment's trouble and, thanks to that electric fan, warm up was much improved and the horrible whine of the standard Capri's mechanical effort banished. Acceleration is of the flashing variety in the Bullit and the improvement over the standard product is thoroughly worthwhile, the latter car hardly qualifying as a motorised mimser anyway. Those who like facts and figures can add up the seconds saved throughout the range from the tables at the end. Far more important to the tester was that the runs were made with no effort and only the slightest indication of axle tramp. On the road we found that the other traffic was apparently all travelling at 00.1 m.p.h. and this led to a few interesting exercises in testing the Bullit's brakes and dodging ability, both of which are in that legendary bracket where it is found that the car assists one out of trouble, instead of dropping

the unfortunate conductor into the mire, should he plumb the depths of stupidity.

In fact, the Bullit is so much fun to drive that it would probably bore you all to recount its perfect balance whilst cornering on the limit (strictly a test track exercise if officialdom is in the habit of writing unpleasant things within the blank pages of your licence), uncanny peace whilst cruising at anything below 110 m.p.h.—and it's mainly the sunshine roof which upsets the harmony, the buffeting from this source being bearable, but not particularly pleasant, at a steady 120 m.p.h.

With the wide power band provided third gear can cover that 34 m.p.h. second gear gap between the two ratios. The maximum of close to 95 m.p.h. in third gear gives one an idea of the effortless and efficient overtaking capabilities offered. The time of seven seconds which it takes to accelerate from 50 to 70 m.p.h. in fourth gear also effectively illustrates the car's flexibility and is 0.7 sec. faster than the standard Capri 3-litre, which shows that the camshaft and breathing arrangements have not suffered at low speed, whilst providing 6,500 r.p.m. and tyre melting take-off. The gearchange was completely acceptable and seemed to be above the average UK standard, though Broad is hoping to produce a closer set of ratios which would probably have the effect of making this Bullit a match for all but the hottest American pony cars, until 80 or 90 m.p.h. at least, when the effect of six or seven litres is bound to make itself felt.

Judged overall, the Capri suffered more than its fair share of minor ailments which would be rectified by Ford under warranty (the bonnet lock jammed intermittently as an example) but surmounted these by its excellent performance and general balance. The car we tried is just an example of Broadspeed's talents, for the intention is to tailor each car exactly to the customers' requirements. Seating, steering wheel design and even a camshaft for automatic transmission can all be specified, as can a £40 limited slip differential which would really ice the cake. With an enormous variety of Ford variations on the Capri theme that are available and the sophistication that Broadspeed can offer, I think the modified 3-litre Capri could well carve out a highly desirable niche in market and make a lot of owners extremely glad they are keen enough to have their production cars improved.

J. W.

PERFORMANCE FIGURES

m.p.h.	seconds	Gear speeds :	
0-30 ..	2.8 (3.0)*	1st ..	42 m.p.h. (39)*
0-40 ..	3.9 (5.0)	2nd ..	60 m.p.h. (53)
0-50 ..	5.5 (7.2)	3rd ..	94 m.p.h. (83)
0-60 ..	7.2 (10.2)	4th ..	126 m.p.h. (114)
0-70 ..	10.1 (13.6)	Overall m.p.g.: 16.6 (19.2)	
0-80 ..	12.9 (17.8)		
0-90 ..	17.3 (25.6)		
0-100 ..	23.2 (39.8)		

Standing quarter-mile : 16.1 sec.
Speedometer error : 3 m.p.h. slow at 70 m.p.h.
Converter : Broadspeed Ltd., Banbury Road, Southam, Warwicks.
Prices : Commence at £1,825, test car valued at £2,400.
  * *Figures in brackets refer to a production Capri 3000 GT XLR.*

Comanche 190

It may have escaped your notice, all twitched up as you are about wringing the last crumb of horsepower from your small block Ford, that the real hop-up news at the moment is coming from the big Capris. We did a piece a couple of months back you will remember on how tuners were at last beginning to realise the big pony's potential —we looked then at Autovita and Superspeed versions.

Since then we've been playing around with our own Allard-blown version of the three litre, have heard secret rumours that Ford of England are seriously interested in the South African Perana Capri with 4.7 Mustang power, and we've seen what Ford of Germany power can do with 2.6-litre sixes. Now we've had the chance to try Jeff 'Mr Engine Swap' Uren's idea of what the Capri should really be like.

Uren is widely known for his well-engineered variants of standard Fords, and achieved lasting fame with his well sorted three-litre version of the Mk 2 Cortina which he called the Savage. Now, staying with the Red Indian kick, we have the Comanche which starts life as a Capri three litre before getting the Uren handling/suspension sort out and one of a choice of Weslake conversions on the engine. What you get is a high performing good handling GT car that at once lifts the Capri out of the Jew Boys' Express bracket and into a more refined slot occupied by BMWs and the like.

Weslake are a concern of many parts but for the average street car user they are best known for their efficient top-end jobs on production engines which through reworked heads, manifolds and cams realise a high increase in power over the manufacturers' standard output. On the Ford V6 you can get your Weslake

power in three stages—170, 180 and 190bhp. Reworked heads with bigger valves, coupled to more efficient manifolding and modded Weber improve breathing by a significant amount and, with a wilder cam, result in 169bhp against the standard 144. Dropping in higher compression pistons with this package realises a further 10 brake and more head work then brings in the full 190 version as fitted to our test car. With the 190 you end up with a free revving and cammy engine which will rev to over 6500, whereas the standard lump comes over all breathless much over 5000 with a theoretical red line at 5850. Difference now is that the engine really happens at higher revs and for purely speed stuff it's worth holding on to the revs. What you lose though is the low down flexibility of the stock engine and around 2750rpm is needed to keep the engine from dropping off cam.

As we explained last month when comparing the Weslake car to our own Capri this creates certain traction problems in that to keep the car from bogging down you need to keep the revs on—pop the clutch too quickly and there's a satisfying howl from the rear but not too much in the way of g-forces. Trick is to feed the clutch in more slowly but rather your clutch than mine. On the move though the Comanche really shifts and honks on right up to 125mph which is a good 15mph more than standard. Sounds quick too with the twin megaphones and the clamour of a finely tuned engine. As we said, acceleration was not quite as quick as our blown Capri but over three runs it was a very near thing —see table right.

No way is the stock three litre suspension up to coping with that sort of power. For one thing the back axle on its

semi elliptics tramps wildly even with the standard output, so Uren has applied his track science to the road and come up with a suspension package that answers just about all the criticisms of the factory version. I was sufficiently impressed to immediately put my car into Uren's to have the same package and so far I can't say anything but good about it.

Basic problem with the big Capri is a lack of directional stability both in a straight line and in cornering. You never quite know where that long front end is going to point next and when motoring hard it becomes a problem to keep the thing anywhere near where you want it to be on the road. Stock suspension is very firm anyway so merely jacking up the shock absorbers (as some converters do) isn't going to help much. Uren has tackled it front and rear. Rear has flatter springs which locate the axle much more securely and prevent wind-up under fierce acceleration. Back end also has adjustable shox and special Uren radius arms. Front has uprated struts with stiffer springs and castor and camber angles have been evolved to point the car more precisely with more surefooted fast handling, though at the expense of slightly increased tyre drag at low speed cornering forces. Apart from the actual handling characteristics, the most noticeable difference from the outside is the slightly lower set of the car—about an

inch lower than norm.

Together the engine and suspension mods give a car with very genuine high speed grand touring characteristics. It goes, it handles, it looks good (well I think it does anyway) and it sounds good too. Fuel consumption comes down to about 17mpg which is fair considering the performance, and a credit to the efficiency of the Weslake mods.

Jeff Uren will sell you a ready packed Comanche on the 3000GT for £1931.69 in 190bhp form, which compares very well with anything offering a similar standard of performance. Uren will also supply and fit engine conversions to your existing car for £184.40 for the 170bhp, £278.50 for the 180 and £288.50 for the 190. That's including labour and fitting charges. Not cheap but you're buying a lot of extra performance. Suspension build as a separate job costs £86.

Worth it? Well these days I only get really turned on by big cars and I'd rather start with something with a good kick of power like a V6 Capri than with something with only half the power which needs a temperamental screamer of an engine to get anywhere near the same output. The Capri 3000 is good value anyway and with performance and handling like this it becomes a very desirable package. Seems at the moment as if we're getting more usable power for less money with the blower route —turn to page 50 to see how we're making out. **MH**

	Comanche	CC Blown Capri	Vita 6	Standard
0—30	2.6sec	2.4sec	2.8sec	3.2sec
0—40	3.8sec	3.8sec	3.9sec	5.0sec
0—50	5.2sec	5.0sec	5.6sec	6.8sec
0—60	6.6sec	6.4sec	7.6sec	8.8sec
0—70	8.8sec	8.0sec	—	11.2sec
0—80	11.6sec	11.2sec	—	—
0—100	18.8sec	not yet taken	—	—
SS¼	16.0sec	15.4sec	—	17.8sec

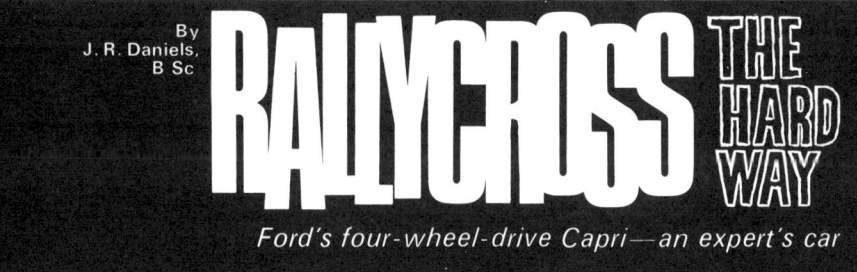

By J. R. Daniels, B Sc

RALLYCROSS THE HARD WAY

Ford's four-wheel-drive Capri—an expert's car

This works Capri is the most sophisticated car in rallycross. It won the ITV/Castrol Championship at Cadwell Park with Roger Clark driving. We test it and find that the combination of high power, low gearing and four-wheel-drive poses problems that only the best drivers can fully sort out

THE day was lovely, which was more than could be said for the car we had come to drive. Not only did it look a bit second-hand (one careful driver— Roger Clark; never raced or rallied—just a full season's rallycross); worse still, it wouldn't start. Power was coming from a massive battery trolley plugged into the back of the car, because the car itself had no generator and only a small battery. Ether was being squirted into six massive intake trumpets under the raised glass fibre bonnet. Mick Jones, well known to thousands as the man who was trying to tell the works drivers how to change a MacPherson strut through the fence of a *parc fermé* in the BBC Wheelbase film of the World Cup Rally, was sitting in the driving seat and exercising patience and the accelerator pedal.

For some time, nothing was heard but a repetitive whirr-splutter-graunch; then the thing lit up on two cylinders and brought in the other four in rapid succession. It was no longer possible to hear anything very much. Mick took the car out to the track to warm it up (we could hear it over the far side) and we learned something about it.

Late last year, three four-wheel-drive Capris were built for the rallycross season. Two of them had a modest 212 bhp, and were to be run by Rod Chapman and Stan Clark. The third, for Roger Clark, was a much more whole-hog device with 250 bhp under the bonnet. The power unit started as a standard 3-litre vee-6, of which little but the block remains. The cylinder heads, Weslake-built, were de-

signed by Len Bailey to take full advantage of a racing type Lucas fuel injection system, with the pump driven by a toothed belt from an auxiliary pulley on the front of the crankshaft. The oil system was completely changed to a dry sump system, based on a 2-gallon oil tank in the boot and a Holbay racing pump. The original pump was retained to act as the scavenge pump. The distributor had to be run off a skew gear, because there was no longer any room for it in its original position. An electronic cut-out was fitted to limit the revs to 6,500 rpm so that the throttle could stay wide open with the car airborne, and steel main bearing caps were fitted so that they wouldn't be hammered out while this was going on.

Despite the hairy nature of the engine, the car's main interest inevitably lies in the four wheel drive system. The heart of it is the Ferguson torque-splitting centre differential, which comes as a sealed unit from Ferguson and Ford don't touch it except to put it into the car and take it out again. The units are available with several different torque ratios; Ford use one which gives a 40:60 split front to rear, so that the back wheels can be made to spin first and set the car up sideways. The front drive passes through the engine beneath the crankshaft. Front final drive ratio is 4·71, an Escort ratio which was as close as Ford had to the back axle ratio of 4·63. The slight difference in ratios appears not to matter, although an experiment with a much greater difference rapidly ended in disaster. A 75 per cent limited-slip differential is used at the back, and there is a spin limiter in the centre differential as well (the car was tried without it, and proved very difficult to control). There is no limited slip on the front final drive.

The main source of unreliability has been drive shaft breakage. This apparently comes about because the constant velocity joints have a maximum design working

angle of 19 deg, and this is handsomely exceeded when the car is suffering the combined effects of full lock and full rebound.

Surprisingly little has been done to strengthen the body, which speaks well for the basic Capri design. Most of the work has gone more into making the car as light as possible, with glassfibre bonnet, boot and doors and plastic windows. One point which is fairly obvious is that the upper housings for the Mac-Pherson struts are massive turrets looking like part of some miniature military emplacement. Strength is necessary here, but the turrets are also needed so that they can mount the struts higher to clear the front drive shafts.

Figures first
Apart from just driving the car, we also wanted to take some standing-start performance figures. A snag arose when we found that there was no way in which our fifth wheel bracket could be readily attached to the bumperless back end of the Capri. Then the helpful Ford instrumentation people next door offered to lend us some of their own test equipment, the sort of gear which makes a road tester wish that he was working for a major manufacturer. . . .

The upshot of this was that colleague Ray Hutton ended up crouched in the back of the Capri, with just a cushion between him and the oil pipes which (we were warned) would get very hot. Facing him was a massive box of tricks—the electronic incremental speed timer, giving the time taken to cover 5 mph or 10 mph increments during an acceleration run— wedged between a spare inner tube and the roll-over bar. I strapped myself in the front, shut the lightweight door with a very un-coachbuilt clatter, and pulled up the plastic window with the sort of strap device you used to find in railway carriages.

Starting was just a matter of ignition on, electrics master switch on, and press the starter button. In contrast to its behaviour when cold, the car started straight away, and Ray and I at once realised the impossibility of trying to communicate by anything but sign language. If the noise outside was bad, the noise inside was terrible, and most of it came very clearly from the massive plain exhaust pipes which ended under either door sill.

I carefully depressed the clutch all the way, engaged the first of the five gears in

RALLYCROSS THE HARD WAY

the ZF box, and gingerly explored the consequences of unleashing the beast. To my surprise, it neither stalled nor shot off through the nearest fence. It just ambled amiably out of the gate, under the guard-rail across the test track entrance, and on to the track itself and the appointed straight. All was ready for the acceleration runs.

I didn't want to invoke the ignition cut-out, because that always ruins this sort of run. Nobody knew exactly how accurate the rev counter was, so I decided to change up at 6,400 rpm, giving me 100 rpm in hand if it was accurate. There was just a trace of clutch slip, which if anything was a help. The gearchange, in true ZF tradition, was excellent. We motored briskly down the straight, making sure we knew where the quarter-mile posts were and what was a reasonable braking marker.

There was now no further excuse for postponing a proper run. Setting up 3,000 rpm, I slid my foot off the clutch. With a great squeal of tyres, the car leapt forward in a surprisingly smooth start. The rev counter rocketed, and I snatched second with the wheels still spinning. There was hardly any drop in revs, nor any appreciable drop in the rate of acceleration, and I had to slam the lever into third before I had a chance to let go of it, or so it seemed. Third was better. It lasted me all the way from 40 to 55 mph before I ran out of revs, a matter of 2 sec or so (said the incremental timer). Fourth was ludicrously close to third, and was only just good for 60 mph, but top gear was a good deal more relaxed —it took almost 3 sec to get from 60 to 75 mph, at which point the rev counter said there just wasn't any more to come. So we sat there at 75 mph until the quarter-mile post came past. . . .

The time for the standing quarter was 15·6 sec.; not bad considering it included four gear changes and a rev-limited final 200 yards. We reached 60 mph in 7·9 sec (including three changes) and 70 mph in 10·4 sec. Later—too late—we discovered that the rev counter was extremely pessimistic, and that my 6,400 rpm had been a true 5,000. Thanks to the mass of information from the timing apparatus, it was possible to extrapolate a pretty accurate picture of the performance had the full range been used. It gives the following figures: 0–30 mph, 2·4 sec; 0–40, 3·5; 0–50, 5·2; 0–60, 7·0; 0–70, 8·9; 0–80, 11·3; 0–90, 13·8. Maximum speeds in the gears emerge as 39, 52, 71, 78 and 92 mph.

Clearly, all the gear changing cuts something from the performance, not only on acceleration runs like this but also on the rallycross circuit. Ford would prefer to use a four-speed box, but there is no existing close-ratio unit which can stand the power, fit the Capri, and mate with the Ferguson transmission; so the ZF it has to be.

Sideways progress

The final stage in the day's operations was to try the car in its natural environment— in this case, a rough little figure-of-eight track laid out on one of the old Boreham

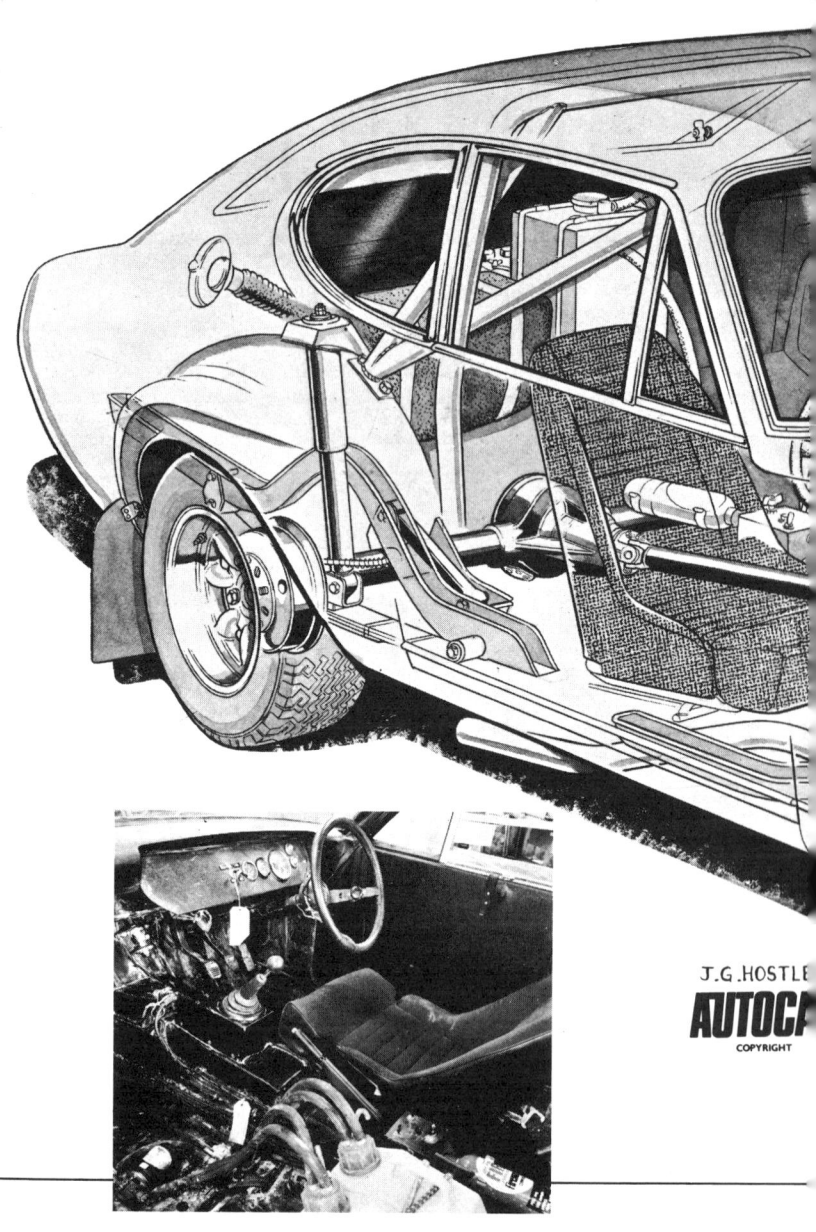

J.G. HOSTLE

AUTOCA

COPYRIGHT

Above: *Gutted interior has minimal instrumentation and very comprehensive screen washing apparatus. The panel behind the handbrake has ignition, starter, wiper and washer switches*

Left: *Our improvised passenger seat alongside Ford's impressive electronic speed timing apparatus, which includes a digital speedometer*

Right: *The boot is occupied by a Marston Excelsior rubber bag fuel tank, tandem high-pressure fuel pumps, the oil tank for the dry-sump system and the battery. Since there is no generator, power for starting is from a plugged-in power pack*

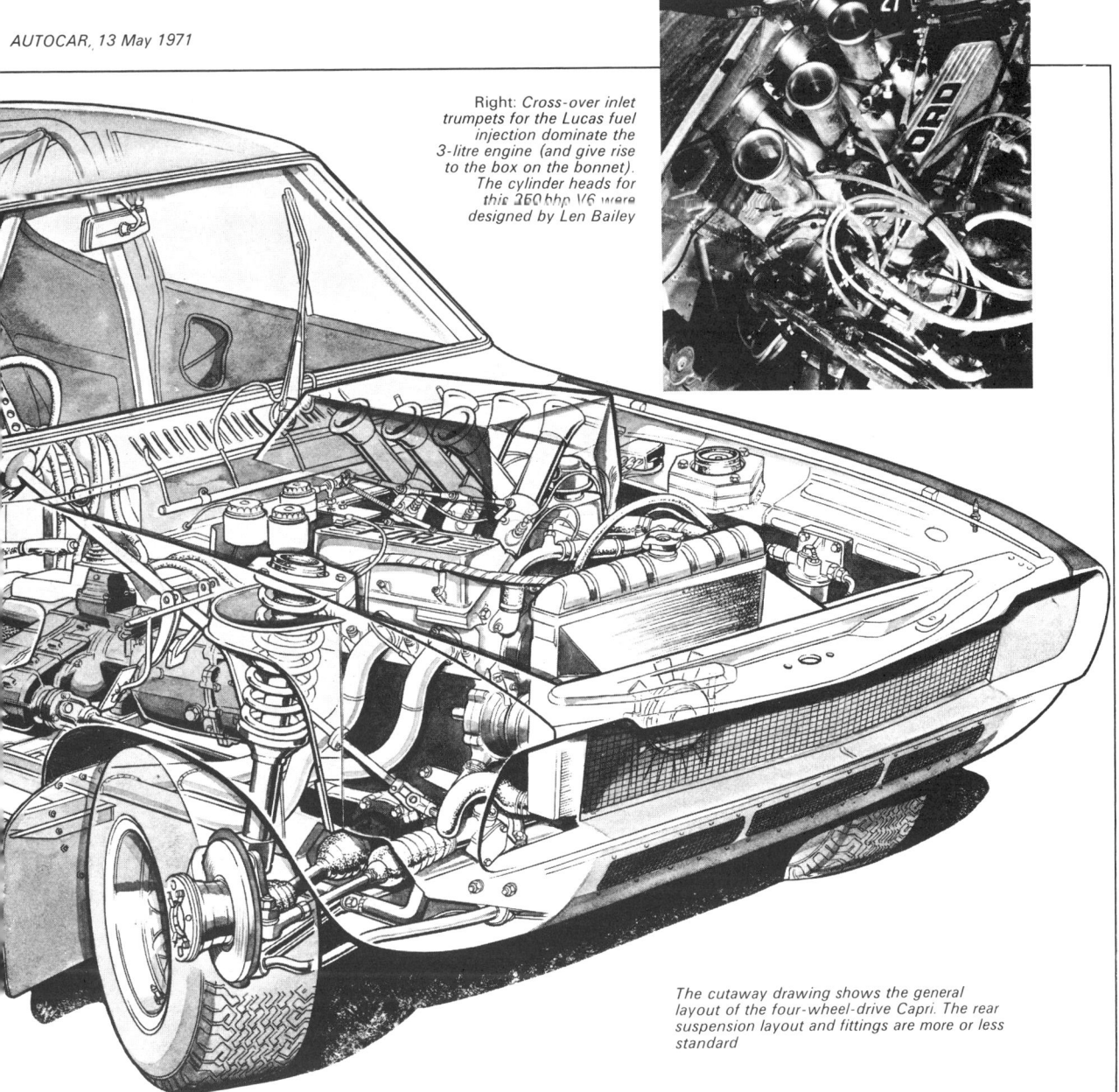

Right: Cross-over inlet trumpets for the Lucas fuel injection dominate the 3-litre engine (and give rise to the box on the bonnet). The cylinder heads for this 260 bhp V6 were designed by Len Bailey

The cutaway drawing shows the general layout of the four-wheel-drive Capri. The rear suspension layout and fittings are more or less standard

dispersal areas. Driving the car round the track, one or two more impressions had formed very strongly. The steering was very heavy on a smooth surface, and opening the throttle always tried to straighten the front wheels; and the brakes were dead and far from reassuring. Apparently the brakes have a tandem-piston arrangement to meet the Group 6 regulations under which the car was sometimes run, and these do not give as good results as the standard system.

On the rough ground of the dispersal area, however, things were different. In such a restricted area, we spent most of our time in second, occasionally taking third when we felt brave. Apparently the Ford works drivers reckon that once the thing gets too far out of line, there is nothing which will catch the tail. "Out of line" to them must mean literally sideways, because I can vouch for the fact that the car shrugs off a 45 deg. slide and regains the straight and narrow with no trouble at all.

Whether it is the *right* straight and narrow is another matter altogether. Ray Hutton and I both tried the car, each commenting that it seemed faster from inside than it looked from outside. Peter Browning, who was also on hand, then tried his luck. Driving the car much more like a Mini, he was impressively faster than either of us. But even he sometimes ended up letting the car go where it wanted to, rather than sticking to a predetermined course.

What does become clear when you are driving a car like this is that the interaction between the power and the steering becomes very complex indeed. Of course it is nice to have the traction of four wheel drive beneath you, and the car feels very impressive when it is pulling its way out of a situation. But pouring on the power doesn't just push the tail out; it pushes the nose out as well, makes the steering heavier, and in extreme circumstances almost wrenches it out of your hands. The best technique for cornering seemed to be

to get the tail out fairly early with a combination of power and wheel twitching, get the attitude stabilized, and *then* attack the corner with steering alone, applying power a few yards past the apex.

You hardly have to worry about the brakes; it is much easier to twitch the car sideways and lift off. Rallycross doesn't place a great premium on brakes anyway. To our credit (I suppose) none of us managed to spin the car. Perhaps we just weren't going fast enough.

One gets used to the noise after a while, but when you are out of the car, the quietness takes some time to filter through. In other respects, it is not too bad a physical experience. The ride is fair-to-good, thanks to the Bilstein dampers and the excellent seat (Roger Clark and I, apart from being virtually the same age, are also virtually the same size). One of the worst things about the car is the visibility. The big bonnet hump over the intake trumpets really gets in the way, to the

RALLYCROSS THE HARD WAY

Fast take-offs on the loose provide the interesting spectacle of all four wheels spinning. Thanks to a torque split biased to the rear it is possible to hang the tail out (inset). The nose-up acceleration shot (below) accentuates the visibility problem created by that bonnet hump

point where it is impossible to see the front left hand corner at all. Visibility in the mud is ensured by a wiper-washer system fed by five gallons of water via a Jabsco bilge pump. The driver can select intermittent or continuous washing; the latter, at full pressure, uses up all the water in about 2½ min!

All in all, a very entertaining day in a splendid and interesting car; our thanks to Bill Barnett and all the Competitions Department staff at Boreham. We carried away with us a much better idea of the way

this sort of work may eventually benefit production cars. It would be foolhardy to deny that four-wheel drive at this level poses engineering and driving problems. It says much for Roger Clark's driving ability that he can get so far towards solving them—and in public. The point is that he is not just doing it for himself; he is doing it for all of us who may one day drive a production four-wheel-drive Ford. In the final analysis, that is one of the things competition is all about.

CAPRI RS 2600

*You'll have to build the tuned version yourself
but the results will be worth the time and money*

PHOTOS BY RAINER SCHLEGELMILCH

OKAY, OKAY. So it's not available in the U.S. But there's no reason why an enterprising American enthusiast can't make up a reasonable simulation of it when the Capri 2600 GT is available in the U.S. in 1972. So, Capri enthusiasts, read on for inspiration, and after you're finished get out your wrenches and wallets.

In Europe the Capri can be ordered with a tremendous variety of engines, ranging up to a 3-liter V-6 in England and 2.6-liter V-6 in Germany. The German 2.6 is the fastest of the lot, and for a year now a racing version of it has been dicing with the racing BMW 2800CS for top honors in European sedan racing. A few months ago Ford Cologne brought a "road version of the racing version" to the market: the RS 2600. We had been excited about the RS ever

since we saw the first pictures of it, and a trip to Europe afforded us the opportunity to try it in an environment where it makes great sense—the roads and autobahns of Germany.

The regular Capri 2600 GT's V-6 engine displaces 2551 cc and produces a healthy 125 DIN bhp on a 9.0:1 compression ratio with twin carburetors—that's about 145 bhp in traditional U.S. thinking. The U.S. edition, with reduced compression ratio, should have 5-10 bhp less. For the RS, Ford bores the cylinders 2.2 mm more for 2637 cc, raises the compression ratio to 10:1, installs a more radical camshaft and freer exhaust system, and tops it off with a Kugelfischer mechanical fuel injection system similar to that used on the BMW 2002 tii. The result: 150 bhp DIN @ 5800 rpm. And performance in abundance.

The whole car is lowered one inch by lower springs—it looks even squatter—and 13 x 6 aluminum or magnesium wheels by Minilite with 185/70 radial tires are fitted. Bilstein ⟫→

CAPRI RS 2600

gas-pressure shock absorbers, like those used on the fancy German cars, are installed at the rear for better control of the live axle and the rear springs become single-leaf instead of multiple. At the front a small amount of negative camber results from the lowering.

Inside, there's complete instrumentation, unlike that of the 4-cyl Capris we have but standard on the 2600 GT, and a small, thick-rimmed racing steering wheel with deeply recessed hub. The front seats are a fine pair, contoured with lots of lower back and thigh support and thick side bolsters for lateral location of the driver and passenger. Racing buckets are available as an option.

Outside, the RS has quad headlights that look like those on the U.S. version but are high-output quartz-halogen units. The hood is painted flat black, that color following the body contours back under the side windows; rocker panels and the rear lighting-license panel are also flat black. And the bumpers are simply not installed, the holes through which their brackets would protrude covered by parking lights similar to the ones that reside inboard the headlights on lesser Capris. A few other holes are left unstamped, and most of the side chrome is omitted. These changes, all relatively simple, result in an exciting, aggressive, muscular look that turned the head of every healthy human being we passed and drew peace signs even from hitch-hiking youths we didn't pick up! So what if there are no bumpers and very little ground clearance?

The fuel-injection engine behaves like the highly tuned pushrod unit it is. It's a reluctant starter from cold, usually dies at least once after the first start, and doesn't really respond well from idling to "go" even when fully warmed up. If it had carburetors we'd call it overcarbureted! At idle (1100 rpm) it rumbles quietly—a sort of small-scale reproduction of the idle of a high-output U.S. V-8.

Give it plenty of gas getting off from rest, though, and it's underway with whatever amount of wheelspin the driver decrees. In 1st gear it's out of revs very quickly—the gearbox, with its stump-pulling 3.65:1 ratio, is shared with the "fours." But the other gears are plenty useful if one interprets the tachometer's red sector (which begins at 5800 rpm, the power peak) liberally, as we did. Third took us to 96 mph, and the 0-100 time of 20 sec shows that even in 4th there's still a good head of steam at 100 mph. At U.S.-style cruising speeds the engine is lazy and quiet; for autobahn work it hums a happy song in the 5000-5800 range for hours on end. One enters the red sector at 120 mph but there's enough left to pull the Capri on to 126 @ 6200.

The RS's quick steering, virile engine and surefooted braking invite its driver to push really hard. Unfortunately the Uniroyal 185/70-13 tires on our test car didn't quite deliver. The car is a basic understeerer and, even with the tires set to higher-than-recommended 32 psi all around, they protest audibly in hard cornering. At that the RS has more cornering power than 98 percent of drivers can use, but the most capable pilots will want something better. The selection of 185/70 or A70 radials is small in the U.S.; those who are willing to sacrifice a bit of general good behavior for ultimate cornering power might prefer a bias-belted A70-13.

With the radials the RS's steering reminds us of a Porsche 911 on big Michelins—there's a feeling of very direct connection with the front wheels, complete with lots of feedback on bumpy turns. Speaking of bumpy turns, the stiff springing and live rear axle also make themselves known—the RS can be skittish under these conditions. At high speed one familiar Capri characteristic—lack of straight-line stability and extreme sensitivity to crosswinds—is nicely under control on the RS, for what reason we can't say. And the prevailing understeer makes it equally stable when cornering at high lateral loading even over 100 mph.

Disc/drum brakes wouldn't be adequate for the real racing Capri, but on the RS they do a workmanlike job. We didn't get into any situations where they let us down, despite a lot of nip-and-tuck autobahn driving, but neither did we run our fade test because we don't take that test equipment abroad.

The seats really work, and we liked their corduroy upholstery; they are adjustable well back for long-legged drivers and the backs recline. Other aspects of comfort are just so-so; the ride is really harsh, and at truly high speeds the racket is plentiful. At 70 mph, where the RS's potential is wasted, one could enjoy the 5-band radio perfectly well.

That's the Capri RS 2600. Not everyman's car, but a bundle of fun if you've got a good place to use it and the nerve to extract its potential. No, you can't order it, but if you start with a 2600 GT (which will have plenty of power for American driving), install a free-flow mellow exhaust system, lower it, fit the big wheels and tires, remove the bumpers and chrome, fill the appropriate holes and do the paintwork, you'll have a stunning Capri and a good time.

ROAD TEST RESULTS

PRICE

List price, W. Germany .app. $4400
List price, U.S. . . . . . .not available

ENGINE

Type	ohv V-6
Bore x stroke, mm	90.0 x 69.0
Equivalent in	3.53 x 2.71
Displacement, cc/cu in	2637/160
Compression ratio	10.0:1
Bhp @ rpm	150 DIN @ 5800
Equivalent mph	116
Torque @ rpm, lb-ft	
	165 DIN @ 3500
Equivalent mph	70
Fuel injection	Kugelfischer mechanical
Type fuel required	premium, 96-oct
Emission control	none

DRIVE TRAIN

Transmission	4-sp manual
Gear ratios: 4th (1.00)	3.22:1
3rd (1.37)	4.41:1
2nd (1.97)	6.33:1
1st (3.65)	11.75:1
Final drive ratio	3.22:1

CHASSIS & BODY

Layout	front engine/rear drive
Body/frame	unit steel
Brake type	9.6-in. disc front, 9.0 x 2.3-in. drum rear, vacuum assisted
Swept area, sq in	217
Wheels	cast alloy, 13 x 6J
Tires	Uniroyal T5 185/70 HR-13
Steering type	rack & pinion
Overall ratio	17.7:1
Turns, lock-to-lock	3.7
Turning circle, ft	34.0
Front suspension	MacPherson struts, coil springs, tube shocks, trailing arms, anti-roll bar
Rear suspension	live axle on single-leaf springs, tube shocks

ACCOMMODATION

Seating capacity, persons	2+2
Seat width, front/rear	2 x 20.0/51.0
Head room, front/rear	40.0/36.0
Seat back adjustment, degrees	70

GENERAL

Curb weight, lb	2315
Test weight	2645
Weight distribution (with driver), front/rear, %	55/45
Wheelbase, in	100.8
Track, front/rear	54.2/53.2
Overall length	165.0
Width	64.8
Height	49.7
Ground clearance	4.0
Overhang, front/rear	28.6/37.6
Usable trunk space, cu ft	7.0
Fuel tank capacity, U.S. gal	15.3

PERFORMANCE

Top speed, high gear, mph	126
0-1320 ft(¼ mi)	15.0
Speed at end of ¼ mi, mph	88
Time to speed, sec:	
0-30 mph	2.8
0-40 mph	4.0
0-50 mph	5.6
0-60 mph	7.3
0-70 mph	9.8
0-80 mph	12.3
0-100 mph	20.0

CALCULATED DATA

Lb/bhp (test weight)	17.6
Mph/1000 rpm (4th gear)	20.0
Engine revs/mi (60 mph)	3000
Piston travel, ft/mi	1360
R & T steering index	1.25
Brake swept area sq in/ton	164

FUEL CONSUMPTION

Normal driving, mpg	19.5
Cruising range, mi	295

SPEEDOMETER ERROR

30 mph indicated is actually	29.0
40 mph	39.0
60 mph	58.0

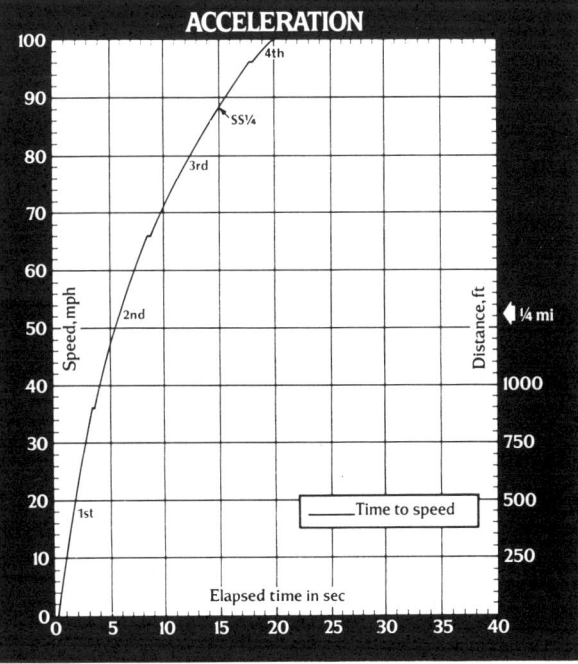

ACCELERATION

Tech expert David Vizard takes a break from "conventional" methods of tuning and looks at Allard's supercharged big Ford.

tuning V6's

THE CONVERSION KIT WAS, TO ALL INtents and purposes, a basic supercharger kit. By that statement I don't mean that anything about the supercharger kit itself is basic, but rather that it could be termed a Stage 1 supercharger conversion. The kit can be had in two forms, the first at £248 utilizes the standard 40 DFA Weber for carburation. The second version, and the one which we tested, costs £268, and instead of the Weber, uses a single 2in SU.

The price of this may sound high, but the kit is very comprehensive. It supplies virtually everything you will need to convert a V6 to a supercharged engine right down to the last detail such as boost gauge, bonnet bulge, gaskets, Kenlow electric fan, reduced compression heads, etc. The only addition to the kit on my test car was that of a high performance exhaust system priced at £48. In view of the inadequacies of the standard system, this new system seemed worthwhile on the basis of power and the exceedingly powerful sounding rumble it emitted.

Okay, some £300 including the exhaust system, is a lot of money to spend on a conversion, so what do we get for the money in terms of power and performance? Well, I asked Alan Allard just how many horsepower he thought the engine produced and he admitted (honest fellow that he is) that the engine had not yet been on a dyno, primarily because they are in the process of moving their dynomometer. However, he did say that since it was at least as fast as other tuned V6's, it must be around 190 bhp.

As later events were to prove, the Allard supercharged Capri was considerably faster than most other Capris tested and yet our own measurements of the horsepower were somewhat short of the 190. This, I think, seems to show that somebody is claiming exaggerated horsepower figures.

Our power curves show the installed flywheel horsepower of both the standard engine and the Allard supercharged engine. These figures show the horsepower actually at the flywheel, when all other losses are catered for, that is, all the power absorbed by the ancilliary equipment, brake servo, and the fact that the engine is breathing hot under-bonnet air. Under normal test bed conditions the V6 engine shows about 10 bhp higher than on our graph. However, it is the installed horsepower that pushes us along the road and not the theoretical test bed power.

By spending £300 on a supercharger kit, then, one can be buying some 60 bhp for the V6 engine or, to look at it another way, a 55 per cent increase in power. When taking the power figures I was somewhat surprised to find that below about 2200 revs, the output of the supercharged engine was slightly less than the standard engine. However, this could be easily accounted for when one considers that we borrowed the car from Allards before the development had been finished. Neither the carb needle profile, nor the advance curve of the distributor, had been finalised at the time of my acquaintance with the car.

Since there is often a lot of controversy as to how much power is lost in the transmission, I took the Allard Capri down to a couple of rolling road dynos to measure the power at the wheels. The first of these, Morspeed Performance, Livery Street, Birmingham, showed that the Capri had 150 bhp at 6000 rpm. This was not peak power, as the graph shows, but the rev limit of 6000 prevented us from taking the figures any higher up the rev range. As a check on the figure obtained at Morspeeds, I then went along to a second rolling road dyno at Kenilworth Motor Racing Services Ltd., Kenilworth Road Garage, Hampton-in-Arden, Solihull. On their dyno the Allard Capri showed 153 bhp at the wheels.

The power curve for the Allard V6 Capri then is, to say the least, pretty impressive, even if it is somewhat short of 190 bhp. It would seem that these high horsepower figures claimed by most tuners have been brought about by Fords original, and perhaps optimistic claim of 144 bhp for the standard engine. To avoid an embarrassing situation where tuners are claiming for the initial stages of tune less power for their engines than Fords are for their standard engines, the tuners have added on their horsepower increases to the original figure. Such practices are misleading, but we can hardly blame the tuners for practices forced upon them by Fords propaganda dept.

As I said earlier on, this kit can be regarded as a Stage 1 kit. Although it gives a very substantial increase in horsepower on its own account it can, when used with other components, give even higher power outputs than those achieved. For instance, the addition of a good camshaft with a little more overlap and lift than the standard item would add at least 15 and possibly 20 bhp to the output. A pair of fully gas flowed big valve heads should add at least another 10.

It should be remembered that the heads supplied with the kit have little else done to them apart from the reduction of the compression ratio from 8.8 down to 8.4. A good transistor ignition system should be worth at least another 6 bhp, whilst a high boost pulley, one which gives the supercharger a 20 per cent overdrive, should be worth at least another 10.

A cross drilled crank, which would allow higher rpm to be used, would also benefit the power. It doesn't take much imagination then to realise that in its supercharged form, the V6 could easily be capable of power outputs of 180-190 at the wheels. (On standard V6 suspension the thought of all that power is little short of terrifying.)

So much for power curves, technicalities

and the like, now how does the car really go on the road?

Turning the ignition key brought the engine to life after rather more turns than one would expect from an unsupercharged car. This, however, can be easily explained by the long induction track from the SU right through the supercharger to the valves. Apparently quicker starting is brought about by use of the 40 DFA Weber mounted on top of the supercharger.

Pulling away and driving in the London traffic presented little problem. Indeed, were it not for the slight hiss of the SU carb, one would be hard put to tell that this car was, in fact, modified at all. Its docility and road manners in traffic conditions are almost beyond criticism, especially so if you are used to high performance cars which do have a degree of caminess.

Having got fully acquainted with the car, I tried some quick driving and it soon became apparent, even before we put the stop watch on it, that this car was going to be fast.

Doing a standing start away from the traffic lights could turn out to be a really spectacular event for the nearby populace. Too much throttle would produce screaming tyres, very thick black lines on the road, and a huge cloud of tyre smoke. A slightly uneven road surface in terms of grip or camber would mean that the car would leave the line with the tail end wagging a couple of feet or so either side if one became too enthusiastic with the loud pedal. I am sure that if the standard 5½in wheels were replaced by suitably shod wider items, the car would have been quicker off the line. Bearing in mind the 57/43 weight distribution biased to the front, the use of wider

wheels and tyres would have meant more grip which would lead to a bigger weight transfer to the rear, thus leading to a much better off-the-line performance.

During the week I had the car to test, the weather conditions were anything but conducive to good traction.

However, given a dry piece of road one could, by running a few hundred revs into the red on the tacho, do a 0-60 in six seconds. On one occasion when the road had dried out and we found some real traction we did a 0-60 in 5.2 seconds and did a standing start quarter in 14.9. However, before we could do another run, it rained, so we couldn't back up these figures.

The question of top speed for the Allard Capri was a purely academic matter. A vast increase in power meant that the standard gearing was now too low to make use of this extra power. At 120 mph the rev counter needle reached the red zone. This meant that the top speed was limited by the rpm gearing combination used. A few calculations based on the bhp available at the wheels of this Capri reveals that it has sufficient power, given the correct gearing, to push it well over 140 mph. An overdrive would be an ideal solution to the problem.

A look at the boost gauge under various conditions of rpm and speed showed that one could maintain high cruising speeds yet still not have any boost on the engine. The delightful part of this conversion was that one could be travelling along at 100 mph or so on small throttle openings and then suddenly give the car full throttle, the boost gauge would rip around to about 4lbs boost and the car would immediately roar off as if 100 mph had been snail's pace.

By adding the supercharger, the noise level within the car was increased. However, the supercharger noise could only be heard whilst accelerating, since at normal cruising speeds the boost would drop down below zero and the supercharger noise would disappear. The noise could in no way be termed excessive.

The only criticism that I could level at this conversion of any consequence was that of fuel consumption. The best that could be achieved was about fifteen to the gallon and during performance testing this dropped to about eleven to the gallon. However, it should not be overlooked that the needle profile of the carburettor had yet to be finalised and a check with a mixture analyser did show that the car was running rich throughout the rev range. There seems little doubt that by the time the needle profile has been got right that the fuel consumption figures will be considerably better than this.

To sum up, the addition of a supercharger on a V6 Capri makes this car a lot of fun to drive. It retains all the docility needed for Granny to use it as a shopping car, but when the power is unleashed little can stay with it except the most exotic of cars.

THE FIGURES

	Allard V6	Standard car
0-30	2.5 secs	3.0 secs
0-40	3.5	4.7
0-50	4.5	7.0
0-60	6.0	10.0
0-70	8.1	12.9
0-80	10.1	16.2
0-90	12.9	22.6
0-100	16.3	30.0

Maximum speed (limited by gearing) 120 mph
Allards are at 51 Upper Richmond Rd, London SW15

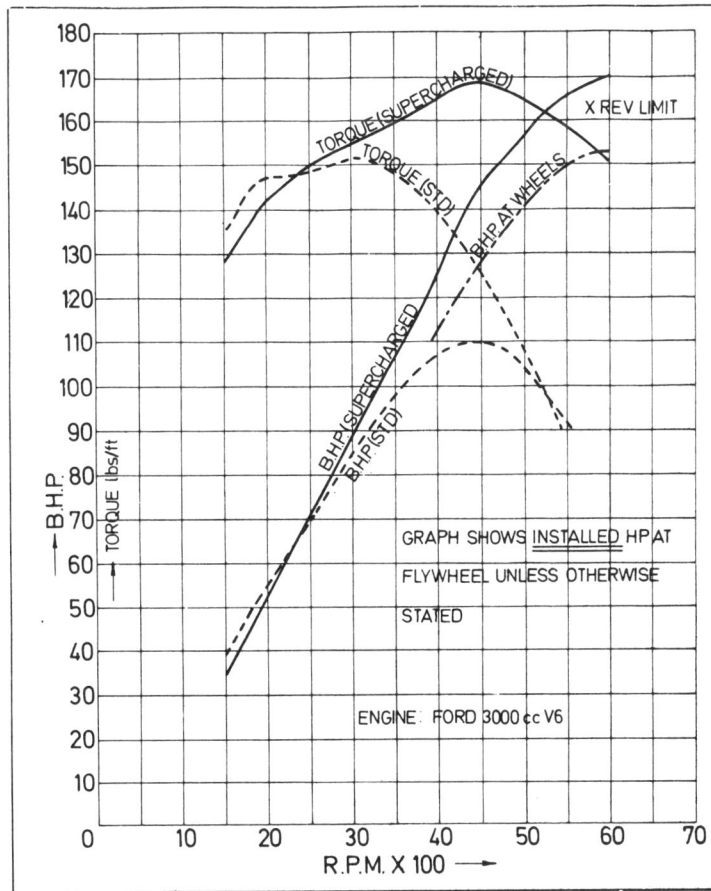

GRAPH SHOWS INSTALLED HP AT FLYWHEEL UNLESS OTHERWISE STATED

ENGINE: FORD 3000 cc V6

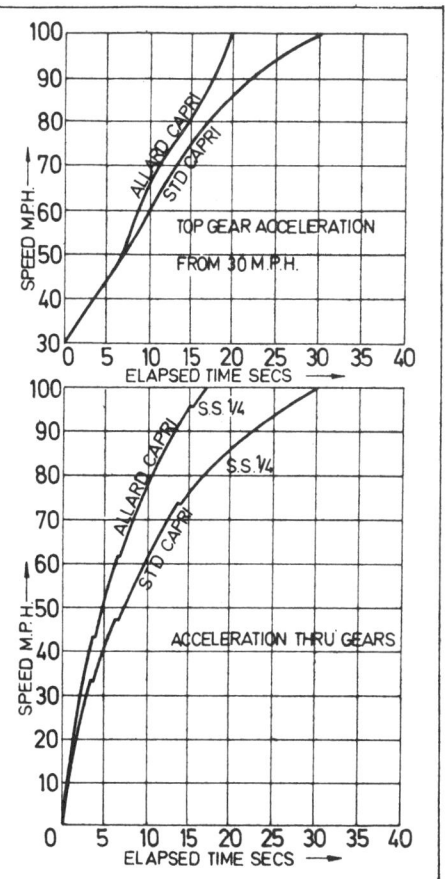

TOP GEAR ACCELERATION FROM 30 M.P.H.

ACCELERATION THRU GEARS

Publisher's 170S : front spoiler, Dunlop wheels and non-standard paint give the Capri an aggressive look.

EDITED BY TONY TOWN

A clutch of Capris from Lumo

SIMON TAYLOR describes owning standard and Lumo-ised 3000s, and tests the latest Lumo 180S

You can make a car fast with lots of revs, camshafts and close-ratio gears ; or you can make it fast with plenty of cubic inches and top gear torque. I've always been a fan of the latter method, and I reckon the best recipe for a rapid road smoker that's not too expensive to buy or maintain is a goodly-sized engine in a fairly compact chassis. When Ford put their excellent 3-litre V6 into the Capri back in 1969 I felt that this must be a workmanlike combination, and about a year later the secondhand prices had come down far enough for me to be able to afford one of the very first, actually about the sixth off the production line.

Although it had done 15,000 miles — and did about another 20,000 during my ownership, at high speed in all weathers, often towing trailered racing cars and never getting more than minimal servicing attention — it remained fast, quiet, effortless and utterly reliable. The engine never wanted to rev much above 4500 rpm, by which time the cooling fan sounded like a kettle coming to the boil, and the suspension was rather harsh, while both final drive and gearbox ratios were ill-chosen, but I developed great affection for it. By now Capris were very common but it was also, I thought, a good-looking car, finished in a nice shade of aubergine, with lines that were effective and not over-decorated.

When my Capri became rather long in the tooth I cast around for something different, mainly because I wanted a change after 18 months' motoring in the same car. But having failed to find anything else approaching the same price which would give me the same combination of torquey power, quietness at high cruising speed, reliability and cheap maintenance, I bought another Capri — this time a white 3000E, with such luxuries as vinyl top and sliding sunshine roof.

I decided to make this car into something rather special as far as funds allowed, so over the next few months it grew a British Vita front spoiler (which really worked in keeping the nose down on rain-soaked motorways at over 100 mph — without it the steering could become disturbingly light in the wet) and fibreglass boot lid (which made no difference to aerodynamics but just looked good). In those days, even though Cortina 1600Es and the like were on 5½J rims, the heavy and rather ugly Rostyle wheels on the Capri were only 5 inches wide, so a set of Dunlop Formula cast-alloy wheels replaced them—light, strong, good looking and not at all expensive. Setting off the exterior of my Mini-Mustang was a superb paint job with metallic dark blue side panels and gold coachwork lines, beautifully executed by the spray specialist at the Surrey garage of prolific motor racing entrant D. J. Bond.

Inside I fitted Terry Hunter seats, a hip-hugging bucket for me and an ultra-comfortable recliner for my passenger, and eventually managed to afford an eight-track stereo tape player, although I was down to one tape for weeks because they're three quid each! A Kenlowe thermostatic fan removed the fan noise at a stroke and, as we later proved on a rolling road, gave another three brake horsepower *at the back wheels* which the multi-bladed standard fan had been consuming. Cibié Caprima headlights transformed night vision, and I also fitted one of the very complex, scientific—and effective— sound-deadening kits from Sound Service of Oxford.

The 170S

So far I had a good-looking, comfortable and rather individualist Capri. But it still didn't want to rev much above 4500 rpm, it still lurched around in an understeery sort of way when it approached the limit of its roadholding and, while it was pretty quick, we all like going faster. So I went to Dunstable and discussed 3-litre Capris with Lumo Cars Ltd : a week later, for little more than £250, my car had become a Lumo 170S, and a very different animal indeed.

The engine was completely transformed : fully balanced and with a special cam and flowed heads and ports (while still retaining the standard compression ratio and the ability to run happily on three-star fuel), it would send the rev-counter needle rushing up to 6500 rpm and beyond, with a hard, smooth sound resembling nothing more or less than a Dino Ferrari. With this greatly improved rev-range the widely-spaced gear ratios no longer mattered much, for low-speed torque seemed unimpaired. Uprated front springs and completely new rear springs working with adjustable dampers gave a ride that fortunately wasn't much harsher than standard, but now, as the car approached its roadholding limit, breakaway was progressively smooth and controllable.

During my year's ownership I loved this car which, apart from a burst heater hose (Ford heater hoses must be made from the world's cheapest materials, for they do go with monotonous regularity) and a flat battery (caused by the clots who fitted the tape player and wired it up wrong), never let me down in any way, despite its higher state of tune, and never developed a thirst for oil. It would also return 20 mpg on long journeys when cruised at three-figure speeds for hour after hour. When, with great regret, I put it up for sale in the back of AUTOSPORT to make way for an extravagant device with two more cylinders, two fewer seats and 2700 more cc, people queued up to buy it. First in the queue was former Formula 3 racer Dave

"Daisy" Williamson, who bought it the day the advertisement appeared and is now, I trust, enjoying it as much as I did.

The 180S

When, at last year's Motor Show, Ford announced their "uprated" version of the 3-litre Capri, many people saw it as the death-knell of the modified Capri marketed by firms like Lumo. Ford had flattered the specialists by imitation: a new camshaft, improved breathing and different jets in the twin-choke Weber produced more power and reduced the original V6's marked unwillingness to rev. At the same time the car was improved in three areas which had been heavily criticised before: gear ratios, springing and braking. Repeated hard applications from high speed on the early big Capris could overheat the brakes and induce fade (although on my 170S harder pads and linings had gone a long way to curing this), so the front discs were moved further inboard on the stub axles to give them more cooling air. Spring rates were changed, softening the previously very bouncy ride, and, glory be, at last the Capri had a higher back axle ratio and lost that giant gap between second and third gears. Everyone who drove it agreed that the 1972 Capri 3000 was a good car made better.

But Lumo lost no time in evaluating one of the new cars against their 170S, and their development engineer, Humph Johnson, got to work. By March the 170S's successor, the 180S, was on the market.

The basis of the 180S conversion follows the same pattern as before: the engine is stripped and meticulously assembled with modified heads, a new Piper cam, rejetted carburetter, and subtle changes to ignition, inlet manifold and valve gear. The heads are polished to a high standard, combustion chambers are equalised, and the inlet and exhaust ports are flowed and matched to their respective manifolds (the V6 engine has as standard very efficient tubular exhaust manifolding). Part of the turnout is a smart blue coat of heatproof paint for the engine. If desired, all moving parts — crank, pistons, rods, clutch and flywheel — can be fully balanced, in which case Lumo say the engine is safe to well over 7000 rpm. Also available is a straight-through exhaust system, with a balance pipe just aft of the manifolds and twin rear exits, one each side of the car, which is not much louder than standard but whose sound complements the "Dino in Dagenham clothing" image.

Suspension-wise, the changes are again similar to the 170S: the rear springs are replaced with completely new four-leaf components working with Spax adjustable dampers, while the front struts are lowered slightly and uprated, now using new, higher rate coil springs.

I recently borrowed Lumo's 180S demonstrator for a fast weekend, just after it had been tested by another magazine who pronounced it "The perfect road Capri." Rather impressively, Lumo had resisted the temptation to dress up their demo car with all sorts of other expensive extras: it had the full 180S conversion with engine balance and twin exhaust system, but otherwise it was a plain 3-litre Capri, no Kenlowe fan, no special wheels, not even a radio.

First impression is at once one of smooth power, lots of it. The engine revs astonishingly easily — in neutral a touch of throttle sends the tachometer needle spinning round the dial — and yet, apart from the hum from the exhausts, it is no noisier than the standard car. Lumo claim 180 bhp from this engine — rolling road before-and-after tests show a 23 per cent gain at the rear wheels — and it is a lot quicker than the current standard car, while there is just no comparison with the earlier model. The closer gearbox ratios and higher back axle combine to produce a very steep acceleration curve indeed, for if one really does use 7000 rpm—which doesn't seem to betray any sign of strain from the engine — well over 70 mph is possible in second gear, and third is good for a sensational 100 mph. Without unduly caning the transmission or spinning the back tyres into oblivion, I repeatedly got 7 s times from standing start to 60 mph. But 0-70 in under

Taylor's car had spoilered glassfibre bootlid as well as the Lumo twin exhausts.

10 s (still in second), and 0-100 in just on 20 s are even more impressive from a substantial four-seater that can be put on the road new for £1800.

But it is during high-speed top-gear cruising that the real charm of the car becomes evident. A comfortable gait of 115 to 120 mph comes up very quickly on motorways, and given a longer stretch the 180S will build up to a genuine 130 mph. And when you have to slow down to 60 there's no need to change down — a quick top-gear squirt past the obstacle and you're doing 100 mph again.

This 180S was fitted with those first-class new Dunlop Formula 70 tyres rather than the more usual Goodyears, and they must have contributed a lot to the solid, precise feel of the car, particularly in the wet. Part of my spell with the car included a run down the M3 in torrential Sunday morning rain to keep a commentating engagement at Thruxton, and at high cruising speeds in the wet the 180S was rock steady.

Naturally, with so much power on tap, the tail can be swung out on sharp corners, but with the modified suspension of the 180S everything happens progressively and predictably. The taut feel of the car inspires tremendous confidence and, while the ride is firmer than on the softer 1972 car, it still feels a lot more comfortable than the earlier ones. Long, open corners on fast roads become a real delight, the car understeering at constant throttle openings just enough to feel

stable and undramatic.

Part of the charm of this 180S was that — unlike my rather extrovert 170S — it looked outwardly completely standard, apart from the second exhaust pipe. At traffic speeds it remained quiet and docile, going below 20 mph in top without fuss, and, while really furious motoring could bring the fuel consumption down to around 18 mpg, driving more steadily the car seemed no more thirsty than its standard sister.

The Ford Capri 3-litre is a mass-produced car that is already fast, inherently safe and good value for money. Lumo have added a further refining process and, at probably considerably less cost than competitive conversions, have turned a good car into something exceptional. The Capri, Ford's success story of the late 1960s, will be with us for a long time yet: further detail improvements are due shortly, and no doubt Lumo (who, as well as selling an awful lot of bread-and-butter Fords along with the rest of the Luton Motors Group, also do a hot Granada called the MD) will continue to please a select but growing number of customers with their unflamboyant but very rapid grand tourer.

Lumo 180S engine conversion: flowed, matched and polished heads, Piper camshaft, rejetted carburetter, modified ignition, etc: £160.
Full engine balance: crankshaft, con rods, pistons, clutch, flywheel, etc: £65.
Lumo 180S suspension conversion: lowered, uprated front struts, higher rate front coil springs, special four-leaf rear springs, Spax adjustable dampers: £60.
Twin exhaust system with balance pipe: £39.
Lumo Cars Ltd, 55 London Road, Dunstable, Beds.

Unless you spot the twin-pipe exhaust system, there is nothing to distinguish the very potent Lumo 180S from a standard 3-litre Capri.

BRIEF TEST

FORD CAPRI 3000E

When the Ford Capri was introduced in February 1969, it caused a near-sensation in the motor industry with a spread of engine options ranging from a modest 54 bhp 1300 unit right through to the 128 bhp 3-litre V6 (brought out in November 1969). The 3000 was the sovereign of the range with a virtually unbeatable combination of handling and performance at the price. However, our enjoyment of it was marred by several faults: the good handling was achieved at the expense of a poor ride; fan noise was excessive at high revs; low overall gearing made it fussy for high-speed cruising; second gear was too low; and the minor control layout was extremely muddled.

On the second generation Capri 3000 most of the original faults have either been cured

	Ford Capri 3000 E 1972 model	Original Ford Capri 3000 GT (*Motor* Road Test Nov. 8, 1969)
Maximum Speed		
Lap	119.5 mph	110.5 mph
Mean Maximile	117.0	109.0
Acceleration		
0- 30 mph	3.1 sec	3.0 sec
0- 40	4.5	4.8
0- 50	6.1	7.0
0- 60	8.6	9.5
0- 70	11.7	12.7
0- 80	15.0	16.4
0- 90	19.5	22.6
0-100	26.5	29.5
Standing ¼ Mile	16.6	16.9
In Top		
20- 40 mph	7.7 sec	6.9 sec
30- 50	7.7	6.9
40- 60	7.7	6.1
50- 70	8.1	6.4
60- 80	8.5	7.4
70- 90	9.9	9.4
80-100	12.2	13.4

or improved, making the model truly outstanding value for money. Revised suspension settings have markedly improved the ride (though it is still not good), arguably at the expense of handling at the absolute limit. A new fan (still engine-driven) has reduced noise and the more powerful engine is a lot more willing. Both the final drive and second gear ratios have been raised with consequent improvements in cruising, acceleration and driver appeal. The muddled minor controls remain, however, and overall, the car is still noisy when extended.

Engine power output has been raised from 128 bhp (net) at 4750 rpm to 138 bhp (DIN) at 5000 rpm although torque has remained almost the same at 174 lb ft (DIN)—it was 173.6 lb ft (net)—still at 3000 rpm. This has been achieved by a revised camshaft, inlet tracts and exhaust system and a rejetted carburetter. The effect is immediately noticeable—the engine revs willingly with a sporting exhaust note (which some thought too noisy) making the 5800 rpm red line a lot more realistic than before.

Starting from cold was always instantaneous but the automatic choke of the down-draught Weber carburetter did not cut out soon enough. Getting the engine to normal temperature took about three minutes in the relatively warm (for January) weather that prevailed during our test. Obtaining warm air from the heater was consequently only marginally quicker. During this period the engine ran too fast on choke (presumably to use weaker mixture) giving an idle speed of 1800 rpm—about 21 mph in second gear. It was also prone to stalling when the choke cut out.

But these minor problems were perhaps quirks of our particular test car: what matters is that the performance is now terrific. The revised gear ratios and increased power have paid handsome dividends. We lapped MIRA's banked circuit at 119.5 mph (the old 3 litre managed 110.5 mph) which is just about as fast as you can go round the banking and achieve a meaningful result. Even at these speeds some speed is lost due to tyre scrub; a mean of two straight-line runs in opposite directions would certainly give over 120 mph.

At 119.5 mph the engine is spinning at 5450 rpm which is well past its peak—it's a pity that overdrive is not available to make high speed cruising even faster and less fussy.

There are four-seaters around that can beat this Capri on top speed but the nearest one in price is the Lotus Elan +2S 130 which costs over £900 more at £2659. And don't forget that you can get the mechanically identical 3000 GT for only £1534 (nearly £200 less than the 3000E).

For acceleration it's even more difficult to find any competitive four-seaters. The Capri is in the exclusive Lotus and BMW class. Predictably, the Lotus is the quicker all the way, but the 2002 Tii (£2299) and the Capri are virtually neck-and-neck up to 80mph when the Capri draws away — reaching 100 mph 2.3 sec. quicker at 26.5 sec. The next cheapest four-seater that we've tested to beat the Capri's 0-50 mph time of 6.1 sec. is the Porsche 2.2 911E (with the 2.4 engine now available it costs £5401 — over three times as much). Against four-seaters of similar price (as in our comparison charts) the Capri

The only way of recognising the new, uprated Capri 3000E is by its pseudo-magnesium wheels. Under the bonnet, below, the only clue is the revised air cleaner

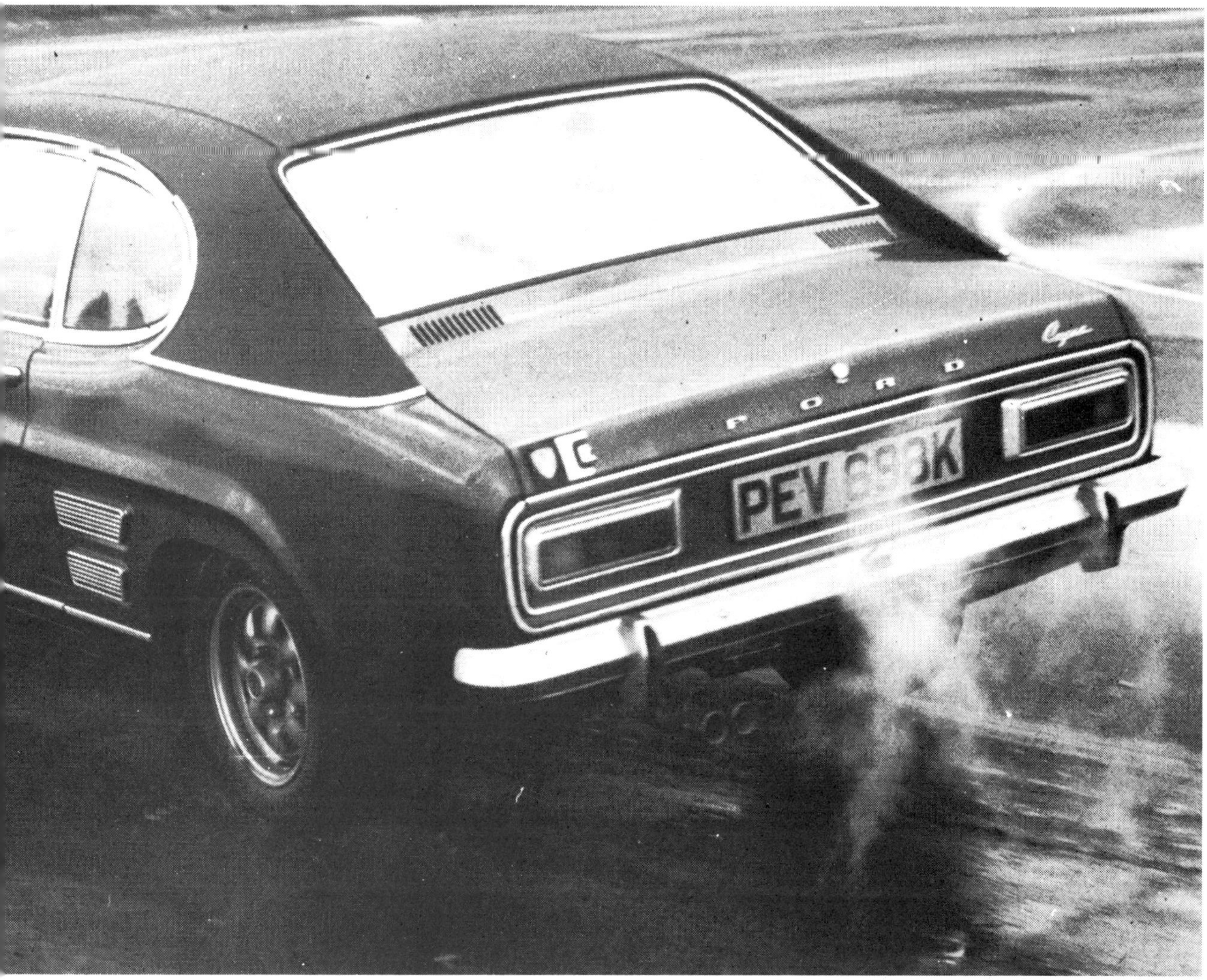
FORD

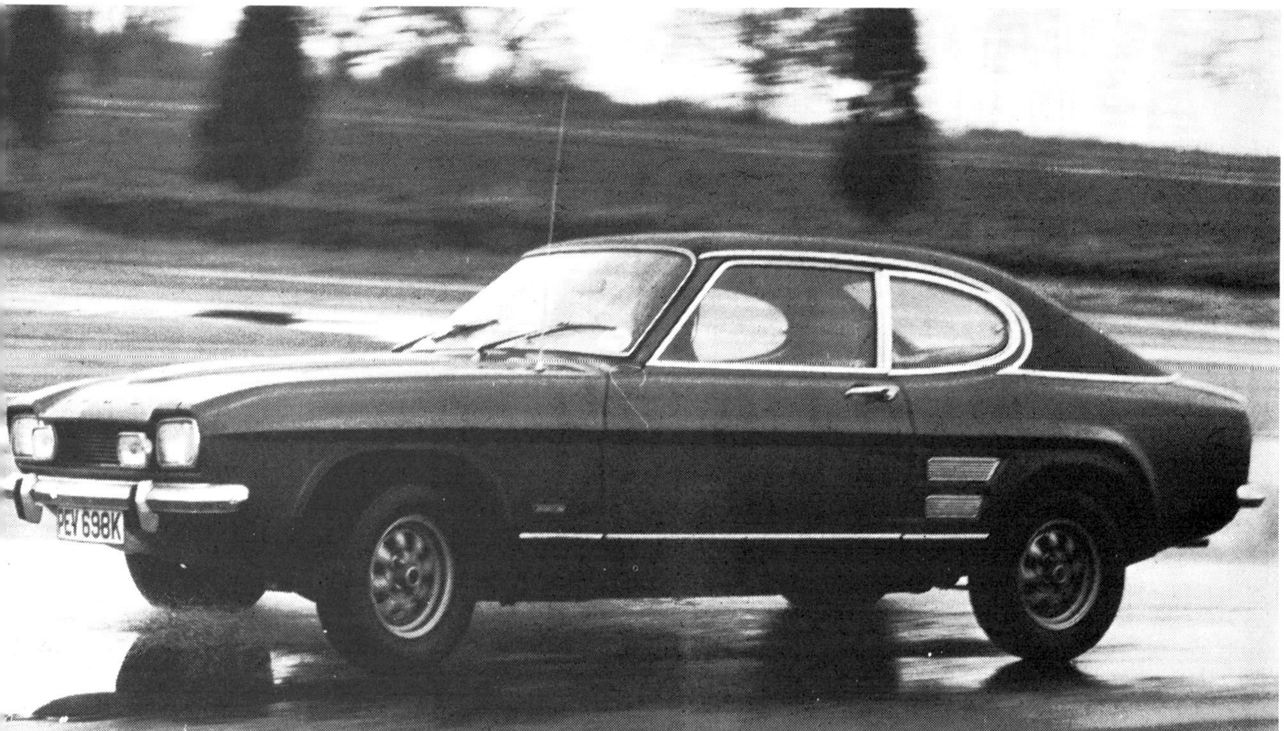
PEV 698K

Motor Brief Test No. 72 Ford Capri 3000E

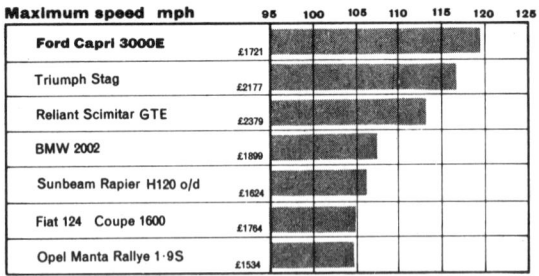

Maximum speed mph

		95	100	105	110	115	120	125
Ford Capri 3000E	£1721							
Triumph Stag	£2177							
Reliant Scimitar GTE	£2379							
BMW 2002	£1899							
Sunbeam Rapier H120 o/d	£1624							
Fiat 124 Coupe 1600	£1764							
Opel Manta Rallye 1·9S	£1534							

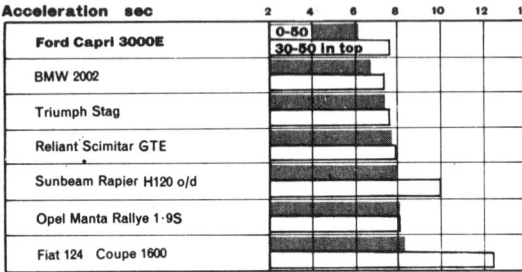

Acceleration sec

	2	4	6	8	10	12	14
Ford Capri 3000E (0-50 / 30-50 in top)							
BMW 2002							
Triumph Stag							
Reliant Scimitar GTE							
Sunbeam Rapier H120 o/d							
Opel Manta Rallye 1·9S							
Fiat 124 Coupe 1600							

Fuel consumption mpg

	5	10	15	20	25	30	35
Opel Manta Rallye 1·9S (Touring / Overall)							
BMW 2002							
Sunbeam Rapier							
Fiat 124 Coupe 1600							
Triumph Stag							
Ford Capri 3000E							
Reliant Scimitar GTE							

Performance tests carried out by *Motor's* staff at the Motor Industry Research Association proving ground, Lindley.
Test Data: World copyright reserved; no unauthorized reproduction in whole or in part.

Conditions
Weather: Windy and sunny.
Temperature: 36-47°F
Barometer: 29.6 in. Hg.
Surface: Damp tarmacadam
Fuel: 98 octane (RM)
4-Star rating

Maximum Speeds
	mph	kph
Mean lap banked circuit	119.5	192
Best one-way ¼-mile	121.5	196
3rd gear	90	145
2nd gear } at 5800 rpm	66	106
1st gear	40	64

"Maximile" speed: (Timed quarter mile after 1 mile accelerating from rest)
Mean	117
Best	118.5

Acceleration Times
mph	sec
0- 30	3.1
0- 40	4.5
0- 50	6.1
0- 60	8.6
0- 70	11.7
0- 80	15.0
0- 90	19.5
0-100	26.5
Standing quarter mile	16.6
Standing Kilometre	30.6

mph	Top sec	3rd sec
10- 30	—	5.6
20- 40	7.7	5.3
30- 50	7.7	5.1
40- 60	7.7	5.1
50- 70	8.1	5.4
60- 80	8.5	6.2
70- 90	9.9	7.7
80-100	12.2	—

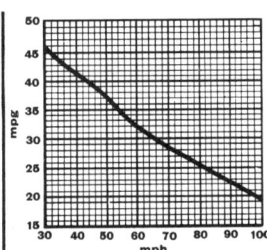

Fuel Consumption
Touring (consumption midway between 30 mph and maximum less 5% allowance for acceleration) ... 24.7 mpg
Overall ... 19.4 mpg (= 14.6 litres/100km)
Total test distance ... 1082 miles

Speedometer
Indicated	30	40	50	60	70
True	30	40	50	58	67
Indicated	80	90	100		
True	77	86	95		

Distance recorder ... 3% slow

Weight
Kerb weight (unladen with fuel for approximately 50 miles) ... 21.1cwt.
Front/rear distribution ... 57/43
Weight laden as tested ... 24.9cwt.

Engine
Block material	Cast iron
Head material	Cast iron
Cylinders	6in vee
Cooling system	Water
Bore and stroke	93.7mm (3.69in.) 72.4mm (2.85in.)
Cubic capacity	2994cc (182.7 cu.in.)
Main bearings	4
Valves	Overhead pushrod operated
Compression ratio	8.9:1
Carburettor	Weber compound downdraught with automatic choke
Fuel pump	Mechanical
Oil filter	Full flow

Max. power (DIN) 138 bhp at 5000 rpm
Max. torque (DIN) 174 lb.ft. at 3000 rpm

Transmission
Clutch . Single dry plate mechanical operation on diaphragm spring.
Internal gear box ratios
Top gear	1.00
3rd gear	1.41
2nd gear	1.95
1st gear	3.16
Reverse	3.35
Synchromesh	All forward speeds
Final drive	3.09:1

Mph at 1000 rpm in:—
top gear	22.0
third gear	15.5
second gear	11.3
first gear	6.9

Chassis and body
Construction .... Steel integral construction with controlled collapse front and rear sections. Electrocoated for corrosion resistance

Brakes
Type Hydraulic disc/drum with vacuum servo assistance
Dimensions . 9.63in. dia. disc front; 9.0in. dia. drum rear

Suspension and steering
Front . Independent by coil springs. Track control arms and anti-roll bar
Rear . Live axle: asymmetrical semi-elliptic leaf springs, twin upper radius arms
Shock absorbers
Front	Telescopic
Rear	Telescopic
Steering type	Rack and pinion
Tyres	185 HR 13 Goodyear Grand Prix radial
Wheels	Sports style pressed steel
Rim size	5½J x 13

Coachwork and equipment
Starting handle	None
Tool kit contents	Wheelbrace, jack handle, jack
Jack	Screw pillar type
Jacking points	4
Battery	12 volt negative earth 38 amp hrs capacity
Number of electrical fuses	6
Headlamps	Sealed beam 60w/60w
Indicators	Self cancelling flashers
Reversing lamp	Yes
Screen wipers	2 speed, self parking
Screen washers	Foot operated with wash/wipe
Sun visors	2

Locks:
with ignition key	Ignition switch/steering lock
with other keys	Driver's door and boot with 2nd key, petrol filler cap with 3rd key
Interior heater	Fresh air
Upholstery	Pvc or optional fabric trim
Floor covering	Cut pile carpet
Alternative body styles	None
Maximum load	924lb.
Maximum roof rack load	100lb.
Major extras available	Metallic paint

Maintenance
Fuel tank capacity	12.2 galls
Sump	8.0 pints SAE 20W/50
Gearbox	3.25 pints SAE 80
Rear axle	1.94 pints SAE 90
Steering gear	0.25 pints SAE 80
Coolant	19.8 pints (2 drain taps)
Chassis lubrication	First at 27,000 miles then every 30,000 miles to 4 points
Maximum service interval	6000 miles
Ignition timing	10° btdc
Contact breaker gap	.025 in.
Sparking plug gap	.023 in.
Sparking plug type	Autolite AG32
Tappet clearance (hot)	Inlet .010in. Exhaust .018in.

Valve timing:
inlet opens	29°btdc
inlet closes	67°abdc
exhaust opens	71°bbdc
exhaust closes	25°atdc
Front wheel toe-in	0.06 — 0.25in.
Camber angle	0.67°
Castor angle	1.33°
King pin inclination	7°

Tyre pressures: Normal/Fully laden
Front:	26/28 psi
Rear:	26/28 psi

is head and shoulders above the rest. The old maxim "there's no substitute for litres" has never been more apt.

Raising the overall second gear ratio from 7.11: 1 to 6.02: 1 means that it's now possible to do 66 mph in this gear (first and third are good for 40 mph and 90 mph respectively), thus eliminating a gear change during the all-out 0-60 mph acceleration which is reduced by nearly a second—from 9.5 sec. to 8.6 sec. Reductions in the acceleration times become progressively greater as the speed increases until the 0-100 mph time is cut by 3 sec. to 26.5 sec. These figures show the substantial gains that can be made in top speed and acceleration using a relatively small increase in power with far better choice of gear ratios.

Predictably economy at steady speeds is also improved. Our touring fuel consumption is almost the same as before at 24.7 mpg but it is calculated from the considerably higher maximum speed of the uprated car. If one takes advantage of the effortless 100 mph cruising speed now available it averages a good 19.5 mpg—the old car was considerably worse at 17.5 mpg. Fuel consumption overall is little changed at 19.4 mpg but at slightly higher average speeds.

Raising the final drive ratio has caused some loss in flexibility. In top gear, the 20 mph incremental times are all slightly slower than for the previous Capri 3000 until above 80 mph when the gain in power offsets the higher gearing. But on the road this slight loss in flexibility is hardly noticed at all and is more than compensated for by the engine's eagerness to rev, as well as by the excellent gearbox.

As with all Ford boxes, the gearchange is one of the best in its class. This isn't to say it's perfect—the spring loading protecting reverse is still too strong, for instance. But in all forward gears it's slick and easy. The clutch seems to have longer travel than before—some drivers were fooled into putting the seat too far back to be able to release the clutch properly—and the take-up is still a little sharp and unprogressive. Once properly seated, though, few would find fault here, especially as the pedal is quite light for a 3 litre.

By eliminating a lot of the earlier bumpy harshness, the ride has been improved, we'd say from atrocious to mediocre. The back end still tends to crash and thump over bad disturbances though, especially at low speeds. Whether the handling has suffered in consequence is something we couldn't agree on here: either way it's marginal and the car's general behaviour is much the same as before.

Accelerating on the turn on a wet surface will, at low speeds, cause excessive inside wheel spin and, at higher ones, cause the tail to breakaway sharply. So you have to be wary of using too much throttle in poor conditions — unless you're proficient in powering the tail round, a technique to which the big Capri responds well at modest speeds. On a dry road, the cornering power on the Goodyear Grand Prix radials is high on a smooth surface (bumpy ones can throw the car off course). The steering on this latest car was not as heavy as we remember so that parking and tight turns don't call for undue exertion. The old weakness of instability at speed in a crosswind remains, however.

Ford have considerably modified the brakes—even though we couldn't fault the original ones—using a deeply dished design that is more in the air flow. Although they gave excellent feel, hard braking from high speed in our test car caused some weaving and they juddered at about 75 mph.

The E package has all the refinements of the GT XLR (less map light) plus a push-button radio, heated rear screen, special padded facia and a crackle paint finish on the tail. In addition, our test car was equipped with the optional fabric seat trim, vinyl roof and Golde sliding roof.

Overall it is quite a relaxing car to drive if not always a very quiet one; at speed, wind, engine and tyre noise are pretty loud in combination. The seats are comfortable with plenty of adjustment (although the rake adjuster could have finer notches). Short drivers may find the seat cushion too low to see over the bonnet and the rear three quarter view remains bad.

The most disappointing thing about the car is the muddled minor controls; an opportunity to improve badly missed. Why Ford should opt for a melee of horizontal rocker switches with the light switch down below the driver's fresh air vent we cannot understand. We liked the wash-and-wipe floor button, though, which works well.

In its latest form the big Capri doesn't really have a competitor in sight—no other major manufacturer has anything of similar conception that can offer such exhilarating performance and accommodation.

Above: roll is a lot less evident in the car than this picture would suggest. Below: switchgear for 1972 is completely unchanged, including the horizontal rocker for the lights, tucked away under the driver's fresh air vent. Confusingly, it works in the opposite sense to the other switches

Make: Ford
Model: Capri 3000E
Maker: Ford Motor Company, Dagenham, Essex.
Price: £1377.00 plus £344.25 purchase tax equals £1721.25. Vinyl roof with sliding sun roof £63.63. Fabric trim £6.14. Inertia reel seat belts £15.50. Total as tested £1806.52.

AUTO TEST

FORD CAPRI 3000 GXL

Executive sports car — 1973 style

AT-A-GLANCE

Latest version of Ford's successful 2+2 with quieter engine, much softer ride and improved interior. Slightly better performance, handling as good as ever. More luxurious and comfortable. Very desirable package, sensibly priced.

WHEN Ford leapt into the sports car market with both feet back in 1969, they billed the Capri as "the car you've always promised yourself". Some of the smaller-engined versions had difficulty in living up to this claim, even though their style and handling were well up the league, but the "muscle" version with 3-litre vee-6 power unit fell into a different category altogether. In the performance-for-money stakes it was unmatched, bearing in mind the two-plus-two accommodation long list of standard equipment and extensive Ford service network.

Just over a year ago the Capri 3000 was improved drastically by a new uprated version of the engine and a much more acceptable four-speed gearbox without such a large gap in the ratios between second and third. For last year's London Show even more improvements were made, in line with revisions right across the model range and the net result is easily the

best Capri yet. A lot of market research and owner reaction went into the new versions, the engineers even taking note of criticisms in the press. The details of all the changes made are so involved that it is best to deal with them in turn in the appropriate part of the test which follows.

Ford's 3-litre vee-6 engine is fitted with an automatic choke which worked well and reliably on the test car. It must be cocked by pressing the accelerator once with the engine cold, starting then being immediate providing the car has not been standing more than a day or so. After a longer period of idleness a fair amount of churning is required to replenish the float chamber with the mechanical fuel pump. Our long-term experience with the same engine in our Granada reveals that this control is liable to go out of adjustment between regular service intervals, but it can easily be reset.

With the choke working properly the engine runs evenly and without hesitation right from cold. As the temperature rises the choke phases out progressively so that the driver can really just forget it once the engine has started. It takes at least a couple of miles for the temperature gauge to move off its bottom stop, however, and even longer before the heater pumps out hot air on a cold morning.

A noticeable characteristic of the Ford vee-6 is a rumbly kind of harshness when accelerating hard, but in this respect Capri 3000 GXL seemed much better than its predecessor and the Granada, although individual examples seem to vary. On a light or trailing throttle the unit is delightfully smooth and quiet, so the change when accelerating is only occasional and rather sporting.

Unlike the earlier 3-litre which had a very low power peak and was the kind of engine which preferred to slog from low revs, the latest version feels much better suited to a sports car with even torque delivery and a rev range which usefully runs up to over 5,500 rpm. The flat shape of the torque curve is well illustrated by the top gear acceleration figures where every increment from 20 to 70 mph is between 7.2 and 7.6sec.

One of the latest improvements is the fitting of a viscous coupling for the cooling fan which restricts blade speed and prevents the excessive whirring noise we complained about at high revs. This gives the engine a rated output of 140 instead of 138 bhp (DIN), which in part explains the improved acceleration figures.

Compared with the Capri 3000E we tested on 20 January 1972, the latest GXL was no quicker (except for a tenth picked up on better standing start) up to 80 mph. From rest to 100 mph though we beat the old time by 2.4sec, most of this being explained by the total lack of wind at the time the figures were taken. On top speed too there was no difference between the two cars, 122 mph being reached and maintained very quickly.

To overcome slight notchiness in this latest top-opening gearbox the gearlever has been lengthened by about two inches and this brings the knob nearer to the steering wheel rim as well as easing the effort required for shifting. Although it feels a little bit long, the overall improvement is very worthwhile. Due to rather small pads on the pedals the clutch effort of 35lb feels heavy, but the travel is short and the take-up very progressive. Clutch disc diameter has been increased by 0.5in. and there was always more than enough bite for quick getaways and steep hill starts.

Tremendous ride improvement

The weak point of the 3-litre Capri has always been the ride, which erred much too much towards firmness, especially at the front end. For this latest version the wheel rates have been

Below: Engine accessibility is good and there is an inspection lamp under the bonnet. Bottom left: The car here is fitted with special alloy wheels available from Ford Advanced Vehicle Operation at Aveley. We used them with spiked tyres on the Monte Carlo rally route

Right: Latest version of the Capri 3000 (now called a GXL) features twin quartz-halogen headlamps and a moulded rubbing strip along the peak of side pressing. Sports road wheels and over-riders are standard but the vinyl cover and sunroof are extras. The radio is standard too on the GXL

Left: The steering wheel now has only two spokes and the instruments easier to read. Lamp switches are in the lower facia rail. Below: The twin-pipe exhaust system is standard but only the GXL has the fluted tail panel between the rear lamps

FORD CAPRI 3000 GXL (2,994 c.c.) — TOTAL AS TESTED ON THE ROAD £1,949.66

ACCELERATION

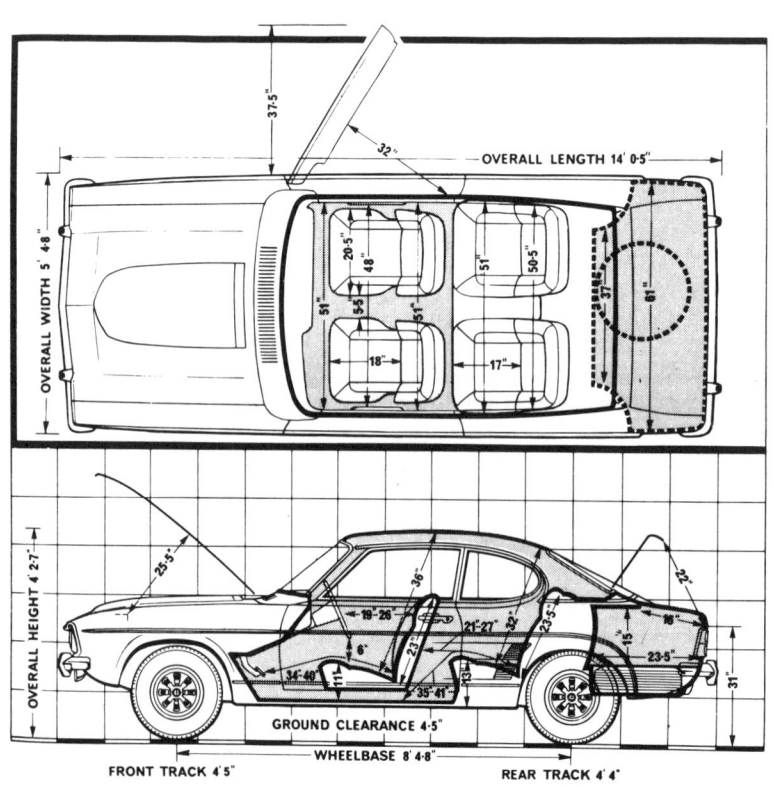

SPEED MPH TRUE (INDICATED)	TIME IN SECS
30 / 31	3.0
40 / 41	4.3
50 / 51	6.0
60 / 62	8.3
70 / 72	11.2
80 / 82	14.6
90 / 91	18.9
100 / 101	25.1
110 / 110	35.1
120 / 120	—

GEAR RATIOS AND TIME IN SEC

mph	Top (3.09)	3rd (4.36)	2nd (6.03)
10-30	—	5.3	3.6
20-40	7.6	5.0	3.5
30-50	7.2	4.8	3.5
40-60	7.2	4.9	3.9
50-70	7.5	5.6	5.1
60-80	8.3	6.5	—
70-90	9.5	8.3	—
80-100	11.6	—	—
90-110	16.6	—	—

Standing ¼-mile
16.6 sec 83 mph
Standing Kilometre
30.6 sec 106 mph
Test distance
3.145 miles
Mileage recorder
1.3 per cent over-reading

PERFORMANCE

MAXIMUM SPEEDS

Gear	mph	kph	rpm
Top (mean)	122	196	5,650
(best)	122	196	5,650
3rd	92	148	6,000
2nd	66	106	6,000
1st	41	66	6,000

BRAKES

FADE
(from 70 mph in neutral)
Pedal load for 0.5g stops in lb

1	35-28	6	40
2	38-32	7	40
3	35	8	40
4	38	9	40
5	38	10	40

RESPONSE
(from 30 mph in neutral)

Load	g	Distance
20lb	0.25	120ft
40lb	0.60	50ft
50lb	0.81	37ft
60lb	0.93	32ft
65lb	1.0	30.1ft
Handbrake	0.32	94ft
Max. Gradient	1 in 3	

CLUTCH
Pedal 35lb and 5in.

COMPARISONS

MAXIMUM SPEED MPH
Datsun 240Z	(£2,398)	125
Ford Capri 3000 GXL	**(£1,831)**	**122**
Reliant Scimitar GTE	(£2,348)	121
Triumph TR6 PI	(£1,678)	119
Vauxhall Firenza Sport SL	(£1,379)	103

0-60 MPH, SEC
Datsun 240Z	8.0
Triumph TR6 PI	8.2
Ford Capri 3000 GXL	**8.3**
Reliant Scimitar GTE	8.9
Vauxhall Firenza Sport SL	11.4

STANDING ¼-MILE, SEC
Datsun 240Z	15.8
Triumph TR6 PI	16.3
Ford Capri 3000 GXL	**16.6**
Reliant Scimitar GTE	16.9
Vauxhall Firenza Sport SL	18.0

OVERALL MPG
Vauxhall Firenza Sport SL	22.2
Datsun 240Z	21.4
Reliant Scimitar GTE	20.8
Ford Capri 3000 GXL	**20.7**
Triumph TR6 PI	19.8

GEARING
(with 185/70-13in. tyres)

Top	21.7 mph per 1,000 rpm
3rd	15.4 mph per 1,000 rpm
2nd	11.1 mph per 1,000 rpm
1st	6.9 mph per 1,000 rpm

CONSUMPTION

FUEL
(At constant speed — mpg)

30 mph	35.1
40 mph	34.5
50 mph	31.7
60 mph	28.8
70 mph	26.2
80 mph	22.5
90 mph	20.2
100 mph	17.8

Typical mpg 22 (12.8 litres/100km)
Calculated (DIN)mpg 23.8(11.8litres/100km)
Overall mpg 20.7 (13.6 litres/100km)
Grade of fuel. Premium, 4-star (min 97 RM)

OIL
Consumption (SAE 10W/30) Negligible

TEST CONDITIONS
Weather: Misty Wind: 0 mph.
Temperature: 2 deg C. (35 deg F).
Barometer: 29.7in hg. Humidity: 90 per cent.
Surfaces: Damp concrete and asphalt.

WEIGHT:
Kerb Weight 22.5 cwt (2,519lb-1,144kg)
(with oil, water and half-full fuel tank).
Distribution, per cent F, 55; R, 45
Laden as tested: 26.3cwt (2,949lb-1,339kg).

TURNING CIRCLES:
Between kerbs L, 34ft 6in; R, 34ft 9in.
Between walls L, 36ft 8in; R, 36ft 11in.
Steering wheel turns, lock to lock 3.3.
Figures taken at 3,200 miles by our own
staff at the Motor Industry Research
Association proving ground at Nuneaton
and on the Continent.

OVERALL LENGTH 14' 0.5"
OVERALL WIDTH 5' 4.8"
OVERALL HEIGHT 4' 2.7"
GROUND CLEARANCE 4.5"
WHEELBASE 8' 4.8"
FRONT TRACK 4' 5"
REAR TRACK 4' 4"

STANDARD GARAGE 16ft x 8ft 6in.

SPECIFICATION

FRONT ENGINE, REAR-WHEEL DRIVE

ENGINE

Cylinders	6 in 60 deg vee
Main bearings	4
Cooling system	Water; pump, thermostat and viscous coupling fan
Bore	93.66mm (3.69in.)
Stroke	72.42mm (2.85in.)
Displacement	2,994c.c. (182.7 cu.in.)
Valve gear	Pushrods and rockers
Compression ratio	8.9-to-1. Min. octane rating: 97RM
Carburettor	Weber compound twin-choke 40 DFA
Fuel pump	AC mechanical
Oil filter	Full-flow, disposable can
Max. power	148 bhp (DIN) at 5,300 rpm
Max. torque	173 lb.ft. (DIN/SAE) at 3,000 rpm

TRANSMISSION

Clutch	Diaphragm spring, 9.5in. dia.
Gearbox	4-speed all-synchromesh
Gear ratios	Top 1.0
	Third 1.41
	Second 1.95
	First 3.16
	Reverse 3.35
Final drive	Hypoid bevel, 3.09-to-1

CHASSIS and BODY

Construction	Integral with steel body

SUSPENSION

Front	Independent; MacPherson struts, coil springs, anti-roll bar
Rear	Live axle, semi-elliptic leaf springs, anti-roll bar, telescopic dampers

STEERING

Type	Rack and pinion
Wheel dia.	15.3in.

BRAKES

Make and type	Girling disc front, drum rear
Servo	Vacuum type
Dimensions	F 9.63 in. dia.
	R 9 in. dia. 2.25 in. wide shoes
Swept area	F 189.5 sq. in. R 127 sq. in.
	Total 316.5 sq. in. (240.5 sq. in./ton laden)

WHEELS

Type	Sculptured pressed steel disc 5 in. wide rim

Tyres—make		Various, Pirelli on test car
—type		Cinturato CN36 radial ply tubeless
—size		185/70HR-13in.

EQUIPMENT

Battery	12 Volt 55 Ah.
Alternator	35 amp
Headlamps	120/120 watt (total)
Reversing lamp	Standard
Electric fuses	6
Screen wipers	Two-speed
Screen washer	Standard foot plunger
Interior heater	Standard, air-blending type
Heated backlight	Standard
Safety belts	Extra
Interior trim	Pvc (cloth optional), seats, pvc head-lining
Floor covering	Carpet
Jack	Screw-pillar type
Jacking points	Two, one each side under sills
Windscreen	Zone toughened, laminated optional
Underbody protection	Electrocoat primer with part under sealing of front and rear wings and front transmission tunnel area

MAINTENANCE

Fuel tank	13.5 Imp. gallons (61.5 litres)
Cooling system	16.4 pints (inc. heater)
Engine sump	9.8 pints (5.5 litres) SAE 10W/30. Change oil every 6,000 miles. Change filter every 6,000 miles
Gearbox	3.25 pints. SAE 80. No change
Final drive	1.94 pints. SAE 90EP. No change
Grease	No points
Valve clearance	Inlet 0.010-0.020 in. (hot) Exhaust 0.018-0.022 in. (hot)
Contact breaker	0.025 in. gap; 38-40 deg. dwell
Ignition timing	10 deg. BTDC (static) 10 deg. BTDC (stroboscopic at 800 rpm)
Spark plug	Type: Motorcraft AGR-22-DB. Gap 0.023-0.027 in.
Compression pressure	145-175 psi
Tyre pressures	F26; R 26psi (normal driving) F 28; R 28 psi (high speed) F 28; R 28 psi (full load) F 28; R 33 psi (full load; high speed)
Max. payload	706 lb (320 kg)

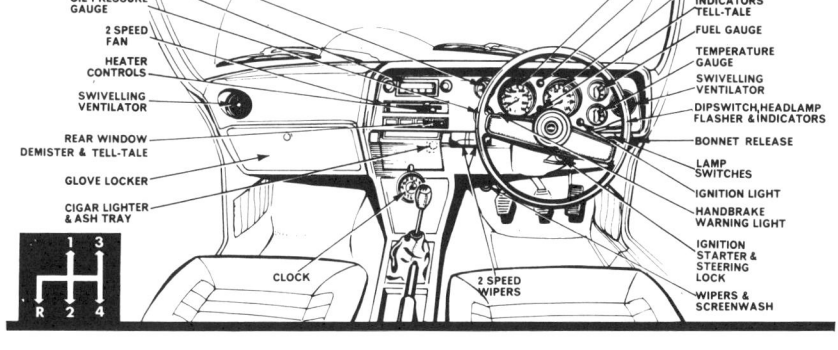

Service Interval	6,000	18,000	36,000
Labour	£6.65	£6.90	£8.60
Oil	£1.76	£1.76	£1.76
Oil Filter	£1.77	£1.77	£1.77
Breather Filter	—		—
Air Filter	—	£1.19	£1.19
Contact breaker points	£0.41	£0.41	£0.41
Sparking plugs	£2.40	£2.40	£2.40
Total cost:	£12.99	£14.43	£16.13

ROUTINE REPLACEMENTS:	Time (hr)	Cost	Spares	TOTAL:
Brake Pads	0.55	£1.65	£5.45	£7.10
Brake Shoes	0.85	£2.55	£2.20	£4.75
Exhaust System	1.05	£3.15	£26.35	£29.50
Clutch	2.30	£6.90	£23.05	£29.95
Dampers — front pair	3.05	£9.15	£23.50	£32.65
Dampers — rear pair	0.75	£3.75	£9.10	£12.85
Replace Drive Shaft, each	0.80	£2.40	£7.00	£9.40
Generator	0.45	£1.35	£8.60	£9.95
Starter	0.40	£1.20	£42.80	£44.00

softened by 30 per cent and the improvement is dramatic. The Capri now has some of the same qualities as the Granada, which we rate very highly indeed in this respect, and insulation from road disturbances is most impressive.

Usually a change of this nature brings with it, corresponding reductions in handling and cornering power, but on the Capri a clever new dual-function rear anti-roll bar offsets most of the snags. Roll angles when cornering fast are noticeably greater, but there is much less understeer and better traction on bumpy turns taken under full power. On a long sweeping bend with a good surface there is now an unpleasant kind of diagonal pitching which sets a lower control limit, but the previous rear-end liveliness is completely absent. These characteristics only begin to show up at very high cornering speeds and most drivers in most situations will not fail to be impressed with the improvements.

More than previously it is possible to provoke axle tramp, especially when making a brisk turn from a standing start — such as when joining a main road traffic stream — but one has to be fairly brutal to do it.

Although nothing specific has been high-lighted about steering improvements, we are finding the latest Ford rack and pinion mechanisms much less sticky and this Capri had a particularly smooth and responsive steering control. Front-end weight with the 3-litre engine makes the steering quite heavy when manoeuvring, but as soon as the wheels are turning the load required drops right off. Castor action is strong enough to pull the wheel straight after a turn without introducing artificial heaviness. There is no power-assisted option and, despite only 3.3 turns between compact locks, we doubt if many would deem it desirable.

Large diameter Girling disc brakes are used at the front with divided hydraulic circuits and a powerful vacuum servo. Rear lining width has recently been increased by 0.5in. and on wet surfaces we found the rears locked first before the fronts had reached optimum efficiency. On a dry road the balance was much better and we easily achieved 1g for a modest pedal effort of only 65lb. There was virtually no fade during repeated stops from 70 mph but when braking from 110 mph we noticed some rumbling from the front. The handbrake held securely on the 1-in-3 test hill facing up, but when facing down, the car slid forwards dragging the locked rears.

Fuel consumption

Despite virtually the same engine in the same car with the same gearing, this GXL used more fuel than the previous 3000E throughout the speed range. Differences amounted to almost 4 mpg at 30 mph in top to 0.6 mpg more at 100 mph, and overall we recorded 20.7 compared to 21.5 mpg before. The Capri runs happily on normal 4-star Premium and most owners in this country should get around 22 mpg which is very good for a sports car with this kind of performance. Once abroad, however, where 100 mph can be maintained for long periods on motorways and *autobahnen*, the consumption tumbles below 20 mpg and on a trip to Monte Carlo and back with the GXL we recorded only 18.5 mpg.

In typical Ford fashion the engine required no oil throughout the test which on this occasion meant a total distance of over 3,000 miles.

Fittings and Furniture

Without departing too far from the original layout Ford have made some worthwhile improvements to the interior of this ultimate sort of Capri. New instrument faces are much easier to read and the addition of three small zeros after each digit on the rev counter eliminates any

AUTOTEST
FORD CAPRI
3000 GXL . . .

possibility of confusing it with the speedometer. On the right of the speedo (which has a trip recorder with an excellent push-button reset control) are the fuel gauge and coolant thermometer. On the right are the oil pressure gauge and an ammeter, public opinion preferring this to the previous voltmeter.

On the left there used to be vertical row of confusing rocker switches for the wipers and lights but these have now been set into the lower facia rail, lights on the right, wipers on the left. Although there is now no possibility of confusing the two very different controls, it is still possible to switch off the sidelamps when trying to turn on the headlamps, the two push buttons being side-by-side and very similar to the touch. What is really wanted is some form of concealed lighting for their identity symbols, like that used for the heater.

Red and blue blobs for the temperature control as well as the distribution arrows are illuminated somehow from behind and at night it is very easy to operate the controls. In the old Ford tradition (now abandoned on the Granada) there is a progressive air-blending temperature slide and an independent fresh-air system for facia vents boosted by the fan. On its slow setting it is very quiet and on its noisier fast position extremely effective.

Under the heater panel is a row for supplementary push-button switches, one being used for the heated backlight which is a standard fitting on the GXL. Above the heater is a Bosch Blue Spot push-button radio (another standard item on the GXL) which had excellent tone and precise station tuning. Under this part of the panel in the centre of the car is a deep dropdown ashtray with concealed cigar lighter.

Instead of a purely stylized centre console fore and aft of the gearlever, the GXL now has useful compartments and a deep bin under the central armrest between the seats. Twice we broke the securing clip for its lid, so this is obviously a weak point. Supplementing the small open trays on the tunnel are two elastic-topped map pockets on the outboard sides of the front footwells. An innovation on the Capri is a proper glove box in front of the passenger with lockable lid. Previously there was only an open shelf here.

Seats have been reshaped to give better support and they certainly grip their occupants well without having hard edges. The test car had the optional cloth centre panels which at only £6.42 extra are worth every penny. Backrests are adjustable for rake and the cushions appear to be raised slightly which overcomes our earlier criticisms of sitting too low in the Capri. In the back there is no longer a folding centre armrest, but we doubt if this will really be missed. Rear seats are shaped for only two and adults sit rather cramped up; head and legroom are not at all bad for this class of car. Front backrests are unlocked by levers mounted near the top, a big improvement over the fumbly controls at the base used on previous Capris.

Wipers have two speeds and there is Ford's usual floor mounted pedal which operates a-washer plunger and starts the wipers. Despite anti-lift wiper blades they lifted off the screen at speeds over 90 mph. Twin-tone horns are fitted to the GXL but their carrying power is insuf-

Top: There is now a locking glove box in front of the passenger and open trays in the tunnel cover moulding. Under the centre armrest is a deep bin. Above: The spare wheel is under the boot mat with the jack and wheelbrace in a canvas bag on the left

ficient at speed and one developed a "frog" for part of the test.

One of the biggest improvements of the GXL over the 3000E and all other Capris is the fitting of four quartz-halogen circular headlamps. Their range and brilliance on main beam was fantastic and the illumination when dipped was in a totally different class from the normal rectangular style used on other Capris.

The boot of the Capri can be opened only with the key and the lid itself is relatively shallow. There is a high sill at the rear (31 in. above the ground) and not much depth inside. The spare

wheel is under the floor mat in a well and the tools (such as there are) are held down on the left by an elastic strap.

Living with the Capri GXL

With a car so comprehensively equipped it is hard to find any extras worth adding and for an on-the-road price of £1,871.62 you really do get a complete car. We would certainly add on the insignificant £6.42 asked for cloth trim on the seats and most likely the £45.24 for the sliding steel sunroof. Unfortunately this does not tip up at its rear edge for extra ventilation like the one

labour charge instead. Unless anything unto-ward happens mechanically outside the normal 12,000-mile/12-month warranty period, the Capri should prove very cheap on garage bills.

Our test car developed a very unusual fault on the way back from Monte Carlo, the symptoms being a knocking on tickover, loss of power and some intermittent misfiring. This was traced to a camshaft bearing retainer ring coming loose and allowing the camshaft to float back and forth. No permanent damage was done and the trouble quickly rectified.

One of the items of standard equipment on the GXL is an under-bonnet inspection lamp mounted on the lid, which must be propped by hand. Accessibility of the alternator is exception-ally good, this being mounted right up on the right-hand side of the engine and the distributor is also easy to get at just behind the radiator. Brake fluid reservoir (the clutch is cable operated) is towards the rear but again mounted well up, the most difficult filler really being that for the oil. The dipstick hole is buried and hard to find in the dark (although the inspection lamp helps). Ford now recommend a 50 per cent anti-freeze long-life coolant fluid, so apart from checking the concentration there is very little winter pre-paration involved.

The only tools provided are a jack and wheel-brace and even these are extremely basic in design. The jack is a screw pillar which has a long side arm and a swing-over handle allowing half turns of the pillar. There is only a single jacking point each side. Jacking with the door closed is a slow and laborious process.

Although the boot is 60in. across at its widest point there are intrusions from the rear wheel arches and very little length or height. The lid aperture is only 16in. from front to back and the height inside only about 14in. Maximum payload is quoted as 706 lb which means less than 30 lb luggage for each adult when travelling four-up. Assuming no weight problem the Capri is hardly the car for family touring, unless you are prepared to add a roof rack.

The strongest asset of the Capri is that you feel at home in it right from the first moment behind the wheel. In its latest form it is much more comfortable and refined, offering a better solution than ever to the problem of combining beefy performance with a practical package. All our drivers found the 3000 GXL a most en-joyable machine with a lot to be said in its favour.   □

Above: The rear seats are shaped for only two. Cloth trim panels are extra but the little rear armrests and the opening rear quarter-lights are standard on the GXL together with a Triplex Hotline heated backlight. There is no longer a folding armrest in the back

fitted by Ford to the Granada range.

If even £1871.62 is too much for you, re-member that for £177 less you can buy a Capri 3000 GT with exactly the same performance but minus the radio, heated backlight and many of the luxury touches.

In line with their improved standards of rust prevention across the board Ford give the GXL the full treatment before painting and a generous application of bitumen-based sealer afterwards under the wheel arches and forward part of the transmission tunnel. Much of the bright metal

is stainless steel and the latest sculptured sports road wheels are much more durable than the original Rostyle ones. The paint finish on the test car was particularly good, Sebring red con-trasting effectively with the matt black tail panel and black vinyl roof cover (£21.18 extra).

Ford service intervals are 6,000 miles apart and there is now no intermediate oil change at 3,000 miles after running in. The latest type of disposable canister oil filters cost about three times as much as the old renewable elements, but they are much easier to fit correctly. There is no fixed time for routine services but an agreed

MANUFACTURER:
Ford Motor Co. Ltd.,
Warley, Essex.

PRICES

Basic	£1,515.00
Purchase Tax	£315.62
Total (in GB)	£1,830.62
Seat Belts (inertia reel)	£16.20
Licence	£25.00
Delivery (no charge)	
Number plates	£5.00
Total on the Road	
(exc. insurance)	**£1,876.82**
Insurance	Group 6
EXTRAS (inc. PT)	
Steel sliding roof	£45.24
Vinyl roof covering	£21.18
Cloth seat trim	£6.42

Mister Muscle meets the Hatchback

A Ford exercise in grit and glamour

Friday. Tim Britten, one time editor of Australian magazine Motor Manual, calls in to see us at the office. Sinking a few tubes (old Colonial saying) he tells us how the muscle car has died the death Down Under just as it did in the USA. Which is kind of strange because two hours later Grimwood and I are sitting in a South London traffic jam on our way to collect Ford's RS 3100 Capri. The first (and last) of the British high power sporty cars?

As the little Opel Kadett — doing good service as a temporary replacement for the Editorial Manta which is much the worse for wear after an argument with a hedge — noses into the press car garage at Brentford we see the RS. Squat, much lower than the standard car with front quarter bumpers, striping around the bonnet bulge and spoilers front and rear. It's one of those wagons that looks like it's doing 100 mph standing still. We also see the tail of the new 1974 Capri poking out of a corner, take a brief look around it and then clamber into the RS. Sign on the dotted line for workshop manager Alf Belsen and off into the no-power afternoon.

No power in a thing like that! V6 engine bored sixty thou to give a total capacity of 3.1 litres. Heads gas flowed, engine carefully put together, net power output 148 brake horse being put down to the road by 185 section low profile Goodyears mounted on 5½ in wide alloy wheels. From the moment you turn the key there's obviously a lot of go in this V6 motor and — although the changes over the standard engine are confined to the power unit itself — somehow it sounds different. Much more of a burble. Finding a gap in traffic round about Kingston on Thames I put my foot down just to see what its like. Suddenly we're illegal, in second gear with six thousand revs on the one clock and just under 70 mph on the other. In a 50 mph limit energy crisis Britain it all seems ridiculous. Still, the car does rumble along nicely at 30 in top and everybody else in the traffic queue is looking at the front air dam and big boot spoiler. Ford say they actually work.

Sitting in the traffic I take a good look around the 1973 spec interior. The facia with big, clear instruments is much better than earlier models and the switches are all the horizontal push button type that first saw the light of day on the Granada. This, like the rest of the appointments, the RS shares with all the super de luxe Capris. Only thing is this interior comes, as Henry once said, only in black. Driving position is good, seats are comfortable and the view of the long bonnet is fair. Only irritation was a persistent squeak from the passenger seat.

Driving over the roads of suburban London on the way home the suspension showed itself to be harsh at low speeds. Lowered all round, with single leaf (instead of multi) rear springs and Bilstein dampers you could feel every bump. Definitely a lot more hard than the normal production item which, in turn, has been softened considerably since introduction allowing the fitting of the rear anti-roll bar which the RS also sports. The Goodyears gripped the dry road well but transmitted one hell of a lot of road noise, a point noticed before on other makes of car fitted with this tyre.

Over the weekend I thought about the RS 3100. Kind of anachronism really. A super sporty version of the Capri released at a time when the new body '74 model was almost complete. At first it looked as if Ford wanted to make 5000 of the cars — designed at AVO but in fact made on the normal line at Halewood — but now it seems it will never be a Group One car. At £2412 the most expensive Capri ever, and in an outdated body shell at that. Limited production special appeal with lots of performance and a definite feeling you're driving one of the new 3.4 litre four cam racers that operate from Ford Cologne. Real ego trip, but sod all use with a fifty limit.

Monday. Life is fun even at 50 in an RS 3100. Taking the twisty route from Edenbridge to Phil Whitehead's garage at Bromley the car proved just how easy it is to drive fairly quickly and how difficult it must be to drive flat out. Because flat out is very, very, fast. Despite the front end weight the steering is not too heavy, it's responsive but does tend to be too affected by bumps or road markings. The faster you go the more stable it becomes. Brakes seem to work well even when tried repeatedly, no doubt the 9.75 in diameter ventilated discs take that credit.

Tuesday. Rail strike today. Bad traffic on the way to our test track at Chobham and furthermore it's raining which promises fun when we get down to the acceleration tests. Grimwood and photog Hodson are already there and we wait around for most of the morning hoping the sun will shine. It does

(while we are in the pub) so back to the track with stop watch at the ready.

In the wet the Capri handles well and brakes even better but I never feel as if I can use all the power that's available. On the dry track there's no trouble at all and the RS runs off a very consistent set of times:

0- 30 mph	3.0 secs
0- 40 mph	4.4 secs
0- 50 mph	6.0 secs
0- 60 mph	7.8 secs
0- 70 mph	10.0 secs
0- 80 mph	12.4 secs
0- 90 mph	15.9 secs
0-100 mph	21.4 secs
Standing Quarter	15.7 secs

Hold the engine at 5000 revs, drop the clutch and watch the needle float around 4-6000 as the wheels spin and then grip. First gces to 40 mph; into third at 68 mph with a chirp as the rear tyres bite then through to top at only four mph under the 100 mph mark. Very quick, and the car feels more stable the faster it gets — can the air dam and spoiler really be working? On the dry circuit I try a few laps without stopping for acceleration runs, the car sitting squarely on the road with just a touch of tail out on the sharper bends and a feeling of slight understeer at lower speeds and on long curves. In all cases the right foot on the throttle controls the attitude of the car. Those vented front discs do their job too, and the Goodyears don't seem all that bad either — wet or dry. Living with a car tends to change opinions.

Top speed I can't say. Speed limits, the limitations of the track and the bad weather mean that 110 mph is all I managed in my

week's ownership. Ford say 125 mph and I reckon that's on the conservative side.

Wednesday. Grimwood arrives in the office announcing the RS drivers seat back collapsed while he was going around a roundabout in Richmond. Phone call to Ford press man Graham Simons attracts the comment: 'what have you been doing in the seats then?' Followed by various other insinuations including that perhaps my left foot got caught in it while attempting Position 29 or somesuch. Decide it's easier to stick the spare wheel behind the backrest until the car is returned to the Ford workshops.

Grimwood shares my opinion of the car. Good power, fine brakes and safe handling just as long as you don't go mad. Thinks the rear spoiler makes a very good advertisement hoarding.

Thursday. Through the Dartford Tunnel (smelly and ancient) up to Ford's test track at Boreham in 'my' 1973/74 Capri to see the **real** 1974 model. On the way consider that the RS should have a limited slip differential as standard to complete the pack.

Boreham is cold and windy. The new Capri — announced end of February but all models not available 'till early May — looks good. Very much a cleaned up model on the Mustang shape recently announced in the USA. But far better lines.

Capri 11 models come in five engine options — 1300 (57 bhp), 1600 (72 bhp), 1600 GT (88 bhp), 2000 (98 bhp), and 3000 (138 bhp) — and four different trim packages. The 1300 motor is the Kent series pushrod, both the 1600's and the two litre are the usual single overhead cam and the three litre is the Granada/Capri 3000 V6. Not, of course, the hopped up RS 3100. Mechanically, apart from a few spring setting changes to compensate for varying weights, the cars are identical to the previous Capri with strut front/leaf spring rear suspensions and disc front/drum rear brakes. The big difference lies in the body.

Although still a two door, four seat coupe Capri 11 has a fold down rear seat and a lift up tailgate. Sort of sporting estate wagon. Top of the range in trim packs are the Ghia models on 1600 GT, 2000 and 3000 chassis. Extra instruments, vinyl roof, high back front seats, alloy wheels are all part of the Ghia spec along with a rear seat that — sensibly — folds down in two halves to make the car a 2, 3 or 4 seater. Facia panel is the same as the 73/74 model.

I take a drive in 1600 and 3000 models. The 1600 feels very light and twitchy on the rear end during hard cornering but the big one sits tight albeit with far more roll than the RS 3100. The Capri 11, however, is one hell of a lot more comfortable for everyday cruising. Works nicely with auto transmission as well.

All in all the new Capri looks and feels a nice package. The plan is to continue the RS 3100 in the older body shape for some months while all other models are replaced by the new range. The RS, of course, is being homologated for Group Two (so that the racing Capris can run at 3.4 litres or larger) and anyway it seems a better bet for this year's racing programme as the body is 200 lbs lighter (on three litre models) and also should be stiffer, not having the opening rear.

Back into the RS 3100 after lunch and return home thinking that a 3 litre Capri 11 with Bilsteins all round to cut down a bit of the softness of the ride might make a very good form of editorial transport. Must be able to get more spare wheels in the back than the Opel boot!

Friday. Through south London again to return the RS to its owners. A low test mileage but still enough to be impressed. Work out fuel consumption for test — 20.45 mpg which is one whole empeegee better than the stock 3000 we tested twelve months ago. But still can't help thinking that in the current gloom we may never see the likes again. Which reminds me, whatever happened to the pointed nose, five speed box, Vauxhall Firenza? **PD.**

MANY-OFF SPECIAL

Look at the records and you'll find Ford are pretty used to winning. Their Cosworth tuned V8 has dominated Grand Prix racing for over half a decade now, they initiated one of the world's most successful racing formulas and their Cortina is still monopolising home market sales. Small wonder then, that they took exception to their Capri being so soundly beaten by BMW in last year's European Touring Car championship. Though not obvious at first sight, the Capri RS3100 is their way of trying to make sure it never happens again.

Motor racing rules that before you can compete in the ETC championship, you must manufacture at least 1000 road going examples of your proposed racer. This homologation, as it is called, must include things like spoilers—hence the massive growth on the boot of the RS3100. The choice of engine capacity is less obvious. That odd figure of 3093 cc for the road car is arrived at by boring the ordinary 3-litre Essex block and fitting standard oversize pistons. However, ETC rules themselves allow a specified amount of over-boring, so the racer ultimately has a full 3412 cc.

Basically, for your £2413 you get only one of the racer's four camshafts, you don't get the alloy heads, the Lucas fuel injection or the extra 300 cc that all help to produce its whacking 400 plus bhp. You do have 99 cc more than standard and other mods to give 148 bhp at 5200 rpm (the standard unit gives 138 at 5000) as well as that big tail, modified suspension, brakes and fat alloy wheels. The resulting car may not be a race-winner, but it is a four-seater saloon that will comfort-

ably out-corner and out-accelerate most other road users and if you can tolerate the heavy steering and appalling ride is one that will give considerable and lasting pleasure.

From the outside, the RS version of the old Essex is recognisable by its smart blue rocker covers. Underneath are bigger 95.2 mm bores, a 9.1 : 1 compression and worked manifolds and head ports. It has fabricated exhaust manifolds too. At present Ford quote the ordinary 3-litre torque figure, but our acceleration times suggest there has been a considerable improvement in torque and power. A mere 7.2 s were needed to reach 60 mph and 21.2 s for 100 mph. A second is shaved from the already good 30-50 mph top gear time and the engine is so flexible that you could almost afford to throw the gear-lever away.

In its fastest form, the Capri is a mite quick even for MIRA's high-speed banking and we undoubtedly scrubbed off a lot of speed on the turns. Nevertheless, we averaged 122.8 mph on the straights and saw 125.0 mph on the best flying quarter.

This outstanding performance is a joy on the road, too, for the engine is totally without temperament and is just as happy accelerating from 15 mph in top as it is pulling 6500 rpm in third. You are certainly not short of power for overtaking, or for anything else for that matter.

Standard 3-litre transmission is retained and seems as good as ever. Gearchanges can be made as fast as your hand will move and even if there was a gap in the ratios, it would be masked by that tremendous engine torque.

Large ventilated discs and heavy duty pads and linings distinguish the brakes from stan-

Roadgoing racers have the large rear wing and a spoiler at the front. Below: it's more powerful, but from the outside the engine looks pretty normal

Lower, sleeker racing version with huge front spoilers, and wing. Below: four-cam racing engine with fuel injection and 400+ bhp

GXL trim is supplied as standard

Car : Ford
Model : Capri RS3100
Makers : Ford Advanced Vehicle Operations, Arisdale Avenue, South Ockendon, Essex RM15 5TJ
Price : £2026.45 plus £166.86 car tax plus £319.33 VAT gives a total of £2512.64.

	Standard Capri 3-litre	Capri RS3100
MAXIMUM SPEED		
Lap	119.5	122.8
Best ¼ mile	121.5	125.0
ACCELERATION		
mph		
0-30	3.1	2.7
0-40	4.5	4.0
0-50	6.1	5.4
0-60	8.6	7.2
0-70	11.7	9.6
0-80	15.0	12.5
0-90	19.5	15.8
0-100	26.5	21.2
Standing ¼ mile	16.6	15.7
Standing km	30.6	29.2
In Top		
mph		
20-40	7.7	6.5
30-50	7.7	6.7
40-60	7.7	6.7
50-70	8.1	6.7

60-80	8.5	7.3
70-90	9.9	8.5
80-100	12.2	10.6
90-110	—	15.5
In Third		
10-30	5.6	4.8
20-40	5.3	4.5
30-50	5.1	4.1
40-60	5.1	4.3
50-70	5.4	4.8
60-80	6.2	5.2
70-90	—	6.5
FUEL CONSUMPTION		
Steady mph		
30	45.7	37.5
40	41.2	37.2
50	37.2	34.2
60	32.0	31.2
70	28.3	28.2
80	25.4	25.1
90	22.3	22.1
100	19.4	18.8
Overall	19.4	22.2
Touring	24.7	24.5

dard. We found them most effective, but prone to judder after continuous heavy usage.

Even more changes are found on the suspension, which is stiffened out of all recognition. Up front Bilstein struts are coupled with the shorter RS2600 coil springs, and re-located track arms give a touch of negative camber. At the rear, massive single leaf springs and Bilstein dampers give the necessary stiffness and location.

The result is a harsh and devastatingly knobly ride but very predictable handling. If anything, there is too much roll-stiffness and on grippy surfaces full power slides are prevented by premature spinning of the inside wheel. A limited slip differential would, of course, cure this problem, but we feel the handling characteristics might then be a little sudden for road use. As it is, the car corners very fast and safely though perhaps disappointingly for those who enjoy a little opposite-lock motoring. Fat 185/70 Klebers fill the 6 in. RS alloy wheels and gave good dry but indifferent wet weather adhesion. The large offset of these wheels is responsible for very heavy steering that makes for difficult parking. However, it is full of feel for main road use.

Outwardly, the smart RS3100 is unmistakable. The low stance, big wheels, quarter-bumpers, spoiler and air dam hit you a mile away — metaphorically that is. Matt black paint is in abundance and colour matching stripes adorn the bonnet and flanks. The car which will retain the old two-door shell until the end of the year, is available in seven colours. Trim is as for the GXL and is black on all models.

Theories about the working range of that spoiler will doubtless be forwarded in the bar for months to come. Though we don't doubt it is invaluable at 130 mph we're not saying at what speed we think it starts to take effect. However, we can recommend it for two unclaimed qualities. One is for keeping the rear screen remarkably clean and the other is for retaining the filler cap when it was inadvertently left lying on the boot lid.
Gordon Bruce

With Fifty Superseded Fliers...

FORD TAKES ON THE TORANA V8s

The fifty Australian Capri RS3100s, all of them Mark I models, will be arriving in Australia as you read this. DOUG NYE has driven the RS3100 already in Britain. Here he discusses the car and what's involved in converting it to the wildest racing tin top you ever saw . . .

IT LOOKS slightly unusual. It was painted bright yellow, with gold pin-striping. Low-slung, it squatted purposefully on wide mag wheels and fat Goodyear radial tyres gripping the ground. A matt-black air dam was tucked coyly out of sight beneath the nose, while a brash tail-spoiler loomed large above the boot-lid.

This was the ultimate in road-going Mark 1 Ford Capris; the British-built 'homologation special' performance car which ended the popular line before the Mark 2 Model received its late-February release.

The RS3100's story goes back to the early part of the '73 racing season, when BMW's 3 and 3.5-litre touring cars sprouted roof-top slots and elevated rear wings and began to blow Ford Cologne's works Capris into the weeds. The hard-driven Capris lacked cubic inches and aerodynamic stability in taking on the BMW challenge, and sure enough the Munich company wrested the increasingly prestigious European title from Cologne.

The German Ford's V6 engine began its performance car life in the Capri as the RS2600 unit. It was stretched to a full three-litres but reached its limit there, so Ford of Dagenham sponsored Cosworth development of the British V6 — the three-litre Essex unit. Keith Duckworth and Mike Hall in Northampton produced the 3.4-litre belt-driven DOHC engine now so well publicised. This unit's road-going pass-card to Group 2 touring car homologation has been the Ford Advanced Vehicles-produced 3.1-litre RS3100.

We recently sampled one of the early RS3100s and visited the competitions department in Cologne to see the specialist chassis developments that have been made to accommodate 415 Cosworth horsepower . . .

Basic spec of the RS3100 is straightforward. The Essex block has been bored out by .060 in. to 93.76 mm, while the standard 72.4 mm stroke is retained to give 3093 cc of swept volume. Cylinder heads are gas-flowed, with hand-polished ports and 9:1 compression ratio, and a single twin-choke Weber 40DFA carburettor is attached which combines to produce a smooth 148 bhp at 5200 rpm. The standard 3-litre mill is good for 132 bhp.

One of those beautifully slick four-speed Ford gearboxes provides transmission, while suspension modifications include shorter springs to decrease ride-height by 1 in., and Bilstein gas-filled dampers front and rear. Front brakes are 9.75 in. diameter ventilated discs (instead of 9.6 in. solids) with dual circuits, and 9 in. diameter rear drums. A vacuum servo is used.

Ford-made RS mag-alloy road wheels are 13 x 6 and carry Goodyear HR radial tyres. The front track control arms are mounted farther apart on their cross-members to give slight negative camber.

Out on the road, this Capri feels very much 'smaller' and more manoeuvrable than any we've driven before. It has enough torque to heave itself away from a standstill in third gear without serious

This is Ford's European sedan racing weapon, based on the Capri RS3100. This is not the car we'll see, you understand, but it shows you just what can be done with a standard RS3100.

FORD TAKES ON TORANAS

complaint, and will pull cleanly in top from below 900 rpm, or about 15 mph. Combining this turbine-like smoothness and flexibility with vivid (if not neck-breaking) acceleration through the gears and you have a nice car. Times of 7.8 seconds 0-60 mph, and 13.0 seconds 0-80 mph speak for themselves. Gearing gives about 40 mph in first. 65 in second, 86 in third and a quoted peak of 125 in top, but there was no red-line on the tachometer, and it is common to drive these cars on their valve-springs!

That's a tricky thing to do under Britain's 50 mph speed limit, crisis conditions, but at 6000 rpm (over the recommended 5750 limit) fourth gear provides 130 mph and that was reached in many one-way runs during pre-release testing.

The RS3100 is a nice Ford; one of those cars which you can nose nicely into the apex of a medium-fast corner, then sit down on the outside rear wheel and power away from the turn in a nicely squatted attitude.

Tight corners show up Ford's mistake; the Capri should have a limited-slip differential as standard. If ever a car needs one, this is it, for the inside rear wheel lifts and spins at the slightest provocation. Lurid opposite-lock slides are good fun, but slow, untidy and time-wasting.

We don't like the new vented front brake system very much, either. On first heavy applications the

The three varieties of Dunlop racing rubber being used by Ford in the European Touring Car Championship.

Front discs are 12-inch turbo ventilated with twin pot calipers and a boosting system which works via a high pressure electric pump.

retardation is uneven, with the nose darting disconcertingly about. The brakes need to be cooking well and truly before the pads achieved a stable working temperature. With them good and warm braking effect is equalised and the Capri stops predictably. On a cold day you really can't go storming down a long, long straight at 125 mph and then expect predictable braking into a tight corner at the end. Pity . . .

Of course the car must be examined in its context — as a short-run 'homologation special' built purely to legalise the larger engine and aerodynamic aids in the European Touring Car Championship works team cars for '74.

While we were testing the RS3100, the '74 Cosworth Capris were being built in the German Ford competitions department in a modest part of the Rhineside Cologne-Niehl plant.

For a full works team in the grand old style so sadly missing from Formula One, the Ford operation is surprisingly small. Mike Kranefuss heads a staff of three main design engineers and about 18 mechanics. Thomas Ammerschlaeger is chief engineer, a thoughtful, intense man, deeply involved in his subject. Under him are Gerd Knoezinger, the chassis man, and Bruno Schutzbach, in charge of engines. The mechanic force includes the chassis builders — who stay with their particular 'babies' throughout the season — engine and bodywork specialists, an electrician and a test cell engineer.

The department has a fairly comprehensive machine shop, and tucked away in one corner is the dynamometer cell with a Schenk 400 instrument installed. The advent of the 415 bhp Cosworth V6 made this device obsolete overnight.

Since the start of the racing Capri RS2600 program, the engines have been developed and produced by Weslake Research down at Rye on England's south-eastern coast.

The '73 Capri racers were based on a batch of RS lightweight cars, built in Cologne and featuring glass fibre doors, bonnet and boot-lid. For the '74 cars such plasticity is not homologated, and they will be heavier, weighing about 1000 kg instead of 950-960 kg.

Bare body shells are prepared in the pilot plant at Niehl before entering the works team assembly room. They are fitted with the same heavy-duty suspension plates as standard models sold to rough-road countries. The wheel arches are extended inwards to help accommodate racing-width tyres, external glass fibre spats are added, and special engine and rear suspension mounts are welded-on.

Suspension and other mechanical parts are fitted by Kranefuss' men. The letter of the Group 2 law is adhered to throughout. Rubber front strut top mounts are replaced by aluminium units carrying a ball-joint, on which special gas-filled Bilstein struts are hung. Last year these struts were threaded into the cast hub-carrier, but this year their aluminium barrels are bonded into a new magnesium upright which carries peg-drive wheels on a centre-lock hex-nut system. Loktite is used for the bonding process.

The track-control arms are specially-made with threaded joints at both ends to adjust wheel camber, and the compression arms are also threaded to adjust castor.

CONTINUED ON PAGE 54

A '74 Capri racer during recent testing. Rear radiator and spoiler are fitted to Mark I body. Mag alloy wheels allow track adjustments.

Latest output for Cosworth-developed 3.4 litre V6 is 415 reliable brake horsepower!

FORD TAKES ON TORANAS
Continued from page 52

The anti-roll bar is 25 mm solid stock, but a tubular replacement is on the way.

At the rear the famous leaf spring — adopted years ago — is retained to fulfil the "standard" regulation, while co-axial Bilstein dampers and coil-springs do the real work.

A standard axle casing is carried, with brackets welded-on to carry radius arms picking-up on the chassis in box mounts let into the rear seat tray. A new axle cover is adopted, mounting the transverse Watts linkage pivot on an adjustable pin. This adjustment allows the rear roll-centre to be altered. The outboard linkages pick-up in mounts welded to the chassis side-rails.

Damper barrels are threaded at front and rear for almost their entire length to give ride-height adjustment on the spring platforms. Ammerschlaeger comments: "You know, last year tyre developments by Dunlop were so fast that spring-rates and roll-bars grew ridiculously. We now have enormous springs, like a railway wagon's! Side forces were so high cars cornered on two wheels; even with their independent suspension BMW had similar problems, tyres were so efficient. When Jackie Stewart drove for us we had to run Goodyears on his car, but they were consistently slower than the Dunlops . . ."

In fact the workshop's front store is packed with '74 pattern Dunlop tyres, the wet and intermediate treads on which have been *hand-cut* into incredibly complex patterns. Some people think Dunlop pulled out of Formula One to save money on tyre developments. Just one look at their technical investment in touring car racing (as with sport and small single-seater classes) shows that spending is still vast — the saving was on driver contracts.

Naturally, the racing Capris have disc brakes all round, with 32 mm thick x 11.97 in. diameter turbo-ventilated front discs and 22 mm thick x 10.51 in. diameter rear discs with more easily cast true radial venting.

German Teves twin-pot calipers are used, and an innovation for '74 is the use of a Teves-developed power-assistance system. This employs not vacuum, but a high-pressure electrical pump which boosts a reservoir to a pressure of 150 atmospheres, from which assistance is then valved to the hydraulic system.

Road wheels are beautifully cast magnesium split-rim types. These wheels allow a wide range of simply adjustable offsets, and are booming in popularity in European touring car circles.

Having equipped the new shells, sprayed in white-top Ford livery for this coming season, with their rolling gear, we can have a look inside the cabin. It is dominated by a massive roll-over cage, with its extreme elements extending down both sides of the engine bay and rearwards into the boot. This cage proved very strong last year in three write-off accidents suffered by the team.

One side of the cage is sealed, and has the Deugra fire extinguisher bomb piped up to it. Holes drilled in the left-side members direct extinguishing gas into the boot, down onto the driver, and into the engine bay, in an accident or fire. This system saves the added weight and complication of a separate pipe circuit, and is a neat solution, nicely-made.

The boot is packed with equipment, starting with the 120 litre fuel tank, fitted with giant filler and breather pipes. A 10-litre oil-cum-air separator tank stands to the right side, while an undersized spare wheel and tyre lie on the left. Fuel pumps are housed here for the Cosworth's Lucas injection system, and

electrics come from a hefty Deta battery installed in the rear seat pan. Near-standard matt black trim, with special racing seats in a lurid dayglo orange upholstery, complete the interior.

When the Capri RS program began, the V6 engine gave about 255 bhp in race tune. A five-speed ZF gearbox was adopted, and was still in use, transmitting 325 bhp, last season. When 415 bhp became available this year, a BMW-like Getrag gearbox was considered, but early tests of the prototype "hack" quickly proved the incredible ZF box man enough to transmit all the extra power and torque, although it is rather borderline in first and second gears. Luckily they are not much used in this class of racing, and the ZF is still fitted.

Ammerschlaeger is experimenting with a rear-radiator system, and although it is not yet completely sorted out, it seems likely to race this year. He says: "This mounting gives great advantages in the balance of the car because with water inside there's 12 kg taken off the front and put on the back. Unfortunately airflow beneath the car is masked by the front spoiler, and is not enough to cool adequately.

"So we have been running two supplementary radiators ahead of the rear wheels in either wheel spat. This is where the oil coolers were last year; the axle cooler behind the right-rear wheel, and the gearbox cooler behind the left-front wheel. I would have liked to have sealed off the nose air intake completely — this gives terrific advantages on the straight — but that is the only place for the engine oil cooler now. Airflow at the back would demand a bigger radiator if I put it there, and there isn't enough space for that.

"Weight distribution was a problem last year, and without spoilers the front end stuck like hell while the tail was always sliding around. We have wind-tunnel tested the new layout with spoilers and

with the tail radiator I think we have found a good balance . . ."

Certainly a second under the lap record in testing at Ricard indicates great progress, and the engineers beam with delight when Cosworth was mentioned. The much-publicised new engine ran well right out of the box, and has been free of mechanical trouble throughout — there haven't even been any oil leaks!

The Lucas fuel injection system was strange to the German team at first, for it suffered badly if there was any air in it at all, whereas their familiar Kugelfischer injection ran happily with air present in the system. So a system of multiple pumps and air-filters has been devised to keep the Lucas system absolutely air-free.

The test program has been done at the Ford Lommel test-ground in Belgium, at Nivelles and Zolder and Ricard, and Mike Kranefuss is running this year's program with Jochen Mass, Toine Hezemans, Dieter Glemser and Niki Lauda as his drivers.

With those men in the cockpits, and Cosworth power under the bonnet, Cologne's sophisticated Capris are simply the (Mark I) ultimate.   *

BLACK GOLD

Touring the twisting roads & high-speed motorways of Europe with a superfast Capri V 6

BY RON WAKEFIELD
European Editor

SUPPOSE THE FORD man in Cologne called you and said, "How would you like to drive a very special, very fast Capri?" Suppose, further, that you're going to the Eifel region of Germany, just an hour's drive from Cologne, anyway. And suppose, finally, he says you can keep that special Capri for two weeks and that between northern Germany and Munich, where you live, lie about 350 miles of *Autobahn,* mostly without speed limits? What would you do?

I did just what you'd do. I flew to Cologne and picked up the Capri. It's a one-of-a-kind car, built by Ford Cologne (where Capris are built for America as well as Europe) to try out some ideas that might find their way into production later on. The Ford folks started out with their special black-gold Capri, a car that was sold in Europe in a limited quantity with a John Player Special-style paint job and is now for sale in the U.S. Nearly everything is black, even the door handles and bumpers, and there's an interesting network of gold stripes, the wheels are gold and so are some of the emblems.

And they went from there. The German Capri comes with a variety of engines, two of which are V-6s: a 2.3-liter of 108 bhp and a 3.0-liter of 138 bhp. The 2.3 is a German engine, the 3-liter a British one. There used to be a German 2.6, and these days there's a German 2.8-liter for the U.S. and Canada only—just why, I haven't been able to find out. But it was this 2.8 block the Ford Competition Department, under Michael Kranefuss, used as a basis for a very hot engine. Before the Capri got its new body and became the Capri II there was a hunkered-down, fuel-injected version of the 2.6 called the RS 2600. It developed 150 bhp and went like a bat, as I found when I drove it in 1971 (see December 1971 R&T). Kranefuss

used the RS trimmings and other means to bring the 2.8 from its modest 109 bhp all the way to 170: Kugelfischer mechanical fuel injection, a rather bold camshaft, big valves and a 10.5:1 compression ratio. He also installed an engine oil cooler and an electronic rev limiter to protect the eager engine from overly eager pilots.

A limited-slip differential and a heavy-duty clutch were also installed, but otherwise the Capri's normal drivetrain with 4-speed gearbox was used. The chassis, however, got a thorough treatment. The Capri RS springs—stiffened, shortened coils at the front and light single-leaf springs at the rear—were substituted for the normal parts to lower the car nearly an inch as well as give it more roll resistance. Bilstein gas-filled shocks, tailored to give firmer ride and handling than the normal Capri's but not so stiff as that of the old RS, were installed. Kranefuss also specified Ford's ventilated-disc-brake kit for the front in place of the standard solid discs, and to all this he fitted a set of Ford's 13 x 6 cast aluminum wheels and Dunlop Radial Formula 60 tires of size 205/60HR-13.

Bodywork and interior got attention too. A special fiberglass spoiler was faired into the lower front bodywork and a commercially available one was added to the rear hatch. Kranefuss also added a spoiler to the rear-window wiper to keep it in place at speed! Inside, Scheel shell seats were installed front and rear, the instrument dials were done up with green numerals and red pointers as on last year's racing Capris, and Blaupunkt's fanciest radio-cassette player-recorder was installed. Naturally, the black-gold Capri was also fitted out with all the factory options such as Ford's two-way sunroof, the Ghia interior trim, an inside-adjustable outside mirror and a small thick-rim steering wheel. Most of this equipment is available from Ford's own Rallye Sport line in Europe (5 Cologne 60, West Germany, Postfach 60 04 02), but as far as I was able to determine there is no U.S. distributor for this interesting line of products for Capris and other European Fords.

When the Capri was turned over to me I was warned that the fuel injection was not tailored exactly for the 2.8 engine, having been brought over directly from the 2.6, and that the mixture was therefore a little rich in city driving or very fast highway work. In fact there were extra sparkplugs in the center console in case a plug fouled. As it turned out the plugs did foul in city driving, and the engine idles more like a race engine than one meant for the road. Once above 2000 rpm, though, it pulls without hesitation.

The Ford V-6 engine, being a pushrod unit, is not a truly high-speed engine, but set up this way it pulls strongly and smoothly to and past its power peak of 6000 rpm. The rev limiter says "halt" at 6200, so you have to be sure and begin your upshift at about 6100; but even with this modest rev lid 2nd gear takes you over 70 mph and 3rd over 100. Top speed is governed by the rev limiter too, and from the ease with which the Capri attained 210 km/h (130 mph) on its accurate speedometer I'd say that if it had a 5th gear it would probably approach 140. In the acceleration tests it would lay down any length of rubber I wanted, knock off 60 mph in 7.7 seconds and reach 100 in just 21.0. Considering all this performance the fuel economy—measured on a run between Frankfurt and Munich at speeds mostly between 75 and 120 mph—isn't bad either at 17 mpg. But the Capri's tiny (12.7-gallon) tank won't take you far at that rate.

With the lumpy low-speed running and the stiff clutch Black Gold was a Capri to be seen in, not to drive, in the city. But what a car to be seen in. In Germany every male from 10 on noticed the "2.8" emblems on the sides, obviously knowing there isn't any such thing, and many of them asked me about it. Male and female alike simply ogled the car—it is unmistakeably something special—and they seemed to enjoy watching my wrestling with the steering wheel as I maneuvered into parking places with wide tires and without power steering.

There were problems of the kind you expect in a one-off job like this. On a particularly warm day, perhaps with fuel that was a bit substandard as it didn't happen but once, the engine overheated and detonated at 100-plus mph and I had to ease off. And the limited-slip differential, especially when hot, graunched loudly in low-speed city cornering. There were some strange rattles from the normally quiet Capri body too. On the other hand the car was far better worked out than the typical highly modified road machine.

I discovered how well Black Gold handled on a delightful winding route through the Eifel. Even if Black Gold isn't as stiffly sprung as the old RS, it *is* hard, and you don't corner briskly on a crude surface without the tail ends—yours and the car's—bouncing around occasionally. The handling characteristic is basically understeering, though not to an inhibiting degree, and with 8-in.-wide tires there's a fair amount of cornering power. But the British Dunlops do inhibit, as they squeal badly (even at 32 psi) and seem much too soft for this sort of car. They also "sing" when you're driving in a straight line, usually a clue to good rain traction, and a cloudburst proved that they are good in the wet, both in cornering and in braking.

Out on the motorway I discovered that the Dunlops were also an inhibiting factor. They shook badly at any speed between 75 and 100 mph, just the range where the thick German traffic usually held me, and a call to Ford established that this was normal for them. So I just tried to stay under 75 or over 100, preferably the latter. At such speeds the Ford is satisfactorily stable, the spoilers holding it down well. As I had the misfortune and embarrassment of destroying the front one on an unexpected tree root in a parking lot, I can say that without it the nose lifts and the car is markedly less stable above 80 mph.

The brakes, improved as they are with the vented front discs,

PHOTOS BY RAINER SCHLEGELMILCH

handle the hot Capri's performance well, but there are reservations. They brought it to a rapid, well controlled stop from 80 mph and showed little tendency to fade in hard work on a winding road. But at really high speeds the car had a tendency to dart when they were applied, and once when I entered a sweeping curve a little too fast I'd have spun if it hadn't been for my gentle foot. In the panic-stop test the pedal went hard, indicating a lack of vacuum to the booster, and if I ever had to tap the pedal twice while coasting in slow city traffic I was out of boost too. I think the problem was inadequate vacuum because of the engine's big valve overlap.

The all-black Capri cockpit was a dramatic place to sit, if not an altogether comfortable one. For one thing, I wouldn't have a black car if I couldn't have air conditioning, and Black Gold didn't have it. The Scheel seats are superb in front, retaining all the adjustments of the normal ones but giving a lot more thigh support and lateral holding. In the rear they're beautiful, but that's about all. Though their backs are set up to release as in the Capri Ghia, they would not even approach folding over flat because of the side bolsters, and they rob the Capri's rear compartment of needed legroom and headroom. Otherwise, the interior was standard Capri Ghia except for the special instrument faces and blacked-out chrome, and I cannot understand why Ford persists with those dumb push-push headlight, parking-light and windshield wiper-washer switches.

About that radio. Called the Blaupunkt Berlin and selling for the equivalent of about $600 [$1200 in the U.S.!—Ed.] in Germany, it has its five-band receiver mounted on a flexible-cable stalk so that it can be moved to the most convenient spot. One turns it on by pushing the top righthand button or one of the tuning buttons. Both the volume control and signal-seeking are power-operated at the touch of two bars at the bottom, the latter sending two little red lights blipping across the dial. There is no manual tuning except for setting up the pushbuttons, and anytime the radio is turned off—which also happens when you use the engine starter with normal wiring—it has to be turned back on and retuned. The "off" bar is on the right side, easily bumped, and stereo balance and tone controls are on the back side. A cassette player-recorder goes in the normal radio spot on the dash and its microphone hangs beside it. Interesting, and very good from tonal and reception standpoints, but more gimmicky than functional.

At the end of the appointed two weeks I drove Black Gold back to Cologne, once again enjoying its strong acceleration, high-speed cruising ability and all the attention it attracted, stopping once for fuel and answering the friendly questions of gasoline-station attendants. It was an experience I won't forget for a long time. How about some of those goodies for an American version of Black Gold, Lincoln-Mercury?

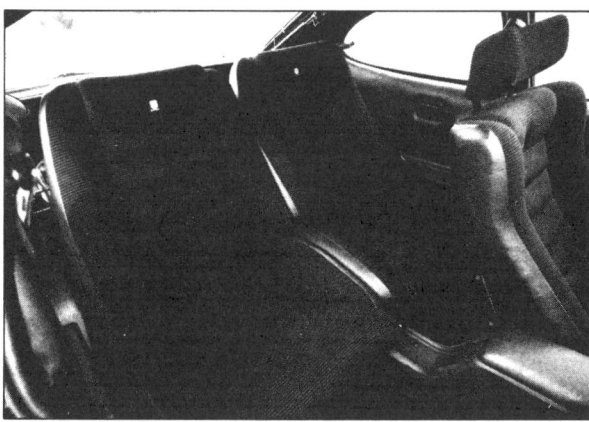

BLACK GOLD CAPRI V-6
SPECIFICATIONS

GENERAL
Curb weight, lb	2420
Weight distribution (with driver), front/rear	54/46
Wheelbase, in.	100.8
Track, front/rear	53.3/54.5
Length	171.5
Width	66.9
Height	50.0
Fuel capacity, U.S. gal.	12.7

CHASSIS & BODY
Body/frame	unit steel
Brake system	9.8-in. vented discs front, 9.0 x 2.25-in. drums rear; vacuum assisted
Wheels	cast alloy, 13 x 6
Tires	Dunlop SP Sport Super Radial Formula 60, 205/60VR-13
Steering type	rack & pinion
Turns, lock-to-lock	3.4
Suspension, front/rear: MacPherson struts, lower lateral arms, coil springs, tube shocks, anti-roll bar/live axle on leaf springs, tube shocks, anti-roll bar	

ENGINE & DRIVETRAIN
Engine type	ohv V-6
Bore x stroke, mm	93.0 x 68.5
Displacement, cc/cu in.	2792/171
Compression ratio	10.5:1
Bhp @ rpm, net	170 @ 6000
Torque @ rpm, lb-ft.	170 @ 4000
Fuel requirement	premium
Transmission	4-sp manual
Gear ratios: 4th (1.00)	3.09:1
3rd (1.41)	4.36:1
2nd (1.94)	5.99:1
1st (3.16)	9.76:1
Final drive ratio	3.09:1

CALCULATED DATA
Lp/hp (test weight)	15.6
Mph/1000 rpm (4th gear)	21.0
Engine revs/mi (60 mph)	2850
R&T steering index	1.11

ROAD TEST RESULTS

ACCELERATION
Time to speed, sec:	
0–30 mph	3.0
0–50 mph	5.9
0–60 mph	7.7
0–80 mph	11.0
0–100 mph	21.0

SPEEDS IN GEARS
4th (6200 rpm)	130
3rd (6200)	103
2nd (6200)	74
1st (6200)	39

FUEL ECONOMY
Fast driving, mpg	17.0

BRAKES
Minimum stopping distance, ft;	
From 80 mph	255

SPEEDOMETER ERROR
62 mph (100 km/h) indicated is actually	60.8
75 mph (120 km/h)	73.5
99 mph (160 km/h)	99.0

Ford Capri 3000S

**Latest version of biggest-engined Capri,
with suspension changes and power steering to make the most of 3-litre output.
Excellent performance and handling, surprisingly good comfort, first-class equipment.
Hatchback and "split" back seat for versatile loading.
Highly competitive on price**

FORD'S CAPRI, which started life as "the car you always promised yourself", has been progressively developed to the point where it lives up to the image. The main advance was of course the introduction of the Mark II Capri with its hatchback rear door and lower waistline, but there have been continual chassis changes, always to the car's benefit and nowhere more evident than in the versions with the 3-litre V6 engine. Thus equipped, the original Mark I Capri

felt short of suspension movement, was both uncomfortable and unpredictable in its handling on anything but a smooth surface. Later cars were softened, perhaps too much for the liking of hard drivers. Now the up-market Capris are available with the sporting S specification. This includes rerated springs and gas-filled dampers, a front "beard" spoiler and alloy road wheels. With the 3-litre engine, the brakes are also uprated and power steering is fitted as standard. Bright

trim is replaced by matt-finish black, and standard equipment includes a pushbutton radio, head restraints, halogen headlamps and a tailgate wipe/wash arrangement.

From a basic engineering point of view the Capri 3-litre is much as before, with a fairly close-ratio four-speed gearbox and a 3.09 final drive giving overall gearing of nearly 22mph per 1,000rpm. Front suspension is by MacPherson struts, while the live back axle is located by carefully-tuned semi-el-

liptic springs, assisted by the anti-roll bar.

Performance and economy

Our last Capri 3000 test (8 March 1973) was carried out before the change to the Mark II body. It is interesting to compare the figures obtained then with those reached by the current car, and to speculate on the reasons for the differences.

Maximum speed is down from

122mph to "only" 117mph, but even this takes the engine some way past its moderate power peak. As is now Ford practice, there is no red line on the rev counter which reads to 7,000rpm. The reduced maximum speed, which suggests an effective loss of some 15bhp, must be due in the main to engine changes aimed at meeting exhaust emission laws (which were in their infancy three years ago). Apart from that there is the power absorbed by the power steering pump to be considered, together with the air dam. Although succeeding in its aim of reducing front-end lift, the dam is unlikely to have reduced overall drag.

The loss in engine power may be more clearly seen in the acceleration figures in each gear. In second, third and top the current car is the loser. As an example, the 40-60mph time in second gear goes up from 3.9 to 4.6sec; in third gear from 4.9 to 5.9sec; and in top, from 7.2 to 8.6sec. There are also signs that the latest-standard engine runs out of breath more quickly at the top end — though not nearly as badly as the first 3-litre Capri which was further hampered by the poor ratios in its Zodiac-derived gearbox. In its present form the Capri runs (in round figures) to 40, 70 and 90mph in its lower gears and these limits, coupled with the engine's wide spread of torque, mean a complete absence of "holes" in the performance when overtaking or driving fast on a twisting road.

Given the deficit in each gear's performance, it is not surprising that the present test car lost ground to the 1973 car in standing-start acceleration. The high first gear does not help the getaway, and it is interesting that the Capri could not quite match the 0-30mph time of the 2-litre Cortina recently tested. Once it is under way, however, it is quick indeed with a time of 9sec to 60mph (8.3sec for the 1973 car) and 30.3sec to 100mph (25.1sec in 1973). A glance at comparative — mostly more expensive — cars will show that such times are highly competitive.

There should be some compensation for the slight loss in performance (apart, that is, from a cleaner exhaust), and in the Capri's case it is found in flexibility and economy. The S was prepared to pull from 10mph in top gear, which previous Capri 3-litres were not; this may be due as much to driveline as to engine improvements, but in any case the low-speed smoothness makes it easier to drive in town. As for economy, our steady-speed figures show the S to have a substantial advantage over the old GXL except, oddly enough, at 70mph where the two figures were virtually identical. The improvement is most marked at lower speeds (40.6mpg- instead of 35.1mpg at 30mph). Our overall consumption figure was 20.7mpg for the GXL; in the S it improved to 23.1mpg. Our best brim-to-brim figure was 25.7mpg, while hard driving in difficult conditions saw the worst figure of 19.3mpg.

Handling and brakes

Ford's adoption of power steering as standard on a sporting Capri may strike some drivers as sacrilege. We remember, though, that the older 3-litre cars were too heavy for comfort, partly because the steering was sensibly geared rather than forcing the driver endlessly to twirl the wheel for a sharp corner. In the Capri S the same gearing (3.2 turns from lock to lock) has been retained, and the power assistance has taken the drudgery out of travelling quickly on a winding road. For the most part we thought the assistance well judged, except that it was light enough to cause some tendency to weave when settling into a corner of tightening radius.

With some 55 per cent of its kerb weight on the front wheels, the Capri is bound to be an understeering car and this governs its behaviour when driven in a "touring" sort of way. As so often happens, the power steering disguises the characteristic unless the driver looks carefully, but in the end the Capri will run wide of its intended line no matter how much lock is applied. Front tyre scrub slows the car quickly if the driver releases the accelerator at this point, but a nervous stab at the brakes will send the nose wider still.

However, the sporting driver can change the whole picture by skilful use of gears and power. He will spend most of his time on winding roads changing between second and third gears; the ability to reach nearly 70mph in second is a great asset. There is enough power available to balance the handling with precision, and the smooth action of the accelerator linkage is a great help. Given the right balance the Capri's cornering ability is improved, and so is its behaviour at the limit. The trick is to avoid overdoing things and provoking the back wheels to slide.

In current Mark 2 form, Capri has more glass area than original version, and high-lifting tailgate. The S-package includes a beard-type spoiler which reduces front end lift and greatly improves high-speed stability, while matt black trim is used instead of brightwork

AutoTEST
Ford Capri 3000S

The brakes, up-rated for the 3-litre engine, proved light in operation and yet pleasantly progressive. A pedal pressure of 40lb sufficed for firm check braking, while an increase to 70lb gave the best stop of exactly 1g. Any further increase caused the front wheels to lock, the car slewing slightly to the right as it stopped. We were not quite so happy with the results of the fade test, in which the pedal effort needed for a 0.5g stop rose gradually until the tenth and last stop, which showed the first signs of recovery. On the other hand there was no smell of linings, and pedal travel remained steady, so presumably it was a question of relatively hard brake linings taking some time to warm fully.

The handbrake worked well when used alone on the level, giving a 0.35g stop despite the lightly-laden back wheels. It also held the car facing in either direction on the 1 in 3 test gradient. A restart on this hill, however, called for skill and restraint. It was easy to succumb to over-enthusiasm, and spin the clutch rather than the rear wheels when getting away.

Comfort and convenience

Ford have been careful in their rerating of the Capri's S-pack springs, and none of the softness of the ride has been sacrificed. The S ride is certainly in contrast to the rock-hardness of the very first 3-litre Capri, and it pays dividends not only in comfort, but also in stability and control on poor sur-

faces. In absolute terms the ride is not soft, yet it avoids any feeling of harshness. The damping is excellent, and the use of anti-roll bars at both ends of the car keeps down body roll to the extent that the car's occupants are scarcely aware of it. The rear anti-roll bar also helps to locate the back axle, and it was impossible to provoke the axle-tramp of which we have complained in previous 3-litre Capri tests. On rough surfaces, the ride remains good up to high speeds, though a certain amount of crashing and banging let the driver know that the wheels are moving a great deal more than the body. Eventually the suspension does begin to run out of travel, usually at the back, and sets a limit. Up to that point, the handling remains good and straight-line stability is little affected. On motorways the Capri runs straight with little conscious effort from the driver, and sidewinds do not greatly deflect it from its course.

Most of the top-range Ford seats look good these days, and those in the Capri S are no exception apart from their garish striped upholstery, which drew a very mixed reaction from our staff. Cushion and squab are shaped to provide good sideways support, much appreciated in hard cornering. But as we have noticed before, the seats do not provide proper lumbar support and allow their occupants to develop a round-backed posture which can lead to aches on long journeys. Large drivers seem worse affected than small ones. Otherwise the seats have a considerable range of fore-and-aft movement and the

relationship of steering wheel to pedals seems right for most people, even though the wheel is not adjustable.

The back seats are interesting in that they are shaped to support two passengers and discourage the squeezing in of a third — as does the limited width and the relatively low rated payload of the car. The back seat squabs may be folded forward together or individually: the latter is a handy arrangement when travelling three-up with a lot of luggage, or (as we found) to allow mother to sit in the back seat alongside a carry-cot on the extended half of the load platform. Purely from the accommodation point of view, the back seat is rather poor with limited leg and headroom for large people; nor is it easy to climb in and out. With the front seat headrests in place, the forward view is restricted.

As we have said, the driving position is comfortable for drivers of most sizes, and the controls are well laid out. The three-spoked sports steering wheel has a trimmed rim which makes it comfortable to hold, and the use of power steering has enabled it to be made smaller. The pedals are well spaced, with room to rest the left foot clear of the clutch; the clutch itself is now light and progressive, with a 22lb force needed to clear it rather than the 35lb of which we complained in the 1973 test. As in all Fords, the gearchange is light and precise, with excellent synchromesh which we were unable to beat even during the snatched changes of our acceleration runs.

The minor controls follow the

Main instruments are tachometer (left) and speedometer, with total and press-zero trip distance recorders. Smaller dials are ammeter and oil pressure gauge on left, fuel tank contents and coolant temperature on right. Steering column levers are for screen wash / wipe and (hidden) driving lamps on right, and direction indicators and head lamp dip / flash on right. Press button switch under heater controls for rear wash / wipe and heated rear window, with ashtray and concealed cigarette lighter beneath. Clock is rather remote, ahead of gear lever

Specification

ENGINE	
	Front; Rear drive
Cylinders	6, in 60deg vee
Main bearings	4
Cooling	Water
Fan	Viscous
Bore, mm (in.)	93.7 (3.69)
Stroke, mm (in.)	72.4 (2.85)
Capacity, cc (in³)	2,994 (182.7)
Valve gear	ohv
Camshaft drive	Chain
Compression ratio	9.0-to-1
Octane rating	97 RM
Carburettor	Weber twin-choke
Max power	138 bhp (DIN) at 5,000 rpm
Max torque	174 lb ft at 3,000 rpm

TRANSMISSION		
Type		

Gear	Ratio	mph / 1000 rpm
Top	1.0	21.67
3rd	1.41	15.37
2nd	1.94	11.17
1st	3.35	6.47

Final drive gear	Hypoid bevel
Ratio	3.09-to-1

SUSPENSION	
Front — location	MacPherson struts, lower links
springs	Coil
dampers	Telescopic
anti-roll bar	Yes
Rear — location	Live axle
springs	Semi-elliptic leaf
dampers	Telescopic
anti-roll bar	Yes

STEERING	
Type	Rack and pinion
Power assistance	Yes
Wheel diameter	14.0 in.

BRAKES	
Front	9.75 in. dia. disc
Rear	9.0 in. dia. drum
Servo	Vacuum type

WHEELS	
Type	Light alloy
Rim width	5½ in.
Tyres — make	Various (Goodyear on test car)
— type	Radial-ply tubeless
— size	185 / 70-13 in.

EQUIPMENT	
Battery	12 volt 44 Ah
Alternator	55 amp
Headlamps	Halogen, 130 / 100 watt (total)
Reversing lamp	Standard
Hazard warning	Standard
Electric fuses	10
Screen wipers	2-speed plus intermittent
Screen washer	Electric
Interior heater	Air blending
Interior trim	Cloth seats, pvc headlining
Floor covering	Carpet
Jack	Screw pillar
Jacking points	2 each side under sills
Windscreen	Toughened (standard)
Underbody protection	Phosphate electro-coat primer

MAINTENANCE	
Fuel tank	12.7 Imp. galls (58 litres)
Cooling system	16.4 pints (inc. heater)
Engine sump	8.8 pints SAE 20W/50
Gearbox	3.5 pints SAE 80
Final drive	1.9 pints SAE 90 EP
Grease	No points
Valve clearance	Inlet 0.013 in. (cold) Exhaust 0.022 in. (cold)
Contact breaker	0.025 in. gap
Ignition timing	10 deg BTDC (static)
Spark plug	Motorcraft
— type	AGR 22
— gap	0.030 in.
Tyre pressures	F 23; R 23 psi (normal driving)
Max payload	760 lb (345 kg)

AUTOCAR, w/e 13 November 1976

Maximum Speeds

Gear	mph	kph	rpm
Top (mean)	117	188	5,400
(best)	119	191	5,490
3rd	92	148	6,000
2nd	67	108	6,000
1st	39	63	6,000

Acceleration

True mph	Time secs	Speedo mph
30	3.0	31
40	4.6	41
50	6.5	51
60	9.0	61
70	12.2	72
80	16.4	82
90	21.6	92
100	30.3	103
110	44.0	113

Standing ¼-mile:
17.0 sec, 81 mph
kilometre:
31.6 sec, 101 mph

mph	Top	3rd	2nd
10-30	10.2	6.0	4.2
20-40	8.8	5.6	4.0
30-50	8.6	5.8	4.2
40-60	8.6	5.9	4.6
50-70	9.2	6.5	6.3
60-80	10.3	7.7	—
70-90	11.7	10.5	—
80-100	15.1	—	—
90-110	22.4	—	—

Consumption

Fuel
Overall mpg: 23.1
(12.2 litres/100km)
Calculated (DIN) mpg: 23.7
(11.9 litres/100km)

Constant speed:

mph	mpg
30	40.6
40	36.7
50	33.3
60	29.8
70	26.1
80	24.1
90	21.6
100	20.1

Autocar formula:
Hard driving, difficult conditions
21.0 mpg
Average driving, average conditions
25.4 mpg
Gentle driving, easy conditions
30.0 mpg

Grade of fuel: Premium, 4-star
(97 RM)
Mileage recorder: 1.3 per cent over reading

Oil
Consumption (SAE 20W/50)
1,500 miles/pint

Brakes

Fade (from 70 mph in neutral)
Pedal load for 0.5g stops in lb

Turns, lock to lock: 3.2

1	40/43	6	45/55
2	40/45	7	50/55
3	45/47	8	55/60
4	45/50	9	50/55
5	45/55	10	55/50

Response (from 30 mph in neutral)

Load	g	Distance
20lb	0.20	150ft
40lb	0.47	64ft
60lb	0.80	38ft
70lb	1.00	30ft
Handbrake	0.35	86ft

Max. gradient 1 in 3

Clutch

Pedal 22lb and 4¾in.

Test Conditions

Wind: 0-5 mph
Temperature: 16 deg C (61 deg F)
Barometer: 29.45 in. Hg
Humidity: 70 per cent
Surface: dry asphalt and concrete
Test distance: 1,006 miles

Figures taken at 2,200 miles by our own staff at the Motor Industry Research Association proving ground at Nuneaton.

All Autocar test results are subject to world copyright and may not be reproduced in whole or part without the Editor's written permission.

Regular Service

Interval

Change	6,000	18,000	36,000
Engine oil	Yes	Yes	Yes
Oil filter	Yes	Yes	Yes
Gearbox oil	No	No	No
Spark plugs	No	Yes	Yes
Air cleaner	No	Yes	Yes
C/breaker	No	Yes	Yes
Total cost	**£20.19**	**£27.61**	**£32.34**

(Assuming labour at £4.30/hour)

Parts Cost

(including VAT)

Brake pads (2 wheels) — Front	£8.19
Brake shoes (2 wheels) — rear	£6.51
Silencer (s)	£40.19
Tyre — each (typical advertised)	£22.00
Windscreen	£26.57
Headlamp unit	£11.61
Front wing	£26.92
Rear bumper	£10.91

Warranty Period
12 months/unlimited mileage

Weight

Kerb, 23.0cwt/2,574lb/1,168kg
(Distribution: F/R, 54.9/45.1)
As tested, 27.3 cwt/3,060lb/1,388kg

Boot capacity: 14/25 cu. ft.

Turning circles:
Between kerbs
L, 35ft 5in; R, 34ft 3in
Between walls
L, 36ft 6½in; R, 36ft 4½in
Turns, lock to lock: 3.2

OVERALL LENGTH 14' 3"
OVERALL WIDTH 5' 7"
OVERALL HEIGHT 4' 3"
GROUND CLEARANCE 6"
WHEELBASE 8' 5"
FRONT TRACK 4' 5"
REAR TRACK 4' 6.5"

Test Scorecard

(Average of scoring by *Autocar* Road Test team)

Ratings:
6 Excellent
5 Good
4 Better than average
3 Worse than average
2 Poor
1 Bad

PERFORMANCE	4.33
STEERING AND HANDLING	4.67
BRAKES	4.40
COMFORT IN FRONT	4.17
COMFORT IN BACK	2.71
DRIVERS AIDS	3.88
(instruments, lights, wipers, visibility etc.)	
CONTROLS	4.00
NOISE	3.83
STOWAGE	3.67
ROUTINE SERVICE	2.90
(under-bonnet access, dipstick etc.)	
EASE OF DRIVING	4.73
OVERALL RATING	**3.88**

Comparisons

	Price £	max mph	0-60 sec	overall mpg	capacity c.c.	power bhp	wheelbase in.	length in.	width in.	kerb weight lb	fuel gall	tyre size
Ford Capri 3000S	2,927	117	9.0	23.1	2,994	138	101	169	67	2,574	12.7	185/70-13
Alfa Romeo Alfetta GTV	4,799	118	8.9	23.3	1,962	122	95	165	65	2,423	11.9	185/70-14
Datsun 260Z 2+2	5,247	120	9.9	23.9	2,565	150	102½	174	65	2,632	13.2	195/70-14
Lotus Elite 503	9,782	124	7.8	20.9	1,973	155	98	175½	71½	2,552	14.8	205/60-14
MGB GT	3,060	102	13.0	23.7	1,798	84	91	158	62	2,260	12.0	165-14
Triumph Stag	5,419	116	9.3	20.7	2,997	146	100	174	63½	2,720	12.7	185-14

AutoTEST

Ford Capri 3000S

Above: The V6 engine sits neatly in the bonnet space, although the dip stick and sparking plugs are not too easy to reach

Centre right: A fold-away panel covers luggage, but it does not lift with the tailgate panel

Right: The spare is stowed beneath the boot floor, with plenty of space around it for oddments and tools

Above The rear seats fold flat individually to extend the load space, but the wheel arches take up some useful room. Centre left: The front seats have catches to lock the backrests in place; the head restraints are standard. Left: Fashionable striped upholstery is used on all the seating; those at the rear are shaped for just two occupants

now-established Ford pattern with three column-mounted stalks for all the most frequently-used items including lights, wipe/wash, indicators, and horn. The heater controls — two horizontal slides and a switch for the two-speed fan — are situated in the centre of the facia, beneath the radio and above the push-push switches for the heated rear window and rear wipe/wash. A full set of instruments comprises two very large dials for the rev counter and the 130mph speedometer (with press-to-reset trip recorder), and four small ones for ammeter, oil pressure, water temperature, and fuel contents. A clock is mounted at the forward end of the centre console, well away from the driver's eye-line.

Visibility from the driving seat is good in the current Capri, with none of the severe over the shoulder blind spots of the first version. Although the bonnet is long, it is not difficult to judge where the car ends; and there is only a short tail aft of the lower edge of the rear window. Ford have taken no chances with the rear vision, fitting electric demisting and a wipe/wash facility as standard. The main wipers clear a good area of screen and stay in contact at

high speed except when there is also a stiff crosswind. The electric washers are most effective. At night, the output of the high-wattage (65 watts per main beam) halogen lamps is rather disappointing and fails to match the performance of the car. The dipped beam pattern is well-controlled with plenty of light down the nearside.

Thanks to its air-blending heater, the Capri's interior can be warmed quickly to the desired temperature and held there without difficulty; the heater controls work smoothly and logically. The fan is quiet on its slower speed, though noisy when used on full boost when clearing the screen of mist (which it does very rapidly). Through-flow ventilation, via two eyeball inlets at either end of the facia, proved adequate except on a couple of hot, humid days when the windows needed to be opened at low speeds. Noise levels were generally low. The engine gave the expected throaty growl when accelerating hard, but was quiet when cruising at up to 90mph. Road noise was well suppressed but the level of wind noise was disappointing, while the tyres (Goodyear G800S on the test car) squealed rather too readily.

Living with the Capri 3000S

Given the high standard of equipment in the Capri S, which includes comfortable inertia-reel safety belts as well as the other items already mentioned, there is little to be added in the way of options. Since the S is supposed to be the sporting version of the Capri, automatic transmission is not available (though you can of course have an automatic L, GL, or Ghia). Probably the most popular extra

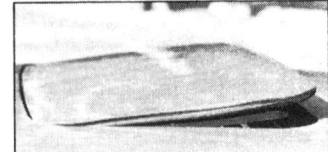

The sun roof panel can be tipped up at the rear as well as being wound fully open.

will be the slide/tilt roof as fitted to the test car, which worked well and did not create too many draughts inside. A laminated windscreen is available, together with tinted glass and a remotely-controlled driver's door mirror.

The big tailgate opens high to make loading easy even for tall

people. We have already commented on the split folding arrangement of the back seat, which adds an extra touch of versatility to the load capacity of the car. With both seat backs folded, the space is considerable and awkward, bulky objects can be carried — though care must be taken that they do not foul the big rear window when the tailgate is closed. The spare wheel lives beneath the false floor of the boot, so luggage must be unloaded to reach it.

With the fuel capacity of nearly 13 gallons, the Capri has a comfortable cruising range although inevitably, the bigger-engined versions such as this 3000S will not travel quite so far on a tankful. Even so it should manage 250 miles between fills even when driven hard. At the other end of the car there is a great deal of space under the big, manually-propped bonnet, and the 3-litre V6 engine looks quite small.

Where it fits in

The Capri 3.0S is one of two 3-litre versions of the car — the other is the 3.0 Ghia in which automatic transmission is standard. The "S" pack may also be had with the 1.6-litre GT or 2.0-litre engines. The 3.0S price of £3,081 verges on the remarkable for what the car offers — it is a good deal cheaper than anything that might be regarded as competitive in performance. It competes in an area of the market where many people would not dream of buying a Ford, despite the Capri's demonstrable superiority in several ways. This is an attitude which the company is gradually overcoming; it is important that it should have such a sound product to offer. Those who can overcome their prejudices will relish not only its performance, good equipment, and reasonable economy, but also its lack of temperament and ease of driving.

MANUFACTURER:
Ford Motor Co Ltd,
Eagle Way,
Warley,
Brentwood, Essex.

PRICES:

Basic	£2,633.48
Special Car Tax	£219.46
VAT	£228.24
Total (in GB)	**£3,081.18**
Seat Belts (inertia)	standard
Licence	£40.00
Delivery charge (London)	£41.00
Number plates	£7.50
Total on the Road	
(exc insurance)	**£3,169.68**
Insurance Group 6	

EXTRAS (inc VAT)

Remote control door mirror*	£16.99
Sliding roof*	£105.60
Tinted glass*	£31.70
Laminated windscreen*	£36.44
*Fitted to test car	

TOTAL AS TESTED	
ON THE ROAD	**£3,360.41**

SOUTH AFRICA'S CAPRI
V8

ENGINE bay is not-too-crowded despite bulk of V8. Compact front suspension gives the engineer plenty of room to play.

CONTINUED FROM PAGE 15

0-100 mph in 17.4 seconds — at over a mile above sea level.

Due to the Capri's space-saving strut type front suspension, the V8 slots in with lots of room to spare and it's not a one hour job to change the plugs, as it is with most of the American V8 compacts. Positioned well to the rear of the engine bay, the 302's trim 460lbs dry weight helps to keep the Capri's weight distribution to a very desirable 53/47 ratio and a dry all up weight of only 2390 lbs. With only 21 cwt. to push along, reasonable frontal area, and some 260 bhp on tap, it's not difficult to see where the performance comes from.

The prototype sports a solid lifter Ford high-performance cam, a four barrel carb, and a 7,000 rpm rev limit. Otherwise it's standard. It pulls sweetly all the way from 1000 rpm

and if you plant your foot at anything over 3,000 rpm you get that lift-off feeling.

Docile

Bearing the performance figures in mind, driving the Capri V8 in everyday conditions was not quite the frightening experience I had expected. It is surprisingly docile, and will lope around in traffic in second and top gears in typical V8 style. Press the accelerator a little harder and the Capri takes off with a pleasant V8 roar.

Revving more like a one litre than a five, the V8 spins all the way to 7000 with gusto, providing second and third gear maximums of 85 and 112. Passing acceleration makes for ridiculously easy overtaking at speed — it's just a matter of tapping the throttle at 80 in

top for example, and you are past and over the ton in less than five seconds, and that's really moving. You get the same sensation at 120 mph. This engine just loves to go and the gearing of the prototype seems just about ideal.

To drive it very quickly through a corner requires a fair degree of courage, and confidence in your ability but with the power on, you can place the back beautifully with the throttle and just steer it through on the power.

Naturally enough the front understeers in tight corners, but judicious use of the throttle overcomes this instantly, and if you feel brave or just like it that way, you can hang the back out, power on. It's all beautifully controllable with the very accurate standard steering.

Rushing through a radiused 60-70 mph corner full tilt is an exhilarating experience. Driving the Capri V8 really quickly is something of an acquired art — it doesn't require the finesse you'd exercise with a 911, but you need a fair measure of judgement and reactions that very few production cars call for.

As a touring car the Capri V8 is an effortless runner. It cruises at the ton with only 4500 rpm on the clock, and it seems just as happy at 120 mph (5500 rpm). At any speed up to its maximum the Capri is satisfyingly stable and straight-running, little affected by cross winds, though bumpy bitumen does promote pitching in movement in the firm suspension.

Ford Australia no doubt are well-advanced on preparing their own version of the V8 Capri. It will be a real "Monaro-masher" and well worth waiting for. ●

SPECIFICATIONS

ENGINE
V8 water cooled ohv engine, thin wall cast iron block.

Capacity .... 302 cu. in.
Bore/Stroke .... 4.0in. x 3.0in.
Compression ratio .... 9.5 to 1
Maximum power ... 260 bhp at 6,500 rpm
Maximum torque ... 300 ft/lb at 2,600 rpm
Electrical system ...... 12 volt 35 amp/hr battery with alternator
Fuel pump .... Mechanical
Carburettor .. Four throat Holley 460 CFM

TRANSMISSION
Type: Four speed all synchro box. Floor shift.
Clutch: 10" diameter single dry plate hydraulically operated.
Ratios:
1st 2.32
2nd 1.69
3rd 1.29
4th 1.00
Final drive: 3.08 to 1 mph/1000 rpm top gear 22.0.

PERFORMANCE:
(Maximum speeds in the gears using 6,500 rpm).
1st .... 62 mph
2nd .... 85 mph
3rd .... 112 mph
4th .... 143 mph
Acceleration from rest:
0-50 .... 5.3 secs
0-60 .... 7.2 secs
0-100 .... 17.4 secs.
Top speed: (Average two way runs) 143.7 mph.
Fuel consumption: 23 mpg normal driving, 15 mpg high speed cruising and performance work.

Black, polished so black that if it were not for occasional flashes from the gold stripes and wheels it would be nearly invisible in the night. Looking quietly competent but with the chillingly-sure suggestion of potential for an assertive explosion. So low that, even if you are fairly short, it will easily pass under your outstretched arm. Just enough changes to the stock Capri II body to add purpose without excess; the exterior is a study in taut self-control. You know that, if this machine were a halfback, off the field it would dress with timeless good taste, in its social life it would treat women with respect, in the huddle it would seldom speak and with the ball it would score a lot. But the identification is as sparse as the breaks in the polished black surface. No screaming chrome signatures. Just a few small, quiet markings, two on the hood and one almost hidden under the whale-tail, that say *RSR Turbo.*

A Capri II, altered and massaged to be the best Capri II in our experience. The Capri has long been a favorite with the sporty-car set, with appeal based on looks, quality, price and availability, but with some things that have always needed fixing. Like handling which was only fair and engine response which was only mediocre. But the basic car was there, just waiting for someone with the right resources, motivation, concepts and restraint to give it that careful kneading and take advantage of what has been there all along but has been snagged under a net of minor yet entangling design deficiencies. So the RS in RSR stands for ROKSTOCK, an Oregon aftermarket business specializing in the Capri, and the ROK in ROKSTOCK stands for Rick O. Kizer, who owns the business and the car, and who will also build you a Capri just like his.

His is serious. It catches the eyes of only the knowledgeable. It

Two lessons in turning the sexy Europeans into Cobra killers.

Capri II RSR Turbo &

PHOTOGRAPHY: LARRY GRIFFIN

is a car not to be taken lightly. As such, it is, on the spectrum of emotional appeal, a long way from our other subject, the Chastain S/3 Capri II.

Because the Chastain S/3 is a neon sign of a car. Monstrous fender flares with enough vents and NACA-style ducts for a whole IMSA GT team. Big black pop rivets securing the fiberglass panels to the body. Stripes everywhere; over the hood and down the back and streaming out of one vent only to go straight into another. Letters identifying it to anyone within three city blocks, with a big "S/3" on the fender and an even larger "CAPRI II" captured in that stripe on the door. Wheels so wide they could almost be used for racing, and tires, B.F. Goodrich Radial T/A 50s, that *have* been used for racing.

If the RSR Turbo is for the few who go for the mountain passes, the Chastain S/3 is for the many who go for the boulevards. In Las Vegas the RSR driver would play five-card

stud and the S/3 driver would be found at the slots; both doing the same thing, really, but not the same thing, really.

So they are for different things. The Chastain S/3, the product of Roger Chastain who has set up shop in Long Beach, California, will be available through your friendly Lincoln-Mercury dealer, fully factory-warranteed because, under the star-spangled hood, the drivetrain is just like it was when it got off the boat from Europe. But the body is the loudest visual statement of any mass-produced car we can think of. Short of a full Kalifornia Kustom or a crazy kit car, nothing on the street turns heads like the S/3. Opinions may differ as to whether or not it is pretty—some of the lines in the flares don't seem to follow the basic Capri shape too well, and so the swoopy, stylized look of it sometimes comes across as a disjointed collection of random shapes that were really meant for something else—but *everyone* agrees that it attracts attention. It attracts so much attention that if you are a

Chastain S/3

little self-conscious, and you start fidgeting when people look at you, wondering if there is something wrong about the color match of your pants and shirt or if you didn't get that cowlick combed down, then you ought not to get into it. Because people *will* look at you.

Their stares will betray what is on their minds: *Is it really as fast as it looks?* Well, how fast does it look? If it looks like 200 mph then no, and no if it looks faster than a stock Capri II, unless you're talking about going around corners and then it's yes. With the same drivetrain as the stocker and about 200 extra pounds worth of body parts, tires and wheels and air conditioning the S/3 was slower to 60 by a full second compared to a bare-bones version. When the road began to bend, however, the wider wheels and tires and the suspension changes—which include lowering, different shocks, larger anti-roll bars (built by ROKSTOCK), and rear radius rods—helped the S/3 come closer to living up to its visual reputation. It felt a lot stickier and it was; where the stock Capri II would get around the skidpad at about 0.73g the S/3 is significantly quicker at 0.78g. So the answer to the yes-and-no question of the stares is no and yes. It won't go any faster, except you can drive it faster because it goes around corners faster. It also stops a lot quicker, and for a car that had good stopping distances before, that's an accomplishment. The wide tires and lowered center of gravity pay benefits besides those you may find in the parking lot outside the disco; from 60

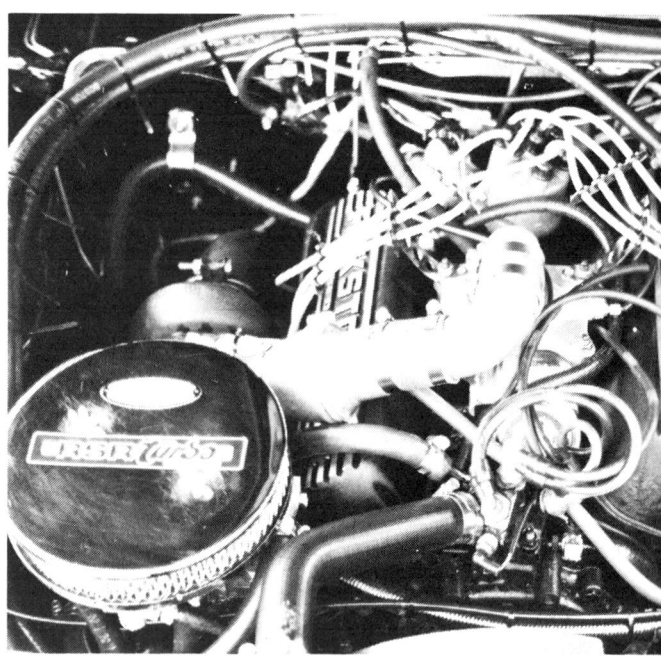

mph the S/3 stopped in 130 feet—the shortest we have ever recorded—and it was straight and true. With repeated hard use that distance would certainly increase, as the brakes are unchanged from stock, but for that one hard time when you need it most the fat tires really come to grips with the asphalt.

Everybody stares at the S/3 and wonders if it's really that fast. Only the ones that notice that sort of thing stare at the RSR, but their stares are just as betraying because written across their faces is the clear message that they *know* it is fast; they are just slightly wary of asking *how* fast. What Rick Kizer did to make it fast was simple. One fine day he opened the hood, then he bolted a turbocharger onto the engine, then he closed the hood. The actual pieces are from Ak Miller, that well-known wizard of the turbo, and the installation is so neat and tidy it could almost be from the factory. There are no other changes necessary, although on this particular car Kizer has replaced the stock timing gears with steel and alloy versions. The boost is limited to about seven pounds, which is mild as turbos go but just about right for street use, and even though the engine has never been on a dyno, Miller calculates it to have around 180 horsepower at 4700 rpm. The turbo is mounted in the right forward section of the engine area and it draws from the carburetor instead of pressurizing it; consequently there is a fairly long path of intake plumbing from the carburetor, through the blower, to the intake manifold of the engine, and so throttle response suffers from a typical turbo lag. With such a long stream of air it takes time for the opening of the throttle plates to cause a noticeable movement of the speedometer needle, but when the needle does move it certainly does it faster than the speedometer engineer originally intended. The technique takes practice; the best acceleration was achieved by using a lot of revs at the start and dropping the clutch, thus maintaining wheelspin *and* boost pressure. With the boost up it would stay there through the shifts, and while not particularly quick off the mark, once into second and third gear the turbo began to make its presence felt with acceleration that had no discernible peak. Third and fourth gears were impressive, because at the point when a normally-aspirated car starts the ultimately futile battle with the wind in a tapering of the acceleration curve, the RSR was really storming. Nothing illustrates the upper-end punch better than comparative numbers. The RSR was only 1.3 seconds quicker to 30 mph than the stock-engined S/3, but it beat the S/3 to 80 by 9.5 seconds, and it was one of the few cars we have tested that was in the 15-second bracket at the quarter-mile. The answer to the speed question is yes.

Which is the same answer to the cornering and braking questions. The suspension changes included in the RSR package are complete. Kizer leaves practically nothing undone. The front springs are heavier wire and cut shorter, the rear springs are single-leaf (manufactured especially for him) and are stiffer than stock and available in one-, two- and three-inch lowering increments. Kizer had springs on this car that lowered it two inches front and rear, but the suspension travel was so limited that the car easily bottomed on rough roads and the ride was, uh, firm. For future cars Kizer is planning on lowering the car just one inch which will be much more satisfactory for general use. If you are really self-destructive Kizer will put the car right on the ground for you, but it's not necessary for optimum handling. In addition to the spring changes the car has Koni shocks—for this test they were on the hard setting with predictable effects on the ride—and big front and rear anti-roll bars which are also manufactured and sold by Kizer. The front bar on the Capri determines the anti-dive, and Kizer installs blocks which lower the bar mounting position and increase the anti-dive, although it's hard to tell whether the minimal nose dive under braking was due to these blocks or just the stiff nature of the chassis. The bar diameters are 1.00 inch front and 0.75 inch rear, which means that this Capri does not lean very much. Finally, to control wheel hop, there are traction bars on the rear springs. In the braking

department the car has Repco pads to reduce fade. For wheels and tires it has enormously gummy (and noisy) Dunlop 225/60 HR 13 SP Supers mounted on 13x6.5 Cromodora wheels, just like the Ferraris use.

When you do all these things to an unsuspecting Capri II you will have a car that gets around the skidpad at 0.81g—it would take you just two fingers to count the others we have tested that are that good—with perfect manners and predictability. It will not turn around and bite you for your small lapses. And you also have a car that will stop from 60 in 135 feet with no unnecessary drama, no muss or fuss, and do it as many times as you care to stab the pedal.

The RSR Turbo is a real performance car. No doubt about it. On performance the S/3 doesn't have the measure of the RSR, but it is still a big slice above the standard Capri II. Cars like this are nice, if you can live with them. If it is your only car, you *have* to live with them.

Living with the S/3 is really no different than living with a regular Capri, except this one looks like the circus came to town and is therefore impossible to hide, impossible to keep from the eternal inquiries of the parking lots. The interior of the S/3 is just like the one your secretary has, except for a little chrome plate around the shift lever that tries to look like a shift gate but is really just a place to lose pennies and gum wrappers. From inside the car the only indication you are in something out of America's transportation mainstream is the black stripe over the hood and the rear window louvers which inhibit vision out the back. If you do not order your S/3 with power steering you will keep your mother-in-law from driving it simply because she can't; the wide wheels and tires also contribute to a drastic increase in steering effort. It is not just bad, it is *very* bad. Get the power steering.

Otherwise it's your basic Capri II. Comfortable seats. Logical

dashboard. Nice level of fit and finish. Funny steering wheel with a rim that's too small. Awkward shift lever with first and third too far away (a complaint we have registered before and which would be a no-cost fix on the assembly line; just let the lever be straight instead of bending it). Awful throttle response with a pedal-to-carburetor ratio that gives a whole lot at first to make you think it's going fast, but requires constant manipulation to hold at an even speed.

The nice thing about the RSR is that most of those things have been fixed. Capri seats were always fairly good, but with the RSR you get a gen-you-wine imitation race seat, with high side bolsters and all. Once seated the driver is on the far side of comfortable, but the problem for some will be getting in, because the low silhouette, smallish doors and bolstered seat imply a lot of crunching and scrunching before you finally get to look straight out the windshield. But *plunk*, you're in there. Gone is the funny steering wheel, replaced with a real Racemark leather-rimmed unit that may be the best you can buy. The different seat also gets you a different reach to the shift lever, so although Kizer hasn't changed anything there, it still feels better. The dash is the same except Kizer manufactures a gold applique with big-as-life letters to help you find the "TACH" and "SPEEDO" and other items of interest. You strap yourself to the machinery with a three-inch-wide competition belt that is really kind of hard to use and peer out at the rest of the world. Your vision takes in the gold striping on the hood and in the mirror you see the rear window louvers which are, in a sort of balance-of-payments arrange-

aimed at different markets and both satisfying those respective markets perfectly. Roger Chastain plans to build a lot of his complete cars and kits for distribution in relatively large numbers through Lincoln-Mercury dealers, and his program has the FoMoCo seal of approval. He knows his fender flares are not really suited for real racing, but he also knows the real racers don't buy cars like his anyway. What he is really building is a Capri II Cobra II, a counterpunch for the L-M dealers to throw back at the Mustang. Plastic surgery on an old familiar face to spruce it up a bit even if the old girl is still the same underneath. Which is not all wrong, because for a lot of buyers in that class there are a lot of good useful miles in the old girl.

Rick Kizer is going for the smaller market, for the hard-core. Cars like the RSR are more hassle; you have to pay attention to them more, and so not as many will buy them. But those that do will get one very fine Capri. ∎

ment, made by Chastain and identical to the ones on the S/3. One last thing, the boost gauge down on the floor in front of the shifter.

It starts easily, unless it's cold, and settles down to a low rumbling idle that is reminiscent of the big V-8s we used to run on the streets at night. For driving around town the effect of the Turbo is scarcely noticeable. It should be that way, with a stock engine, and all you really notice is the improved throttle linkage, which you wouldn't even notice at all if you weren't familiar with Capris. The only trick to make it go is to just drive it. When you hit it hard it goes but not right away, because if you've been trundling around it will take some time to build up the boost. But once you've got some boost, well, then, aha . . .

The only thing we didn't like about the car was the ride, and we understand that if you are the local sports club hot shoe and you drive at ten/tenths all the time, even when taking your kids to school in the morning, and you have forty-seven Konis at each wheel, all set on MAXIMUM HARD and that you think even go-karts are sometimes a little soft, you'll think it's fine, but the ride of the RSR was too hard and harsh.

But we applaud everything else about the RSR. It has a kind of race car feel, that solidity over bumps, that firmness to the mechanism, that conveys the impression that everything is bolted solidly together. It feels like a car you could count on, a tough, honest little car that will be able to handle itself.

Two Capris, both starting from the same point and directed towards enthusiasts, but different kinds of enthusiasts. Both

The Bottom Line

Where do you sign? If you want the visual statement of the S/3 you can get it at: Roger Chastain Associates, 2180 Temple Avenue, Long Beach, California 90804; (213) 439-6841.

If you drive your Capri into their shop or your L-M dealer, $1950 later you will have the S/3, which includes the flares, spoilers, stripes, rear window louvers, wheels and tires. For $1300 they will give you the parts and you can put them on yourself, which isn't really so hard; you paint them to match the car before they go on then just get out the pop riveter and go to it. For another $1500 Chastain will install its suspension parts, giving you the equivalent of our test car.

On the other hand, if the RSR is what lights your fire, send to Rick Kizer at: ROKSTOCK, 9035 SW Burnham, Tigard, Oregon 97223; (503) 620-5126.

Added to your Capri the RSR Turbo package will cost you $2495 for the kit or $3095 installed. If you're handy you could do all of it yourself, but if you're not, it would be wise to part with the extra 600 bucks and have it done right. In Southern California you can have it installed at: Champion Muffler, 14426 E. Whittier Blvd., Whittier, California; (213) 698-8166.

SPECIFICATIONS

ENGINE

Type	OHV V-6
Displacement, cu in	170
Displacement, cc	2792
Bore x stroke, in	3.66 x 2.70
Bore x stroke, mm	93.0 x 68.5
Compression ratio	8.2:1
Hp at rpm, net	180@4700 (est.)
Torque at rpm, lb/ft, net	NA
Carburetion	1 2-V w/turbocharger

DRIVELINE

Transmission	4-spd manual
Gear ratios:	
1st	3.36:1
2nd	1.81:1
3rd	1.26:1
4th	1.00:1
Final drive ratio	3.09:1
Driving wheels	rear

GENERAL

Wheelbase, ins	100.8
Overall length, ins	174.8
Width, ins	66.9
Height, ins	48.5
Front track, ins	53.0
Rear track, ins	54.3
Trunk capacity, cu ft	22.6
Curb weight, lbs	2700
Distribution, % front/rear	54/46
Power-to-weight ratio, lbs/hp	15.0

BODY AND CHASSIS

Body/frame construction	unit
Brakes, front/rear	disc/drum
Swept area, sq in	314.6
Swept area, sq in/1000 lb	116.5
Steering	rack & pinion
Ratio	17.4:1
Turns, lock-to-lock	3.3
Turning circle, ft	32.0
Front suspension: Independent, MacPherson struts, coil springs, tubular shocks, anti-roll bar	
Rear suspension: Live axle, trailing arms, leaf springs, tubular shocks, anti-roll bar	

WHEELS AND TIRES

Wheels	13 x 6.5
Tires,	225/60 HR 13
	Dunlop SP Super
Reserve load, front/rear, lb	521/739

INSTRUMENTATION

Instruments: 0-140 mph speedo, trip odo, 0-7000 rpm tach, oil press, amps, fuel, coolant temp, vacuum/boost

Warning lights: directionals, high beam, door ajar, seat belts, brake failure, hazards, charge

PRICE

Factory list, as tested: $8240.80

Options included in price: Capri II plus: "S" option—$241.00; V-6 engine—$272.00; AM radio—$71.00; Rokstock RSR Turbo package installed—$3095.00; cocoa mats—$28.95; radar detector—$79.95; Repco brake pads—$21.95; steel and aluminum timing gears—$69.95

TEST RESULTS

ACCELERATION, SEC.

0-30 mph	2.7
0-40 mph	4.1
0-50 mph	5.7
0-60 mph	7.3
0-70 mph	9.8
0-80 mph	12.4
Standing start, ¼ mile	15.9
Speed at end ¼ mile, mph	88.6
Avg accel over ¼ mile, g	0.25

SPEEDS IN GEARS, MPH

1st (5500 rpm)	34
2nd (5500 rpm)	65
3rd (5500 rpm)	97
4th (5500 rpm) (calc.)	120
Engine revs at 70 mph	3200

SPEEDOMETER ERROR

indicated speed	True speed
40 mph	39 mph
50 mph	48 mph
60 mph	58 mph
70 mph	68 mph
80 mph	78 mph

INTERIOR NOISE, dBA

Idle	58
Max 1st gear	87
Steady 40 mph	71
50 mph	75
60 mph	76
70 mph	78

FUEL ECONOMY

Overall avg, RT cycle	22 mpg
Range on 15.3 gal tank	336 miles
Fuel required	premium

BRAKES

Min stopping distance from 60 mph, ft	135
Avg deceleration rate, g	0.89

HANDLING

Max speed on 100-ft rad, mph	34.8
Lateral acceleration, g	0.81
Transient response, avg spd, mph	24.8

RATING

Graph Of Recorded Data Expressed in Percentage of 100 (100 = best possible rating)*

0   5   10   15   20   25   30   35   40   45   50   55   60   65   70   75   80   85   90   95   100

- Acceleration
- Brakes
- Handling
- Interior Noise
- Tire Reserve
- Fuel Economy
- Overall Rating
- Highest Rated To Date — Volkswagen Super Scirocco Saab EMS, Porsche Turbo Carrera

*Acceleration (0-60 mph): 0% = 34.0 secs., 100% = 4.0 secs.; Brakes (60-0) mph: 0% = 220.0 ft., 100% = 140.0 ft.; Handling: skidpad lateral accel., 0% = 0.3 g, 100% = 0.9 g, transient response, 0% = 20 mph, 100% = 25 mph (average skid pad and transient response for overall handling percentage); Interior Noise (70 mph): 0% = 90.0 dBA, 100% = 65.0 dBA; Tire Reserve (with passengers): 0% = 0.0 lbs., 100% = 1500 lbs. or more; Fuel Economy: 0% = 5 mpg, 100% = 45 mpg or more. Test Equipment Used: Testron Fifth Wheel and Pulse Totalizer, Lamar Data Recording System, Esterline-Angus Recorder, Sun Tachometer, EDL Pocket-Probe Pyrometer, General Radio Sound Level Meter.

SPECIFICATIONS

ENGINE

Type	OHV V-6
Displacement, cu in	170
Displacement, cc	2792
Bore x stroke, in	3.66 x 2.70
Bore x stroke, mm	93.0 x 68.5
Compression ratio	8.2:1
Hp at rpm, net	109 @ 4800
Torque at rpm, lb/ft, net	146 @ 3000
Carburetion	1 2-V

DRIVELINE

Transmission	4-spd manual
Gear ratios:	
1st	3.36:1
2nd	1.81:1
3rd	1.26:1
4th	1.00:1
Final drive ratio	3.09:1
Driving wheels	rear

GENERAL

Wheelbase, ins	100.8
Overall length, ins	174.8
Width, ins	72.5
Height, ins	51.0
Front track, ins	54.0
Rear track, ins	55.3
Trunk capacity, cu ft	22.6
Curb weight, lbs	2870
Distribution, % front/rear	56/44
Power-to-weight ratio, lbs/hp	26.3

BODY AND CHASSIS

Body/frame construction	unit
Brakes, front/rear	disc/drum
Swept area, sq in	314.6
Swept area, sq in/1000 lb	109.6
Steering	rack & pinion
Ratio	17.4:1
Turns, lock-to-lock	3.3
Turning circle, ft	32.0

Front suspension: Independent, MacPherson struts, coil springs, tubular shocks, anti-roll bar

Rear suspension: Live axle, trailing arms, leaf springs, tubular shocks, anti-roll bar

WHEELS AND TIRES

Wheels	13 x 7.0
Tires,	BR50-13
	B.F. Goodrich Radial T/A 50
Reserve load, front/rear, lb	330/720

INSTRUMENTATION

Instruments: 0-140 mph speedo, trip odo, 0-7000 rpm tach, oil press, amps, fuel, coolant temp

Warning lights: directionals, high beam, door ajar, seat belts, brake failure, hazards, charge

PRICE

Factory list, as tested: $8728.00

Options included in price: Capri II plus: V-6 engine—$272.00; AM/FM stereo—$216.00; air cond—$429.00; Chastain S/3 package installed—$1950.00; handling package installed—$1500.00

TEST RESULTS

ACCELERATION, SEC.

0-30 mph	4.0
0-40 mph	6.2
0-50 mph	8.7
0-60 mph	11.9
0-70 mph	16.2
0-80 mph	21.9
Standing start, ¼ mile	18.4
Speed at end ¼ mile, mph	74.5
Avg accel over ¼ mile, g	0.18

SPEEDS IN GEARS, MPH

1st (5500 rpm)	32
2nd (5500 rpm)	61
3rd (5500 rpm)	91
4th (5500 rpm) (calc.)	113
Engine revs at 70 mph	3400

SPEEDOMETER ERROR

Indicated speed	True speed
40 mph	39 mph
50 mph	48 mph
60 mph	58 mph
70 mph	68 mph
80 mph	77 mph

INTERIOR NOISE, dBA

Idle	52
Max 1st gear	87
Steady 40 mph	71
50 mph	73
60 mph	75
70 mph	78

FUEL ECONOMY

Overall avg, RT cycle	24 mpg
Range on 15.3 gal tank	367 miles
Fuel required	unleaded

BRAKES

Min stopping distance from 60 mph, ft	130
Avg deceleration rate, g	0.92

HANDLING

Max speed on 100-ft rad, mph	34.1
Lateral acceleration, g	0.78
Transient response, avg spd, mph	24.0

RATING

Graph Of Recorded Data Expressed in Percentage of 100 (100 = best possible rating)*

- Acceleration
- Brakes
- Handling
- Interior Noise
- Tire Reserve
- Fuel Economy
- Overall Rating
- Highest Rated To Date — Volkswagen Super Scirocco, Saab EMS, Porsche Turbo Carrera

*Acceleration (0–60 mph): 0% = 34.0 secs., 100% = 4.0 secs.; Brakes (60–0) mph: 0% = 220.0 ft., 100% = 140.0 ft.; Handling: skidpad lateral accel., 0% = 0.3 g, 100% = 0.9 g, transient response, 0% = 20 mph, 100% = 25 mph (average skid pad and transient response for overall handling percentage); Interior Noise (70 mph): 0% = 90.0 dBA, 100% = 65.0 dBA; Tire Reserve (with passengers): 0% = 0.0 lbs., 100% = 1500 lbs. or more; Fuel Economy: 0% = 5 mpg, 100% = 45 mpg or more. Test Equipment Used: Testron Fifth Wheel and Pulse Totalizer, Lamar Data Recording System, Esterline-Angus Recorder, Sun Tachometer, EDL Pocket-Probe Pyrometer, General Radio Sound Level Meter.

ROAD IMPRESSIONS
The Ford Capri III 3000S

Excellent performance and driveability. Fantastic value

THE CAR doing all the winning in the Tricentrol British Saloon Car Championship is the Ford Capri III 3000S. As always, a successful car on the circuit is as chalk and cheese to its road-going sister (though Group 1½ cars would be almost road-legal with silencers fitted), and the owner of a 3000S straight off the German production line, from whence all current Capris emanate, would be shocked were he to take the wheel of a racer. Clever, competitive race engineered improvements not withstanding, a successful racing saloon is usually only as good proportionally as its standard sister. Few saloons prove the point quite so strongly as this latest 3000S.

Right from the early versions with agricultural steering, handling, trim and wide-ratio gearbox, the 3-litre Capri has presented an astonishing ratio of pound sterling against performance. Versatility and improved refinement accrued with the various hatchback Mk. II versions. Now the Capri III – almost certainly the last variation on the theme – gives even better confirmation of Ford's extraordinary flair for budget-price production engineering, at least in the version road tested. At £4,593 I don't think there is any better value than the 3000S.

I "had a ball" with this car. It felt like a Big Healey treated to modern equipment, four proper seats and a steel roof: a bellowing, muscular, long-legged engine, handling which was a total joy, though without the splendid Abingdon cars' need for strong-armed elbow twirling, thanks to high-geared power steering. In character – and it shows plenty of that, to the driver if not to the observer – the 3000S is a fixed-head sports car. It just happens to combine the versatility of a four-seater hatchback. Although 3-litre Capris don't have the charisma of traditional sports cars, they seem to have developed a strong following amongst enthusiasts and racing drivers who appreciate tough, high performance, reliable work horses.

Only two 3-litre versions of this latest series of Capri are available, the 3000S (Sport) and the luxury Ghia. The mechanical recipe of the III is as for the II. The big difference lies in the more aerodynamic body: the bonnet line is lower, its lip drooping down over a grille which has bars angled to act as aerofoils and a spoiler is integrated into the sheet metal-work below the new black, wrap-around front bumper of all models. A rubberised tail spoiler mounted on the boot lid is exclusive to the 1600S, 2000S and 3000S models. Ford claim that the front-end treatment has reduced drag by more than 6% on all models, from 1.3 upwards; the rear spoiler on the S brings the total drag reduction to 12.6%, a very appreciable saving. Sidewinder transfers down the flanks are an unfortunate boy racer part of the S package. All models have four headlamps and ridged, stay-clean rear lights, à la Mercedes.

The whole of the very real character of the 3000S stems from that simple, cast-iron V6 engine. This is the familiar British built, 2,994 c.c. Essex version, not the 2.8-litre German V6 recently adopted by the Granada range. In its current European emission form this 93.77 mm x 72.4 mm, bowl-in-piston, 60 degree V6 delivers 138 b.h.p. DIN r.p.m. and a healthy 174 lb. ft. torque at 3,000 rpm. It is such a basic, solid design that I have always had visions of a Dagenham blacksmith beating it out on an anvil and, indeed, its character is akin to a shire horse: totally untemperamental, uncannily flexible, effortlessly powerful. If the throttle pedal is depressed once to the floor to activate the automatic choke on the Weber twin-choke, downdraught carburetter, the engine starts at the merest flick of the starter motor. The lazy power is instantly and smoothly available without hiccuping protestations at low temperature. The test car's choke was sometimes slow in retiring and needed prompting with another flick on the throttle. The flexibility of the V6 is such that the sporting 3000S will trickle along almost at walking pace in top gear, in which it will accelerate cleanly from 1,000 r.p.m. and 1st and 2nd gears are rarely required in town except for restarting.

Such docility is deceptive: the response to small or large throttle openings is instantaneous and given a vigorous thrust of the right foot there aren't many mass-produced cars capable of staying with the 3000S. Full use of the 6,000 r.p.m. limit gives nearly 70 m.p.h. in 2nd gear, close on 95 m.p.h. in 3rd. Sixty m.p.h. comes in 8¼ seconds. 100 m.p.h. in 28 seconds and a long enough stretch of motorway (sorry, *autobahn*) should wind the needle round to about 125 m.p.h. at 5,700 r.p.m.

The improved aerodynamics really do seem to have made a difference. This Capri III test car felt noticeably quicker than a Capri II 3000S borrowed from Ford not long before the model was discontinued, yet the power was the same and 23.5 cwt. kerb weight practically identical. Even more marked was the improved stability at speed, particularly in cross-winds. The changed bonnet line has removed some of the annoying flapping of that large piece of steel, too.

Superb ergonomics contributed to my very great liking for this 3000S. The fixed steering wheel, the pedals, the switchgear (at long last moved to the steering column on the Capri III),

The optional Recaro seats "added £2,000 to the feel" of the 3000S. The S version has black vinyl facia trim.

the seating position – all contribute to relaxing the driver in a natural position. As the feelings of this 5′ 7″ writer were supported by a 6′ 5″ ex Leyland development engineer, who was loathe to vacate the driving seat, I think it safe to say that this should be a comfortable car for most drivers. I fear that my feelings were coloured by the test car's Recaro seats, however. These are a £76 optional extra, available on the S model only. Never was there a greater bargain: they add £2,000 to the feel of the car. These firm, form-hugging competition seats give a seat of the pants tautness to the handling; the similarly trimmed standard seats are like blancmange in comparison. At first they feel uncompromisingly hard, uncomfortable. It takes a few miles for the body to accustom itself to the lumbar support, the firm cushion which curves down under the knees so that no sharp edges cause discomfort, the prominent side-pieces of the backrest which stop one's body rolling about under cornering. The backrests have micro-adjustment. Net centres to the head restraints (fitted to the standard seats too) help the driver's view for reversing and stop claustrophobic feelings in rear seat passengers. All the seats have tartan cloth inserts, in pleasant pastel shades in the metallic green test car.

Like the gutsy engine, the handling is modern vintage, superior to its roadholding and consequently great fun – and much safer than 3-litre Capri behaviour used to be. The familiar McPherson strut front suspension and leaf sprung, live rear axle – the latter making itself obvious on occasions – are unchanged in this new model. Gas-filled shock-absorbers (from various suppliers, no longer Bilstein solely) on all four corners tauten the handling and stiffen the ride on the 3000S. The Capri II referred to earlier, which was on Bilsteins, had been too stiff for comfort; the Capri III test car was a much better compromise. The ride improves with increasing speed, but limited travel of the live axle shows up abruptly over bad bumps. That marvellous spread of engine torque combined with a responsive chassis means that this Ford can be put into virtually any attitude the driver cares for by playing with the throttle and steering. Without provocation, the normal tendency is towards understeer, as might be expected with that big lump of iron in the nose, but any experienced driver will soon learn to neutralise that and even enjoy himself on opposite lock when nobody is watching. The rear axle is free from tramp, despite its meagre location, but wheelspin can be a problem, particularly in the wet. The test car's 185/70 HR-13 Goodyear tyres showed a great improvement in wet weather road-holding compared with the Pirelli CN 36s I have been used to on 3-litre Capris.

Cam Gears power assistance is a standard fitment to the rack and pinion steering. At first I felt cynical about it. I grew to positively enjoy it. Although light, it is very direct and positive with no lost motion, the 14″ soft-rimmed wheel needs a reasonable 3.3 turns lock to lock and there is plenty of feel for changing surfaces/adhesion. So equipped, the once heavyweight 3-litre Capri can be chucked around, slotted through traffic and parked more effortlessly than an Escort. However, a colleague who was equally enthusiastic about the steering of another Recaro-equipped Capri III 3000S is finding the power steering of his own, subsequently acquired 3000S, to be more vague from the soft cushion of his standard seat. As I have said, the Recaros really are worth having; with them you wear the car, become a part of it, and it responds much more accurately.

The new rear parcel shelf in the hatchback. Much of the Capri's character stems from the lusty 3-litre Essex V6.

The brakes on the test car were light and effective under normal circumstances, but they began to feel suspect under a real hammering. Hard braking gave a slight trace of the usual shimmying around the McPherson struts, a common fault with 3-litre Capris which worsens

with mileage. A gearbox which can be as light and easy to operate as this one was, whilst transmitting vast torque, deserves nothing but praise. But it clonked into reverse if not handled delicately. The clutch was sticky in action and I have always disliked the way the toe of the clutch foot is forced to press against the angled pedal arm of Capris. Although much quieter than earlier models, the 3000S continues to suffer some wind noise, but I shall not complain about that healthy noise from under the bonnet, which starts in a burble, rises to a bellow at 3,000 r.p.m. and gradually softens to a deep drone as the revs rise.

Readers must be as familiar as me with Capri detail specifications. Suffice to remind that the S has the basic black vinyl facia trim, that alloy wheels, a Ford push-button radio and rear screen wiper/wash are standard, that the heating and through-flow ventilation is first class and that rear-seat occupants suffer poor head and knee room. The fuel tank holds 13 gallons; its 4-star content can be swallowed at rates varying between 17 and 25 m.p.g., depending upon enthusiasm, and 20-21 should be considered the norm. Ford claim that the revised aerodynamics have improved consumption, which is probably true for consistent high-speed motorway cruising, but is difficult to assess in general use. A detachable rear parcel shelf is a welcome addition to the Capri III equipment; it attaches simply to the hatch back with looped, nylon cord. The rear seats fold down individually to make this a versatile, high speed express. I regret that the engine capacity is no longer shown on the front wings, but the wide tyres and twin tail pipes – one each side – are instant recognition points for the 3-litre cars.

The test car was fitted with one of those marvellous, tilt and slide, Ford sunshine roofs, which I would not be without, though it costs £146 extra, high-pressure headlamp washers (£56), a remote-control door mirror (£23) and those Recaro seats.

Ford engineering may be cheap and cheerful, but there is no disputing the effectiveness of the assembled recipe. By any standards, the 3000S is a very desirable motor car, with a high standard of performance and driveability. At its price, even with extras fitted, there is no other big-engined performance car to approach it. – C.R.

Black, wrap around bumpers, a very effective rubber tail spoiler, new rear lights and twin tail pipes distinguish the 3000S III from the rear.

Long Term Report

Ford Capri 3000S (12,000 miles)

By Tony Howard

"What a lucky boy you are!"

THERE IS a long-standing joke about motoring writers who — if they cannot really find much to fault in a car — complain about the ashtrays. In this case, however, it is not the ashtrays but the colour — a strident "kiddy-colour" green. It yells that you have arrived as you pull into the kerb. It is highly visible, and thus gives other drivers plenty of warning that you are coming — a good safety feature.

But it is not for me — the colour that is. Nonetheless, this has in no way diminished the sheer pleasure the Ford Capri 3000S has given over the last 12,000 miles. When John Miles heard in March that the car had been allocated to me, he warned: "You're really going to enjoy that. It's just so good, so well sorted, and smooth. And it just goes to show what can be done with pretty basic components. The rear suspension proves my theory it's hard to beat a properly located live axle — and there's not that much point in going to all the trouble of an independent rear end." John was right.

Mini Ferrari

A septuagenarian Argentino-Italian millionaire who rode in the Capri was not at all put off by its extrovert exterior. "What a car!", he exclaimed. "What a wonderful car! It's like something out of a James Bond movie — and it has performance to match. What a lucky boy you are." Another friend — a racer of ERAs — was wont to enquire "How's the 'mini Ferrari' going then?"

Both their responses to the Capri are very much part of my own.

It is a car that makes you feel pretty good every time you drive it and it is the first — for a long time — in which I have felt completely comfortable behind the wheel. Much more expensive cars notwithstanding.

The 3000S is very much a sporting car and, yet, it is extremely practical in so many ways. It is this lack of niggling impracticality that makes it so easy to live with, and enhances one's enjoyment of it.

The state of the mass-market car builder's art is such that, once a good overall design has been achieved, derivatives of widely different character can be drawn off the mainstream. So, by adding all the extras that characterise the 3000S, Ford have been able to create a car that is different from the bottom-of-the-range Capri 1300 as chalk is from cheese.

The current Capri III body introduced about nine months ago is, of course, common to all the cars in the range. Ford's figures suggest that its drag has been lowered 2.5 per cent as a result of a lowered bonnet line, new aerofoil section grille, and a front spoiler that is an integral part of the sheet metal. On the S-cars, a rear spoiler, made of soft black urethane so as not to damage two-wheeler riders in a rear-end collision, has been

Not to everyone's taste, but the external "decor" certainly gives the Capri 3000S a distinctive look. Black varying-density 'S' stripe combines with black bumpers to have dramatic lowering effect on the look of the car

added to reduce drag a further 5 per cent and improve high-speed stability.

In a departure from our normal long term test practice, we did not run this Capri from new, but rather took it over from Ford after Autotesting it in March. At that time it had covered 3,000 miles from new and we have since run it for a further 12,000 miles.

The comprehensive Ford catalogue claims a maximum speed of 124 mph. Despite the aerodynamic improvements, no way did we achieve this when we " figured" the car at the MIRA proving ground for the Autotest published on 4 March, and again last month for this report. The first time, we saw a best of 118 mph, and a mean 117 mph. The

second time, on a gusty day which made discretion feel definitely the better part of valour on the MIRA bankings, the best was 119 mph, while the mean was 116 mph. No doubt, Ford's claim is based on a good long tear along an *autobahn* in limit-free Germany.

In neither case did we equal the catalogue acceleration figures. Their 0-60 mph in 8.0 sec was matched by our 8.6 and 9.8 sec respectively, and their 30-50 mph top gear acceleration in 6.7 sec compared with our respective 7.4 and 8.1 sec. Despite — or because of — a full service at a Ford dealer three days before our second MIRA session with the car, its acceleration reflected a distinct decline. We subsequently discovered that the ignition had been retarded by 14deg. in servicing — and this car will be re-run at MIRA before our next report.

However, overall fuel consumption has shown a very marked improvement from our 19.5 mpg

Autotest figure to 23.9 mpg over the longer period. From April to October, it has covered more than 12,000 miles in our hands, in a hectic schedule, during which it has served well as an effortless "executive express", and has been used for commuting in rush hour from outside London as well as within it. On the open road, both in Britain and on the Continent, this Capri has been driven enthusiastically, and that combines with a considerable rush-hour mileage to provide the least advantageous conditions for good economy. All the more gratifying, then, is this 4.4 mpg improvement with age.

No doubt, this good fuel consumption under the circumstances is a by-product of the 2,994 cc V6 engine's great flexibility. (This also serves to make the car extremely docile and restful when you want it that way.) It allows you to trickle along through rush-hour in second or third gear without having constantly to shift up and down the box or open the throttle very wide when traffic speeds up.

Once the road opens up, you can then make use of the car's splendidly long stride with an unfussy 70 mph second gear and 100 mph third. Through most of the rev range, snap throttle response was impressive and reassuring. But this is not a car with which to make a tyre smoking getaway from rest on a dry road because of its high first gear and well located rear axle.

This Capri is nicely taut without

Above: Well laid out facia is finished in matt black, as is the rest of the interior, save for the loud check seat facings and perforated white headlining. Clear main instruments are rev counter (left) which lacks orange or red line, and speedometer with trip. These are flanked on left by oil pressure gauge and ammeter, and, on right by water temperature and petrol gauges. Instrument lighting is dimmable, but headlight main beam warning is too bright. Radio and controls for excellent heating / ventilation are well placed in centre; below them are sensibly grouped pushbutton for rear window demister element, tailgate window wiper, and washer. Locker in front of passenger is a useful size, and tray on top of gearbox is handy for oddments like wallets or cigarette packets. Ashtray with built-in cigarette lighter is big enough to satisfy long-distance chain smokers. Clock would be better placed on facia. Auxiliary controls are by Ford's good standardised three-stalk system.

Below: This view shows one of the fishnet front headrestraints, designed to reduce claustrophobia in rear passengers and help driver's rearward vision when parking. Rear spoiler helps high-speed stability, reduces drag considerably, and is made of soft material to lessen likelihood of injury to riders of two-wheelers. Sunroof is open in tilt mode which is a great help to ventilation. Rear quarters create slight blind spots which are largely overcome by a mirror on each door

too much roll, and the ride improves as speed rises. It gives the driver a clear "message" so that he is not confused into giving those wrong responses that make him and his passengers feel unhappy in soggier, less well-developed cars. There is a good balance which allows the car to be cornered in a stable and neutral condition that is free of disconcerting quirks.

In the wet, over-enthusiasm with the throttle is met with wheel spin and snaking, in a straight line, while the tail comes out smartly in a corner. All of this can be countered immediately, so one never feels the

situation is getting out of hand.

Apart from successful attention to suspension and tyres, two other features must play a significant role in the sense of command engendered by the test car. The 3000 S rack-and-pinion steering has power assistance as standard. And, even at risk of disagreement with more learned colleagues, I would go so far as to say it is among the best around. In addition to good steering response, there is always plenty of feel.

The front seats of the test car come in for high praise too. They are Recaro sports seats offered as an option on the S models for £78.80 —

money well spent for they complete the car's character.

Not everyone will agree with me, but I was impressed by the seats' firm support for back and thighs as well as by the excellent lateral location. They were definitely less fatiguing than more conventional seats, and made one feel very "close" to the car. They afforded a very comfortable posture from which to manipulate the controls, and I shall have a job to find another car with a driving position that suits me so well.

In the "cockpit" all is as it should be — neat, practical, unconfusing, and done out in matt black, relieved

rather garishly by check fabric seat facings. The soft-feel three-spoke steering is placed just right. So is the gear lever which has a light, precise action not too far removed from the proverbial butter cutting. Pedals, too, are well placed for the heel-and-toe driver. However, the clutch has rather a sharp take-up fairly high up the pedal travel and this takes the first-time driver a little by surprise.

Ford's excellent three-stalk auxiliary control system is employed, and there is clear and comprehensive instrumentation with dimmable green illumination to minimise distraction while driving at night. By contrast, I found the blue main-beam warning light too bright, and thought the rev counter could have done with orange and red lines.

Quickly-understood controls for the highly-effective heating / ventilation system are placed at eye level — as is the radio — in the centre of the facia. (Other manufacturers please note — on all counts.) Two face-level eyeball vents provide bags of cool fresh air, while the feet can be toasted — rare or well done — as desired. And the two-speed blower, scarcely needed for other purposes, quickly clears the screen of mist or frost.

All this is greatly helped by the optional steel sunroof (£152.28) which has proved good value. And I have used it every day — winter or summer, rain or shine. In the tilt mode, it provides a very effective fresh air exhaust that lets no water in during the heaviest rain, provided you keep moving. Fully opened, it is surprisingly draught-free, even at

AUTOCAR, w/e 21 October 1978

maximum speed, and helps one maintain a vestige of a tan.

The pushbutton medium/long wave radio, fitted as standard to the test car, had a speaker mounted in the top of the facia and aimed at the screen. As there was quite a lot of wind noise, whether the sunroof was open in either of its modes or closed, the radio had to be turned right up. But the speaker was not of good enough quality to cope happily with this. And it struck me it would be well worth paying extra for a set-up with a pair of high-quality door mounted speakers.

Another extra I now wish had been fitted in the first place is an electric aerial. The Capri has briefly joined the growing ranks of cars with a dry cleaner's metal coat hanger stuffed in the socket where once stood a proper aerial. Yet another victim of that particularly incomprehensible branch of vandalism that finds aerial snapping an amusing or satisfying or whatever way to waste time.

Ford catalogue options that are fitted to the test car include headlamp pressure jet wash system (£58.31), a remote-control driver's door mirror (£23.59), while a wash/wipe system is fitted as standard to keep the rear tailgate window clear. It has its own reservoir, placed rather awkwardly under the boot floor (difficult to replenish with a load aboard), but it works well and is handy in slow traffic while it is raining. The headlight wash system is better than nothing (the addition of wipers would be even better), but it is only effective when it is raining already. Bugs splattered on the lights in summer still have to be removed with elbow grease and a wet chamois.

The screen wipers (two speeds and intermittent) make a good sweep, but lift off the screen at speed. Rather oddly, the washers will not function until the wipers are switched on. Sensibly, the headlight washers do not spray until the headlights are on, and there is a vast screen wash reservoir under the bonnet.

Lock-out

Call me a silly b . . . . . , if you like, but I have absent-mindedly locked the ignition key inside this Capri three times during my period of "ownership." The one key serves the two doors and the tailgate (not self-locking) as well. While it is undoubtedly super-convenient to be able to step out of the car, pressing down the lock as you go, and shut the door — locked — behind you, it is far from idiot-proof. I'm all for that quick-lock idea on the passenger door/s but — after experiencing that sinking feeling so many times now — I'm convinced that the driver should only be able to lock his door with the key.

The tailgate opens easily on its gas struts; the package tray lifts with it to give easy access for suitcases. If you need more room — and are not too concerned about concealing your treasures — step one is to remove said tray. That's easy. So is step two — folding forward one of the rear seats to create a three-seater with extra luggage floor. Step four, of course, is folding forward the other

High-back Recaro seats are extras well worth having. They are firm, provide excellent support, and "make" the car. Steering wheel, gear lever and handbrake are well positioned.

Separate rear seats also provide good support, but legroom behind tall driver is a bit limited. Access is reasonable for the young and nimble.

Versatile rear load area can accommodate a lot of gear. It is seen here with the "package tray" removed to allow more height, and the left-hand seat folded forward.

rear seat to create enough space to keep your lady happy when she goes mad with the weekend luggage or shopping.

Put the seats up again and there is accommodation which seemed to suit the nimble and not too tall well enough. Personally, I would not fancy sitting in the reasonably comfortable rear seats for all that long, but nobody complained — thought it was rather cosy, in fact. Leg room was adequate on the left but fairly restricted behind the driver's seat for I like it well reclined. The high backs of the front seats rather restrict the view for the rear passengers, but fishnet front head restraints are an attempt to ease the problem. Rear windows that open would be a welcome — if expensive — inducement.

At one stage, oil consumption appeared alarmingly high — about 1 litre every 400 miles. And although

AUTOCAR, w/e 21 October 1978

sked to check for leaks at every ervice, garages have reported that here was no apparent problem. However, consumption dropped off onsiderably and, overall, it has veraged 1 litre every 1,100 miles. part from normal engine service arts, the only things needing eplacement so far have been a set of ront brake pads, at the 12,000 mile ervice, a headlight smashed by a tone, and that radio aerial. Not bad or so many miles of hard motoring, nd a reliability that is an important part of the car's appeal.

It might not have an exotic or very up-market label on it. It might be rather garishly dressed-up. But you have to admire the Capri 3000S for its many qualities. Not least, it is a cleverly put-together package that must rate as excellent value for £4,619 plus an additional £313 for those options. Look around. You'll be hard pressed to find a car that provides a combination of so much performance, convenience, reliability and fun for anything like the money.

Optional headlight washers operate simultaneously with screen wash, but only when headlights are switched on. The system is better than nothing, but more expensive wipers would do a better job removing squashed insects in summer.

Under-bonnet accessibility is on the whole good. Battery and huge screen wash reservoir are easy to replenish as are brake master cylinder and power steering reservoir. But it was difficult to pour oil into filler on left-hand rocker box cover without spillage.

WHAT THE CAPRI HAS COST

Total: 12,000 miles £1,098.62. **Cost per mile:** 9.16p.

Consumable items:	Life in miles	Unit cost £	Cost per 12,000 miles £
Fuel: 4-star (gallon)	23.9	0.83	415.51
Oil: topping up between changes (litre)	1102.8	0.96	10.45
Brakes:			
Front pads (unit cost = set of 4)	12,000	12.89	12.89
Rear linings (unit cost = set of 4 on exchange)	24.000	14.34	7.17
Tyres: Goodyear 185/70HR13		35.42	
Front pair	24,000		35.42
Rear pair	20,000		28.33
(unit cost = single tyre)			

Service and repairs:		
Recommended charges for service at £6.50 per hour (labour only)	6,000 miles	£36.35
	12,000 miles	£40.45
Service costs incurred with our car in the past 12,000 miles (inc. oil and materials)		£76.80
Repair costs incurred		£32.63
Total maintenance costs incurred		£109.44

STANDING CHARGES per year	
Insurance (see note)	£108.30
Tax	£50.00
Depreciation:	
Cost of our car when new £4,834	
Its estimated value today £4,500	
Decline in value over 7 months	£334.00

Note: *To put all our cars on equal footing for insurance cost, the figure given above is a typical quotation for a "good risk" driver — with clean record, and car garaged in Oxfordshire, a "middle range" risk area. Full n.c.b. discount has been deducted, as has the saving for £25 excess. The actual figure given is the middle one of five quotations ranging from £95 to £134. Source: Quotel Motor Insurance Service.*

MAXIMUM SPEEDS

	LT		RT	
Gear	Mph	Rpm	Mph	Rpm
Top (mean)	**116**	**5,300**	117	5,350
(best)	**119**	**5,450**	118	5,400
3rd	**93**	**6,000**	93	6,000
2nd	**68**	**6,000**	68	6,000
1st	**41**	**6,000**	41	6,000

IN EACH GEAR

mph	Top LT	RT	3rd LT	RT	2nd LT	RT
10-30	—	—	6.1	5.5	4.6	3.8
20-40	8.7	8.0	5.9	5.3	4.0	3.6
30-50	8.4	7.8	5.4	5.1	3.9	3.8
40-60	8.1	7.4	5.8	5.0	4.6	4.5
50-70	8.9	7.8	6.4	5.6	5.8	5.6
60-80	9.8	8.7	7.7	6.8	—	—
70-90	11.5	10.2	10.0	9.4	—	—
80-100	14.4	12.7	—		—	—

ACCELERATION

FROM REST

True mph	Speedo mph	Time (sec) LT	RT
30	31	**3.2**	2.9
40	41	**4.8**	4.4
50	52	**7.25**	6.4
60	62	**9.8**	8.6
70	74	**13.2**	11.5
80	85	**18.2**	15.5
90	95	**23.8**	20.0
100	106	**32.6**	28.1

Standing ¼-mile:
LT **17.8** sec 79 mph
RT **16.6** sec 83 mph

Standing km:
LT **33.7** sec 101 mph
RT **30.6** sec 103 mph

CONSUMPTION

Overall mpg:
LT **23.9** mpg (11.9 litres/100km)
RT 19.5 mpg (14.6 litres/100km)

Note "RT" denotes performance figures for Road Test of Ford Capri 3000S tested in Autocar of 4 March, 1978.

SPECIFICATION

ENGINE
	Front, rear drive
Cylinders	6 in 60 deg V
Main bearings	4
Cooling	Water
Fan	Viscous
Bore, mm	93.7 mm (3.69)
Stroke, mm	72.4 mm (2.85)
Capacity, cc	2,994 c.c (182.7)
Valve gear	ohv
Compression ratio	9.0-to-1
Carburettor	Weber twin-choke downdraught
Max power	138 bhp (DIN) at 5,000 rpm
Max torque	174 lb ft at 3,000 rpm

TRANSMISSION
Gear	Ratio	mph/1,000rpm
Top	1.00	21.84
3rd	1.41	15.49
2nd	1.94	11.26
1st	3.16	6.91
Final drive gear	Hypoid bevel	
Ratio	3.09	

SUSPENSION
Front—location	MacPherson struts lower links
springs	Coil
dampers	Telescopic
anti-roll bar	Yes
Rear—location	Live axle
springs	Half elliptic leaf
dampers	Telescopic (gas filled)
anti-roll bar	Yes

STEERING
Type	Rack and pinion
Power assistance	Yes
Wheel diameter	14.0 in

BRAKES
Circuits	Dual split front/rear
Front	9.75 in. dia. disc
Rear	9.00 in. dia. drum
Servo	Vacuum type

MANUFACTURER:
Ford Motor Company Ltd,
Eagle Way,
Warley,
Brentwood, Essex.

PHOTOS BY WM. A. MOTTA

CAPRI II RSR TURBO

It may be Rokstock, but it ain't no stone

BY JOHN DINKEL

BACK IN JANUARY 1976 R&T published an article called "Black Gold" which described a one-of-a-kind, very fast Ford Capri II built by Ford in Cologne, Germany. Although the unique black-with-gold-pinstriping paint scheme, front and rear spoilers and gold-colored alloy wheels turned heads wherever the car was driven in Germany, Black Gold was much more than a visual attention getter. Under the hood and attached to the chassis were the sort of pieces that start an enthusiast's pulse racing: mechanical fuel injection, 10.5:1 compression, 170 bhp, a hunkered-down stiffer suspension, Bilstein shocks, body-hugging Scheel seats, special instrumentation and various convenience and comfort options such as Ford's 2-way sunroof.

When that story appeared, Capri owners from around the country wrote to find out where those specialized components could be purchased. All of them were very disappointed because at that time we knew of no U.S. distributors. But we know of one now, a company called Rokstock (located at 9035 S.W. Burnham, Tigard, Ore. 97223; 503 620-5126). Rokstock has been designing, developing and engineering specialty equipment for the original Capri and the Capri II for more than six years, and already has specialty components developed for the 1979 U.S.-built Capri/Mustang.

As you might expect, the $3.00 Rokstock catalog contains the usual assortment of hard-core enthusiast and dress-up items, ranging from special exhaust systems, clutches, intake manifolds, flywheels and carburetors to driving lights, padded steering wheels, shift knobs and even sheepskin seat covers and drinking mugs. But we were particularly intrigued with a section dealing with a limited-edition RSR Turbo Capri Rokstock builds, and it was this model that I drove and tested during a trip to Oregon.

There are two ways to purchase an RSR Turbo: The customer

can furnish Rokstock with any German-built Capri (Capri II with V-6 only) which Rokstock will convert to RSR specs for around $7000. If the customer doesn't own a Capri, Rokstock will buy a 1976–1977 Capri II and convert it into an RSR Turbo for $12,000.

If that seems high, consider what goes into an RSR Turbo. First, the engine is disassembled and all components are cleaned and inspected. Clearances are checked and then the engine goes back together with an AiResearch turbocharger, reworked carburetor and distributor, special head gaskets, exhaust manifolds and timing gears and all the trimmings, including steel-braided hoses and high-performance sparkplugs and wiring.

From the engine compartment you have to work yourself under the RSR Turbo where you'll encounter 40-percent stiffer front coil and rear mono leaf springs that lower the car about 2.0 in., larger-diameter front and rear anti-roll bars and Bilstein shock absorbers. But that's just the beginning because to fine tune the chassis Rokstock includes rear radius rods to reduce axle hop during hard acceleration and braking, a steering kit containing aluminum mounting brackets to eliminate the rubber mounts on the steering rack and 50-percent higher-rate polymere bushings for the front lower arm and rear leaf spring. In addition, at each corner you'll find Repco brake pads or shoes for improved braking and a Cromodora 13 x 6½JK magnesium wheel shod with a Dunlop 205/60HR-13 radial (the car I tested had optional 225/55HR-13 Dunlops).

Rokstock doesn't stop here. To give the RSR its distinctive appearance, Chastain-designed window louvers plus a front air dam and a whaletail rear spoiler are added. Cibié driving lights replace the stock headlights and the finishing touch is a new paint job.

Not content with the stock interior, Rokstock redoes the Capri

decor. Inside you'll find deeply contoured driving seats, a leather wrapped steering wheel and a turbo boost gauge. In essence, when you purchase an RSR Turbo, you're getting a car that's been totally revamped from wheel to roof and from bumper to bumper.

At the beginning of my 4-day stay in Portland, Richard O. Kiser, Rokstock's chief designer/builder, handed me the keys to his personal black RSR Turbo Capri II and said: "Let the engine warm up before you give it boost, use 5000 as a redline and have fun." And that I did, driving the car on some of the numerous twisty roads around the Portland area and also at Portland International Raceway where I conducted acceleration and slalom testing and spent some time lapping the demanding PIR road circuit. According to Kiser, the turbo V-6 develops 180–200

CONTINUED ON PAGE 86

MOTOR week ending November 17, 1979

Great X-packtations

Add a Ford Rallye Sport Series X kit to your Fiesta, Escort, Cortina or Capri and you can make it look, stop, corner and even go faster. We've been testing a 3-litre Capri with a full-house X-pack conversion that gives it near-supercar class acceleration, but at a Porsche price.

IN THE 1960s, Ford established themselves as experts at producing custom-pack "specials". Based on their standard saloons, these models have offered extra performance, better handling and a smarter appearance at a relatively modest cost, and, in most cases, without affecting the standard warranty.

Despite the closure of the production line at Ford's Advanced Vehicle Operations centre nearly five years ago, the flow of RS and other performance models has continued to attract customers, and to maintain Ford's sporting image. The latest set of "specials", the Series X range, was announced more than two years ago, but this is the first opportunity we have had of testing an example.

The Series X cars differ from previous low-volume Fords in offering the customer greater flexibility of choice: a Series X car can be either a "cosmetic" conversion of the standard model, or a performance conversion, or both, and the range of options is almost endless. Series X "packs" are available to owners of Capris, Escorts, Cortinas and Fiestas, and are fitted by Ford's chain of 80 RS dealers; there is no specific limit on the age or mileage of the car to be modified, and there is no effect on the standard Ford warranty.

Perhaps the most exciting of the Series X conversions is based on the Capri, and it was virtually a "full house" treatment of the 3.0 S which Ford loaned us for appraisal, with substantial modifications to the engine, suspension, transmission, brakes and bodywork.

First the engine: though it has the standard capacity (2,993 cc), it is fitted with "Big Valve" heads, special head gaskets (though the 9.0:1 compression ratio is standard), a set of triple Weber 42 DCNF carburetters with a special inlet manifold, a high-capacity electric fuel pump, a high-capacity radiator, and free-flow silencers. The standard camshaft is retained. These parts alone account for approximately £1,000, even before labour costs are taken into consideration.

Though the gearbox and clutch remain standard, a Salisbury limited-slip differential is fitted to the live rear axle (£263.63). Ford's aim with the suspension was to combine more sporting handling with a tolerable ride, and to this end the rear suspension is unchanged, apart from the use of Bilstein gas-filled dampers (£53.61), but the front end has Bilstein struts (£164.43) and

uprated springs (£36.11). There is also an anti-dive kit (£83.90).

Our test car was fitted with low-profile Pirelli P6 tyres (205/60 × 13), which cost approximately £55 each, on 7½in RS alloy rims (£297.86 for a set of five, including nuts and RS caps), which necessitate fitting glass fibre flared wheel arches (£200.76). It is possible, incidentally, to fit 7in rims to a Capri without any need for wheel arch modifications.

This Series X Capri was fitted with a Granada-type ventilated front disc kit (£218.36), with the standard rear drums unchanged.

Ford estimate that the total cost of our test car, including all labour charges, would be in the region of £9,625. As a complete package on a new car, this pitches it into a totally different market sector from that in which the standard 3.0S Capri (£5,574) has to compete: potential buyers will have to dismiss such attractive (if less uncompromisingly sporting) alternatives as the BMW 528i (£10,115), Rover 3500 (£9,052), Peugeot 604 TI (£9,258), Porsche 924 Lux (£9,582), Saab Turbo 900 three-door (£9,910) and Vauxhall Royale Coupé (£10,069). However, costs could be considerably reduced by basing the conversion on a good used Capri S, and by opting for 7in rims.

On our first evening with the car, something blew in the engine department, causing clouds of smoke to gush out of the exhaust pipe and from under the bonnet; Ford returned the car to us, saying that the car had mistakenly been fitted with standard head gaskets, and that one of them had blown. At a later date, the Facet fuel pump failed. However, we are prepared to put these events down to misfortune, for the car seemed otherwise untemperamental for such a high-powered beast.

With 175 bhp at 5,000 rpm and 194 lb ft of torque delivered at 4,000 rpm (standard figures are 138/5,000 and 174/3,000), and despite an increase in weight of over 1 cwt, this Capri certainly moves along. We were unable to measure the top speed precisely, but it is easy to pull 6,000 rpm in fourth (equivalent to 128 mph) and perhaps a little more. The standing start acceleration is inter-

MOTOR week ending November 17, 1979

esting when compared with the (much lighter) RS3100, another special conversion (to a Capri Mk 1) of about five years ago, which had a larger capacity (as the name suggests) as well as modifications to the camshaft, heads, and inlet and exhaust manifolds: up to 100 mph there is no difference between the cars at all, both machines accelerating from 0 to 100 mph in 21.2 sec, and it is only thereafter that the Series X has a significant advantage.

This acceleration, with 0-60 mph in 7.4 sec,(the equivalent figure for the standard Capri is 8.9 sec, and it manages 0-100 mph in 27.3 sec) is not far off the "supercar" league. Top gear pull is also impressive, with 30-50 mph in 7.2 sec and 50-70 mph in 7.6 sec (7.7 sec and 8.2 sec respectively for the standard car). But this flexibility is, however, no match for the much lighter RS3100: it returned 6.7 and 6.7 sec respectively.

This leads us to question the value of fitting triple carburetters without a slightly more potent camshaft. Despite the improved breathing, the engine runs out of steam at about 6,000 rpm, just when the carburetters should be coming into their own. The engine is also rather rough at idle and at low engine speeds, and we suspect that an RS3100 style of conversion provides a more pleasant engine for the road at a lower cost. Fuel consumption is poor — we managed only 17 mpg, compared with 22.1 mpg for the standard car.

The standard clutch is well up to coping with the 27 per cent increase in power, and the Capri gearchange is among the best in any modern car, though the movements of the lever are longer than average.

If we are less than entirely enthusiastic about the engine conversion, we have few reservations about the modifications to the suspension: in this respect the Series X is a great advance on the RS3100, as it combines superbly taut handling (which the RS 3100 had) with a tolerable ride (which the RS3100 lacked). The P6 tyres provided outstanding grip in the wet as well as in the dry, and they also add weight to the power-assisted steering, though it still hasn't as much feel as we like. The firmer damping and stiffer front springs give excellent balance and surefootedness. In tight bends there is fairly strong understeer under power, but on fast country roads the Series X is virtually neutral, with final but easily controllable oversteer. There is some tendency to hop about over bumps. but this is not excessive.

We are uncertain of the value of the limited-slip differential; besides making unpleasant noises when the car is cornering at low speeds, its response is slow. We doubt that wheelspin would be excessive without it, such is the grip of the tyres.

It was with some surprise that we discovered our Series X test car to be fitted with the ventilated disc brake kit, as the brakes seem no better than those of a standard Capri: the pedal has too much travel, and has a spongey feel to it, and the brakes tend to pull the car up unevenly. However, the anti-dive kit is clearly worth fitting, as it adds to the good balance provided by the

well-tuned suspension, and makes the transition from throttle to brakes and back to throttle again very smooth indeed.

As 6,000 rpm are approached, the engine becomes very loud; indeed our noise recording equipment broke fresh ground at 93 dB in 2nd gear. However, this is mostly induction and exhaust noise, and if a measure of restraint is observed, the engine, if never quiet (at low speeds, the carburetters can be heard "spitting back"), does not become intolerably noisy. Wind noise is fair, but above average for a £9,500 car. Road noise, even with the fat Pirellis, is remarkably low. The groaning of the limited-slip diff becomes irritating around town.

In other respects, our Series X was just like any other Capri S. It is a successful two-plus-two with comfortable seats, a good driving position, a useful amount of luggage space, clear instrumentation, and good heating and ventilation. But is it worth £9,625?

Like the curate's egg, the Series X Capri is good in parts: the conversion we would approve of more wholeheartedly would have the RS3100 engine, and Series X suspension modifications, and 7in rims (on which the 205/60 Pirellis fit). This would obviate the need for the well-styled but ostentatious flared arches, which are liable to attract unwanted attention. With improved brakes, this would in our opinion be a superb sports coupé, and at a relatively low cost.

Barely visible under the massive air-cleaner are no fewer than three twin-choke carburetters, fed by a high-pressure electric pump that's located in the rear nearside corner of the engine bay

PERFORMANCE

Stand'g ¼	15.6	Stand'g km	28.8	

CONDITIONS

Weather	Sunny; wind 0-12 mph
Temperature	47°F
Barometer	29.5 in Hg
Surface	Dry tarmacadam

ACCELERATION IN TOP

mph	sec	kph	sec
20-40	7.1	40-60	4.4
30-50	7.2	60-80	4.5
40-60	7.4	80-100	4.6
50-70	7.6	100-120	4.8
60-80	8.0	120-140	5.7
70-90	8.7	140-160	6.3
80-100	9.8		
90-110	13.5		

MAXIMUM SPEEDS

	mph	kph
	See text	
Terminal Speeds:		
at ¼ mile	89	143
at kilometre	111	179
Speed in gears (at 6000 rpm):		
1st	40	64
2nd	66	106
3rd	91	146

FUEL CONSUMPTION

Overall	17.0 mpg
	16.6 litres/100 km
Fuel grade	97 octane
	4 star rating
Tank capacity	12.8 galls
	58.0 litres
Max range*	256 miles
	412 km
Test distance	612 miles
	985 km

ACCELERATION FROM REST

mph	sec	kph	sec
0-30	2.7	0-40	2.1
0-40	4.1	0-60	3.7
0-50	5.6	0-80	5.5
0-60	7.4	0-100	7.9
0-70	9.6	0-120	10.9
0-80	12.4	0-140	14.9
0-90	15.9	0-160	21.0
0-100	21.2		
0-110	27.4		

*Consumption midway between 30 mph and maximum less 5 per cent for acceleration.
**Based on a touring consumption of 20 mpg.

NOISE

	dBA	Motor rating*
30 mph	64	10
50 mph	74	21
70 mph	76	24
Max revs in 2nd		
(1st for 3-speed auto)	93	79

*A rating where 1 = 30 dBA and 100 = 96 dBA, and where double the number means double the loudness.

SPEEDOMETER (mph)

Speedo							
30	40	50	60	70	80	90	
True mph							
28	38	47	57	66	75	84	

Distance recorder: 4.7 per cent fast

WEIGHT

	cwt	kg
Unladen weight*	24.0	1219
Weight as tested	27.7	1407

*with fuel for approx 50 miles

Performance tests carried out by Motor's staff at the Motor Industry Research Association proving ground, Lindley.

Test Data: World Copyright reserved; no unauthorised reproduction in whole or part.

GENERAL SPECIFICATION

ENGINE

Cylinders	60° V6
Capacity	2993 cc (182.5 cu in)
Bore/stroke	93.7/72.4 mm
	(3.69/2.85 in)
Valves	Pushrod ohv
Compression	10.0:1
Carburetter	Triple Weber 42 DCNF
Max power	175 bhp (DIN) at 5000 rpm
Max torque	194 lb ft (DIN) at 4000 rpm

TRANSMISSION

Type	4-speed manual; limited slip differential

Internal ratios and mph/1000 rpm	
Top	1.00:1/21.3

3rd	1.41:1/15.1
2nd	1.94:1/11.0
1st	3.16:1/6.7
Rev	3.35:1
Final drive	3.09:1

BODY/CHASSIS

Construction	Unitary steel, with glass fibre wings

SUSPENSION

Front	Independent by Bilstein Macpherson struts, uprated coil springs, anti-roll bar.

| Rear | Live axle located and sprung by semi-elliptic leaf springs; telescopic Bilstein dampers; anti-roll bar. |

STEERING

Type	Rack and pinion
Assistance	Yes

BRAKES

Front	Ventilated disc
Rear	Drum
Servo	Yes
Circuit	Dual, split

WHEELS/TYRES

Type	RS Alloy, 7½J
Tyres	Pirelli P6, 205/60 VR 13

COMPARISONS

	Capacity cc	Price £	Max mph	0-60 sec.	30-50 sec.	Overall mpg	Touring mpg	Length in.	Width in.	Weight cwt.	Boot cu. ft.
Ford Capri Series X	2993	9625	128**	7.4	7.2	17.0	—	172	73	24.0	8.5
BMW 528i	2788	10115	129**	8.3	9.1	17.9	—	182	67	27.8	13.0
Ford Capri 3.0 S	2993	5574	118.4	8.9	7.7	22.1	24.1	172	69	22.7	8.5
Porsche 924 Lux	1984	9582	121.3	9.3	7.3	25.2	—	166	67	20.2	4.8
Saab 900 Turbo 3-dr, 4-sp	1985	9910	119.0	9.3	10.1	21.6	—	187	66	24.2	11.9

*Approximate cost of new Capri 3.0 S with full conversion (see text)   **Estimated

EVER SINCE the Model A, Ford have been expected to offer value for money. The expectation almost exclusively evolved into covered family cars of various sorts, but latterly a good money's worth from Ford has included some distinctly sporting cars. The best example in value is the current 3-litre Capri. From slightly dubious beginnings — the early examples disappointed with their heavy understeer — the one Capri which has the power and performance its size and shape suggests has evolved into a singularly pleasing car, at any rate in 3000S form. What else can you buy for £5,574 which has a 117 mph maximum, an 8.6sec 0-60, comfortably easy flexibility, good steering, fair handling and a just tolerable ride in a body that is usefully versatile given the limitations of a close-coupled four-seat coupé?

Rightly, partly for their own competition homologation purposes and partly to encourage the customer who is keen to make his Capri different from the others, Ford offer a good list of parts and modifications. Briefly, you could make your Capri into a faster car that looked no different from original, or you can go the whole hog and add sundry body modifications — Q-car or poseur's car. The example of an X-pack 3000S offered to us for test is a not too showy combination of both.

Under the bonnet, it has three instead of one carburettor — Weber downdraught twin-choke 42 DCNF on a short inlet manifold (rather than horizontal Webers on a cross-over manifold with longer tracts). The head gasket is a special one and there is a Facit high capacity electric fuel pump. The silencers are "free-flow" ones, but apart from cosmetically altered tail pipes (their ends are flattened slightly), the exhaust is otherwise standard. Ford say that the uprated radiator fitted is necessary with the engine changes.

Suspension changes include Bilstein gas-filled front struts, similar rear dampers, uprated front springs and anti-dive modifications. Brakes remain standard at the back, but in front the discs are ventilated and the calipers larger, Granada-sized ones. Wheels are 7½in.-rimmed RS alloy with 205/60 Pirelli P6 tyres. In the back axle there is a clutch-type limited slip differential.

Most obvious change is to the body, which has the extended glass-fibre Series X wings (which incidentally allow the fitting of 225 section tyres if desired) and a deeper front spoiler. Clutch, gearbox and axle are otherwise standard. Thus modified — the changes are not do-it-yourself ones, but must be done by any of the 75 Ford Rallysport dealers — the cost increases by around £4,000.

Performance

The result is an exciting-looking, exciting-performing Capri. It sounds exciting too, even if on first driving the car round a town corner would certainly suggest to anyone unused to limited slips that someone had put broken glass in the back axle — the musical crunches and tings from behind as the Powr Lok sticks and gives are surprisingly loud. The engine rumbles away quite heartily, promising great things on the open road if something less than great refinement.

Tractability isn't quite as good as the standard car's, because inevitably with the lower gas speeds brought in with the train of those extra carburettors, there is a loss at the very bottom end. Try to pull in top gear from

below 15 mph and the engin fluffs and coughs; even at ar after the 20 mph start used f our top gear acceleration runs, was necessary to ease the rig foot down gently to avoid tim wasting misfiring. This shows the figures — 8.3sec 20 to 4 mph in top compared with th original Road Test car's 8.0sec

All is well by the time 30 or s comes up, the X-pack beginnin to get going. It is at the top er that it really shows its true co ours, from 70 mph onward constantly lengthening its lea over the standard car — 0.1se quicker from 60-80, 0.7se from 70-90, 2.0sec from 80 100 and a handsome 5.6sec from 90-100. Its straight roa maximum speed is a resoundin 125 mph which is 8mph quicke than normal. It would be highe still given higher gearing, sinc the engine is clearly past it 5,000 rpm peak at this speed.

Standing starts are highly en tertaining. Our best times wer done dropping the clutch a 4,700 rpm to leave two strips c black on the MIRA twin horizontal tarmac — just th right length, backing off th throttle slightly for the tyres t grip fully at around 4,000 rpm and changing gear at 6,000 (4C 67 and 90 mph). So driven, i just tolerable conditions (10-2 mph wind, 29.1in. baromete 80 per cent humidity and 50de F), the X-pack gets to 60 mp saving 0.9sec on the standar car's time, 1.9sec for 80, 5se for 100 and 7.7sec for 110.

A tale of two Capris

Ford's X-pack three-carburettor Capri 3-litre — and a single carburettor 3.2-litre alternative

By Michael Scarlett

X-pack Capri nearest camera — and the WM Developments 3.2 Capri beyond. You can of course have an X-pack without the giveaway body changes

Economy naturally suffers. e best we saw was 21½ mpg, t it was alarmingly easy to get wn to around 14½ mpg if one ed the performance a lot. This reflected in our 17.7 mpg erall figure; as the steady- eed consumption graph ows, the car is a thirsty animal, en at low speeds, where dging from the flattened be- nning of the curve it is not nning efficiently.

The extra performance is cked by excellent road man- rs. The grip of the P6s is markable, particularly in the et, giving one great confidence all circumstances, including pping. The car doesn't dersteer too much, in spite of e extra traction given by the ited slip differential; highly joyable power slides are there r those who can afford the tyre ll. Ford are remarkable for parently responding to con- ructive criticism — we noticed welcome example of this in the caro seats, which we faulted the 4 March 1978 Road Test r poor back support. Extra dding is now provided, greatly proving the seat. It is only the pack's noise levels which duce its otherwise great enjoy- ent for all sorts of journey, long short.

n alternative

There is another way to prove a car's performance. creasing the engine size — by oring it out say to 60 thou. and inding a crankshaft blank to give perhaps 96 thou. more stroke — is a good start. Lightly fettle the normal inlet manifold's plenum chamber and alter the inlet ports to make them more of a swirl type (along Weslake lines) but still leave them rough, and you can retain the standard carburettor, giving it a smaller accelerator pump jet but the European emission-meeting main jets (which are 0.03mm smaller bore). Do a variety of minor adjustments, blueprint- style — make sure that the new pistons run to the top of the cylinder bores at top dead centre (in standard form they can be anything between top of bore to 20 thou. down), get the float chamber levels right, set the automatic choke to run at no more than 1,200 rpm, time the camshaft symmetrically (the normal one runs advanced, to close the exhaust early for better emissions), re-time the ignition to run 42deg before top dead centre total advance instead of 44 and fit a reliable electronic ignition system (Piranha in this case).

The bore and stroke go up from 93.67×72.42mm (2,994 c.c.) to 95.19×74.85mm — 3,196 c.c. Compression ratio goes up from 9 to 9.8 to 1, because of the extra swept volume. On the brake, this en- gine gives a flat-topped 155 bhp at 5,000 rpm, compared with the standard claim of 138 bhp at the same rpm. The aim is "to make the car more efficient and in so doing it performs better and more economically." The philo- sophy is Harry Weslake, but the speaker is my colleague John Miles, speaking for himself and for his friend Martin Murphy, of WM Developments who with John's help carried out the conversion.

I can't remember a case where *Autocar* has tested a car tuned or modified by one of its own staff. The last occasions were I suppose when (before I joined in 1966) we drove Ronald Barker's Napier, or whenever we have tested any Twin Cam Lotuses or Fords prior to the BDA engine (the old Ford-based Lotus Twin Cam engine cylinder head was designed by my illust- rious predecessor Harry Mundy). It is happily easy for me to wholeheartedly refute any charges of incipient nepotism by explaining (a) that the modifica- tions to John's car are entirely his and Martin's private venture, (b) that we — *Autocar* — only agreed to write about the car given our usual Road Test con- ditions, and (c) that what follows is an entirely honest and un- biased report. I have to point out

X-pack interior is actually standard 3000S (except for fire extinguisher)

WM Developments engine compartment (far left top) looks standard apart from Piranha electronic ignition box on nearside; X-pack engine (lower far left) is dominated by different air cleaner hiding the triple Webers

COO 260T

X-pack is beautifully stable at high speed on MIRA's banking

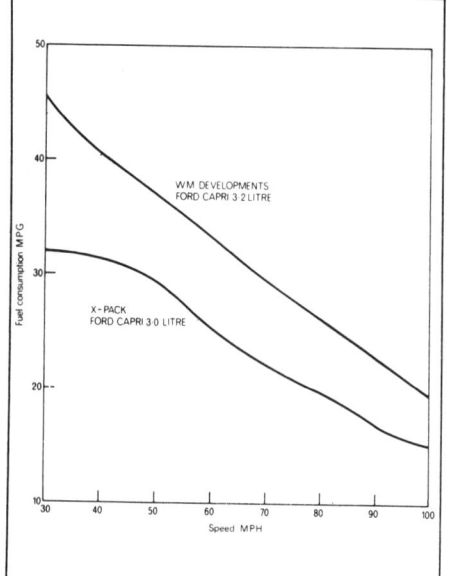

that anyone who knows the diffident Mr Miles will appreciate that there are few other people around who would be tempted to apply less pressure on the tester, so it hasn't been difficult to treat the car and the case entirely professionally.

Returning to the car, readers with good memories for numbers will recall that VHK 494S was *Autocar's* original Road Test Capri 3000S which then became a long term test car. John bought it from its owners after we returned it — but the engine now installed actually began its life as one in a Granada, in which it did perhaps 80,000 miles. The original pushrods, rockers and so on are in the rebored engine. Unlike the X-pack, which was supplied with its vacuum advance disconnected, the WM Developments car has its one connected.

Other changes are the substitution of Bilstein gas inserts in the front struts, and the effective lengthening on the rear anti-roll bar to prevent it interfering at all

with the axle on full droop, to reduce the tendency towards one wheel spinning in a bend taken under power. Front suspension pivot bushes are stiffened to improve response. The rear dampers are the original 35,000-mile heavy duty Fichtel and Sachs gas-filled units standard on the S-pack car. Brakes are unchanged except for special Mintex pads in front which though giving near enough the standard car's response, are exceptionally fade-resistant.

It depends on your taste of course, but as far as I am concerned, it is much better to drive a car that looks normal than one that looks faster. The WM car is completely standard outside, including wheels and tyres, but it is something else to drive. As the figures show, it is a shade less quick than the X-pack — 0.3sec behind to 60 mph, 0.7sec at 80, 1.2sec at 100 and 2.1sec at 110. But as the figures also show, it is appreciably more flexible, both than the X-pack

and the original. It doesn't fluff low down, so we managed to take figures from 10 mph without difficulty. It lapped MIRA's tight banking at a confident and beautifully stable 123 mph.

This translates on the road into the most relaxed and rewarding Capri I have ever tried. You spend an absurd amount of time in top when not in a hurry, the car pulling so easily from ridiculously low crankshaft speeds. On the other hand, if the mood takes you, it will rev beautifully easily too, with the most delightful eagerness and zest. For the acceleration runs, we changed up at 6,000 rpm — 6,200 rpm was tried with neither loss or gain; the car's low speed power was underlined by the starts, full-blooded wheelspin ones done by dropping the clutch in at 3,500 rpm — again, once the start itself had been made, it paid to back off very slightly to get the tyres engaged with the surface again.

Noise is not high, although the use of an old exhaust system

may have been the reason slightly more exhaust sou than I remember. The chang brake pads made themselves f with graunchy noises, but oth wise work very well. The c steers very well indeed and ultimate handling is a delight not too much understeer, f lowed by final oversteer if yo provoke it. Any improvement resistance to inside wheel-sp would have to be proved with back-to-back test against the o iginal; it certainly seeme improved in this respect.

What happens to econom Bigger engine equals mo thirst, surely? Not if you increas the compression ratio sensibl and do the other changes me tioned. To the driver, the W Developments car feels easy an eager, and particularly flexibl All the same, it is a surprise see what happens to the co sumption. Brim to brim, v never saw less than 17.7 mp over the actual testing period; c two occasions, which include plenty of commuting plus som

X-pack at speed — note deeper spoiler'd front

Handling of both cars is excellent — here WM Developments 3.2 Capri demonstrates its easily controlled oversteer in the hands of its co-modifier, John Miles. Graph of steady speed fuel consumption against speed shows how the bigger-engined single carburettor'd WM car scores in efficiency; graph in a way parallels relative flexibility of each car

Ford X-pack Capri parts price
(inc. VAT)

Triple carburettor kit	£574.7
44.5mm inlet valve (std d 41.1mm) — set	£33.6
41.1mm exhaust valve (std di 36.9mm) — set	£36.0
Cylinder head gaskets	£45.0
High capacity radiator	£225.6
High capacity fuel pump	£31.4
Limited slip differential	£263.6
Gas-filled front struts (2)	£164.4
Front springs — pair	£36.1
Anti-dive kit	£83.9
Gas-filled rear dampers (2)	£53.6
Ventilated front discs and larg calipers — set	£218.3
RS al. alloy wheels 7½in. x 13in. - set of five	£375.1
Wheel nuts — set	£17.3
RS wheel hub emblems	£5.3
Glass fibre wheel arch extension and front air dam	£200.7

NB. These prices do not include labour. As labo charge will vary according to customer specifica tion and dealer concerned, exact price of X-pack Capri is not available, approximate pric of test car is given as around £9,500.

normal open road driving, we recorded just over 24 mpg. This was confirmed when we took steady speed figures at MIRA, as the graph shows; the car *is* less thirsty than both the X-pack (which isn't surprising) and the standard 3000S. The last time I remember this sort of difference was almost each time we tested a Downton conversion — more performance for less fuel.

The run-off

We couldn't resist trying the cars side by side when the opportunity occurred. The WM car was for these runs re-shod with some wide Goodyear 195/60 NCT tyres on 14in. diameter alloy rims. These lowered its gearing very slightly from standard, but marginally less than the X-pack had been on its Pirellis. We tried accelerating from the same speed in top — and each time the WM car pulled initially away thanks to its better low speed power, to be held but not overtaken by the X-pack as that car's top end power came into play. In standing starts — in the wet — the X-pack's limited slip helped it keep just ahead at the beginning, but it could not gain anything on the 3.2-litre car higher up until we were beginning to run out of straight. The X-pack sounded faster, but effectively there is very little in it — and,if petrol matters, then the mechanically simpler cheaper WM car is a handsome winner.

There is a difference in price too. WM Developments offer their conversion for £863 which added to the standard price comes to £6,437 (on a second-hand car, you add £1,213.25). For the Ford X-pack, talk to your nearest Ford Rallysport dealer; for the 3.2-litre alternative, WM Developments are at 1 Lancaster Garages, off Lamholle Place, London NW3 (tel: 01-586 7149). □

Left: Top gear acceleration runs, begun with both cars running side by side at 20 mph — X-pack (trailing) has not regained its initial loss even by ¼-mile after start. Unlike acceleration runs for both cars which were done in the dry, these runs were made in damp conditions

Left: Neck and neck at the same spot after a simultaneous standing start — the X-pack only began to out-drag the 3.2-litre car towards the very top end

PERFORMANCE

Maximum speed	Capri 3000S	X-pack Capri 3000S	WM Developments Capri 3.2S
mph (rpm) mean	117 (@ 5,350)	*125(@ 5,900)	123 (@ 5,650)
best	118 (@ 5,400)	*128 (@ 6,050)	124 (@ 5,700)

NB: X-Pack Capri's maximum speeds, level road; others, MIRA banking

Acceleration (sec) mph			
30	2.9	2.8	2.8
40	4.4	4.1	4.2
50	6.4	5.7	5.8
60	8.6	7.7	8.0
70	11.5	10.5	11.0
80	15.5	13.6	14.3
90	20.0	17.7	18.5
100	28.1	23.1	24.3
110	38.7	31.0	33.1
Standing ¼ mile	16.6 (@ 83mph)	16.1 (@ 87mph)	16.5 (@ 87mph)
Standing km	30.6 (@ 103mph)	29.6 (@ 108mph)	30.1 (@ 107mph)

Top gear acceleration mph			
10-30	—	—	8.8
20-40	8.0	8.3	7.2
30-50	7.8	7.2	6.9
40-60	7.4	7.2	6.9
50-70	7.8	7.9	7.2
60-80	8.7	8.6	7.8
70-90	10.2	9.5	8.9
80-100	12.7	10.7	10.4
90-100	19.2	13.6	14.6
consumption	19.5mpg	17.7mpg	22.6mpg

CONTINUED FROM PAGE **79**

bhp, depending upon whether the customer opts for 7- or 9-psi maximum boost; his car has the latter. I have no reason to doubt those claims as the black RSR zipped to 60 mph in 7.2 seconds and covered the quarter mile in 16.0 sec at 93.0 mph. That's damn quick and compares to times of 10.6 and 18.0 sec, respectively, for a stock 2.8-liter V-6 Capri II R&T tested in July 1975.

But what's even more impressive than the sheer exhilaration of that sort of performance is that none of the V-6's normal flexibility has been sacrificed. The compression ratio is stock and up to about 3500 rpm the engine runs like a normally aspirated V-6. Then the turbo really starts twisting, the boost pegs at 9 psi and the tach needle makes a quick climb to 5000 rpm. And it does this in every gear. I encountered no detonation during my driving, probably a result of Kiser installing a Spearco electronic water injection system to cool the intake charge. Neither was there any indication of overheating during some extended slow-speed 1st- and 2nd-gear driving. Also, the engine was never cantankerous, starting easily when cold and warming up quickly. My only complaint, and a minor one, is that an exhaust resonance caused an annoying buzzing at 2000 rpm.

I also had an opportunity to briefly drive a customer's RSR with slightly different tuning and boost limited to 7 psi. That engine exhibited slightly better mid-range flexibility—positive boost started around 3200 rpm—at the expense of some top-end performance.

It took only a few trips through the slalom to discover how well the Rokstock RSR handles. The car is balanced and forgiving when thrown from pylon to pylon. With the wide tires and rims, the steering is heavy but it's also precise and accurate, and on the dusty PIR straightaway the RSR averaged 59.6 mph through the 700-ft slalom course compared to 55.5 for a stock Capri II.

The real fun, however, was on the road course. The RSR's suspension is very firm and although I never bottomed the front spoiler either on the road or the track, I'd be concerned about taking dips and culverts at stock Capri speeds. The firmness of the suspension translates to minimal body roll and a precise surefooted feel that give the driver enormous confidence when cornering near the limit. The car understeers but not to an inhibiting degree. If you back out of the throttle when cornering hard it understeers less; there's no tendency for the tail to come around. About the only change I'd make would be the addition of a limited-slip differential to prevent spinning the inside rear wheel when exiting tight low-speed corners. Luckily, Kiser has an open pipeline to Germany and Rokstock can order locking differentials and other hard-to-find limited production parts such as 5-speed gearboxes and fuel injection systems for the V-6 engine direct from the factory.

Aiding and abetting my enthusiasm for spirited cornering was the lateral and side support provided by the high-sided driving seat. The one in Kiser's car is a prototype and he has settled upon similar Carrera racing buckets in the RSRs currently under construction. One complaint of a personal nature: The seat was mounted higher than I like, and as a result the steering wheel interfered with my right thigh, effectively aborting my attempts at heel-and-toe downshifting. Also, the thicker rim of the steering wheel blocked my view of the ammeter and fuel level gauge. On Kiser's personal RSR the rear seats were replaced with deeply contoured buckets, but this eliminates the fold-down feature of the stock seats and the customer cars Kiser builds have the stock rear seats re-upholstered to match the fronts.

There's no denying the RSR Turbo is a real eyecatcher, eliciting questions regarding its origin and admiring glances everywhere I drove it. Thankfully Kiser has kept the cosmetic changes to a tasteful and purposeful few while expending a great deal of time and effort in turning the Capri into an outstanding road or track machine. If you're a Capri enthusiast or just enthusiastic about the Capri, you're doing yourself a great disservice if you don't at least leaf through the Rokstock 80-page catalog. I'm betting that after you've read a few pages you'll feel like the proverbial kid let loose in the candy factory.

A super Capri?

road test

JOHN BOLSTER describes a special version of the Ford Capri

Many people think that they would like to own a vintage car. It's an agreeable pipe-dream, but in actual fact they would probably be defeated by the 'crash' gearbox, and the friction-type shock absorbers would shake out their teeth. There are, however, a few modern cars that have some of the vintage virtues, of which the Ford Capri, in 3-litre form, is a prime example. A big, simple engine, lots of torque, moderate weight, and very high gearing, are the main ingredients.

At the time of writing, it would appear likely that this model will be replaced by something more modern in conception but perhaps less appealing. No doubt a well-restored Capri with the 2994cc 'Essex' engine will become a collector's piece in due course, but at the moment it represents imcomparable value among high-performance machinery.

The subject of the present report is a Super-Capri, which has been developed in such a way that the aforementioned vintage qualities stand out even more prominently. It is faster than the standard vehicle, which is a pretty quick car in its own right, but the main emphasis has been placed on improved torque and flexibility or, in a word, 'driveability'. Under normal road conditions, this automatically gives better fuel economy, largely as a result of reduced gearchanging.

The car I tested is the particular pet of John Miles, who is on the technical staff of *Autocar*, after a distinguished racing career. Though he developed this Capri for his own smoking, as the saying goes, similar conversions are to be carried out by WM Developments, 1 Lancaster Garages, Lambolle Place, NW3 (01-586 7149).

Engine tuning has followed two paths. In the first place, the piston-swept volume has been increased to 3.2 litres, which takes the compression ratio from 9.0 to 9.8:1. This was achieved by re-boring to 60 thou oversize and obtaining an un-machined crankshaft blank, which was ground to increase the throw. The result was an engine of 95.19×74.85 mm (3196cc) instead of 93.67×72.42 mm (2994cc), and it was nicely set up to these dimensions.

The second approach came from John's very considerable experience of developing racing engines, with perhaps a *soupçon* of the gospel according to Harry Weslake. Suffice it to say that, although the shape of the ports was very considerably modified, the standard valves were retained; the combustion chambers also received a touch here and there. The production camshaft was used, but set to split the overlap, instead of to give early exhaust valve closing for anti-pollution reasons.

A proprietary electronic ignition system was adopted, but I was glad to see that a reserve 'black box' was installed, with provision for an easy changeover. John had experienced two failures and, although the contact breaker is regarded as the weakest part of the conventional arrangement, it can usually be fiddled to complete a journey, whereas a dead black box is beyond roadside repair. Ask your friendly RAC man.

An enlarged engine, with improved breathing, naturally called for some tuning of the carburettor, including reduced delivery from the accelerator pump. On the bench, the unit developed 155bhp instead of 138, at 5000rpm, but far more important was almost 200lb ft of torque from 2000 to 3000rpm.

Some attention has been given to the suspension, notably by incorporating Bilstein gas-filled dampers in the front struts. Behind, the anti-roll bar has had its geometry modified to allow the axle greater freedom in the rebound direction. This reduces the tendency to pick up the inside rear wheel on roll when cornering, in the interest of improved traction.

As I have often remarked in these columns, I don't know why I try to road-test fast cars in midwinter — I should stick to two-cylinder economy models! However, in a period when everybody, including the coppers,

Above: A Super-Capri which retains all the standard model's vintage qualities. Right: The emphasis has been placed on improved torque. Bottom right: Externally, the appearance is unchanged. Below: The big Capri represents imcomparable value for money. Bottom: Conventional interior.

was spinning on black ice, I had just one day of sunshine and thaw. The roads might have been drier so, like Agag, I had to tread delicately at my getaways and some time was no doubt lost.

Nevertheless, the acceleration figures speak for themselves: 0-30mph 3.0s, 0-50mph 6.2s, 0-60mph 7.9s, 0-80mph 13.8s, 0-100mph 22.8s. For comparison, the standard car recorded 0-60mph in 8.6s under rather better conditions. Even more impressive was the fuel economy, with an overall consumption of 26.5mpg, including the performance testing. Most of the driving was distinctly brisk, though I was careful on those corners where shadows warned of lurking ice. The maximum speed is of little interest nowadays, but a brief dart put the speedometer well past 130mph, which my stopwatch translated as a genuine 125mph, as near as dammit.

With all that torque, there would be little advantage in having a five-speed gearbox. Indeed, I think that a three-speed box would be ample, for only third and top need be used once the car is on the move. Circumstances permitting, if you know what I mean, 100mph

would be a good cruising speed. When required, the engine revs very readily on the lower gears, when it has a more urgent note than a standard unit, though it is not objectionably noisy.

Good traction

The car handles very well, with a moderate degree of understeer that can be cancelled by the usual methods. Traction is quite good, with no sign of axle tramp, though propeller-shaft torque naturally causes the right-side rear wheel to spin first, in the absence of a limited-slip differential. Special brake pads had been fitted, which coped well with reasonably fast driving, though the aforementioned road conditions made it inadvisable to test them to the limit. No Ford gives a really soft ride and this one is a bit on the hard side with only the driver inside, though with a couple of passengers aboard it is quite acceptably comfortable.

Conversions cost £765 with a new engine, or £1035 with a secondhand one. So, grab your Capri while you may, for they could become scarce and expensive! ∎

AutoTEST Ford Capri 2.8i

Straightforward enjoyment

The Capri strikes a familiar slight understeering pose on the test track. Note sideways displacement of the rear axle under these hard cornering conditions

THE CAPRI has, in its various guises, not only provided high performance motoring at low cost, but in 3-litre form a persistently excellent basis for a race winning track car. Perhaps it is this connection with the sport that keeps the model range — even the 3-litre — selling tolerably well. It was nevertheless all too clear that if the big engined Capri was to stay in production it needed updating if only to improve levels of refinement and meet future exhaust emission standards. Hence the obvious move in installing the 2.8-litre Bosch K-Jetronic fuel injected "Cologne" V6 which, besides being potentially "cleaner" than the carburettored Essex, gives 16 per cent more power — 160 bhp at 5,700 rpm though admittedly 7 per cent less torque — 162lb. ft. at 4,200 rpm against the Essex's 174lb.ft. at 3,000 rpm.

It is particularly rewarding to know that these German built cars were developed by the recently formed Special Vehicle Engineering group at Dunton in Essex, many of whom were originally employed at AVO (Advanced Vehicle Operations) which no longer exists.

In the interests of refinement, the new car is based on a shell finished to Ghia specification but with "S" type Recaro seats now more luxuriously trimmed and

> **Ford Capri 2.8i**
> Job 1 out of Special Vehicle Engineering at Dunton, the Capri 2.8 Injection was first seen at the Geneva Motor Show in March this year. By the end of 1981, it will supersede 3-litre Essex engined "S" and Ghia models. Car based on shell trimmed to Ghia specification using 160 bhp 2.8-litre Bosch K-Jetronic fuel injected "Cologne" engine, much revised suspension, alloy wheels, and ultra low profile tyres.

the "S" steering wheel. The gearlever is shortened. Otherwise there is little change to be seen inside. The car sports an "S" type moulded rear spoiler, suitable badging, Ghia side bump strips and can be had either in a single metallic colour or with the very attractive optional two-tone metallic paintwork.

Most interest centres around the chassis (described *Autocar* 23 March). It runs a nominal 20mm lower than the Essex cars and has

PRODUCED BY:
*Ford Motor Co Ltd
Eagle Way
Warley
Brentwood
Essex CM13 3BW*

single leaf rear springs. Front and rear spring rates are higher than presently seen on the 3-litre "S" and these are used in conjunction with Bilstein gas-filled rear dampers and gas dampered front struts. Anti-roll bar dimensions go up 2mm front and rear — to 24 and 14mm respectively. The car uses the vented disc front brake set-up originally seen on the Granada, then Capri racers. At the rear the normal drum system is employed.

Very attractive GKN/Wolfrace Sonic pattern 7 x 13 in. alloy wheels (slightly modified to a Ford specification) are shod with 205/60VR Goodyear NCT tyres — an exclusive fitment — and with an unchanged drivetrain, these leave overall gearing just a little lower, at 21.17 instead of 21.84 mph per 1,000 rpm. As we shall see, the lower gearing matches the higher power peak

reasonably well.

Our test car tipped the scales at the Motor Industry Research Association (MIRA) proving ground at 23.4 cwt, distributed 54.6/45.4 front to rear, the lack of much improvement over the Autotest 3-litre S's 23.6 cwt being accounted for by the combined weight of the engine and fuel injection equipment and high level of trim.

Performance
Exhilarating

Three things are immediately apparent – the engine's superb flexibility, its smoothness, and much greater top end power compared with the 3-litre. A good 3-litre Essex car is still slightly faster in the mid-range but in the 2.8 injection we were able to take acceleration figures from 10 mph in top gear where the engine would pull without hesitation or hiccough (not the case in the Essex). An academic test admittedly, but a tribute to the close matching of the Bosch K-Jetronic fuel injection to the engine's needs. Above 1,000 rpm the car begins to accelerate almost as strongly in top as the Essex until it reaches 80-90 mph, when it takes over decisively.

In a straight line there is no contest. Where the Essex is running out of puff, the 2.8 injection is accelerating hard with a pleasingly raucous cry. In spite of the greatly increased grip provided by those fat Goodyear NCTs and the relatively high first gear, standing starts proved a

Badging and paintwork are distinctive. 2.8 Injection features "S" type rear spoiler, and Ghia side bump strips

Front shot emphasises the much increased tyre width and front end lowness

Rear light treatment and bumpering are unchanged

simple matter, wheelspin (after a dumped clutch, using 4,500 rpm) blending nicely into forward acceleration, to 30, 60, 100, and 110 mph in 2.8, 7.9, 23.4, and 32.0 sec (3-litre S: 2.9, 8.6, 28.1, 38.7 sec).

Equally impressive was the way that in far from still conditions, the car pulled quickly up to its maximum speed. The mean of 127 mph is equivalent to 6,000 rpm - 300 rpm above peak power. One felt it would have gone slightly faster with the wind had the rev limiter (which cut in on cue at 6,100 rpm) allowed it to do so. This and the marginal undergearing, suggests it would readily pull a higher final drive, to the benefit of mechanical refinement and economy at high cruising speeds.

All this translates into a car that goes with wonderful eagerness. The engine has a delightful

Wheels are very attractive 7×13in. GKN/Wolfrace (Ford modified), laquered in silver, and fitted with 205/60VR Goodyear NCT tyres

spread of power and with 66 mph available in second and 92 mph in third, there is always plenty of overtaking acceleration on tap particularly at the top end where the Essex would be struggling. The shorter gearlever makes changes seem crisper than ever, and the clutch requires a moderate 28lb load to free.

In common with all Bosch fuel injected engines driven recently, the early morning starts in the 2.8 injection are immediate, the fast idle soon cutting back as the water temperature rises. Driveability during the warm up period is truly excellent.

Economy
A great improvement

During a fairly short test period fuel consumption varied between 19.6 mpg (mostly testing), and 24.7 mpg when being driven more normally on a mixture of town and country roads. An overall figure of 21.3 mpg should be considered reasonable for a car of the Capri's performance, bettering several much slower 2-litre competitors. The 13 gallon tank gives a quite respectable touring range of around 290 miles, certainly no more, since one is unlikely to spend the time

necessary trying to brim the Capri's tank fully to the filler neck. Oil consumption was negligible during the test period.

Noise
Mainly road and wind

Although the adoption of the fuel-injected Cologne V6 has produced significant gains in mechanical smoothness and refinement the use of low profile tyres has produced an equal if not slightly greater (if such things can be quantified) trade in road induced noise. With the tyres set to the recommended pressures (28psi for normal driving) the car is particularly sensitive to transverse road joints and ripples – any sharp surface change – which produce an above average degree of thump. At high speeds particularly, pattern noise (the roar produced by wide tyres) is

always there and is very noticeable on the coarse concrete motorway surfaces, rougher ones sometimes also introducing a degree of harshness into the car. Lowering the tyre pressures by 4psi all round helped considerably in making the car more comfortable. Wind noise becomes increasingly apparent above 70 mph though never to an obtrusive degree.

When accelerating hard the engine is an absolute joy spinning up to the rev limiter first with an enthusiastic yet muted growl – then an almost BMW-like cry, but for some buzziness over 5,300 rpm. Lift off at around 4,000-4,500 rpm, a habitual change up point and the engine emits a marvellous rasp.

Though one is aware of the engine revving quite highly on the motorway mechanical noise dies away to an acceptable degree on light throttle openings.

The engine is topped by Bosch K-Jetronic plenum chamber. Most of the fuel injection equipment is housed alongside the nearside inner wing. The layout is tidy, and most maintenance items easy to reach

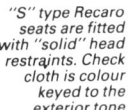

"S" type Recaro seats are fitted with "solid" head restraints. Check cloth is colour keyed to the exterior tone

Individual rear seats are reasonably comfortable

Road behaviour
One for the enthusiast

The ride and handling represents a good compromise, but with previous comment culled mainly from smooth test track experience where the car driven behaved beautifully, we found ourselves just a little disappointed by some aspects of the ride behaviour of this particular test car. We know only too well from our experience with the model, that Ford have had to tread a fine line in making the suspension able to cope with various load conditions, provide acceptable ride on low profile tyres, yet stiffen it to exploit the extra grip; all this in a semi-elliptically rear sprung solid rear axled car having less axle travel than is now considered the norm.

Ride was a mixture. Firm closely controlled yet nicely supple at low speeds it became less happy at medium speeds, on roads where there were ripples and general road wear. The suspension found difficulty in absorbing the small changes in level, leading to rather bumpy and sometimes jerky behaviour. As mentioned, rough motorway surfaces sometimes produced rather hard high frequency inputs in the car. It should be stressed that the car behaved much better and more evenly with two or even three persons on board and with lower than recommended tyre pressure. When working the car hard on undulating or bumpy roads with any reasonable payload one felt the suspension working once more to cushion the occupants. Lightly laden, one was also occasionally aware that the rear is stiffer sprung than the front, for example when running at high speeds in blustery conditions or turbulence, or when turning into a very fast corner where any small degree of wander occurs mainly at the front. Straight line stability in still airs is excellent.

With just over three turns from lock to lock the steering is ideally geared. We have known these power assisted systems to vary somewhat. Ours maintained nice weighting and a good degree of feel at all times. With wheels as wide as seen on racing Capris and NCT tyres the car has a great deal of grip. Cornering roll is well controlled (though when cornered hard it rolls more than some of its counterparts). As the cornering speeds build up one notices that the 2.8 injection remains very neutral right up to the limit of adhesion. Finally it is the front tyres that begin to develop some slip. At the limit of adhesion in balanced throttle cornering the car has a pleasantly reassuring degree of understeer, with the driver always able to balance this with power at the lower speeds or by backing off the throttle at any speed, the change to tail out attitude being perhaps more easily provoked in this car than in other big-engined Capris we have driven. For rear wheel drive addicts the ultimate handling is a delight since the car is so easily controlled at the limit, the front responding to steering and the rear to throttle action. We gained the impression that in tuning the suspension, Ford have been looking for near neutral balance (by the addition of a stiffer rear anti-roll bar), and this seems to have resulted in the car being prone to spin an inside rear wheel when accelerating out of slow corners — particularly on wet roads.

Brakes
Unbalanced in panic

Used normally on road and track the brakes gave nothing but satisfaction. We did however encounter two unusual phenomena during MIRA tests. With the

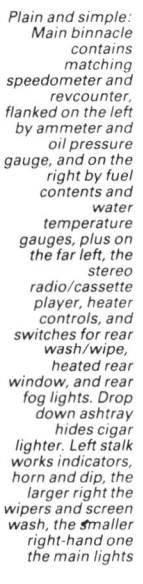

Plain and simple: Main binnacle contains matching speedometer and revcounter, flanked on the left by ammeter and oil pressure gauge, and on the right by fuel contents and water temperature gauges, plus on the far left, the stereo radio/cassette player, heater controls, and switches for rear wash/wipe, heated rear window, and rear fog lights. Drop down ashtray hides cigar lighter. Left stalk works indicators, horn and dip, the larger right the wipers and screen wash, the smaller right-hand one the main lights

brakes displaying a nicely progressive response curve at first it was odd to discover that by varying the rate at which the pedal load was applied towards the top end — say between 60 and 80lb — the front brakes would lock at more than usually differing pedal efforts and deceleration forces. By building pedal loads up quickly to say 70lb, conclusive front locking occurred with between 0.82-0.84 showing on the decelerometer, whereas more progressive application of the brake pedal, would allow between 80 and 90lb to be used and a much better 0.94 stop to be obtained; a situation Ford say is likely to be due to the adoption of a front/rear G sensing pressure limiting valve, apparently dictated by European legislation designed to force manufacturers to make brakes progressively more front biased (or to be more accurate less rear biased) the harder you brake. Fair enough, but in this case the front bias seems to have been carried too far; and inconsistently so.

Fade resistance is excellent — not surprising since the vented front disc set up originally appeared on the Capri as a homologation item for Group 1 racers. The car cast off the *Autocar* fade test — ten consecutive 0.5g stops from 88 mph—with only a moderate rise in pedal pressures midway, pedal loads then recovering almost to starting levels towards the end. However from the fourth stop onwards the front end developed an increasingly severe judder, which in turn excited the steering to wobble. Not once did the problem occur on the road or during circuit running, nor did it occur if the brakes were left to recover between stops.

Behind the wheel
Good as ever

Most agreed that the Capri feels right from the word go. Entry is straightforward, the "S" steering wheel and pedals are ideally placed. The shortened gearlever is appreciated and falls perfectly to hand. The Recaro seats provide excellent lateral location (more important than ever with such a high degree of adhesion available) though are rather hard backed, ours lacking the extra lumbar support that is available and has been seen in similar seats. Fore and aft adjustment is plentiful; enough for 6ft drivers and rake is of infinitely variable type. As before the driver is presented with one of the most pleasingly straightforward control layouts in existence. The dash is extremely simple yet comprehensive, with the large matching speedometer (This over-reads by an illegal 11 per cent) and 0-7,000 rpm revcounter (a mere 100 rpm fast) plainly visible through the top half of the wheel. These are flanked on the left by the ammeter, and oil pressure gauge, and on the right by matching water temperature

and fuel contents gauges. Warning lights (handbrake, charge, main beam, and indicators) are kept to a minimum, and also neatly contained within the main binnacle, are the stereo radio/cassette player, heater controls, and push button switches for rear wash/wipe, rear fog lights and heated rear window. Stalk controls are traditional Ford — solid feeling and crisp in use if ISO patterned — with the left working the indicators, horn and dip, the larger right the wash wipe, and the smaller right hand one the main lights.

As in most coupés the rear seat passengers do not have quite such an easy time of it. Getting in requires a degree of agility particularly if the front seats are in their furthest position. Once installed, the Capri lacks something in rear headroom compared with a Vauxhall Sportshatch, though it remains considerably more roomy in this respect than offerings from Mazda, Porsche or Datsun.

The Capri's long and fairly squared off bonnet, so wasted in the smaller engined versions, gives the car a purposeful feel and makes it a very easy machine to judge widths in, if occasionally an awkward one when nosing out of a side turning. With solid rather than "S" type "racquet" head restraints, the over-the shoulder visibility is tolerably good, though the car's thick C panels do restrict rear quarter visibility.

It is nevertheless a car that continues to score heavily over its rivals on heating and ventilation. The two familiar Ford sliders control an air blending system which gives tremendous heat output, plus fine temperature and directional control. Furthermore the Capri, unlike many other cars, has the traditional outer eyeball vents giving a forceful supply of

fresh air (even without the fan which is noisy if run fast), quite *independent* of the main system. The only thing missing is a side window demist.

Living with the Capri 2.8 Injection

Revisiting the Capri, so to speak, one is struck by its comparative simplicity in aspects of maintenance (with prospects of easy spares availability) and general day to day running. Once you have located the bonnet release recessed in the facia in line with the driver's right knee, access to the engine bay service items is excellent with only the plugs being a little inaccessible, the 2.8 Injection motor is a pleasingly purposeful sight. A good point is that by raising the covering panel slightly Ford have found room for the correct sized spare wheel plus jack and wheel spanner in the normal under rear floor compartment. The wide opening rear hatch door is held by gas struts — it would have been nice to see this system adopted for the bonnet — and although the rear sill is rather high, long and bulky items can be loaded with reasonable ease. With both rear seats in place, a moulded shelf covers luggage and valuables and as before the rear seat backs fold individually allowing long loads or a carrycot and one rear seat passenger to be carried. The cloth trim is of good quality, and colour keyed to the exterior tone chosen. We were particularly impressed with the standard stereo radio/cassette player which provided good reception and sound reproduction. The sliding and tipping sunroof is in our experience a particularly worthwhile inclusion on this Capri providing additional ventilation on hot days

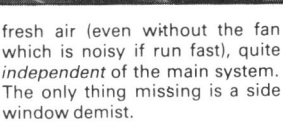

Load space is carpeted and with both rear seats folded down floor is relatively uncluttered. Rear sill is higher than one would like

Rear parcel shelf hinges with rear door and can easily be removed if desired

Split rear seat facility is most useful

without too much turbulence or roar when used in either mode. With no door or seat back pockets oddments space is limited; to a small centre armrest locker, a drop down glovebox of reasonable size and a small tray in front of the gear lever.

Main service intervals are at 12,000 miles with an oil change and simple inspection every 6,000. The ignition is breakerless, so apart from any specialist attention that might be required by the fuel injection, the new car should even provide no servicing difficulties for the DIY owner.

By raising spare wheel cover 1in., car sized spare can be accommodated with jack and wheelbrace in the normal spare wheel compartment

The Capri 2.8 and 3 litre range

Until late this year the 3-litre Essex engined automatic transmissioned Ghia (£7,739) and manual "S" (£6,563) will run concurrently with the new 2.8 Injection manual which costs £7,995, and comes in monotone metallic or with three two-tone metallic choices for £175 extra.

HOW THE CAPRI 2.8 INJECTION PERFORMS

Figures taken at 2,050 miles by our own staff at the Motor Industry Research Association proving ground at Nuneaton

All Autocar test results are subject to world copyright and may not be reproduced in whole or part without the Editor's written permission

TEST CONDITIONS:
Wind: 10-18 mph
Temperature: 18 deg C (65 deg F)
Barometer: 29.7 in. Hg (1,008 mbar)
Humidity: 60 per cent
Surface: dry asphalt and concrete
Test distance: 555 miles

MAXIMUM SPEEDS

Gear	mph	kph	rpm
Top (mean)	127	204	6,000
(best)	129	208	6,100
3rd	92	148	6,100
2nd	66	106	6,100
1st	41	66	6,100

ACCELERATION

FROM REST

True mph	Time (sec)	Speedo mph
30	2.8	34
40	4.2	45
50	6.0	56
60	7.9	68
70	10.7	79
80	13.9	90
90	17.7	101
100	23.4	111
110	32.0	121
120	—	131

Standing ¼-mile: 16.2 sec, 88 mph
Standing km: 30.0 sec, 108 mph

IN EACH GEAR

mph	Top	3rd	2nd
10-30	9.9	6.2	4.4
20-40	8.4	5.9	4.0
30-50	7.9	5.3	3.7
40-60	8.0	5.1	3.8
50-70	8.2	5.5	—
60-80	8.6	6.0	—
70-90	9.3	7.1	—
80-100	10.6	—	—
90-110	13.8	—	—

FUEL CONSUMPTION

Overall mpg:
21.3 (13.5 litres/100km)

Autocar constant speed fuel consumption measurement equipment incompatible with Bosch fuel injection

Autocar formula: Hard 19.2
Driving Average 23.4
and conditions Gentle 27.7

Grade of fuel: Premium, 4-star (98 RM)
Fuel tank: 13.0 Imp. galls (59 litres)
Mileage recorder reads: 6 per cent long

Official fuel consumption figures
(ECE laboratory test conditions; not necessarily related to Autocar figures)
Urban cycle: 19.1 mpg
Steady 56 mph: 34.9 mpg
Steady 75 mph: 27.4 mpg

OIL CONSUMPTION

(SAE 20/50) negligible

BRAKING

Fade *(from 88 mph in neutral)*
Pedal load for 0.5g stops in lb

	start/end		start/end
1	30/30	6	30/70
2	30/28	7	34/55
3	30/36	8	34/48
4	30/60	9	34/44
5	30/70	10	34/44

Response *(from 30 mph in neutral)*

Load	g	Distance
20 lb	0.30	100 ft
40 lb	0.57	75 ft
60 lb	0.83	36 ft
80 lb	0.94	32 ft
Handbrake	0.32	94 ft
Max. gradient: 1 in 3		

CLUTCH
Pedal 28 lb; Travel 6½in.

WEIGHT

Kerb, 23.4 cwt/2,620 lb/1,190 kg
(Distribution F/R, 54.6/45.4)
Test, 26.8 cwt/3,005 lb/1,365 kg
Max payload 749 lb/340 kg

DIMENSIONS

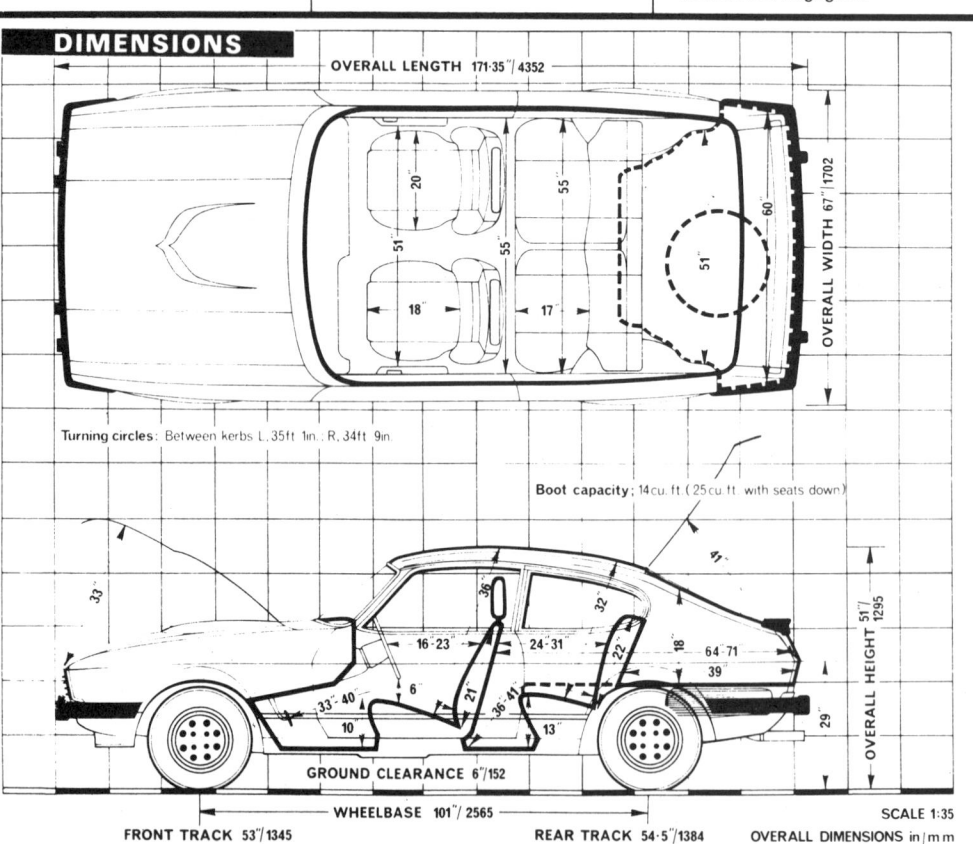

OVERALL LENGTH 171·35"/4352
OVERALL WIDTH 67"/1702
Turning circles: Between kerbs L. 35ft 1in. R. 34ft 9in.
Boot capacity; 14cu. ft. (25cu. ft. with seats down)
OVERALL HEIGHT 51"/1295
GROUND CLEARANCE 6"/152
WHEELBASE 101"/2565
FRONT TRACK 53"/1345
REAR TRACK 54·5"/1384
SCALE 1:35
OVERALL DIMENSIONS in/mm

PRICES

Basic	£6,417.39
Special Car Tax	£534.78
VAT	£1,042.83
Total (in GB)	**£7,995.00**
Seat Belts	Standard
Licence	£70.00
Number plates	£15.00
Total on the Road	**£8,080.00**
(exc. insurance and delivery)	

EXTRAS (inc. VAT)
*Two tone metallic paint £175.00
*Tinted glass £37.78

*Fitted to test car

TOTAL AS TESTED ON THE ROAD £8,292.78

Insurance Group not yet established

SERVICE & PARTS

	Interval		
Change	6,000	12,000	24,000
Engine oil	Yes	Yes	Yes
Oil filter	Yes	Yes	Yes
Gearbox oil	No	No	No
Spark plugs	No	Yes	Yes
Air cleaner	No	No	Yes
C/breaker	N/A	N/A	N/A
Total cost	**£27.15**	**£59.81**	**£68.81**

(Assuming labour at £11.50/hour inc. VAT)

PARTS COST *(including VAT)*
Brake pads (2 wheels) – front	£18.89
Brake shoes (2 wheels) – rear	£12.98
Exhaust complete	N/A
Tyre – each (typical)	£91.26
Windscreen (laminated)	£34.67
Headlamp unit	£38.15
Front wing	£71.32
Rear bumper	£45.39

WARRANTY

12 months/unlimited mileage

SPECIFICATION

ENGINE
	Front; Rear drive
Head/block	Cast iron/cast iron
Cylinders	6 in 60° vee, bored block
Main bearings	4
Cooling	Water
Fan	Viscous
Bore, mm (in.)	93 (3.66)
Stroke, mm (in.)	68.5 (2.69)
Capacity, cc (in³)	2,792 (170.4)
Valve gear	Ohv
Camshaft drive	Chain
Compression ratio	9.2-to-1
Ignition	Breakerless
Injection	Bosch K Jetronic
Max power	160 bhp (DIN) at 5,700 rpm
Max torque	162 lb ft at 4,200 rpm

TRANSMISSION
Type Four speed synchromesh
Clutch Single plate diaphram

Gear	Ratio	mph/1000rpm
Top	1.00	21.17
3rd	1.41	15.02
2nd	1.95	10.86
1st	3.16	6.70

Final drive gear Hypoid level
Ratio 3.09

SUSPENSION
Front—location MacPherson struts, transverse link and anti roll bar
—springs Coil
—dampers Telescopic gas filled
—anti-roll bar Yes 24mm
Rear—location Live axle
—springs Half elliptic single leaf
—dampers Telescopic gas filled
—anti-roll bar Yes 14mm

STEERING
Type Rack and pinion
Power assistance Yes
Wheel diameter 14.0 in.
Turns lock to lock 3.3

BRAKES
Circuits Dual
Front 10.3 in. dia./ventilated disc
Rear 9.0 in. dia./drum
Servo Vacuum
Handbrake Centre lever working on rear drums

WHEELS
Type Cast alloy
Rim width 7 in.
Tyres—make Goodyear
—type NCT
—size 205/60VR-13
—pressures F28 R28 psi (normal driving)

EQUIPMENT
Battery	12V 55Ah
Alternator	45A
Headlamps	55/60W
Reversing lamp	Standard
Electric fuses	
Screen wipers	2-speed plus intermittent
Screen washer	Electric
Interior heater	Air blending
Air conditioning	N/A
Interior trim	cloth seats, pvc headlining
Floor covering	Carpet
Jack	Screw pillar
Jacking points	1 each side under sills
Windscreen	Laminated
Underbody protection	Bitumastic wax and pvc over paint

HOW THE CAPRI 2.8 INJECTION COMPARES

Ford Capri 2.8 Injection £7,995

Front engine,
rear drive
Capacity
2,792 c.c.
Power
160 bhp (DIN)
at 5,700 rpm
Weight
2,620 lb/1,190 kg
Autotest
20 June 1981

Mazda RX7 £8,699

Front engine,
rear drive
Capacity
2,292 c.c.
Power
105 bhp (DIN)
at 6,000 rpm
Weight
2,258 lb/1,024 kg
Autotest
24 November 1979

Audi Coupé £7,475

Front engine,
front drive
Capacity
1,921 c.c.
Power
115 bhp (DIN)
at 5,200 rpm
Weight
2,352 lb/1,069 kg
Autotest
May 1981

Datsun 280ZX 2+2 £9,695

Front engine,
rear drive
Capacity
2,753 c.c.
Power
140 bhp (DIN)
at 5,200 rpm
Weight
2,881 lb/1,307 kg
Autotest
13 October 1979

Lancia Beta HPE 2000 £6,550

Front engine,
front drive
Capacity
1,995 c.c.
Power
119 bhp (DIN)
at 5,500 rpm
Weight
2,400 lb/1,088 kg
Autotest
8 April 1977

Porsche 924 £9,103

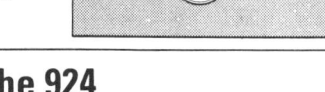

Front engine,
rear drive
Capacity
1,984 c.c.
Power
125 bhp (DIN)
at 5,800 rpm
Weight
2,450 lb/1,114 kg
Autotest
August 1978

MPH & MPG

Maximum speed (mph)

Ford Capri 2.8 Injection	127
Porsche 924	126
Lancia Beta HPE 2000	116
Mazda RX7	113
Audi Coupé	113
Datsun 280ZX	111

Acceleration 0-60 (sec)

Ford Capri 2.8 Injection	7.9
Porsche 924	9.5
Mazda RX7	10.1
Audi Coupé	10.2
Lancia Beta HPE 2000	10.6
Datsun 280ZX	11.3

Overall mpg

Porsche 924	25.0
Audi Coupé	24.8
Ford Capri 2.8 Injection	21.3
Lancia Beta HPE 2000	20.3
Datsun 280ZX	18.4
Mazda RX7	18.2

Other obvious contenders are the 2-litre Alfa GTV (£7,710, 118 mph, 0-60 mph 8.9 sec, and 23.5 mpg), and the soon to be introduced V6 2.5-litre version. There is also the Renault Fuego GTX (£6,888, 113 mph, 0-60 mph 10.0 sec, and 26.0 mpg). With the advantage of cubic inches (and much more power than the Datsun) the Capri trounces the lot on performance, particularly acceleration. It is reasonably economical and at least equally mechanically refined to the Datsun and Mazda rotary, both rather stodgy performers also disappointingly inefficient cars overall – precisely where the slightly rough engined but aerodynamically very efficient Porsche scores heavily. Of the two relatively low powered fwd cars the Audi goes well. It is refined and economical but has nothing like the Lancia's zest. For gutsy performance with tolerable economy it has to be the Ford.

ON THE ROAD

Of the front wheel drive pair the HPE just beats the ultimately equally viceless Audi because of its marginally better ride and crisper response, though some might find its lowish geared non-assisted steering a shade heavy when parking. Afficianados of front engine/rear drive handling have a good bunch to choose from the least likeable aspect of the Porsche and Mazda being their low geared steering. Both need nearly a turn more from lock to lock than the power steered Datsun and Capri, the Goodyear NCT shod Ford having easily the best – quite remarkable – dry road grip if slightly greater understeering tendencies (on a balanced throttle) than the more equally weight biased Mazda, Porsche, and Datsun – all three much less powerful and accordingly less prone to inside rear wheelspin than the Capri when charging out of slow

corners. The Ford has reasonable ride (see text) considering the basic nature of its suspension and running gear, and for sheer "chuckability" the Capri has it from the Datsun (how this car needs more power), Mazda and Porsche, not forgetting the Lancia which vies with any similarly shod fwd car on handling and grip, if not for its water valve heater, a heating system also used by Porsche and Audi. The air blenders in the rest work well, though the Capri is perhaps best ventilated overall because of its strong independant ram fed fresh air supply.

SIZE & SPACE

Legroom front/rear (in)
(seats fully back)

Audi Coupé	40/37
Ford Capri 2.8 Injection	40/36
Datsun 280ZX	44/29
Lancia Beta HPE 2000	40/32
Porsche 924	44/23
Mazda RX7	40/25

Drivers interested in this type of sports saloon car will often be more interested in out-and-out performance rather than in the car's luggage carrying capacity or its passenger accommodation; none the less for a family man the more spacious the car the more practical it must be, a point which favours the Audi and the Capri. The Lancia and Capri clearly offer the most loadable space of the five hatchbacks particularly as the Datsun's spare wheel normally dominates the rear compartment (unless Dunlop Denovos are specified). The Porsche and Mazda have opening rear windows rather than hatch doors, and are simply smaller cars – offering very little more than occasional accommodation for rear seat passengers. Both the Datsun and Ford have split rear seats. Being a Coupé the Audi's rear seat is of course fixed. Its quite reasonable rear seat legroom is matched by good for a coupé boot space.

VERDICT

In terms of roadholding, handling, refinement, looks and performance, the Capri 2.8 Injection is a vast improvement over the now rather agricultural feeling Essex engined "S" and Ghia, and shows how a simple down to earth concept (with the attendant relatively simple maintenance) can be kept more than competitive. It is not as lavishly equipped as the Datsun, or ultimately as fuel efficient as the Porsche (possibly the most corrosion resistant car in the group). Nor does it ride as comfortably as these two or the RX7 on some surfaces, but as a "driving machine" it beats all of these, and assuming one prefers the handling characteristics of a rear drive car, it will be much preferred to the Audi and very competitively priced Lancia. The latest big engined Capri is no longer a relatively inexpensive car. By the same token it offers something extra in most aspects of its dynamic performance – a car that will be particularly relished by the keen driver.

Ultimate Capri

Tickford's Capri 2.8T puts a Ford in the supercar performance league. Autocar *has a special interest . . . .*

By John Miles

Top and right: Modified front panel allows single air inlet at spoiler level. Front and rear bumpering is moulded with inset rubber bump strip. Side bump strips neatly cap sill to body joint. Side turn reflectors and twin motorised mirrors are standard

Below: Normal radiator and battery mountings are removed to make way for intercooler on right radiator and re-positioned Bosch K Jetronic fuel injection equipment. Note dimimutive size of turbocharger

SINCE THE Capri appeared in Mk 1 form some 14 years ago, big-engined versions of the marque have consistently provided unequalled value-for-money performance in an extraordinarily practical car, which has also formed the basis of a successful track machine.

We have seen the Essex 3-litre version phased out in early 1982, to be replaced by the Special Vehicle Engineering developed fuel injection 2.8i. More than ever this car fulfils the need for a practical down-to-earth high performance machine, and in virtually unmodified form, is now winning production saloon car races. It seems that, notwithstanding the appearance of the Sierra XR4, the Capri does not want to die.

There may be more refined and technically sophisticated cars in the class, but few, if any, offer the Capri's blend of performance, mechanical simplicity, small overall size, interior space, hatchback versatility, good

ventilation, ergonomic quality, handling and value. British sales of the 2.8i alone have topped 4,000 units since June 1981.

The time seemed right to build what hopefully will be regarded as the ultimate roadgoing Capri; a car that would retain the practical virtues (and the standard car's useful narrowness) but easily better the mid-range performance of all other cars in its class. It should have a minimum top speed of 140 mph, to be matched by gains in handling, roadholding (and ride) plus lower noise levels. The case for building such a Capri stood, and as the result of the writer's enthusiasm for the project (ultimately fulfilled as part of the development team) Ford and Aston Martin top brass met, a year ago almost to the day, and agreed in principle that prototypes should be built. In turn, the project was handed over to Tickford, the engineering associate of Aston Martin Lagonda Ltd.

Turbo engine

Predictably, turbocharging was considered the simplest and most effective way of obtaining the performance and refinement required without exceeding current emission levels. The Michael May-developed 2.8-litre carburettor turbo engine fitted in a German Ford RS division developed Capri was considered, but this would not fit right-hand drive cars without shifting the turbocharger and associated manifolding. Aston's engine development chief David Morgan felt it absolutely essential in the interests of reduced thermal stress – and greater power outputs still – that the inlet charge air should be cooled, and that if possible the engine should run on the existing Bosch K-Jetronic 2.8i fuel injection. Furthermore, to get the best possible response and efficiency from the system, the turbocharger should be placed at a point equidistant from both cylinder heads, where best use could be made of the heat and exhaust pulse energy.

Instead of the turbocharger being mounted directly on an exhaust manifold with a connecting cross-over pipe, as in the May system, new equal-length stainless steel manifolds, running four pipes (the 2.8i has siamesed exhaust ports) into two just before the turbine inlet, come forward to an integrally wastegated IHI RHB6 turbocharger mounted in front of the engine. The viscous-coupled fan is replaced by an electric unit and the radiator space is now

shared by a new larger capacity water radiator, an enormous 17-row air-to-air intercooler, plus a large 16-row oil cooling radiator. The battery, which is normally tray-mounted on the nearside inner wing, is relocated in a box in the luggage compartment. The turbo compressor now sucks through the Bosch K-Jetronic air weighing mechanism, and blows via the intercooler into the standard plenum chamber and inlet manifold – some might say the treatment the 2.8i's tortuous inlet passage has always needed. Above all, torque, response, and driveability have been the aims, and in this regard Morgan is full of praise for the extraordinarily efficiency and wide airflow range offered by the little IHI turbo – and the way that the Bosch air

weighing mechanism passes the necessary extra flow. The turbocharger has allowed enormous increases in power and torque at the bottom end, yet still permits a fairly large increase in mass airflow required for a substantial increase in top end power, and in this regard Morgan stressed the importance of reducing exhaust back-pressure downstream of the turbo. The 2.8T has an enormous stainless steel downpipe running into an all-new free-flow twin-pipe stainless steel system. Tests have shown that on the standard 9.2-to-1 compression ratio the engine will accept 11 psi boost before detonation becomes a possibility, and 8.5 psi is the maximum boost level chosen, used in conjunction with an otherwise standard 2.8i engine – and that includes the ignition advance curve and pistons neither of which have shown the need for alteration thanks to the intercooler which lowers charge temperatures by up to 55degC. The standard engine is quoted as giving 160 bhp (DIN) at 5,700 rpm, and 162 lb. ft. torque at a rather high 4,200 rpm.

The benefits of an intelligently applied turbo system are apparent especially in the torque figures; a simply staggering 260 lb. ft. (more than all but the four-cam GAA and Zakspeed group 5 turbo racers) developed at 3,500 rpm. Better still, the 2.8T has more torque (165 lb. ft. available at 1,500 rpm) than the standard car has anywhere! And once above 2,000 rpm there is always more than 200 lb. ft. on tap. Peak power is 205 bhp at 5,000 rpm

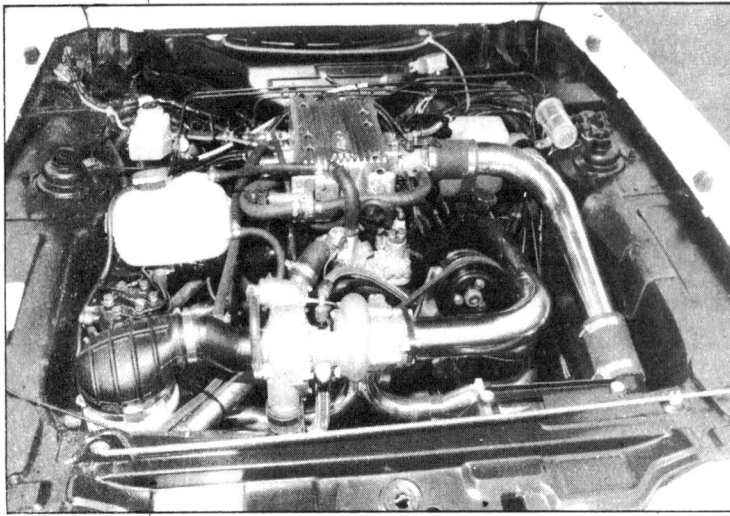

nd stays flat to 5,500 rpm, moreover specific fuel consumption figures for the new engine are very encouraging, articularly at the top end.

At present this lot is passed through a Ford five-speed transmission (a Getrag gearbox is being considered) and of course a limited slip differential. On the standard 3.09-to-1 final drive and 205/60VR-13 tyres overall gearing is raised from 21.2 mph to 25.8 mph per 1.000 rpm. This leaves the engine revving at 5,400 rpm, or right in the power bend at 140 mph, a speed at which cars have been consistently running on Vauxhall's Millbrook test track.

surface and detail finish in GRP, and this includes the side sills, so very necessary to fill out the Capri's obvious tumblehome. The rear bumper moulding includes a tank shield. Both front and rear number plates are recessed into the relevant mouldings, and at the rear end this has allowed the space between the lights to be filled in with a reflective panel.

Flush-fitting wheel trims — another positive aid to drag reduction — are presently formed in aluminium but will ultimately be moulded.

A rather nice refinement will be the addition of a rubber lip seal to the window frame thus closing

Left: Standard instruments are repositioned and a boost gauge included on a burr walnut instrument panel. Door cappings are also in this material. Show car is leather-trimmed throughout

Aerodynamics

The standard wide-tyred 2.8i Capri starts out with a MIRA-measured drag co-efficient of around 0.39. Aerodynamically the Capri is not bad. Its main fault is the degree of front lift. Predictably, the aerodynamic package was dictated to a large extent by the effectiveness of the front spoiler-cum-bumper moulding, itself limited by such considerations as ground and kerb clearances and of course looks. Various options were tried, the final shape achieving a front lift reduction of around 70 per cent. It was then a relatively simple matter to tune the rear spoiler accordingly. For the sake of high speed balance rear lift has been cut back near to zero. Since the front air dam is a source of extremely high pressure air, it has been found possible to duct all the cooling flow necessary at this point (after some sheet metal modifications in the front panel) and blank off the normal radiator grille ala Aston Martin Vantage. Impressively, a large improvement in aerodynamic stability, and the necessary cooling airflow has been obtained with a sizeable reduction in drag. The Cd figure is 0.36.

Presently all the additional panels are moulded. Tickford have achieved excellent levels of

the Capri's rather large frame-to-door opening gap. It should also provide a token reduction in wind noise.

Locating the axle

One of the earliest lessons learnt was that no real improvements in handling, transient stability (or ride) could be had unless rear axle location was improved (particularly in the sideways direction). It was known that in hard cornering the single-leaf sprung rear axle on a 2.8i Capri moves sideways by approximately 1½in., some of this deflection being due to the rubber bushing in the front spring eyes and rear hangers,

and a significant amount also occurs in the springs themselves.

Presently two location systems are under evaluation; one consists of a pair of forward-facing links angled outwards from near the centre of the axle to a mounting on the spring itself, thus triangulating the axle/spring structure. The more likely alternative is a "Bulldog" linkage, of the type first seen on the mid-engined 5.4-litre turbo supercar of the same name (*Autocar* 19 April 1980).

The rear springs are unchanged and the standard anti-roll bar also remains, as it does at the front end. Modified anti-roll-bar-to-chassis pick-up points allow an extra 2 deg caster, a positive aid to straight running, and special strut top mounts permit 1 deg negative camber. To offset the extra front end weight and improve stability and handling, front spring rates are increased by 15 per cent, and the damping forces are altered to a more progressive curve. Dampers and struts are Bilstein. Braking has never been a Capri strong point, and although Tickford engineers have successfully been running development cars with the standard vented disc/drum set-up, albeit with harder than standard linings, production cars are likely to have rear drums replaced with discs.

Trim and interior

On the show car, Connolly hide is used throughout with Wilton carpet for the floor and load areas. For those who prefer a more functional look, cloth will also be available — and cost less. Replacing the standard instrument panel is one in burr walnut. The standard instruments are rearranged and a boost gauge included. Door cappings are also in walnut. The rear wash/wipe now has an intermittent and time delay facility. Both door mirrors are electrically adjustable and the steering wheel features an upholstered crash pad. A new centre console houses cassette/tape player, cassette holder and glovebox.

Prices for the 2.8T have not yet been fixed and will depend very much on trim specification, but Tickford are aiming for an upper limit of £14,000.

Performance

Development cars have been doing 0 to 60 and and 100 mph in 6.2 and 14.6 sec respectively; they run easily to 140 mph. The Capri 2.8T should not only trounce all the direct competition on performance but give many of the currently available supercars a run for their money, especially in the mid range.

Left: Large tray spoiler cuts rear lift to zero. Rear bumper moulding-mounted number plate allows space between rear lights to be filled in with reflective panel.

Super Panda
Fiat make their basic baby more cuddly

A higher specification Fiat Panda, called the Super, comes onto the British market later this year, when prices will be announced. There is no alteration in engine size or output, but changes have been made to the carburetion and ignition to improve response and economy. On the chassis, single leaf rear springs are now being used to provide a more progressive travel and better ride.

A new tweed type of material

has been adopted for seat, door and facia "pouch" trim, while the seats are made more comfortable by better shaping and padding. New too are the black carpets, steering wheel and facia panel. Convenience has been improved with re-designed heater controls, and electric washers for both front and rear screens. Over 660,000 Pandas have been built since the model was launched in February 1980. **ML**

PRACTICAL CLASSICS **SALON** FEATURE

FORD CA
RS 3100

Tony Whiting's RS3100 exhibiting its lowered suspension, with negative camber at the front, four spoke alloy wheels, front quarter bumpers in black and, of course, the spoilers which greatly improved the stability of racing versions.

Michael Brisby tries a Capri with that little bit e

PRACTICAL CLASSICS **SALON** FEATURE

I well remember Ford's launch of the Ford Capri in 1968; at the time I was quite impressed by American muscle cars — the Mustang, the Stingray and the Camaro in their more ferocious forms — and now Ford were giving us a mini-version. But I saw the posters with a picture of a car whose frontal styling did not seem to match the back, and a silly slogan — "Ford Capri — the car you always promised yourself", and then I discovered that the basic model had a mere 52 brake-horsepower under its long bonnet, so I pretty well lost all interest.

My interest perked up considerably when Ford popped a version of their Vee-six 3-litre engine under the bonnet of the most expensive Capris and gave them some real go. Those who had tried the cars did report that in the wet the power was a bit tricky and that while the acceleration was fine, the car was undergeared but it still seemed interesting.

Not long after the announcement of the "big" Capri it became clear that Ford were going to race them and that meant they were going to come into direct conflict with BMW's 3-litre Coupes. At this stage most British people were probably unaware that while British Capris were made at Halewood, there was another assembly line at Ford's Cologne plant, and that German Capri sales had fallen away after a promising start.

The Capri competition programme was master-minded by Ford Cologne and they chose the biggest of the German family of vee-six engines — the 2,520cc — for their racing Capris. At the time it was widely suggested that this was a far better unit than the British engine but, as we shall see, the "Essex" 3-litre would come into use later.

For readers who are not familiar with motor-racing based loosely on production cars I should explain that there is generally a requirement that the racing cars should comply with a pedigree based upon a production model, a minimum number of which should have been built for sale to the general public. This "pedigree" is achieved by a process known as homologation and as this is not a perfect world the minimum production run figures are not always met and the model itself is very often invented to suit racing requirements.

So that the Capri could pose a threat to the BMWs, Ford homologated the RS2600 as a basic ingredient for their racing programme. An artificially low weight was "engineered" and fuel injection gave the car a claimed 150 brake horsepower.

The RS 2600 served its purpose, but BMW outpaced Ford on the tracks with power and aerodynamic advantages. To win any sort of advantage Ford needed to homologate a bigger engined car with air dams and spoilers and that gave rise to the RS3100.

The RS3100 announced in 1974 was, to put it bluntly, a bit of a fraud. Outwardly it had considerable cosmetic appeal — like the RS2600 it sat on wide alloy wheels and suspension alterations made it about an inch lower than normal Capris. Nearly ten years later we have become used to spoilers and air dams but in 1974 such items definitely gave the new performance Capri a "racing" look. There were, however, some pretty obvious disappointments.

Mechanically the engine was just a long stroke, bored-out version of the standard Carburated 3-litre and in terms of power and performance the new RS was no better than the old fuel injected RS2600. Even the impressive looking competition style reclining seats which had been standard on the earlier RS were now an extra — what did the customers feel about this "let-down"?

The RS2600 was always offered to the public in left-hand drive form and although about 4,000 were eventually built, most stayed on the Continent; by contrast the British-made RS3100 was aimed much more at the British market. Its announcement followed an energy crisis and the imposition of blanket speed limits had just preceded the announcement of the three-door Mk II generation of Capris — not surprisingly sales were poor. Having said that it must be added that despite what the governing bodies of motor sport may have been told Ford made very few RS3100's — 200 would be nearer the mark than 1000!

It has been easy to predict that, sooner or later, the preservation enthusiasts would take an interest in the post-1968 Capri. Obviously that interest was going to start with, and centre around, the performance versions so I have recently driven two very entertaining examples.

The first was Joe Callaghan's device which is well-known (or notorious) in the Eastbourne area. Now this car is reputed to have started life as an RS3100. The story goes on to suggest that it was then taken to AVO (what used to be Ford's small division devoted to limited production runs and one-offs) to be dressed up to look like a Ford of Cologne racing Capri. That "dressing-up" did not extend to the interior but did include massively flared wheel arches covering 11 inch wide front wheels and 15 inch wide rears! Were the mechanics altered? Here I can only guess but it may well have been bored out to 3.2-litres and I suspect some camshaft and porting improvements.

(Continued)

The security pins for the bonnet are not original but the four halogen headlamps are correct and offer enormous advantages over the rectangular lights of "normal" Capris.

Nowadays we take spoilers and air dams for granted on some quite modest production cars — in 1974 such aerodynamic aids were most unusual.

(Continued)

The car certainly goes rather well. I had been warned that it was pretty vicious but I found that it was very flexible with a smooth flow of power from fairly low down but

The standard RS3100 may just have been a bored out 3-litre with minor alterations producing 148 bhp at the flywheel — but Tony Whiting's example has been modified to produce over 160 bhp at the rear wheels!

Within less than half a mile I had discovered that in town Tony's outwardly very neat and tidy but not all that spectacular Capri can only accept third gear when the traffic clears or the engine hunts and snatches. Give it the chance to run a little freer and at

3,500 rpm the exhaust gives you a warning — a few more revs and the exhaust note becomes a violent crack and the car fairly leaps forward. You have guessed it — Tony has not got a standard RS3100 either!

Before he bought the Ford, Tony had a very nice Datsun 240Z with one of the Samurai conversions and he had become accustomed to more performance than the standard 148 bhp, 124 mph RS3100 can give. While thinking about this problem a day and a half after buying the car it obliged Tony by running a big end and an engine overhaul was dictated.

Tony decided that he would use this as the ideal opportunity to turn as average RS3100 into a very good one. He sent the engine to the tuning specialists, Burtons, with instructions

no sudden "cam" effect.

I believe that the wheels are far too wide for road use so that it would like to wander about at speed on a dry road and is probably frightening on a wet road. There is considerable kick back at the wheel and the brakes are adequate rather than really good so it adds up to a car with plenty of go that needs a bit of care to get the best from it.

In search of something nearer the true RS3100 I then asked Tony Whiting if I might sample his version. Leaving Tony and his partner, Peter Smee, to run PS Panels — The Kent Stag Centre — I cautiously edged Tony's car out of the clogged streets of Plumstead, London SE18.

FORD CAPRI RS 3100

Look below the air cleaner and you will see the four choke Holley carb. on a Swaymar inlet manifold, but the camshaft, porting and exhaust manifolds are all non-standard.

The interior of the RS3100 was almost identical to that of the standard 3-litre Capri but Tony Whiting's has the optional reclining seats.

to produce something "a bit different but not too far out" while he attended to the body and running gear.

The engine capacity was left standard but the cylinder heads were considerably improved, a steel camshaft with matching cam-followers to Burton's own spec was fitted and a Swaymar inlet manifold was fitted with a four choke Holley 390 CFM carb on top of it. Instead of the standard claimed 148 bhp DIN at the flywheel a trip to a rolling road has revealed that the run-in engine now produces 167 bhp at the rear wheels — that is some difference!

In town Tony's Capri is not a great deal of fun because although the car is reasonably tractable it is not all that brisk — unless the revs rise and once that happens you want open spaces. As a result delivery vans leave you in their wake. Given room to breath the Capri improves and when the opportunity arises can *really* be launched.

The effect is pretty spectacular. With a bark that does not sound at all Ford-like the car comes alive. Other cars that appeared to be accelerating well are transformed into stationary objects that have to be steered around!

Sales literature referred to the car as an RS3100 but there were no special badges — probably because they would have been very expensive for such a small production run. The car could only be obtained from Ford's Rallye Sport dealers.

Obviously it pays to use the power cautiously to avoid exciting noises announcing to anyone who can hear that you are going to break a speed limit or two in the very near future if you have not already done so.

We took the Capri to a quiet road with little traffic, a good surface and sweeping bends and let the car have its head. The results are very, very impressive but I did discover that the shove in the back as the power comes in can be a little unwelcome if you let it happen halfway through a corner. A single standing start, by

no means a violent one was all I needed to accept Tony's hand timed 0-60 mph times of 6.3 to 6.5 seconds — I am pretty well convinced it can be done.

Handling and steering are good without being inspired and while the brakes do their job, they are not fantastic. What it really comes down to is that if you want a Ferrari or a Porsche you have to buy one. The RS Capris are very potent, in modified form they are even more so but they are still Capris.

By coincidence during the course of sampling both Capris it emerged that both Joe Callaghan and Tony Whiting are contemplating selling their Capris to finance their businesses. Both men seemed genuinely reluctant to do so and I can understand why, but they will probably go to appreciative homes — it certainly looks as if the interest in performance Capris is beginning to take off. □

Joe Callaghan's Capri is said to be an RS3100 Capri which the original owner specified should be fitted with the spectacular Ford Cologne competition wheel arches. They give the Capri a striking "wasp-waisted" appearance.

The Cologne look-alike proved to be much more manageable than its appearance would suggest. The wide wheels encourage the front wheels to snatch over bumps but the engine delivers considerable performance over a wide range.

Whilst writing this article I made constant references to two excellent books on Capris — both by Jeremy Walton. They were:- Capri, published by Haynes and Capri Volume 3 of the MRP Collector's Guide to the Sporting Capris.

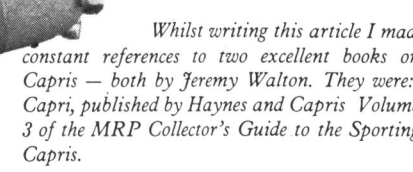

QUICKEST CAPRI APPEALS TO FAST LADIES . . .

Jerry Sloniger drives the Ford Capri Turbo which, in Germany, has been snapped up by fräuleins with a taste for speed!

LIKE DAME Nellie Melba, the Ford Capri seems determined to make a career out of farewell performances — with each new variation more extravagant than the last "final" version. It is no great secret that Ford won't design another car for this Capri class, but that is a very different thing to saying that the current version has reached the end of the (sorry) road.

On the contrary: the very latest Capri from Cologne — called Turbo — came from the Ford Motorsport department close on the heels of the 2.8i, itself briefly billed as the most powerful production car Ford of Europe had ever built. With its 130 mph potential, the 2.8i is no laggard — but it hasn't held the throne long either.

Of course, there won't be nearly as many Capri Turbos made: perhaps 300 or 400 for a start, then as many more as the market demands, all lefthand drive — although the Germans are currently toying with the idea of selling the car in the UK as well. But nor is this final fling merely a homologation exercise.

In fact, Ford sees the car as a road offshoot of the works-backed Zakspeed racers, a publicity bonus if you like, but not as a future Group B competition car as such. Of the first 50 already delivered — they're available only through special Ford RS dealers — over a quarter, surprisingly, have been bought by women. The cars are supplied in plain white for dealers and customers to add their own stripes and shadings.

The new super-Ford draws heavily on the 2.8i. Ford had originally planned a 2.3 turbo with wing flares and gutted muffler to replace the limited-edition 3.0, but by the time it was ready the 2.8i had appeared. Although the Injection was endowed with a little less power than the blown 2.3, it was just as quick as a result of its reduced frontal area and narrower tyres.

Ford Motorsport quickly shifted to supercharging on the 2.8, but used the Granada carburetter version because turbocharger technology with the carburetter (blowing into a sealed airbox) already existed in the form of Michael May's turbos — Michael May being the man behind the Jaguar HE engine. As a side advantage, this method reduces turbine temperatures by some 450 to 500 degrees. About all that's left of the May kit in the final version is the regulator, however, and that component has been improved in quality. Ford even changed the blower from a KKK to an AiResearch model.

Ford engineers are very coy about turbo pressure, apart from saying the figure is 0.38 bar until the 1,000-mile service, when the pop-off spring is changed. Maximum power of 188 bhp is achieved with (probably) 0.48 bar, the official figure for one-off registration in Germany. That is produced at 5500 rpm, with a steep power curve and turbocharging which comes on stream at about 2700 rpm. The torque peak of 199 lb ft is also high at 4500 rpm.

With only a marginal weight increase and the same gearbox and rear axle ratios as a 2.8i (although a 75 per cent limited slip diff is optional), the car is slightly faster at the 6300 rpm red line — there is no rev limiter — with a claimed 133 mph. Part of the added power, incidentally, comes from the gutted exhaust they devised originally to gain 7 bhp in the special 3.0 Capri. Despite the exhaust, maximum noise has been kept down to 79dB, which falls within the ECE-prescribed limit.

Apart from a new manifold and nitrided crankshaft, the engine internals are standard 2.8-litre Ford V6 components except for the head gasket and a vibration damper on the crankshaft.

In like manner, brakes for the 3.0 Special had come from Ford Motorsport's bin and are also used on the 2.8i. The springs and dampers are from the 2.8i, with a slightly thicker front anti-roll bar using lowered mounting points, a common RS anti-dive trick. With wider wheels they normally move the steering box forward, as is done here, to counter weight shifts under braking; Ford offer 6½-inch steel rims for high-speed cruising or 7½-inch alloy rims for ultimate cornering, with 250/60 VR 14 Phoenix tyres (developed in conjunction with Ford) in both cases.

The RS department doesn't bother about wind tunnels. Engineers simply take a base car out on a still, dry day, run it in both directions, then add aerodynamic aids. First came the soft tail spoiler, whose wing part breaks loose under loads in excess of 45 lb as demanded by German federal regulations. That gave so much rear downforce that they added a front air dam (glassfibre, like the flared wings, but in pebble finish to ward off stones).

Inside there is a set of special seats, the only four-spoke wheel fitted to any road Capri (so far) and a standard facia without even a boost gauge, which Ford boss Bottger believes mislead more than they help.

Like all special-order RS cars through the years, this Capri is manufactured on the usual production lines, with both engine and body (the latter with flares added by Zakspeed purely as a supplier)

moving down their respective assembly routes. Thereafter every car is driven up to 25 miles for a final check, without the air dam to restrain the test team; besides, the cars cannot be loaded on to the transporter with the dam mounted in position.

We had the dam mounted and went much further but were unable to check the car's maxima since it was scheduled to be delivered to a Ford director that same afternoon.

The Turbo's handling underlines *Motor*'s findings with the 2.8i, with a ride that tends to be a little sharper over ripples and with good bite into bends. The Ford engineers are rightfully proud of how softly the turbo comes in, but another gear would make driving more restful in speed limit-free Germany. Perhaps the chief advantage over the 2.8i is the Turbo badge by your door handle, but it is also nice to feel closer to the winning team racers too.

Ford is right about one thing — with the long nose and the low roofline the Capri would never be an effective rally weapon. It could serve well, however, as a crowd- and driver-pleasing national-class racer in a couple of years. The company will certainly be selling more than that initial 400.

Prominent turbo, with the all-important RS badge to indicate pedigree

THE X FACTOR

Xciting, xuberant, xtrovert, xpensive . . . Ford's X pack 3-litre Capri is all of these

In a few days time, the Capri will be 11 years old. In the course of the decade just passed, it has undergone three distinct facelifts and its simple, even crude, mechanical specification has been engineered and developed into reliable competence.

Nevertheless, 11 years is a comparatively long time for a model such as this to remain in production, especially a model which comes from a multi-national whose fundamental concepts of merchandising involve planned obsolescence; so it's fair to assume that while the Capri is not a mainstream success in the Cortina/Escort 250 000 plus units-per-annum mould, it's sufficiently successful and creates a suitable enough image in the market place for Ford to continue selling it.

It has of course long since repaid the investment on its tooling costs, since it shares almost its entire running gear with other models in Ford's strongly communal range, and thus today, the Capri represents good value in the image or coupé market.

For a car conceived in the aftermath of the Mustang's impact on America, the Capri has stood the test of time well, and for that, one must look both to the professional competence of Ford engineering and the flair of styling and marketing departments. The Capri still doesn't provide acceptable seating for four people and its luggage space is limited with the rear seats in place, but that's not the important thing for coupé, and particularly Capri, buyers, for in terms of performance-per-pound-sterling (particularly in 3-litre form) the Capri is virtually impossible to beat.

The top of the range 3-litre is now the only Ford passenger vehicle to retain the services of the Essex block V6, and doubtless, in the course of time, it too will be swopped over to German 2.8 litre power (all Capris are now made in Germany in any case). In the meantime, the 3-litre provides enough power, and notably mid and low speed torque, to make the Capri about the fastest thing on four wheels that you can buy for under £5500. With 138 claimed bhp at 5000rpm and an impressive 174lb/ft of torque developed at 3000rpm and maintained usefully throughout the limited rev range (there's no need to take the standard engine beyond 4000rpm since it doesn't appear to relish the experience and performance is not improved) this top of the line boulevard cruiser will manage about 120mph and, in S guise, it at least handles with a certain amount of verve in view of the fact that the rear axle is still located only by its semi-elliptic rear springs! That's what I call development!

So what happens when one introduces an X certificate into a package already recommended for adults? My recollections of 3-litre Capris only go back about 12 months to the days when young Terry Grimwood, sometime race driver, dilletante, and these days resident of Los Angeles, possessed a 3000S as his editorial transport.

I remember that car with a strange mixture of indifference tinged by nostalgia. The uncertain power steering (TG loved it!) didn't seem to me to promote much confidence; the brakes were a joke (but then it's conceivable that Mr. G could have cooked them heartily on several occasions) and in wet or slippery conditions, it was, as expected, a salutory embarrassment.

Cumbersome, crude, and lacking in finesse it may have been; yet it was also at times, fun to drive. It may not have been nearly as quick point-to-point, as an RS2000, and certainly it drank far more fuel in the process; (about 18mpg as I recall). Yet sitting behind that old V6, letting it slug away in top (often the only certain gear, this, as the selector would persist in bending) certainly had its moments.

Overall though, you could say that I am not a Capri afficionado (whereas I could easily get excited about a Dodge Challenger R/T, a *real* Z28, and a handful of other proper muscle cars – RIP) so when we got our hands on Ford's X-pack 3-litre demonstrator a few months ago, I was especially interested to see whether it fulfilled the genuine road burner image which seemed a little veneered with the standard car.

X-packs were first conceived in 1977, in the aftermath of the closure of AVO, to broaden the appeal of the entire Ford range by creating the availability of a personalised car, and also offering Rallye Sport dealers a highly profitable alternative to the relatively specialised competition car market – lucrative though that certainly was (and is).

The idea represents nothing new in marketing terms; it's been a fact of life in America for almost as long as anyone can remember, with the notable difference being that most Americans can personalise their cars with almost anything ex-works – *except* genuine performance parts.

Broadly speaking, X-packs divide themselves into three main areas: engine tuning; chassis modification, and cosmetic/bodywork revisions. Within these three broad categories the owner can specify as much or as little as he wishes/can afford, and the steps that can be taken with a customer's car are not inter-dependent on each other; ie: one can order big wheels and glassfibre arches without anyone so much as going near the engine. Or then again, the customer

THE X FACTOR

could also go for a 200bhp wolf in sheep's clothing.

Personally, I think that from the customer's point-of-view, the secret of X-pack success is to find a good Rallye Sport dealer, for none of the work is going to be cheap, and when one is shelling out the kind of money involved in such transactions, it's good to retain some confidence in the extra-curricular expertise of one's dealer.

The best Rallye Sport dealers should select themselves fairly easily. If they are involved in any active competition then that is in itself an encouraging pointer; but a few well chosen questions, either at the parts desk or a look around the workshop; together with a chat in a showroom; should rapidly reveal to you the general standard of competence or otherwise of the establishment.

Meanwhile, out on the road, the comprehensively X-packed 3-litre is certainly a dramatic machine, both from a visual as well as a performance point-of-view. The car we borrowed had been prepared in Ford's service garage at Brentford to provide a mobile demonstration of X-pack versatility, and not for any over-riding cost considerations.

Thus I found myself sitting in a car which had started its life retailing at £5400, but which now emerged on the road at well over over £9000.

The idea behind the creation of this machine was not to go for outright performance and a consequently peaky engine but rather to endow the car with increased performance without sacrificing any of its more endearing driveability.

Work started on this project in the good old days of five star fuel, so high compression pistons were initally fitted, but with the rapid disappearance of the former, the engine was rebuilt with a standard bottom end (9:1 compression) and a standard camshaft. X-pack larger inlet and exhaust valves have been incorporated in the heads, along with a triple twin-choke downdraught Weber 42DCNF kit and electric fuel pump to meet the increased fuel demand. (X-pack also offers a bigger than standard single twin choke device as an alternative.) A special headgasket, as used in G1 racing, a comparatively minor session of head work which did not apparently involve polishing, and a high fin density radiator (all £200 of it!) complete the engine package. The result of these comparatively minor revisions is about 170bhp (DIN) at 5500rpm, with 195lb/ft of torque developed at 4500rpm.

Two hundred brake horsepower is easily possible with this engine, but for the reasons stated earlier, was ruled out on this particular car.

Modifications to suspension involve harder front springs (145lb as opposed to 120) and an anti-dive kit which lowers the angle of the anti-roll bar; all of which has the effect of lowering the car by about an inch. Bilstein gas dampers are fitted all round, while rear springs are standard spec. The rear axle received a noisy but thoroughly entertaining LSD, and the brakes, something of a weak point with Capris, are beefed up with 10.3in ventilated front discs and larger swept area Granada calipers. Pads and linings were left standard since the larger calipers appear to make DS11s superfluous for road use. However don't expect more than about 6000 miles from a set of pads if you drive the car hard.

A set of extremely smart RS 7½in rim alloy wheels, shod with 205-60 x 13 Pirelli P6s completes the chassis side (the rims will take 225 tyre sizes without problem and seven-inch rims can be fitted without the

need to alter the bodywork) while the latest glassfibre front and rear wheel arch extensions, plus front air dam, complete the cosmetic picture.

The result (depending of course on the quality of the glassfibre work) is a strikingly aggressive yet svelte-looking machine which has few equals in the art of attention-getting. As a poser's wagon alone, this car must be a match for even such exotic ego-gratifiers/eye catchers as the Porsche Turbo, and since the Capri concept is all about image anyway, some people will doubtless be able to justify the substantial extra outlay on this fact alone. To put it bluntly, if you want to get noticed, then this car is a *must*. The latest sculptured arches as opposed to the chiselled Spa types which were formerly available, not only look a perfect integral part of the car, (rather than a bolt-on goody), they will undoubtedly stand the test of time better, since the glassfibre reaches up to the top of the wings and hence makes for a far better and longer lasting finish. These revisions should minimise the risk of an appearance of unsightly cracks between original metal and new glassfibre bodywork.

How much labour time is involved in the fitment of those arches? Hard for me to say; but 80 hours sounds about right, since there is a lot of metal to be cut away and the overall final finish is everything. Add that 80 hours (at say, £8.50 per hour) onto the list of prices at the end of the feature. (Gulp!)

Two excellent Recaro seats (a £100 option with which most S Capris are fitted these days), completes the build.

A car which costs you around £9500 and which shouts performance and masculinity would be an embarrassment if it didn't go. Happily there is no cause for alarm here, as we managed to record a genuine 130mph (this Capri will manage a rather breathless 6000rpm in fourth!) with 100mph coming up in well under 25 seconds and a 0–60 mph time of 7.6 seconds . . . figures which are more than enough to put this Capri in the upper echelon performance bracket, and which are achieved relatively noisily but without fuss.

Road behaviour is also vastly improved, perhaps due as much as anything to the remarkable qualities of Pirelli's P6 tyres

which generate adhesion and steering response which a year or two ago would have seemed quite ridiculous on a Capri. It's virtually impossible to unstick the car in the dry, and the car tracks accurately and safely with far more feel and stability than the standard machine can manage.

On a test track, this Capri is not at its best, since understeer goes on remorselessly building-up, as the speed rises from quick to absurd, but on the road, the machine's point-to-point cross-country abilities are most impressive since one doesn't have to try that hard to set new standards – it's all very civilised.

At low speeds and in towns, the LSD can be annoyingly obtrusive however, and one wonders whether its advantages in terms of traction really outweigh the extra cost and nuisance value. Again, we suspect that those P6s are doing much of the good work.

Fuel consumption can drop to around 15mpg, especially with *CCC*'s leaden clogs at the controls, but then the 3-litre Capri was never brilliant in this respect and one can't really expect genuine economy from three litres and three large downdraught Webers. Despite the modifications, the brakes remain curiously unimpressive.

Is it worth the money? In strict terms the answer is no. There are some very sophisticated vehicles on the market at this price, and the Capri will never be one of them. However, it has real character, tremendous gusto, and it could sell on looks alone.

You may not be able to convert a sow's ear, but you can certainly live in peace with one. **PN** ∎

Cost of Parts (excluding labour and VAT).	
Triple carburettor kit	£499
Inlet valves (6)	£29
Exhaust valves (6)	£31
Head gasket (2)	£39
Freeflow exhaust system	£147
LSD	£229
Ventilated disc brake kit	£189
Anti-dive kit	£73
Front Bilsteins (2) (struts less springs)	£143
Rear Bilstein dampers (2)	£47
Front springs (2)	£31
RS wheels (5)	£376
Wheel nuts	£15
Radiator	£196
Wheel arches and front spoiler kit, in primer	£175
Total. excluding labour	£1990

WHAT CAR? LONG TERM TESTS

Long distance runners

Ford Capri: three litre performance is normally expensive, but our 3.0S has impressed us with its low running costs

A V6 THREE litre engine producing 138 bhp, installed in the pretty Ford Capri bodyshell has to add up to an impressive package. And it does. Our driver has now covered 33,000 miles and it certainly does not seem that the car is now three years old.

In March 1977 we took delivery of a Capri 3.0S which at the time cost £3509 and represented remarkable value for money as a very fast and practical three-door coupe which lacked only the exclusivity of similar cars costing up to twice the amount. Today's equivalent revamped Capri costs £5574, but still is good value for money.

Three years on, the Capri is departing from our test fleet after a somewhat hectic career in the hands of a driver who has always seemed to be needed somewhere else in a hurry. In our major report at 12,000 miles we used the headline "Learning about Ford reliability" and this lesson has continued right up to 33,000 miles despite its hard life.

Up until 12,000 miles only two small things had gone wrong with the car and they seem almost too trivial to mention — a blown fuse for the heated rear window and a faulty reversing light switch.

During this time it also became obvious that we were not going to

have much expenditure on engine oil, for in that time we used only three pints of oil.

The subsequent mileage up to our last **What Car?** fleet round-up has proved to be equally reliable although we reported that the brakes had developed a tendency to pull to the left. They still do, but as we said before the problem is so small that we have never deemed it necessary to pull the car out of its busy working schedule for attention to this elusive fault.

Servicing has always been straightforward and reasonably priced although the relatively short interval of 6000 means that our car always seems to be coming up to its appointed hour of attention.

In fact Ford recommend that this car has a small service at 3000 miles which amounts to an oil change and general tune up but in the light of experience we do not feel that this is absolutely essential unless the car feels slightly "flat".

The latest major service was carried out slightly overdue at 26,000 miles by Pippbrook of Dorking at a cost of £37, thus again proving that running a three-litre sports coupe need not be too expensive. Included in the cost of this service was the fitting of a pair of air horns.

We have commented before

that the brakes on our Capri have become slightly spongy over its lifetime. This became worse and while the driver had pointed this out when the Capri was in for service, he put it back into Pipp-brook of Dorking for specific attention to this problem. After checking the system Pippbrook came up with no solution and told our owner that this was a common problem with Capris and charged us £7. The driver was not very happy with this diagnosis so he decided to go elsewhere. Another garage revealed that the master cylinder in the system was leaking. Once this was replaced at a cost of £50, the brakes were perfect and have given no trouble since, ingoring the pull to the left, that is.

The last time the Capri saw the inside of a garage workshop was for a quick tune up at around 30,000 miles, when the owner reported that the car generally felt "flat". The cost was £29.

Apart from the problem with the brakes our Capri has been a model of reliability and from this point of view alone has been a pleasure to own. Only now, after 33,000 miles, is the car beginning to look anything less than brand new with an odd stone chip here and there. Both the front MacPherson struts have softened up slightly as seems to be the case

with all Fords, but handling has not been unduly affected.

The 33,000 miles with our Capri 3 litre has proved that running such a car need not necessarily be such an expensive business. Insurance is obviously going to be high — it is in group six, but apart from that, running costs can be kept to a reasonable level. Petrol consumption seems to be very much what a driver makes of it; our car has given 25 mpg but on occasions has sunk as low as 16 mpg. Such is the case when a driver has control of 138 bhp under his right foot and can enjoy his motoring.

The costs
Price when new: £3509
Resale value (Feb 1980): £3100

Fuel and oil consumption
Petrol: 33,000 miles at 23.5 mpg (4 star): £1266.85
Oil: 4000 miles per pint £4.12

Servicing
Depreciation: £409
Petrol and oil: £1270.97
Servicing: £329.14
Insurance (3 years): £350
Road Tax (3 years): £140.
Total: £2499.11

Cost per mile: 7.6p

*Insurance quote is for the "What Car? man", a 35-year-old married man with two children, living in London. He has a full no claims discount

TWO AND SIX

The three litre Capri a classic? WM Developments think it is and they've developed engine and chassis modifications to make it even more desirable. Graham Jones investigated and discovered a company capable of tackling anything from a Jaguar engine rebuild to the construction of a powerboat racing motor.

On an engine stand directly in front of me sat a massive 7.4 litre Firebird Trans Am motor, modified to give an estimated 450bhp and awaiting installation, while a two-stroke Mercury V6 outboard motor destined for a Formula One class powerboat was being assembled on a nearby workbench by former Brian Hart and Andy Dawson engine builder, Mark Perry.

In a far corner nestled a 3.8 Jaguar engine and gearbox, soon to be dismantled, completely refurbished and reassembled ready for fitting into a Lynx D-type Jaguar replica.

Stacked neatly on shelves in every available corner of the shop were assorted cranks, pistons, rods, BDA and Jaguar cylinder heads, a four-cylinder Honda racing engine, and several small kart motors.

Had I stumbled accidently into some engine builder's paradise? No, only WM Developments, now occupying the Lambolle Place premises which formerly housed Dawson Auto Developments before the latter's move north to Milton Keynes.

W.M. Developments was formed as the result of a partnership between engine development engineer Martin Murphy and ace spannerman, Steve Whitmore, with former GP driver, John Miles, as a "sleeping" partner in the business. Both Martin and Steve, ex-Hexagon employees, have been heavily involved with racing projects in the past; Martin's career having included spells as agent for Swiss Morand F5000 engines and as engine man for John Middleton during the time he was running Formula Two cars for Derek Bell and the late Carlos Pace, as well as a Formula One effort for Henri Pescarolo.

Other notable achievements included running a Formula Atlantic car for Mike Franey in 1975-1976, and developing and racing some very quick Komet and Parilla engined karts. He was also responsible for developing the well-received BMW 528 turbo conversion which was to be marketed by David Prophet Cars.

The subtleties of engine efficiency are obviously of considerable interest to Martin, and when he moved into the former Dawson premises 18 months ago, it was agreed that he would look after the engine side of the business while Steve would look after the servicing and garage part of the operation. This combination has worked very well, for if Martin builds up a motor for a customer, Steve is then able to fit it to the car, thus offering a package service.

They were soon joined by Mark Perry, Dawson's number one mechanic, who had found that commuting from north London to Milton Keynes every day was not exactly his cup of tea. He was a valuable addition to the little team and his wide experience with such diverse projects as the Attila sports car, the Unipower GT and the development of a 16-valve Imp engine meant he was an ideal choice as mechanic and engine assembly expert.

Which brings us handily back to John Miles, for he approached the little band of enthusiasts with an idea for a 3.2 litre Capri.

He knew it was possible since he had seen a prototype engine during his time at Racing Services, when it was installed in Chris Craft's road car.

The heart of the conversion is a long-throw crankshaft which is ground up from a Ford blank to give a longer stroke, and in combination with a .060in. cylinder overbore, produces a displacement of 3196cc (bore and stroke go up from 93.67 x 72.42mm to 95.19 x 74.84mm).

The project was put largely in Martin's hands, and being a great Weslake fan, he altered the inlet ports to create more swirl while the standard carburettor, with smaller accelerator pump jet, was retained. He freely admits that many of the modifications which now go to make up this 'kit' were thought up as he went along, and are aimed at engine efficiency. Taken in combination, items such as float chamber level, compression ratio, piston-to-deck height, camshaft and ignition timing can liberate considerable amounts of horsepower if they are skilfully manipulated – just ask any exponent of Group One saloon car racing!

The resultant power output of 155bhp at 5000rpm may not seem like a staggering increase when compared with the standard

car's 138bhp, but the figure which really tells the tale is the (approximately) 200lb/ft of torque generated in the mid-range. It brings new meaning to the phrase "tractability in the gears".

Martin Murphy on the theory behind these V6 engine modifications: "The three litre motor is very efficient to begin with, and basically all we have done is tidy it up. If Ford had the chance to do everything by hand, then I think they would have arrived at much the same sort of finished product as we did.

"We just clean up the engines and make them as efficient as they can possibly be with the specification we have set. I think we have succeeded to a large degree since the fuel consumption, at around 24mpg, is significantly better than either the standard 3000S or the X-Pack version. It means the engine is making better use of each pound of fuel that's used."

At this point, WM Developments had an excellent engine in search of an equally good car, and this was where John Miles' highly regarded sorting abilities came to the fore. The target he set himself was "to get the Capri to work on low profile tyres without sacrificing the ride – that is, what the manufacturer would aim for in ride and handling if it were doing the project."

The concept of the car is as a GT rather than a harsh road racer, like the X-Pack Capri. The aim was to achieve refined, smooth performance in combination with a good ride and satisfying handling, which is much more easily said than done. Miles again: "Nearly all low profile tyres affect ride detrimentally to some extent, especially when you have a clunky axle and loads of unsprung weight. The effort has gone into getting a car that rides yet remains ultimately 'chuckable'."

John worked long and hard on the problem, trying numerous combinations of springs, dampers and tyres, to the point where it is now more or less at the specification in which it will be offered to potential customers.

Tyres are Pirelli P6s fitted on some very attractive 14in. diameter Minilites. Suspension changes involve the fitting of specially valved Koni struts at the front and a set of new Koni gas-filled dampers at the rear. The standard 3000S 22mm anti-roll bar was deemed to be stiff enough for the job in hand (the standard Capri item is 19mm), although it has been modified to prevent the possibility of fouling the rear axle on full droop, which in turn causes the inside rear wheel to lift under power in a bend, thus losing traction.

Brakes are the standard issue item fitted with harder Mintex pads at the front to increase fade-resistance.

In fact, Martin has a preference for a slightly different rear suspension arrangement which has been tried on the Capri. This involves the fitting of single-leaf springs in place of the standard multi-leaf springs, the result being a slight reduction in ride quality but a significant improvement in traction since wheel spin under heavy cornering loads is virtually eliminated – one of the most common complaints heard from sporting-minded motorists in relation to 3-litre Capris.

These single-leaf springs are also set to retain the standard car's ride height (as opposed to the units fitted to the RS3100) since both John and Martin feel that any lowering of the car would upset the excellent ride qualities that have been developed.

The only remaining area for modification is the bodywork, and with that thought in mind, a stylist is currently looking at the Capri with a view to cleaning up the front and sides of the car, thereby (hopefully) further improving the high speed stability and petrol consumption. Such modifications would probably involve the addition of a spoiler at the front, a cleaning-up of the sides, and the removal of "that nasty little lip" at the rear.

The stylist concerned has been given a fairly free hand with the project, since it is also aimed at creating a more visually acceptable package, John and Martin being all too aware that nice as a 'Q'-car may be,

the customer who must be persuaded to part with his hard-earned cash frequently wishes to see some external justification for his non-standard vehicle.

Whatever the psychology of it all, by mid-winter the body bits will have been made which can then be adapted to either a Mk2 or Mk3 bodyshell.

Suspension components and exchange motors are available now, the only condition on the latter being that all the major parts must be serviceable. The conversion can be carried out on either a new or secondhand car, although the cost to carry out the necessary work on the latter will be somewhat greater since certain worn components must naturally be replaced.

Having dealt with the technical spec, then, what was the Capri like to drive? That's the best bit about driving modified cars really – you can talk about the mechanics of the alterations for many (and often enjoyable) hours, but the bottom line is: have they actually created an improved motor car?

The answer in this case is an unequivocal and resounding 'yes.' John Miles set himself some difficult targets in the handling and ride departments, and his reputation as a sorter is verified by the fact that he has achieved excellent results with both.

Between the time at which we drove the Capri originally and photographed it a few days later, the front springs were changed and the front damping rate altered, making the turn-in and steering even more precise, again without any noticeable sacrifice in ride.

The first thing you notice about the car as you steer it out onto the main road is the amazing flexibility of the engine – so much so, that it almost renders the gearbox superfluous since it will pull from such low speeds in third and fourth gears without even the slightest hesitation. On the other hand, if you feel like a spot of the old accelerative G-forces, it can be taken up to a self-enforced 6000rpm redline with very satisfying results, the icing on the cake being that restrained, but growing howl from the twin exhausts.

We didn't get involved in any rubber-burning standing starts in deference to the 40 000-mile-old propshaft which, by the sounds emanating from that direction, was somewhat tired of the abuse it had received at the hands of numerous testers.

Martin's claim of a 0 to 60mph time of about eight seconds seemed just about right, while a quick prod on the accelerator had the speedometer needle up to an indicated 120mph very quickly indeed. In fact, it was so entertaining to revel in this engine's performance that one could easily overlook the suspension modifications, and that is probably a true sign of just how effective they are.

The ride was quite excellent, being firm

without any sign of harshness, while the handling allowed easily induced oversteer at the limit – the "ultimate chuckability" mentioned earlier by Miles. Steering and turn-in seemed very precise with the front suspension set-up as originally tested, but the second time around, with the altered dampers and springs, it felt (subjectively, you understand) just that bit sharper, the steering quality on uneven surfaces being notably more reassuring.

So what does all this automotive wonderfulness cost? On a new car, the cost of the WM conversion is £863, while on a second-hand car, where numerous worn items will have to be replaced, the price rises to around £1210 or so. These prices may seem at first glance to be rather large sums of money, but consider that the X-Pack conversion, offered by Ford, adds £2164.42 to the price of a 3000S, not including the glassfibre wheel arch extensions and front air dam. . . .

Admittedly the X-Pack specification includes items such as a triple carburettor kit, high capacity radiator and a limited slip differential, which the WM car doesn't have, but since the latter is able to achieve similar (and frequently better) performance for considerably less money with better fuel consumption, surely the comparison is a valid one.

If you fancy the single-leaf-spring rear suspension specification as part of the package, the fitted cost would be £411.22 plus the dreaded VAT. That price includes four dampers, a pair of single-leaf springs, a shackle kit and labour charges. The most expensive single item is the springs, which account for £125 of the total.

As we drifted back toward London, the engine burbling away contentedly, another question presented itself: why convert a car which is undoubtedly in the final stages of its production-line career?

Martin explained: "It is perhaps slightly convoluted thinking on our part, but we firmly believe that the Capri will become a classic machine. Given that there has been a shift of popularity from open cars to GT-type vehicles, the price and performance of the 3-litre Capri really makes it the successor to the E-Type Jaguar.

"What we are hoping is that when people need an engine rebuild – possibly at 40 000 to 50 000 miles – they will consider putting in a 3.2 litre motor, so they don't change the way the car drives at all, but obtain a sensible increase in performance and fuel economy."

After enthusing over the car with Martin for a short while, conversation turned to the future of WM Developments, and he explained that the company did not want to fall into the trap of *having* to modify cars – that is, having to convert a car against their better judgement: "We want to be able to pick and choose the cars we work on; otherwise, we can't give what I feel is a decent service to the customer."

His eventual ambition, he confided, was to own a firm like Weslake which could undertake advanced research and development work on behalf of motor manufacturers. Being a realist, however, Martin is aware that he will have to continue earning a living by servicing customers' cars for quite a few years to come, and restrict himself to modifying production engines and overseeing the odd racing project.

Still, there has to be a future for someone whose winter project this year is a complete rebuild of a Rolls Royce Merlin aero engine. ∎

MILES
Behind the Wheel

Low profile Capri...

. . . . or one man's struggle to make a mass produced car grip, handle and ride on low profile tyres

IT DOESN'T really need me to tell you that the low profile tyre has been a godsend to the manufacturer of powerful or sporting cars. As the engine men have provided more power, so more grip has been required. To maintain, let alone improve, handling, braking, and roadholding, more rubber is needed on the road and more stability in the tyre. Any such tyre has to work more or less within existing bodywork clearances, and with current thinking on steering geometries (particularly on front-wheel-drive cars) incorporating little or no king pin offset, much of the outer suspension linkage and, of course, the brakes, need to be tucked inside the wheel. It is perhaps stating the obvious to say that a lower-than-usual profile tyre is the only answer to such conflicting requirements. They also look better!

Presumably luminaries at Dunlop (as far as we know the first with a 60-aspect ratio tyre in 1973) and Pirelli, whose fabulous 50 and 55-series P7 arrived in late 1975 as a direct development of a rally tyre, were aware of some of the problems that vehicle manufacturers might be facing in the future. Others like Goodyear, Continental, Fulda, and Firestone have followed the lead.

The lower the number the wider the tyre for its sidewall height. By "low profile" for the purposes of this vehicle, I mean aspect ratios of 60 per cent or less. Among the first to transform the roadholding and

handling of their cars were Porsche and Lotus. Since then the movement has gathered enormous strength with Audi, Fiat, Saab, Volvo, Ford, and Opel offering 60 series tyres, while BMW employ 50 and 55 profile P7s on the M1 as do Porsche on the Turbo, while the 928 and 924 Carrera also use P7s of 50 or 55 section. You do not get something for nothing and even Porsche have had to accept increased levels of ride harshness and noise in return for the extra grip.

My particular interest in the ride and handling conundrum that comes with such tyres started when searching for a reasonable degree of extra grip on my 3.2-litre Capri (*Autocar*, 1 December 1979). We opted for the normal "Plus One" set up; that is to say a 14in. dia. rim shod with 60 profile 195 section tyres (against the standard 185/70-13 Goodyear G800+S).

These left gearing more or less unaltered – important on a car that is already undergeared. They would go into the spare wheel bay and look suitably unostentatious on the car.

The problem was that even with standard springing and damping they left the ride quality unacceptable – to me at any rate – with a much greater degree of high frequency vibration put into the body which was particularly tiring on the motorway. The change demonstrated just how big an influence the tyre has on ride quality, especially in a "crude" car like the Capri.

Somehow we had to find a way of putting back at least some of the damping effect that the standard 70-series tyre sidewall offered. Furthermore it soon became obvious that to exploit fully the extra grip offered by such tyres and keep the car's handling precision and balance it would be necessary to stiffen the front springs *and* the damping to control that springing – though as I was to discover not necessarily on bump and rebound.

By ride quality I am referring mainly to the increased levels of high frequency bumpiness and harshness low profile tyres put into a car. Cars with sophisticated suspension and more favourable sprung-to-unsprung weight ratios than the Capri *may* take to low profile rubber without complaint, though it has to be said that some of the more compromising independent rear suspensions might not react particularly well to wider tyres. There is also a school of thought suggesting that heavy unsprung masses actually improve the absorption of minor surface imperfections by putting more work into the tyre.

Tyre performance

Lateral stability	Violent overtaking and recovery
	Change in attitude after abrupt lift off
Steering	Speed of response
	Precision around the straight ahead
Dry road adhesion	Good road
	Bad road
Harshness (ability to absorb minor road surface imperfections)	
Straight running	Cambered and rough road
	Smooth surfaces
Noise	Squeal
	Thump

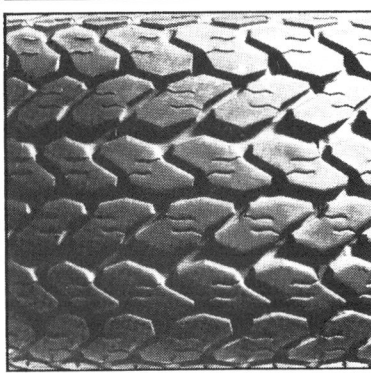

Wide P6 tread has centre grooves and angled blocks

NCT has five rib tread and tough looking shoulders. Note pronounced unequal phasing of tread and shoulder blocks

D3 has very open tread design with no obvious grooving, and a comparatively complient shoulder

Modifications

After a longish struggle I feel I may be getting somewhere in trying to get the Capri to grip, handle, and, most important, ride acceptably without lowering the car or re-engineering the suspension (far too expensive). Before we get on to the part different tyres have to play in the equation, perhaps I can explain some of my findings in the suspension area.

Firstly, it is my experience that where coil springs are concerned, a reasonable increase in rate does not necessarily result in a reduction in ride quality. It is however very important to get

the damping right, and not ask the damper to do the work the spring should be doing on bump. Here Koni were very helpful in reducing the bump setting on their "Sport" inserts (the rebound is adjustable externally). These are currently being used with a 145 lb.in. spring (standard 136 lb).

The rear end has proved more of a problem. Cart springs are heavy and suffer leaf-to-leaf interference; furthermore, they are connected to a heavy axle working against the lightest end of the car. Low profile tyres put sharper accelerations into that axle and thence into the car. Here again damping rates and

characteristics are critical. Ideally what seems to be required is a "regressive" damper, one that is firm over the longer undulations, B road surfaces, etc, yet can operate freely at very high frequencies thus allowing the tyre to follow the road faithfully (in a controlled way) over the small surface imperfections that cause all the trouble. Certainly with the Esprit Turbo Lotus have proved that it is possible (by subtle tuning of springing damping and compliance bushing) to get even a comparatively light car to ride and handle on low profile rubber. When such matters are discussed with Lotus' development

driver/chassis engineer Roger Becker, he is the first to admit that "damping is still something of a black art where one still has to use experience and, experimentation to find the right valving compromise to cope with the widely differing working amplitudes, and frequencies the suspension has to cope with." Experiments conducted at Bristol Cars by engineering chief Dennis Sevier go further and suggest that there is little point in trying to get a damper to oscillate very fast in the first place because even the best damper effectively becomes a solid strut at frequencies over 30 cycles a second, becoming a most efficient transmitter of harshness into the car.

Firestone S660 is a seven rib design again with tough looking shoulders and four wide grooves

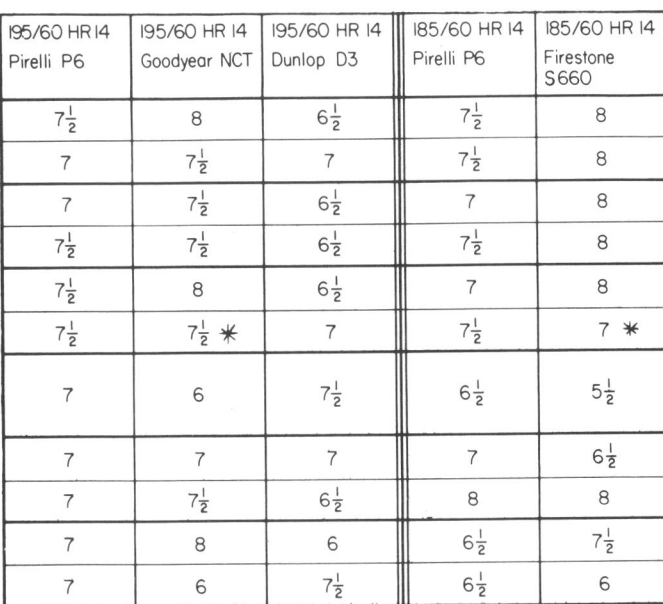

195/60 HR14 Pirelli P6	195/60 HR14 Goodyear NCT	195/60 HR14 Dunlop D3	185/60 HR14 Pirelli P6	185/60 HR14 Firestone S660
7½	8	6½	7½	8
7	7½	7	7½	8
7	7½	6½	7	8
7½	7½	6½	7½	8
7½	8	6½	7	8
7½	7½ ✳	7	7½	7 ✳
7	6	7½	6½	5½
7	7	7	7	6½
7	7½	6½	8	8
7	8	6	6½	7½
7	6	7½	6½	6

*NCT and S660 would have been marked ½ point higher if they had not created some axle hop on rough surfaced corners

Low profile Capri

continued

Our early experiments with single leaf springs resulted in better ride and traction over every type of surface. They seemed able to "flutter" with the road surface more easily. Not so good was their sideways location of the axle. Lateral stability in a transient manoeuvre (swerve from left to right) suffered especially with the greater levels of grip.

So currently we are persevering with the standard multi-leaf (112 lb. in. rate) with off-the-shelf Koni adjustable gas filled dampers. However, we have adopted detail changes to reduce the effect of high frequency inputs. One is to pre-tension the axle eye rubbers against the spring at ride level by tightening the relevant Metalastic bushing with the car laden, thus allowing the spring to "fight" the bushing at ride level. The other, more promising line, bearing in mind Sevier's findings, is to alter the top damper mounts in a manner that allows them to take the lion's share of the high frequency axle movement. Currently we are experimenting with rubber but may soon move on to polyurethane as we know various manufacturers of "high quality" cars including Bristol have already done.

We have also found that it is essential to set the rear anti-roll bar (which is geometrically quarrelsome on the Capri) so that it is not "fighting" the axle at ride level.

These detail modifications have at least made the car bearable. There is of course still

The tiresome side of tyre testing

some room for improvement and we are now working to further the aforementioned "concepts" and refine damper settings.

Tyre tests

Naturally, in all this development we were anxious to discover any special qualities possessed by the available 60 aspect ratio tyres which were the Pirelli P6, Goodyear NCT, Dunlop D3 and very recently introduced Firestone S660.

No wet skid or wear tests were conducted and one has to qualify the results by saying that the NCT, P6, and D3 were in 195 section whereas the only

Firestone S660s available were 185/14s. These are included in a separate panel tested against P6s of similar size.

Testing was conducted on the road and at the MIRA proving ground where we used the bumpy, potholed and variously cambered Ride and Handling circuit, to assess handling and ride on difficult surfaces, also the No. 2 circuit where experiments in violent overtaking (plus the swerve from left to right) ultimate handing and an assessment of grip could be carried out. The steering pad was used to confirm squeal thresholds and levels of ultimate grip (by timing laps). Smooth pavé provided an additional harshness test. The ratings are out of 10 (considered unobtainable). The higher the marking in each section the better the performance.

Cearly inflation pressures have a significant effect on the way a tyre behaves, and here our experience with the Capri (and recommendations from the tyre companies concerned) suggest that 24 psi cold comes close to the ideal for the NCT, P6, and S660. We added a further 2 psi to the Dunlops during road testing.

As any tyre company will tell you, it is very much up to the individual manufacturer to tune his suspension settings around the tyre. It's a sensitive business. We know of at least one case where the switch to a different make of tyre has resulted in the chassis engineer having to alter compliance bushing to maintain the desired ride/handling compromise. In fact the tyre manufacturer is probably working more closely now than ever with the vehicle manufacturer when it comes to setting a car up on low profile rubber. Even my own experience suggests that very small changes in bushing and damping make significant alterations to the way a car behaves.

A lot also depends on the size of tyre and rim widths being used. The fatter the tyre and the narrower the rim, the better the ride is likely to be, or the less you are likely to notice the change (in ride terms) from the standard set-up.

When it comes to fitting these tyres as replacements, you may well ask if there is any point in going to all the trouble and expense. But then you have only to experience the gains in grip and response to be hooked; in my case, hooked enough to try and find simple solutions to the ride and handling deficiencies that resulted from fitting low profile tyres to a Capri.

My comments are of course based on personal experience. Another wheel and tyre set-up (for instance a 205/60-13 on a narrowish rim) might not provoke the same difficulties on the Capri. But it seems inevitable that a harder ride will result if one adopts the "Plus One" concept, and with any wide tyre a higher level of pattern noise is to be expected – this is the roar of varying intensity one hears depending on the surface.

Conclusions? As the table shows, we found that where low squeal, dry road grip, stability, and response were concerned the Firestone and Goodyear rated highest *on our test cars*. Fairly predictably, their ride quality and ability to absorb minor surface imperfections was lower than average. The soft sidewalled Dunlop provided especially good ride for a 60-series tyre (barely worse than the standard 185/70-13 Goodyear on the Capri) but not unexpectedly lacked the sheer response and grip of the others. And the Pirelli? Though not truly outstanding anywhere it seemed to provide an excellent compromise. □

The forgoing experimentation would not have been possible without assistance from Goodyear, Pirelli, Firestone, Dunlop, Koni, and Dennis Sevier at Bristol Cars.

The Goodyears waiting for track running

Enthusiasm continued

with the new 2.0 litre Capri

By John Miles

ENTHUSIASTS will be relieved to discover that the big engined Capri is destined to continue in production for some time yet — selling as perhaps the best value for money sports saloon package available anywhere today. As we indicated in the Geneva Motor Show report, sales of the new 2.8 injection Capri have already started in Europe, while Britain (presently the 3-litre Essex engined car's best market) will have to wait until late May or early June for the right hand drive version.

For the moment, the new car is intended as a high performance flagship, running alongside existing 3-litre engined Ghia and "S" models until early 1982 when the carburettor Essex engine will no longer be able to meet stiffer European toxic emission regulations. The car itself is an entirely logical development of the MkIII, and first in a series to come out of the newly formed Special Vehicle Engineering group headed by Rod Mansfield and based at Ford Research in Dunton.

There will be one model, based (in the interests of refinement and quietness) on a bodyshell trimmed to Ghia specification,

the only difference being that "S" type Recaro seats with racquet-type head restraints (trimmed with softer cloth) replace the normal Ghia variety. A shortened gear lever is fitted. Customers can choose either a single exterior colour, or go for the rather attractive two-tone option. Badging is pleasantly restrained.

Mechanically there are no surprises. For the Capri, the 2.8-litre Bosch K-Jetronic injected Cologne V6 is quoted as giving 160 bhp (DIN) at 5,700 rpm (against the Essex's 138 bhp at 5,000 rpm). If the smaller German V6 gains considerably in power, it loses to the Essex in the mid-range. Torque outputs for the two units are stated as 162 lb ft at 4,200 rpm for the 2.8 and 174 lb ft at 3,000 rpm for the 3-litre.

No alterations have been made to the Capri's rugged four speed transmission, or to the rear axle ratio, which remains at 3.09 to 1. Bearing in mind the Cologne engine's higher power peak, overall gearing at 21.17 mph per 1,000 rpm is about ideal to achieve the claimed maximum speed of 127mph.

Low profile 205/60VR-13 Goodyear NCT tyres are an exclusive fitment. Ford are full of

praise for the tyre as offering particularly good ultimate adhesion, handling and wear characteristics. They are mounted on very attractive 7 in. wide Wolfrace Sonic wheels (slightly modified to a stronger Ford specification). These are the same width rims as used by the current Group 1½ racing Capris!

Such a choice of wheel and tyre could have easily resulted in a harsh car. In fact, Mansfield and his team have done an extraordinarily effective job in exploiting all the grip potential of the tyres, at the same time obtaining good ride quality. To achieve the optimum road holding and handling, it was not felt necessary to alter any of the front or rear suspension pick up points. However, the car runs 20mm lower than the existing 3-litre models. Bilstein gas-filled front struts carry 122 lb/in. front springs (106 lb/in. on 3-litre S) while the "standard" multi-leaf rear springs (nominal rate 134 lb in. on the "S") are discarded in favour of single leaf springs rated at 140 lb/in. Again Bilstein gas dampers are employed. Anti-roll bar dimensions go up from the existing S's 22 to 24mm at the front and from 12 to 14mm at the rear.

Except for the fitment of Granada/Fordsport type ventilated front discs and the appropriate caliper, the braking system is unaltered, bar the use of a G sensitive valve which is claimed to alter braking balance more effectively in conditions of light and heavy load.

A casual onlooker might have expected the 2.8 injection powered car to weigh less than the one it will eventually supercede. In the event, the fuel injection equipment and high level of trim leave the overall weight of a 2.8 injection engine directly comparable with the 3-litre "S". Even by today's standards, the car still looks like being outstanding value for money. Indications are that it will cost £7,700 including Car Tax and VAT.

Driving Impressions

All the existing 3-litre Essex car's ergonomic virtues are there: a good driving position with, for us, excellently placed pedals and steering wheel. The latest Recaro seats give superb overall support. The Capri's

beautifully simple-to-operate heating and ventilation system remains as effective as any. As a load carrier the Capri may not have as much room in the rear as does a Cavalier Sportshatch, on the other hand it boasts a split rear seat making it perhaps a more versatile proposition.

Frankly, once motoring, it is difficult not to go overboard about this car. It offers so much adhesion, handling and performance, yet is simple and practical, as well as straightforward to maintain. Immediately obvious is the comparative smoothness of the Cologne engine. Where the Essex is at its happiest slogging away, the 2.8 injection unit wants to rev freely to 6,000 rpm. Bar some wind noise, 100 mph is a relaxed cruising speed and there is still some overtaking performance in hand.

The example we drove rode firmly yet without any apparent harshness over a variety of surfaces. Straight line stability was arrowlike. On dry roads, the car is able to generate very high levels of grip, with no apparent handling quirks whatever. Despite the huge increase in grip, roll is well controlled, and there is just the right degree of initial understeer to *lead* the driver into a corner and to give a feeling of security in the faster bends. Too much throttle in a slow turn will spin an inside rear wheel, as it has always done on the more powerful Capris, however, in medium and faster bends there is enough rear end traction and power to drive the rear end out a little — to balance the car. This solid rear axled car's predictability at the limit of adhesion has to be experienced to be believed. It is a supremely "chuckable" car. Of the two cars we drove, the second one (a production car) had more — and sufficient — steering feel. The car responded well to small steering inputs — not in the slightly exaggerated way a Rover SD1 tends to on low profile rubber — and of course the steering is ideally geared with three turns from lock to lock. We know from experience of the Capri racers that the ventilated disc brakes will be well up to the job in hand. All in all it is by far the most refined Capri yet, while it has all the front engine/rear drive virtues, without any significant vices. ☐

SPECIFICATION

ENGINE

Head/block	Cast iron/cast iron
Cylinders	6
Main bearings	4
Cooling	Water
Fan	Viscous
Bore, mm (in.)	93.0 (3.66)
Stroke, mm (in.)	68.5 (2.69)
Capacity, cc (in.³)	2,792 (170.4)
Valve Gear	ohv
Camshaft drive	Chain
Compression ratio	9.2-to-1
Ignition	Breakerless
Fuel injection	Bosch K Jetronic
Max power	160 bhp (DIN) at 5,700 rpm
Max torque	162 lb ft at 4,200 rpm

TRANSMISSION

Type	4 speed synchromesh
Clutch	Single plate diaphram

Gear	Ratio	mph/1000rpm
Top	1.00	21.17
3rd	1.41	15.02
2nd	1.95	10.86
1st	3.16	6.70
Final drive gear	Hypoid bevel	
Ratio	3.09	

SUSPENSION

Front – location	Macpherson struts	
	springs	Coil
	dampers	Telescopic gas filled
	anti-roll bar	Yes 24 mm dia
Rear – loacation	Live axle	
	springs	Half elliptic single leaf
	dampers	Telescopic gas filled
	anti-roll bar	Yes 14 mm dia

STEERING

Type	Rack and pinion
Power assistance	Yes
Wheel diameter	14.0 in.
Turns lock to lock	3.0

BRAKES

Circuits	
Front	10.3 in. dia. ventilated disc
Rear	9.0 in. dia. drum
Servo	Vacuum type
Handbrake	Centre level working on rear drums

WHEELS

Type	Cast alloy
Rim Width	7 in
Tyres – make	Goodyear
– type	Radial ply
– size	205/60 VR-13

EQUIPMENT

Battery	12V 55Ah
Alternator	45A
Headlamps	55/60W
Reversing lamp	Standard
Hazard warning	Standard
Screen wipers	2-speed + intermittent
Screen washer	Electric
Interior heater	Air blending
Air conditioning	N/A
Interior trim	Cloth seats, pvc headlining
Floor covering	Carpet
Jack	Screw pillar
Jacking points	2 each side under sills
Windscreen	Laminated
Kerb weight	2,642 lb (1,200 kg)

SERVICE DATA

Fuel Tank:	13.0 Imp. galls (59 litres)

PERFORMANCE
(Mfrs figures)

Maximum speed (approx.):	127 mph
0-60 mph	8.2 sec

ECE/Government Official Fuel Consumption figures

Urban (manual/automatic)	19.1 mpg
Steady 56 mph (90 kph)	34.9 mpg
Steady 75 mph (120 kph)	27.4 mpg

RoadTest

FORD CAPRI 2·8 INJECTION

Ford's new 2.8-litre Cologne-engined Capri looks good and does 130 mph. But its economy, refinement and handling are impressive too

REGULAR READERS will know that Ford's 3-litre Capri rates among our favourite sporting coupés. There have been plenty of detail changes since its introduction at the 1969 Motor Show, and no shortage of challengers abroad — none of which has altered our opinion of the car. The formula is right: Ford's lazy, lusty Essex V6 gives the stylish and capable Capri an appealingly gutsy, yet effortless character that few rivals can approach, and performance-per-pound value that is simply outstanding.

It's no secret, however, that the Essex engine's days, as a power-plant for the Capri at least, are numbered. This is what prompted British specialist sports car manufacturers like Reliant and TVR, previously long-standing customers for the Essex engine, to go over to the Cologne-built 2.8-litre V6, as used in the Granada for some years now, for their latest models. It also explains, in the light of Ford's understandable desire to retain the successful big-engined Capri formula after the eventual demise of the 3-litre, why a fuel-injected 2.8-litre version of the Capri made its debut at the Genevà Motor Show last March. This car, called the 2.8 Injection, is now on sale in the UK — in addition to the 3-litre models — and we test it here.

Billed as "the fastest production car ever to be manufactured by Ford in

**Above left: Recaro front seats are well-shaped and superbly comfortable.
Above: in the rear, however, legroom is at a premium**

The facia is neat but rather uninspiring, unable to hide its humble origins

Europe'', the 2.8 Injection is the first product of Ford's newly formed Special Vehicle Engineering Department. This department employs a small, flexible team of enthusiastic engineers whose brief it is to develop high performance and specialist derivatives of bread and butter models. Thus the 2.8 Injection retains the 3-litre Capri's three-door hatchback body but gets the Granada's more potent fuel-injected 2.8-litre V6 engine under its bonnet.

In line with the increase in power (up from 138 to 160 bhp) the new Capri enjoys a number of other improvements, the most obvious of which are distinctively styled 7J × 13 alloy road wheels shod with 205/60 VR Goodyear NCT tyres. The suspension, as before, involves MacPherson struts and coil springs at the front with live rear axle located and sprung by semi-elliptic leaf springs. But gas-filled Bilstein dampers have been adopted together with larger diameter anti-roll bars front and rear plus shorter, uprated springs which lower the ride height by about an inch. The rear drum brakes are now paired with ventilated front discs. Otherwise, the mechanical layout is straightforward enough, with the drive being transmitted to the rear wheels via a manual four-speed gearbox (there is no automatic option), and power-assisted rack and pinion steering.

In addition to the mechanical and chassis alterations, the 2.8 Injection can be distinguished from the 3-litre S

and Ghia variants of the Capri by its special alloy wheels and (if ordered) a smart two-tone metallic paint job which incorporates red "Injection" side and rear decals. Inside, there are deeply-contoured Recaro front seats upholstered in blue check cloth, and colour-keyed carpet which extends to the lower sections of the doors. A stereo radio/cassette player comes as standard.

At £7,995, the 2.8 Injection is some £1,432 more expensive than its Essex-engined counterpart in the Capri range, the 3.0S. Its more overtly sporting and undeniably svelte image pushes it up market, to compete against such redoubtable rivals as Alfa Romeo's Alfetta 2000 GTV (£7,710), BMW's 323i (£7,925), Lancia's Beta 2000 HPE (£6,750), Porsche's 924 (£9,103) and VW's Scirocco Storm (£7,362). But when you consider that the Ford can boast an engine half a litre larger than even the BMW's and that it is not only faster than *any* of these cars, but among the most refined and best-handling with a ride, gearchange and quality of trim and finish that are well up to the mark too, it most certainly warrants serious consideration by the enthusiastic driver. For one who appreciates sheer effortless lugging power, on the other hand, the 3.0S might still be the more appealing car, despite its softer character.

Equipped with Bosch K-Jectronic fuel-injection, the 2792 cc Cologne-built V6 engine develops 160 bhp (DIN) at 5700 rpm, against the 138 bhp of the Essex engine. But there is a significant drop in torque. The German unit develops 162 lb ft and the British one 176 lb ft, and at considerably higher revs; 4300 instead of 3000 rpm.

We haven't tested the current 3.0S, but compared with the mechanically similar Mk 2 version of this car we tested back in 1977, some significant gains in performance are clearly evident. The 3-litre car recorded a maximum speed of 118.4 mph, but the 2.8 Injection proved simply too fast to hold "flat" into the banking of MIRA's high speed circuit, as towards the end of the wind-assisted leg it was doing over 128 mph and still accelerating — albeit very slowly. In the light of this, Ford's claimed maximum of 130 mph seems realistic enough, and very impressive too when you consider that even the fastest of our selected rivals, the Porsche 924, lags by some 8 mph.

The 2.8 Injection's 0-60 mph time of 8.2 sec doesn't give it quite such a

decisive advantage, either over the 3.0S (8.9 sec) or the more accelerative of its rivals such as the BMW 323i (8.2 sec) or the VW Scirocco Storm (8.9 sec as tested by us in four-speed GLi form). Higher up the speed range, however, not even these cars can stay with the new Ford, as evinced by its 0-100 mph time of 23.9 sec, which compares with 27.3 sec for the 3.0S and 25.2 sec for the BMW (the VW wouldn't record a 0-100 mph time within the confines of the twin 1-mile horizontal straights).

In top gear, the 2.8 Injection displays respectable but unremarkable flexibility — when it comes to lugging power, the 3.0S (which has very similar gearing to the 2.8) is a hard act to follow. The 2.8's 30-50 mph time of 8.5 sec, for instance, compares with 7.7 sec for the 3-litre car, its 50-70 mph time of 8.7 sec with 8.2 sec. At higher speeds, as you might expect, the tables are turned though only marginally since the 2.8 covers the 60-80 and 70-90 mph increments in 8.8 and 9.7 sec, respectively only 0.2 and 0.3 sec better than the 3.0S can manage. Compared with smaller-engined but lower geared rivals the 2.8 Injection can easily hold its own.

Judged against the old Essex engine, the fuel-injected Cologne-built V6 seems very smooth and refined, but by absolute standards it's nothing special. Its qualities suit this sporting Capri well, however; it revs freely and willingly to 6000 rpm (an ignition cut-out at 6200 rpm prevents over-revving) with plenty of top-end bite and a particularly clean and responsive power delivery. There is an edge of harshness

to the engine note at high revs and a sort of boomy growl that becomes apparent between about 100-110 mph in top, but these things apart, it sounds suitably sporty and seldom obtrusive.

Our overall fuel consumption of 22.5 mpg is excellent for a car of this power and performance and even compares well with figures returned by rivals of 2 litres or less. With an estimated touring consumption of 25 mpg, the 13 gallon tank permits a range of around 320 miles on 4 star petrol.

In typical Ford fashion, the gearchange is quick and snappy with a crisp, baulk-free action through a wide but well defined gate. The three intermediate ratios are quite closely stacked and long enough to allow 65 mph to be reached in second, which is especially useful when overtaking. The clutch was judged to be a little sharp in its take-up — a less endearing Ford trait — and our testers detected some whine in the intermediates.

Despite its basic, even crude, rear suspension the 2.8 Injection has fine, responsive handling and strong grip, a tribute to the engineers who instituted and sorted the chassis changes. Although the power steering lacks much in the way of genuine feel, it compensates with sensible weighting and swift, direct responses which allow the car to be placed on the road with pin-point accuracy and inspire great confidence. On dry roads initial understeer changes to a more neutral attitude in fast sweeping corners and mild oversteer as the impressively high limit of adhesion is approached. In the wet, the excellent NCT tyres continue to bite surprisingly well, though the tail

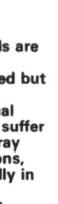

The dials are clearly calibrated but their individual glasses suffer from stray reflections, especially in strong sunlight

can be pushed wide under power virtually at will, but when this happens it is delightfully progressive and controllable. It is clear that the damping is also well judged, as it keeps the suspension in check and the car on line even when severe mid-corner bumps are negotiated at speed, and ensures an even, well-controlled ride in conditions of similarly fast driving. Around town, however, the ride can feel rather firm and jiggly.

Despite a rather spongey pedal feel, the brakes are progressive and sufficiently powerful on the road. During heavy stops from high speed at MIRA, however, they emitted a worrying rumbling noise and suffered from some fade.

Although more than a 2+2, the back seats of a Capri are not the best place in which to travel long distances if you're of average height or taller as headroom is rather limited and legroom is poor. The rear seats can be folded flat to increase the Capri's carrying capacity, though the rear suspension housing turrets do impinge on cargo space. An easily-detached rear shelf protects the boot contents from prying eyes and rises when the rear hatch is opened. Oddments stowage is sparse and amounts to a shallow tray and a small lidded cubby on the transmission tunnel and a rather shallow glove box.

The form-hugging Recaro front seats fitted to the 2.8 Injection as standard found immediate favour with our testers for their firm but correctly placed padding and supportive shaping; they were judged to be superbly comfortable. Their range of adjustment is good too, and it is easy to tailor a relaxed, slightly bent-arm driving position and still maintain a good relationship with all the major controls. The small diameter, leather-rimmed steering wheel is good to handle but partially obscures some of the minor gauges of the well-stocked and clear but reflection-prone

and now dated-looking instrumentation. The three column stalks which operate the lights, the wash-wipe (two-speed plus delay), the horn, and the winkers are sensible but have a rather heavy handed action, though the push-push minor switchgear is neatly and conveniently presented and works well.

Despite a now quite commanding seating position, the expansive bulging bonnet line makes it quite difficult to place the Capri's nose accurately in tight spaces. That accepted, all-round vision is fine, only the slightly heavy rear three-quarter area requiring some neck-straining at accutely-angled T junctions. Though very powerful on main beam, the lights suffer too short a range on dip with rather a sharp cut-off. A nearside door mirror is standard, as is the rear wash-wipe system. A drivers door mirror with a wider field of vision would be useful, however.

The heating and ventilation system follows standard Ford practice and, as usual, functions well. Plenty of warmth is available within a couple of miles of a cold start but on our test car, the temperature slide proved unusually unprogressive and hard to regulate. A powerful airflow, independent of the heater, enters the cabin through two butterfly valve rotating eyeball vents but because these are located at either end of the facia, it is hard to direct sufficient cool air to your face.

Noise in general is low, with little mechanical intrusion at speed and wind and road noise levels that are decidedly modest. Engine noise tends to dominate under hard acceleration, though it is pleasantly crisp and sporting in quality. Tyre bump thump is low.

The interior is well trimmed and finished with good quality materials and colours that harmonise tastefully. Likewise, the two-tone exterior paintwork looks good and gives the familiar Capri shape an attractive visual lift.

The V6 is a snug fit under the Capri's bonnet but all the major service items fall easily to hand

Ford Capri 2.8 Injection
MOTOR ROAD TEST NO 30/81

PERFORMANCE

CONDITIONS
Weather	Wind 20-35 mph
Temperature	60°F
Barometer	29.5 in Hg
Surface	Dry tarmacadam

MAXIMUM SPEEDS
	mph	kph
Banked Circuit	130	209
	(see text)	
Terminal Speeds:		
at ¼ mile	86	138
at kilometre	106	170
Speed in gears (at 6,000 rpm):		
1st	40	64
2nd	65	105
3rd	90	145

ACCELERATION FROM REST
mph	sec	kph	sec
0-30	2.8	0-40	2.2
0-40	4.2	0-60	3.8
0-50	6.1	0-80	6.0
0-60	8.2	0-100	8.8
0-70	10.8	0-120	12.0
0-80	13.7	0-140	16.4
0-90	17.7	0-160	23.4
0-100	23.9		
Stand'g ¼	16.3	Stand'g km	30.0

ACCELERATION IN TOP
mph	sec	kph	sec
20-40	8.4	40-60	5.2
30-50	8.5	60-80	5.3
40-60	8.8	80-100	5.5
50-70	8.7	100-120	5.4
60-80	8.8	120-140	6.1
70-90	9.7	140-160	8.0
80-100	11.9		

FUEL CONSUMPTION
Touring*	25 mpg (estimated)
	11.3 litres/100 km
Overall	22.5 mpg
	12.6 litres/100 km

Govt tests	19.1 (urban)
	34.9 (56 mph)
	27.4 (75 mph)
Fuel grade	97 octane
	4 star rating
Tank capacity	13.0 galls
	59.1 litres
Max range	325 miles
	523 km
Test distance	1226 miles
	1973 km

*Consumption midway between 30 mph and maximum less an allowance of 5 per cent for acceleration.

NOISE
	dBA	Motor rating*
30 mph	63	9.5
50 mph	69	15
70 mph	73	19
Max revs in 2nd	81	34

*A rating where 1 = 30 dBA and 100= 96 dBA, and where double the number means double the loudness.

SPEEDOMETER (mph)
Speedo	40	50	60	70	80	90	100
True mph	37	45	54	63	72	80	89

Distance recorder: 6.4 per cent fast

WEIGHT
	cwt	kg
Unladen weight*	23.0	1168
Weight as tested	26.7	1356

*with fuel for approx 50 miles

Performance tests carried out by Motor's staff at the Motor Industry Research Association proving ground, Lindley.

Test Data: World Copyright reserved; no unauthorised reproduction in whole or part.

GENERAL SPECIFICATION

ENGINE
Cylinders	V6
Capacity	2792 cc (170.4 cu in)
Bore/stroke	93.0/68.5 mm
	(3.66/2.69 in)
Cooling	Water
Block	Cast iron
Head	Cast iron
Valves	Pushrod ohv
Cam drive	Chain
Compression	9.2:1
Carburetter	Bosch K-Jetronic fuel injection
Bearings	4 main
Max power	160 bhp (DIN) at 5700 rpm
Max torque	162 lb ft (DIN) at 4300 rpm

TRANSMISSION
Type	4-speed, manual
Clutch dia	9.5 in
Actuation	Cable
Internal ratios and mph/1000 rpm	
Top	1.00:1/21.2
3rd	1.41:1/15.0
2nd	1.95:1/10.8
1st	3.16:1/6.7
Rev	3.95:1
Final drive	3.09:1

BODY/CHASSIS
Construction	Unitary, all steel
Protection	Underbody sprayed with heavy-duty wax. PVC applied to wheelarches and lower panels. Wax injected into box sections and inside doors

SUSPENSION
Front	Independent by MacPherson struts, coil springs; anti-roll bar. Gas-filled dampers
Rear	Live axle located and sprung by semi-elliptic leaf springs, anti-roll bar. Gas-filled dampers

STEERING
Type	Rack and pinion
Assistance	Yes

BRAKES
Front	10.3 in ventilated dics
Rear	9.0 in drums
Park	On rear
Servo	Yes
Circuit	Dual, split front/rear
Rear valve	Yes
Adjustment	Automatic

WHEELS/TYRES
Type	Cast alloy, 7J
Tyres	205/60 VR 13 Goodyear NCT
Pressures	28/28 psi F/R (normal)
	32/32 psi F/R (full load)

ELECTRICAL
Battery	12V, 55 Ah
Earth	Negative
Generator	Alternator 45A
Fuses	13
Headlights	
type	Quadruple halogen
dip	110 W total
main	220 W total

Make: Ford
Model: Capri 2.8 Injection
Maker: Ford Motor Company Limited, Brentwood, Essex CM13 3BW. Tel: Brentwood 253000.
Price: £6,417.39 basic plus £534.78 Car Tax and £1,042.83 VAT equals £7,995.00. Extra fitted to test car: two-tone paint (£175). Price as tested £8,170.00

TheRivals

Other rivals include the Audi Coupé (£7,475), the Colt Sapporo (£7,649), the Datsun 280 ZX 2+2 (£9,695), the Lancia Gamma Coupé (£9,949), the Renault Fuego GTX (£7,127), and Datsun Skyline 240 K GT (£7,362)

FORD CAPRI 2.8 INJECTION £7,995

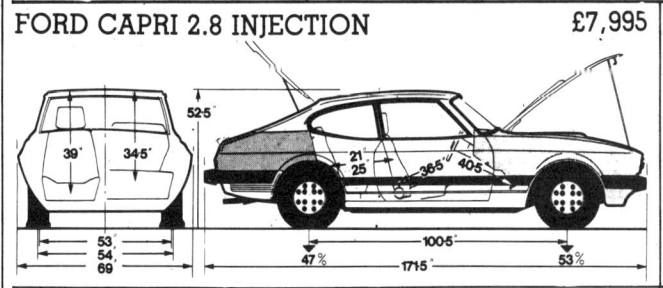

Power, bhp/rpm	160/5700
Torque, lb ft/rpm	162/4300
Tyres	205/60 HR 13
Weight, cwt	23.0
Max speed, mph	130*
0-60 mph, sec	8.2
30-50 mph in 4th, sec	8.5
Overall mpg	22.5
Touring mpg	25.0*
Fuel grade, stars	4
Boot capacity, cu ft	8.5
Test Date	June 27, 1981
*Estimated	

New fuel-injected 2.8 Capri flagship is a fine sporting car which, although lacking the solid low speed torque of its 3-litre counterpart, more than compensates with better outright performance and economy. Its handling is sharper and its ride better-controlled too. Rear seat space remains cramped, however, and facia now looks dated. Finish and trim are smart and well executed.

ALFA ROMEO ALFETTA 2000 GTV £7,710

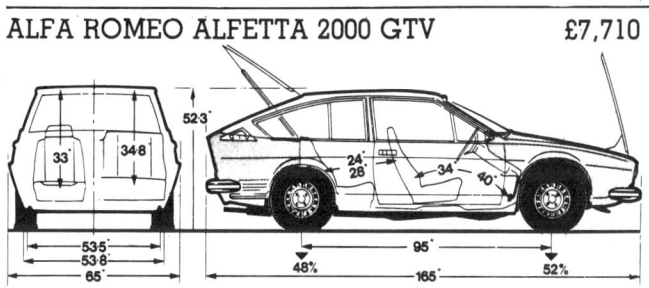

Power, bhp/rpm	130/5400
Torque, lb ft/rpm	131/4000
Tyres	185/70 HR 14
Weight, cwt	21.5
Max speed, mph	118.0
0-60 mph, sec	9.5
30-50 mph in 4th, sec	6.8
Overall mpg	25.4
Touring mpg	27.4
Fuel grade, stars	4
Boot capacity, cu ft	7.9
Test Date	April 16, 1977

Alfa's attractive 2 plus 2 is front-engined but has the gearbox incorporated with the differential at the rear. Evergreen dohc engine gives lusty performance with particularly strong pull from low rpm (latest version has even more power than one we tested) and very commendable economy. Fair ride; excellent traction and stability, but too much low-speed understeer. Odd instruments and a typical Italian driving position.

BMW 323i £7,925

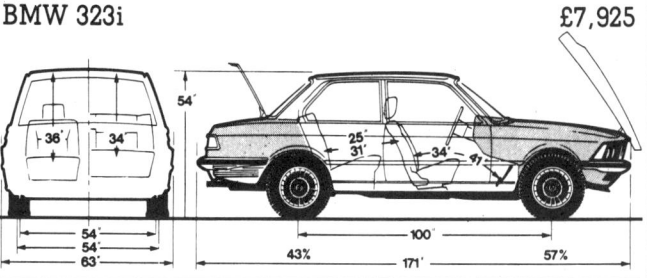

Power, bhp/rpm	143/6000
Torque, lb ft/rpm	140/4500
Tyres	185/70 HR 13
Weight, cwt	23.0
Max speed, mph	118.5
0-60 mph, sec	8.2
30-50 mph in 4th, sec	8.3
Overall mpg	20.0
Touring mpg	—
Fuel grade, stars	5
Boot capacity, cu ft	10.3
Test Date	May 27, 1978

Top 3-series BMW has sparkling outright performance, though not very torquey. Thirsty if driven hard (should be better with optional 5-speed), and engine noisy when revved. Fair ride and powerful brakes, and despite recent controversy over slippery-road behaviour, we found its handling safe and entertaining. Very nice gearchange and driving position, firm but well shaped seats, fine build quality, and now an excellent ventilation system, though heating could be better.

LANCIA BETA 2000 HPE £6,750

Power, bhp/rpm	121/5500
Torque, lb ft/rpm	128/2800
Tyres	175/70 HR 14
Weight, cwt	21.1
Max speed, mph	111.6
0-60 mph, sec	10.0
30-50 mph in 4th, sec	6.9
Overall mpg	23.1
Touring mpg	28.6
Fuel grade, stars	4
Boot capacity	9.0
Test Date	August 7, 1976

Attractive sporting estate version of Lancia's successful front-wheel drive Beta. Noisy and harsh Fiat-designed two-litre engine gives lively performance, average economy. Steering heavy at low speed but handling, roadholding and ride good. Soundly made and finish excellent, inside and out. Very well equipped. Versatile and quite roomy for a car with strong sporting appeal.

PORSCHE 924 £9,103

Power, bhp/rpm	125/5800
Torque, lb ft/rpm	121.5/3500
Tyres	185/70 HR 14
Weight, cwt	20.2
Max speed, mph	121.3
0-60 mph, sec	9.3
30-50 mph in 4th, sec	7.3
Overall mpg	25.2
Touring mpg	—
Fuel grade, stars	4
Boot capacity, cu ft	4.8
Test Date (Group test)	November 24, 1979

Front-engined, rear-wheel drive "baby" of the Porsche range has good performance for a 2-litre and is available in much faster Turbo form, both versions offering excellent economy in relation to their performance. Superb steering, brakes, transmission and handling, but ride is firm, and noise suppression — notably of road roar — and ventilation could be better. As in all Porsches, quality of finish and build is excellent.

VW SCIROCCO STORM £7,362

Power, bhp/rpm	110/6100
Torque, lb ft/rpm	101/5000
Tyres	175/70 HR13
Weight, cwt	17.0
Max speed, mph	112.3
0-60 mph, sec	8.9
30-50 mph in 4th, sec	9.4
Overall mpg	28.7
Touring mpg	34.4*
Fuel grade, stars	4
Boot capacity, cu ft	7.7
Test Date	October 6, 1979
*Estimated	

Plush and be-spoilered version of VW's fuel injected Scirocco. Excellent performance (for engine size) and economy complemented by precise handling and a delightfully slick gearchange. Mechanical refinement is disappointing, however, and the sleek Scirocco body limits space. Well finished and put together but sparsely equipped for its price and not such good value as the Golf GTi.

Road Test

Injected zest!

Lower, squatter and more purposeful than other Capris, the 2.8 Injection looks the part. The car is an amalgam of the best of the existing Ghia and 'S' versions with the added benefits of Ford's Cologne V6 engine with more power and refinement.

MATTHEW CARTER reports on the latest version of Ford's sporting coupé, the 2.8 Injection Capri.

There is but one modern car that is continually cited as one offering exceptional performance at an exceptionally low price. In the pound to power ratio stakes the 3-litre Capri has no peers. And yet not everyone is satisfied.

In recent years the public and press alike have acknowledged the car as being a leader in its field, but have tempered that original enthusiasm criticising its ride comfort, its rortiness . . . in short in rather basic charm.

These criticisms made themselves felt in the new car sales lists, too. Although most manufacturers would give their all to have the sales figures Ford manage with the Capri, the Ford management recognised the need for a more refined version of the car. Enter the 2.8 Injection.

Initially designed to sell alongside the 3.0S Capri, the Injection model should take its place as *the* high performer of the Ford fleet by the end of the year . . . and justifiably, too. Replacing the loved, though elderly Essex V6 with the newer, more powerful and 'cleaner' Cologne V6 — as found in Granadas the TVR Tasmin, and in carburettored form, the Reliant Scimitar — was an obvious move. But the 2.8 Injection is more than just a simple engine option, for Ford have spent much time updating the rest of the package to match.

They started by setting up the Special Vehicle Engineering group (an eighties equivalent of AVO) and letting them get to work on the idea. Using the more luxurious Ghia trimmed version as a base, lessons learnt with the X-pack Capris were used to the full. Like those road burners, the Injection has gas-filled Bilstein dampers all round, and have thicker (by 2mm) anti-roll bars front and rear, higher spring rates, wider wheels and a lower ride height than the standard "S" machines. The wheels are in fact attractive GKN Wolfrace Sonic 7in rims shod with Goodyear NCT 60 series tyres . . . the Capri, born in the sixties, at last has up-to-date rubberware.

The SVE group, in starting with the Ghia versions, did not neglect the best of the 'S' cars. Accordingly the Injection has superb Recaro seats, a boot spoiler, and 'S' steering wheel, while another change is a slightly shorter gear lever.

Externally it is pure Capri, only the Injection badges and — on the test cars — attractive two-tone paintwork telling the tale. That's cars in the plural, for over the past few weeks we have covered more than 1500 miles in two of the machines. The first 500 miles or so was spent on a high speed motorway chase across France, Belgium and Germany to the Nürburgring in one machine, while the other was used in more normal circumstances in England again taking in some motorway travel but with a fair amount of town city and country driving thrown in for good measure, too. And the German made 2.8 Injection came out with flying colours.

On the road the first impression is one of refinement. The Bosch K-Jetronic injected engine starts immediately, warms up quickly and is smooth and flexible throughout the range. It is also considerably quicker than the 3-litre with a top speed of 130mph compared with the 3-litre's 122mph. It accelerates faster, too with 60mph being reached in 7.9secs (8.6secs) . . . and is more economical to boot. Over the test period we recorded a high of 29mpg and a low which included

Attractive Sonic rims and Goodyear NCT tyres mark out the Injection.

Ford's 2.8 V6 in a new home. It develops 160bhp in the Capri.

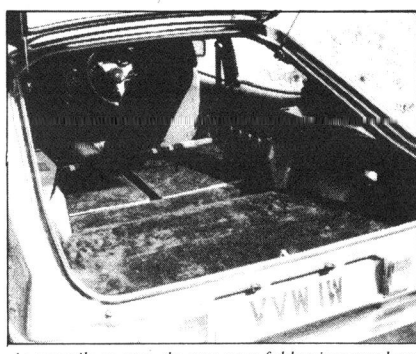

As versatile as ever, the rear seats fold to increase boot space.

performance testing of 19mpg . . . an average figure for the older machine is around the 24mpg mark. The 7000rpm rev counter has no red line but an ignition cutout that operates at 6100rpm. While the car is slightly undergeared . . . it reaches its top speed someway over its peak power reached at 5700rpm.

Every silver lining has a cloud, however, though in this case the cloud cover is pretty sparse. Yes, the Cologne engine lacks some of the torque of the Essex, but, no, it makes little difference. The sheer flexibility and willingness of the German engine makes up for the slight drop in mid-range — anyway the car's ability to accelerate quickly from say 70-90mph is impressive. Indeed the only real black mark that could be levelled against the engine/drive train is Ford's insistent ignoring of a high fifth gear for cruising gains when progress will be quieter — with added benefits in the way of less wear — and more economical still. As ever the gearchange is one of the slickest about, especially so with the shorter gear lever it would seem.

As befits a sporting coupé the Capri's steering is excellent. With just the right amount of power assistance and perfect gearing, the rack and pinion steering ably complements the handling package that Ford have put together. The low squat stance, the wide tyres and the steering combine to make the car a real enthusiast's dream . . . despite the rather basic nature of the single leaf semi-elliptically sprung rear end.

With all that grip available from the tyres it is not surprising that understeer is the initial attitude, especially in the slower corners, but the driver's right foot always has the ability to make the back end step out of line, either by accelerating or by lifting off. Always superbly controllable, the Capri is a model of rear wheel driveability. As ever the ride is something of a compromise . . . after all this is an enthusiast's car, and without independent suspension at both ends the ride is going to suffer.

Having said that, however, it must be recorded that on smooth surfaces the ride is good, and at once on the move some of the low speed jiggly behaviour is lost. The excellent Recaro seats hold the driver and passenger well in place, though it is doubtful whether some of the more rounded Germans bottoms would be able to fit comfortably. The driving position is pure Capri, excellent for controlling the vehicle but not so good when it comes to viewing the instruments . . . the fuel and temperature gauges in particular being 'lost' behind the steering wheel and driver's hands. One minus point concerns the seat belt stalk which rests on the driver's abdomen — not good in an accident.

That the Capri is a modern mass-produced machine became obvious during the test periods with the two cars . . . little irritations irked. That they were found in one car and not the other suggests they could be put right by a diligent dealer, even if they don't come off the production line quite 100 per cent.

The first car suffered that perennial Capri fault of juddering brakes. Although the ventilated discs do the job — though with little feel — the juddering felt through the steering column was off putting. The second car braked perfectly . . . but that had a harshness in the drivetrain missing from the first. The second car, too, had a noisy shock absorber, but at least that would be a simple replacement job.

In all other aspects the Injection has the attributes — and the handicaps — of every other Capri. Although leg and head room in the front is fine, riding for long distances in the rear is no fun for an adult, while rear three quarter vision is as bad, if not worse, than before . . . the Injection seats lack the see-through tennis raquet string head restraints of the 'S'.

Heating and ventilation is excellent, a model for others to work from, and the new model has a tilting sliding steel sun roof as standard, along with a radio/tapeplayer. The rear seats fold individually so the Capri is a versatile carrier, too, while Ford have not skimped on the spare wheel. Unlike so many cars with wide alloy wheels, the Capri's spare matches the four at each corner — no get-you-home spare, here.

And of course it's a Ford. A look under the bonnet will reveal that everything is where it should be and is easy to get at. Service agents are everywhere and, in theory at least, spares and servicing should be cheaper than some exotics on a performance par.

And yet it's that badge that might be the car's biggest enemy. True, it doesn't have the style of an Alfa Romeo or the status of a BMW, but so what? It does the job as well or better than most. And to the driver of another German built sports hatchback (costing considerably more) who said the car was nothing more than a four letter word beginning with 'F', I say this: "You, too, are a four letter word starting with 'F' . . . a fool."

Excellent dry road grip and handling make the Capri a joy, even though our attempts on the daunting Nürburgring were a trifle amateurish . . .

FORD CAPRI 2.8 INJECTION £7995

Specification

Cylinders, capacity	V6, 2792cc
Bore x stroke	93mm x 68.5mm
Valve gear	Overhead valves
Compression ratio	9.2:1
Fuel system	Bosch K-Jetronic injection
Power/rpm	160bhp at 5700rpm
Torque/rpm	162 lb ft at 4200rpm
Gear ratios	1.0, 1.41, 1.95 and 3.16:1
Final drive	Hypoid bevel, 3.09:1
Steering	Power assisted rack and pinion
Brakes	Servo assisted ventilated discs/drums
Wheels	7in light alloy, Goodyear NCT 205/60VR tyres
Suspension (F)	Ind. Struts, anti-roll bar, gas filled dampers
(R)	Live axle, single leaf semi elliptic spring, anti-roll bar, gas filled dampers

Dimensions

Wheelbase	101ins
Track (F/R)	53ins/54.5ins
Length	171.4ins
Width	67ins
Weight	2620lbs

Performance

0-30mph	2.4secs
0-40mph	4.3secs
0-50mph	6.1secs
0-60mph	7.9secs
0-70mph	10.4secs
0-80mph	13.5secs
0-100mph	22.9secs
Standing 400 metres/terminal speed	16.1secs/87mph
Max in 1st	39mph
Max in 2nd	66mph
Max in 3rd	90mph
Max in 4th	130mph
30-50mph in 4th	8.0secs
40-60mph in 4th	8.2secs
50-70mph in 4th	8.0secs

Fuel consumption

Testing	19.8-29.1mpg
Urban/56mph/75mph	19.1/34.9/27.4mpg
Tank size	13galls

VEE-SIX APPEAL

The new Alfa Romeo GTV6 and Ford Capri 2·8i are both powered by potent V6 engines. The Alfa costs more, but is it better? Roger Bell compares two classics.

COMPARE the technical specifications and it looks on paper like a runaway win for the Alfa GTV6, almost a no-contest affair. Beneath Guigiaro's penetrating shovel-nosed bodywork — mildly modified (and better aerodynamically) to distinguish it from that of the evergreen 'tours — is running gear straight from the classic-car textbook: an all-alloy V6 injected engine with hemispherical combustion chambers fed by unusual overhead cam valvegear, with a single camshaft for each bank operating the inlets directly and the exhausts by cross-over pushrods; a rear-mounted five speed transaxle to give a balanced weight distribution (almost 50/50); de Dion rear suspension which reduces unsprung weight and keeps the back wheels upright regardless of vehicle weight or cornering loads; and all-disc brakes, ventilated at the front, inboard behind, again to minimise unsprung weight. The front suspension is by double wishbones and longitudinal torsion bars, the unassisted steering by rack and pinion. Given a blank sheet of paper, it would be hard to conceive a more appetising, uncompromising design than the Alfa's for a four-seater everyday express costing less than £10,000. That of the Ghia-based Ford Capri 2.8i hardly matches up to it.

The engine — Cologne's 2.8 replacing Dagenham's 3 litre which is being phased out — has less sophisticated ohv valvegear, but with its greater capacity and similar Bosch fuel injection, delivers the same 160bhp as the Alfa, and marginally more torque. Drive is through a four-speed engine-mated gearbox to a live back axle, sprung and located by two single-leaf springs à la cart, which are stiffer and lower than those of the 3-litre S. MacPherson struts, controlled by gas-filled dampers (as at the back), suspend the front wheels and the rack and pinion steering is one-up on the Alfa with power assistance. Braking is by a disc/drum setup, in keeping with the car's simple, almost agricultural design. It is results that count, though, not data on a spec sheet, and it's here that the tables, if not totally turned, are at least upset as the Ford exceeds expectations and the Alfa doesn't really live up to them.

You get a hint of the unexpected when first settling behind the wheel: in the Capri you're immediately at ease and relaxed in an embracing semi-bucket Recaro seat which gives a perfect driving position behind a grippy three-spoke wheel and well-aligned pedals placed at just the right height. The comprehensive, no-nonsense instruments and minor switchgear are fine too. In contrast, the Alfa is an ergonomic nightmare: despite height adjustment for the seat and steering column (telescopic movement would be far more useful here), you sit arms stretched, knees bent, Latin-ape style, behind a slippery non-grip steering wheel and a muddled facia with the speedometer isolated from the main cluster of instruments, centrally placed where they're hard to read. (Regrettably, right-hand drive cars have not been graced with the new and much better facia fitted to left hookers.) Advantage Ford.

Both engines fire immediately, idling and pulling from cold without stutter, as good injected engines should. There's little between the two on performance, either: both cars will nudge 130mph, which is cracking on a bit, and rocket to 60mph from rest in a little over 8 seconds. Both excel at the top end of the rev range rather than at the bottom (unlike the old Essex 3 litre which is the other way about), though both will lug smoothly and quite strongly from low revs, the Ford (21.2mph/1000rpm in top) predictably with rather more vigour than the Alfa (22.0mph/1000), as it's lower geared, stronger on torque and 200lb lighter. In voice and delivery, though, even Cologne's flexible, sweet-running V6 is outranked by the turbine-smooth Alfa, which in full cry emits an even more satisfying wail, not unlike that of a distant Grand Prix engine. Only its lumpy idling mars otherwise outstanding refinement. It's far

from quiet but anyone who objects to a noise of such quality doesn't want an Alfa in the first place.

There's not much in it for economy either. Considering their formidable performance, both cars are remarkably frugal, the Alfa more so than the Ford in my hands (official steady-speed figures suggest that it should be), with an overall consumption of 24mpg. The Ford returned 22mpg. Driven gently, the Capri is capable of returning up to 28mpg, the GTV6 over 30, though you can subtract 10mpg from these figures for really hard driving.

With five gears to play with, the Alfa ought to have a decisive transmission advantage over the 2.8i — but it doesn't. For a start, the gearchange is a clumsy affair, with a vague gate and crunchy, obstructive engagement, no doubt because the synchromesh of the rear-mounted gearbox has the additional inertia of propshaft and flywheel to arrest. First and second are also too low — you run out of revs at the 6400rpm limit at 31 and 55mph respectively. What's more, clutch take-up is vague and concentrated at the top of the pedal's travel. The Capri, with one gear less, has a better drivetrain in several respects. It is less snatchy at low revs, particularly when ambling in town, and the change is crisp and precise. Clutch engagement is marginally better too, though as on many Fords it's irritatingly sharp and requires a delicate left foot to avoid jerky starts. With 41mph on tap in first at the 6100rpm rev-limited cut-out, and 66mph in second, the ratio spread is better than the Alfa's, giving more fluid acceleration through the gears, as well as better vigour when slogging in third or top.

The Alfa's flaws don't end there. It's steering is heavy, ponderous even when parking or rounding sharp corners where understeer can set in prematurely, limiting hairpin speeds with front-end plough. It's on fast, smooth, sweeping roads that the Alfa is at its outstanding best, with terrific grip and stability and fine placement control. Feedback through the informative steering is also excellent; you know just where you are with the Alfa. It has no untoward vices and gently forewarns of pending breakaway, if you're brave enough to reach it on dry roads. In the wet, it's easy enough to dislodge the tail under low-gear power, though such provocative oversteer is easy enough to control.

So it is with the Ford, which despite its primitive but very effective rear suspension, handles superbly and if anything clings on even more tenaciously than the Alfa, as well it might with fatter tyres (205/60 Goodyear NCTs on special Wolfrace alloy wheels, against the Alfa's 195/60 Pirelli P6 rubber on Campagnolos). Its power steering is also sharper and more precise than the Alfa's, yet still nicely weighted and by no means lacking in feel. I doubt that the Alfa would have bettered the Ford's handling and roadholding on the fast, lightly trafficked sweeping roads on which I drove the Capri back home from the Nurburgring recently, though it might well have equalled it. Where the Alfa does score over the Capri is on braking and ride. Despite excessive servo assistance, which calls for undue delicacy to 'feather' the pedal on and off smoothly, the brakes of the Alfa are immensely reassuring:

hard road driving betrayed neither fade nor any tendency to lock the wheels. The Ford's brakes feel better under normal use, as the pedal is firmer and response more progressive. But a sudden panic stab can easily lock the front wheels at quite modest g, due to a pressure-limiting valve that's strongly front biased to comply with European regulations, say Ford. If this be the case, the law is an ass and the rules need changing.

Although the GTV6 can become decidely turbulent on uneven corners, rocking rudely under diagonal pitch, it normally rides more smoothly than the rather harsh and jittery Capri. In other respects, there's little to choose between the two for comfort, driving position apart where the Ford is vastly superior. Both cars have comfy, supportive seats and, by coupe standards, acceptable rear seat accommodation, though leg and headroom is cramped for anyone of above average height, particularly in the Alfa. Because it's a true hatchback, with individually folding rear seats, the Capri is also a more versatile and accommodating car than the Alfa, which has a tailgate opening on to a conventional boot. Neither car is particularly quiet, least of all at speed when wind noise begins to intrude, especially in the Capri. But what music from those V6 engines! When it comes to keeping warm and fresh, it's the Ford that excels, with its efficient heating system, tilt-and-slide sunroof (a standard fitting) and effective eyeball ventilation that does a better job than the Alfa's rather crude flap valves.

Although manufactured in Germany, the Capri 2.8i was developed in Britain by Ford's Special Vehicle Engineering operation at Dunton, Essex, under the direction of Rod Mansfield. Rod and I are old Escort Mexico sparring partners so I know better than most that he can drive a bit (he gets his off-duty kicks now from an ocean-going catamaran I believe) as well as sort cars. And there lies the key to the 2.8i's undoubted appeal: it's a car for serious drivers, well sorted by people who are serious drivers. Unlike the Alfa, which is sensationally good in some respects but disappointing in others, the Ford, if not flawless, is uncommonly good for a car of such humdrum origins. What's more, it's £1500 cheaper than the Alfa so I don't need to tell you where I'd put my money. ◬

Specification	Alfa Romeo	Ford
Cylinders	V6	V6
Capacity	2492cc	2792cc
Bore/stroke	88/68.3mm	93/68.5mm
Valves	sohc per bank	ohv
Compression	9.0:1	9.2:1
Induction	Bosch injec.	Bosch injec.
Max. power	160bhp/5600rpm	160bhp/5700rpm
Top mph/1000	22	21.2
Chassis	monocoque steel	monocoque steel
Front sus.	wishbones, torsion bars, anti-roll bar	MacPherson struts, anti-roll bar
Rear sus.	de Dion, Watts linkage, coils	live axle, single leaf springs
Steering	rack and pinion	ass. rack and pinion
Brakes	disc/disc	disc/drum
Tyres	Pirelli P6 195/60	Goodyear NCT 205/60
Performance		
Max speed	130mph	129mph
0-60mph	8.5sec	8.0sec
60-80mph, top	10.3sec	8.7sec
mpg range	22-30	19-28

Alfa, left, has poorer instruments and driving position than the Ford.

Ford's new 2.8 litre, fuel injected, Capri

NOW that I have driven the 2.8i Capri for some ten days, ten days in which the car was driven at very high speed from Germany, at more sedate speeds for commuting and at a relatively leisurely pace down to Cornwall, I am very disappointed. Not with the 2.8 Capri, but with the 3.0S version which I use normally.

Usually, after a road test, I climb back into the 3.0S thinking how lucky I am to have a car which will reach 60 in a shade under nine seconds, cruise all day at 100+ m.p.h., return 22 to 24 m.p.g., depending on how it is driven, and yet costs under £7,000 — a useful yardstick against which to judge other manufacturer's products. If the road test car has been an expensive super-car, I realise that such vehicles are not for normal mortals, and think how lucky I am to have a car which comes reasonably close. If it is a run of the mill saloon, then it is doubly gratifying to hear the snarl of the exhausts as I accelerate through the gears.

The 2.8 has changed all that, for it does everything the 3.0S does, but it does it so much better, in such a refined manner, and I cannot console myself with the thought that it costs twice as much, for its tax inclusive price is under £8,000 — and that includes items which are optional on the S, and which would push the price of the 3-litre to over the £7,000 mark.

It is the first child of Ford's recently constituted Special Vehicle Engineering Department, and was nurtured from conception to birth in a shade over nine months by this small but capable team, led by Rod Mansfield. The recipe is quite simple in outline — take one Capri body shell, trim to Ghia specifications, add a 2.8-litre fuel-injected engine from a Granada, fit suspension, brakes and tyres to match, decorate with "injection" badges to taste and so on. It is to the team's great credit that the fitting of the suspension, brakes and tyres to match has been done so very well, matching the car's handling, roadholding and braking to its extra performance to produce a beautifully balanced, high speed touring car, superior to many costing half as much again. The only quibble that I have is with the "injection" badges — I would have chosen a more discreet size!

The interior of the body is trimmed with very pleasing blue checked fabric and thick carpeting which covers the lower parts of the doors. The head lining is matt black, and the instrument panel is just the same as that fitted to the 3.0S version. The seats are by Recaro, and are the same as those which may be had as an option on the lesser Capris, save that the "tennis racket" style head-rests have been replaced by properly upholstered versions. A stereo radio / cassette player and sunshine roof are standard items.

The subsitution of the German engine for the Essex unit has necessitated a different front cross member and a different bellhousing to mate with the manual-only gearbox. The suspension has been lowered by an inch all round and Bilstein struts are employed at the front with up-rated springs. At the rear, the axle is located simply by single-leaf half-elliptic springs, again uprated, and its movements are damped by Bilstein shock absorbers. Anti-roll bars are fitted front and rear, but these are 2 mm. thicker than those fitted to the 3.0S. The brakes at the front are revised with ventilated discs and heavy-duty pads are employed. The wheels are 13″ × 7″, of a very distinctive design and carry 205/60 Goodyear NCT tyres.

ENJOYING the delights of the Nürburgring with the exhilarating 2.8i Capri.

In Bosch K-Jetronic injected form, with transistorised ignition, the 2.8 engine develops 160 b.h.p. at 6,100 r.p.m. This is delivered very smoothly throughout the range. It is impressive how the car will pull away from below 25 m.p.h. in top gear without any snatch or hesitation, while at the other end of the engine speed scale, it happily whistles up to 6,100 r.p.m. (at which speed an ignition cut-out operates) delighting in being revved, unlike the 3-litre which shouts for an upward change between 4,500 and 5,000 r.p.m. It is only in the middle engine speed range that the Cologne engine is slightly inferior to the Essex unit, for the maximum torque levels are lower, with a consequent deterioration in top gear performance. Gone is that laziness-inducing push in the back when flooring the throttle at about 2,500 to 3,000 r.p.m. in top to pass an obstruction — in the 2.8 you need to change down.

The handling of the car is superb. It is beautifully chuckable and is well behaved on the limit, with no nasty vices. Unlike the 3-litre, which has tendencies towards understeer when pushed hard, the 2.8 is very neutral. The grip from the NCT tyres in all conditions is truly amazing, especially so in the dry, but once they do let go, for instance on a smooth, polished surface, it takes time to regain grip as the car has to be travelling so fast to unstick them in the first place. I learnt about this the hard way, while enjoying a couple of laps of the Nürburgring. Expecting the understeer I am used to from the 3-litre when entering a corner fast, I automatically induced a power-on tail slide. This was a mistake, for it broke the grip of the NCTs and resulted in a fish-tailing exercise. As I gathered everything together and headed off to the next corner, I realised that I should have given the design team credit for improving the handling of the car to such an extent that the minimal natural understeer can be balanced very easily on the throttle alone without having to deliberately put the car into an oversteering attitude. The 2.8 driven almost sedately achieves the same cornering speeds as the 3.0S on the ragged edge, and when the 2.8 is on the ragged edge itself, it handles better than the 3-litre. It amazes me how a single leaf rear spring can locate the back axle so effectively, giving characteristics so much better than many independent set ups.

Leaving the Eifel Mountains, we headed cross country for Belgium and the French coast. On the road, the car is so much quieter than the Essex engined version, the exhaust being especially subdued until the revs rise towards their maximum when a satisfying roar accompanies the car's progress. Charging up and down the forest lined roads, similar to the beter Welsh A roads, I found I was using the gear lever more than I

would have expected, and commented to Rod Mansfield, my passenger, that I thought the change had been improved, even though I knew the gearbox was the same unit. The answer should have been obvious — the gear lever has been shortened, making the travel between the gears that much less, and the change more positive. The ride on rough surfaces is somewhat harsher, which is to be expected in view of the uprated springs, but roll on corners is considerably reduced. The power assisted steering has three turns from lock to lock and has rather more feel than the previous model. This, coupled with the more neutral handling, made the hilly and twisty roads a real pleasure to drive along, although the inside rear wheel tended to spin very easily if power was applied too soon on the exit from a tight bend.

The performance in the gears never failed to delight me. Whether it was charging between corners for the sheer exhilaration of speed, or being employed more sensibly for safe overtaking, it was a source of immense satisfaction. 60 m.p.h. comes up in well under 8 seconds from standstill and second gear will carry the car on to 65 m.p.h. before the limiter comes into operation. Third is good for over 90, and once out on to the autobahn, we discovered that maximum revs can be achieved in top gear, some 130 m.p.h., given favourable conditions. The car is happy cruising at 125, and we covered a large number of miles at around this speed, the stability being very confidence inspiring.

Fuel consumption on the hard and very fast journey to Calais worked out at a very creditable 22.7 m.p.g. — my Essex engined car would have returned well under 20 m.p.g. in its futile attempts to keep up — and rose to a very impressive 24.8 m.p.g. for commuting from Berkshire into the city, rising still further to 27.2 m.p.g. when used gently (but nonetheless at speeds which would have had me in trouble if the boys in blue had seen me) for a long weekend in Cornwall. The car could be made even more economical if a five-speed gearbox was used — it is not under-geared in its present form, but it could easily pull an overdrive fifth which would add enormously to the pleasure of driving the car long distances on motorways.

At £7,995, no-one can claim that it is a cheap car in real terms, but to obtain similar performance and comfort, one has to look at least at a Porsche 924 (£9,100), which only beats the Capri on fuel consumption, or a 2.5 V6 Alfa Romeo GTV at £9,400. The Ford does not have the magic of these names, but it deserves great success for it does the same job at less initial cost and it will almost certainly be cheaper to run.

P.H.J.W.

CAR TEST

FORD CAPRI 2,8i (GERMAN V6)

There we were — running a 200 km/h burst on our test road in a new-model fuel-injected V6 Capri...

Just a dream? No — this was for real: we were trying out the latest Ford Capri, which is also the fastest production model ever to come from Ford of Europe. Using the smooth and vivid Köln V6 motor of 2,8 litres, with Bosch mechanical fuel injection, this Ford sports model was launched 18 months ago, and has proved capable of competing with some of Europe's best in this field.

The Product Engineering Division of Ford South Africa does assessments of most of the important new Ford models announced in Europe, to keep in touch with new developments. We found out that they had the Capri in Port Elizabeth, and managed to borrow it for a few days for this Test.

STILL IN PRODUCTION

While there are quite a few still running around here, we have rather lost touch with the Capri in South Africa.

KEY FIGURES

Maximum speed	199,4 km/h
1 km sprint	30,2 seconds
Terminal speed	172,5 km/h
Fuel tank capacity	59 litres
Litres/100 km at 80 (ECE)	7,62
Optimum fuel range at 80	774 km
*Fuel Index	9,91
Engine revs per km	1 780
British list price	£8 125
(*Consumption at 80, plus 30%)	

It is still in production in Europe, though, and is now nearly 15 years old. There has been a lot of change in the intervening years, of course: revision of everything from suspension to steering, modernisation of the exterior, totally-new trim and interior equipment — and, inevitably, exciting new engines.

But through it all, this is still the racy and distinctive Capri: low, sleek, and exciting. This top model is finished to Ghia specification, with full instrumentation, cloth-upholstered Recaro seats, sports steering wheel, Ford specification GKN/Wolfrace alloy wheels, substantial side protective strips, and front and rear aerofoils. The quad-headlight treatment and modernised rear end also make it different from the Capri we have been used to.

POWERFUL ENGINE

This latest version of the German V6 engine is particularly interesting.

The evergreen Capri is now built in Europe with 2,8 litres of fuel-injection power. We give it a trial here in South Africa...

In Europe, it is replacing the long-established Essex 3-litre V6 right across the board — in Granada, Capri and Sierra top models.

With Bosch mechanical fuel injection, this 2,8-litre pushrod motor develops 16 per cent more power than the Essex 3 litre, though it loses marginally in torque output. On balance, though, it is said to give improved performance and fuel-efficiency, and it is also notable for its smoothness and willingness to rev. There is no red line on the Capri's tachometer, but we found that the engine worked willingly to 6 000 and beyond, while an ignition cut-out limits it to 6 200, to curb its enthusiasm.

The standard Capri four-speed gearbox is used, with a 3,09 to 1 final drive giving good overall gearing.

ROAD PERFORMANCE

In performance tests, this fuel injection Capri is a real tiger. With its fat, ultra-low-profile radials it develops limited wheelspin in sprint starts, and gets going quickly. We reached 80 in 6,3 seconds and 100 in 9,1, and two-way maximum speed came out at a shade under a true 200 km/h — just topping this magic figure one way.

Third gear is enormously flexible — the car pulls strongly from right down to 20 km/h in this ratio, to nearly 150 before the governor comes into effect, with a very fine spread of torque in the 50-100 range in both 3rd and top. There is also very strong gradient ability — including one-in-8,5 in top.

Instrumentation is satisfactorily accurate — the tachometer being particularly precise — though the fact that the main speedo dial is calibrated in m-p-h, with sub-titling in km/h, is a reminder that Britain is still avoiding full commitment to metrication.

FUEL ECONOMY

For reference purposes, CAR's Road Test of the old Capri V6 with Essex 3-litre engine was in the July, 1970, issue. This new fuel-injection model came up faster all round, and based on official ECE (Economic Community of Europe) figures, it also returns superior fuel efficiency (in litres/100 km):

SPECIFICATIONS

ENGINE:

Cylinders	V6
Fuel supply	Bosch K-Jetronic fuel injection
Bore/stroke	93,0/68,5 mm
Cubic capacity	2 792 cm³
Compression ratio	9,2 to 1
Valve gear	o-h-v, pushrods
Ignition	transistorised breakerless
Main bearings	four
Fuel requirement	98-octane Coast, 93-octane Reef
Cooling	water — 7,8 litres — thermo-coupled fan

ENGINE OUTPUT:

Max power I.S.O. (kW)	117
Power peak (r/min)	5 700
Max. usable r/min	6 100
Max torque (N.m)	220
Torque peak (r/min)	4 300

TRANSMISSION:

Forward speeds	four
Gearshift	console
Low gear	3,16 to 1
2nd gear	1,95 to 1
3rd gear	1,41 to 1
Top gear	direct
Reverse gear	3,95 to 1
Final drive	3,09 to 1
Drive wheels	rear

WHEELS AND TYRES:

Road wheels	alloy sports
Rim width	7,0J
Tyres	205/60 VR 13 radials
Tyre pressures (front)	220 to 240 kPa
Tyre pressures (rear)	220 to 250 kPa

BRAKES:

Front	262 mm discs, ventilated
Rear	229 mm drums
Pressure regulation	dual system, anti-lock at rear
Boosting	vacuum servo
Handbrake position	between front seats

STEERING:

Type	rack and pinion, power assisted
Lock to lock	3,3 turns
Turning circle	10,1 metres

MEASUREMENTS:

Length overall	4,374 m
Width overall	1,698 m
Height overall	1,323 m
Wheelbase	2,563 m
Front track	1,353 m
Rear track	1,384 m
Ground clearance	0,152 m
Licensing mass	1 200 kg

SUSPENSION:

Front	independent
Type	coil struts and anti-roll bar, gas dampers
Rear	live axle
Type	leaf springs, gas dampers, anti-roll bar

CAPACITIES:

Seating	4/5
Fuel tank	59 litres
Luggage trunk	260-640 dm³

	Essex 3,0	Köln 2,8
At 60	8,24	6,96
At 80	9,22	7,62
At 100	11,38	8,70

That means something like 20 per cent overall improvement — though to

The 2,8-litre Köln fuel-injection engine is replacing the Ford Essex 3-litre V6 in Europe.

be fair, that was the old Essex motor: it has been improved substantially since then. Nevertheless, this is one of the reasons why Europe is switching to the lighter and more flexible German motor.

SOUND AND BRAKING

Noise levels are good, as well. The fuel-injection motor starts easily, idles smoothly, gives a crisp performance note under pressure, and is smoothly quiet at steady speeds. Wind noise is surprisingly low for what is basically a 1969 model, but road rumble runs a bit high by modern Ford standards, in spite of the big radials.

We did not want to punish this experimental car too hard, so we limited the brake test to five successive stops from 100, registering an average of 3,78 seconds, with good overall consistency, though the pads were becoming smoking hot at stop 5. Balance was good, with a mild front-wheel-locking tendency.

TEST SUMMARY

There may be no particular significance in the fact that Ford SA is doing a detailed assessment of this modern version of the Capri and the 2,8 fuel-injection motor. We know that a similar assessment of the Fiesta was done at PE a few years back, for instance, without any production sequel.

We're pretty sure that there is no intention of reviving the Capri in South African production, but the Ford SA engineers are having a good look at that 2,8 engine. Again, this may have no particular significance, as the Essex 3-litre V6 is built here in South Africa, and is giving wonderful service. But it does show that Ford has alternatives up its sleeve, should they be needed — and we might well see it being phased into South African models in the future.

Be that as it may, it was great fun to test a Capri again — and particularly on one with fuel-injected dynamite under the bonnet!　　　　●

Above: Interior is very different from earlier Capri models — this one ranked as the German 1982 model.

CAR TEST

Left: The rear hatch gives access to a much bigger load space than on earlier luggage-trunk models.

Below: Cloth-upholstered Recaro sports seats are used on this special model.

ACCELERATION

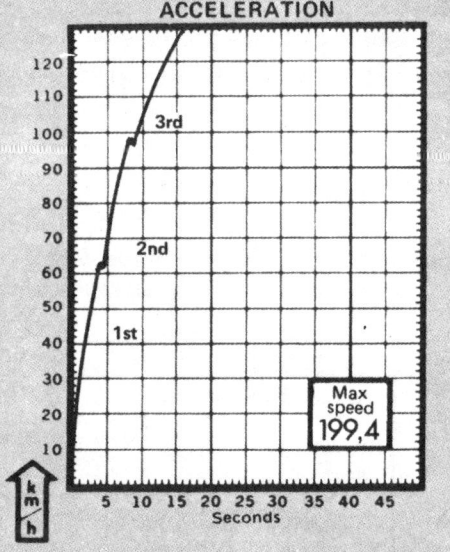

3rd
2nd
1st

| Max speed | 199,4 |

Seconds

BRAKING DISTANCES

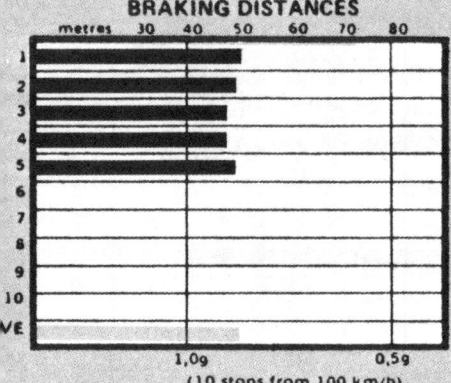

metres 30 40 50 60 70 80

1,0g   0,5g

(10 stops from 100 km/h)

NOISE VALUES

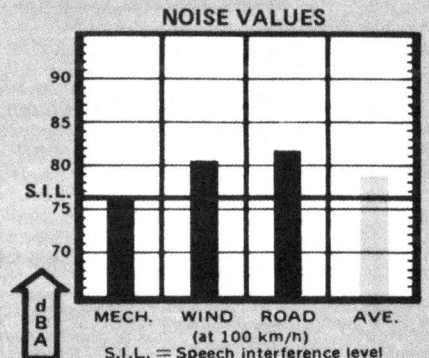

S.I.L.

MECH. WIND ROAD AVE.
(at 100 km/h)
S.I.L. = Speech interference level

CALCULATED FUEL RANGE
(km)

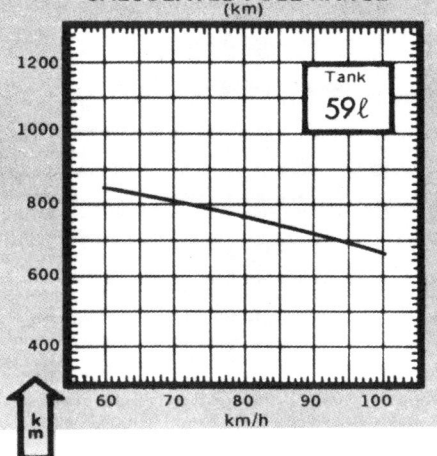

| Tank | 59ℓ |

km/h

---

test Ford Capri 2,8i

PERFORMANCE

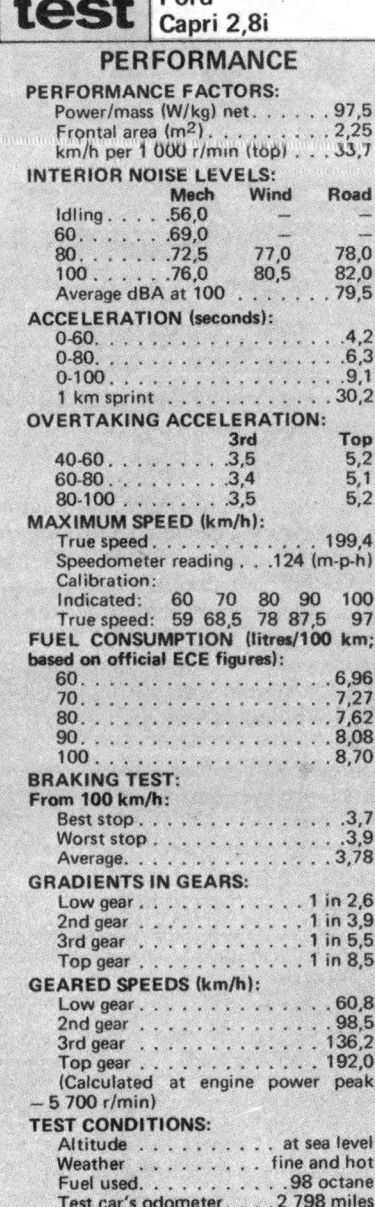

PERFORMANCE FACTORS:
Power/mass (W/kg) net 97,5
Frontal area (m²) 2,25
km/h per 1 000 r/min (top) 33,7

INTERIOR NOISE LEVELS:
	Mech	Wind	Road
Idling	56,0	—	—
60	69,0	—	—
80	72,5	77,0	78,0
100	76,0	80,5	82,0
Average dBA at 100			79,5

ACCELERATION (seconds):
0-60 4,2
0-80 6,3
0-100 9,1
1 km sprint 30,2

OVERTAKING ACCELERATION:
	3rd	Top
40-60	3,5	5,2
60-80	3,4	5,1
80-100	3,5	5,2

MAXIMUM SPEED (km/h):
True speed 199,4
Speedometer reading . . . 124 (m-p-h)
Calibration:
Indicated: 60 70 80 90 100
True speed: 59 68,5 78 87,5 97

FUEL CONSUMPTION (litres/100 km; based on official ECE figures):
60 6,96
70 7,27
80 7,62
90 8,08
100 8,70

BRAKING TEST:
From 100 km/h:
Best stop 3,7
Worst stop 3,9
Average 3,78

GRADIENTS IN GEARS:
Low gear . . . . 1 in 2,6
2nd gear . . . . 1 in 3,9
3rd gear . . . . 1 in 5,5
Top gear . . . . 1 in 8,5

GEARED SPEEDS (km/h):
Low gear 60,8
2nd gear 98,5
3rd gear 136,2
Top gear 192,0
(Calculated at engine power peak — 5 700 r/min)

TEST CONDITIONS:
Altitude . . . . at sea level
Weather . . . . fine and hot
Fuel used . . . . 98 octane
Test car's odometer . . . . 2 798 miles

WARRANTY:
Not specified.

TEST CAR FROM:
Ford Motor Company of SA, Port Elizabeth.

ENGINE SPEED

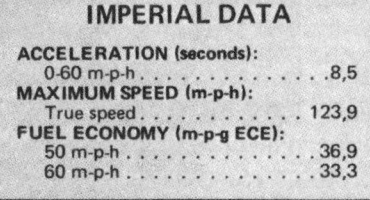

Max torque

Top
3rd
2nd
1st

2000 3000 4000 5000
Revs per minute

IMPERIAL DATA

ACCELERATION (seconds):
0-60 m-p-h 8,5
MAXIMUM SPEED (m-p-h):
True speed 123,9
FUEL ECONOMY (m-p-g ECE):
50 m-p-h 36,9
60 m-p-h 33,3

GRADIENT ABILITY

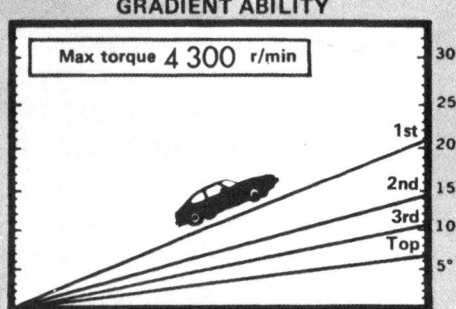

| Max torque | 4 300 r/min |

1st
2nd
3rd
Top

(Degrees inclination)

CRUISING AT 100

Mech noise level . . . . 76,0 dBA
0-100 through gears . . . . . 9,1 seconds
Litres/100 km at 100 (ECE) . . . 8,70
Optimum fuel range at 100 . . . 678 km
Braking from 100 . . . . . 3,78 seconds
Maximum gradient (top) . . . . 1 in 8,7
Speedometer error . . . . 3% over
Speedo at true 100 . . . . . . 64 m-p-h
Tachometer error . . . . negligible
Odometer error . . . . . . not measured
Engine r/min at 100 . . . . 2 965

STEADY-SPEED FUEL CONSUMPTION
(litres/100 km at true speeds)

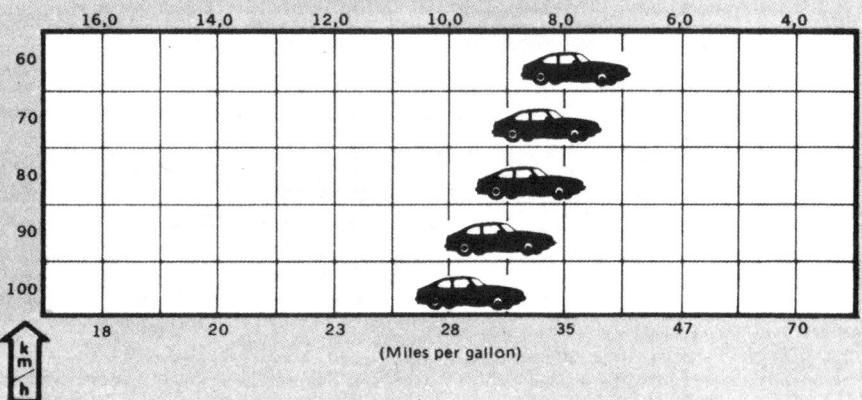

16,0 14,0 12,0 10,0 8,0 6,0 4,0

18   20   23   28   35   47   70
(Miles per gallon)

MILES Porsche eater
Behind the Wheel

Janspeed turbo conversion gives Capri 2.8i near supercar performance

NFB 494Y

Top: Fast and well balanced, the Janspeed Turbo Capri comes out of the Goodwood chicane with a touch of oversteer

CONTRARY TO popular opinion, the big engined Capri has time to run yet. "As long as it sells we will build it," say Ford. As they point out, the Capri does not compete in the same market as the newly introduced Sierra XR4i. One is a relatively sophisticated, refined, fast touring car, with space to spare. The 2.8i Capri remains a niftily small, practical, simple, well-ventilated, easy to manage (in some ways crude) value-for-money performance package.

At Motor Show 1982, the 2.8i got new trim and a five-speed gearbox, and at just over £8,000 it is still selling well. Ever since its introduction, the big engined Capri was ripe for conversion into a race or fast road machine. No matter what the purpose, this leaf sprung, beam axled chassis goes on accepting more and more power without significant modification. It used to be camshaft, cylinder head, and carburation modifications, now it is the age of the turbo.

Janspeed started looking at a turbo kit for the 2.8i Capri six months ago; a conversion that would also suit either Capri or XR4i if need be. Certainly the Capri installation demands a very compact layout if one is not to cut metal or move the basic components, and in this respect, Janspeed boss, Jan Odor, has managed a beautifully neat installation without moving injection equipment, battery or

radiator. The standard engine is untouched. The Rotomaster turbocharger bolts directly to a specially cast nearside exhaust manifold, a cross pipe connecting up from the manifold on the driver's side. Downstream of the turbocharger the standard twin pipe exhaust is replaced with a large bore single pipe Janspeed system. As several tuners — and the manufacturers — have now discovered, the secret of making the standard compression ratio engine stay together with forced induction is to cool the inlet charge. Air is drawn through the standard Bosch K-Jetronic air weighing mechanism (this will pass enough air for a little over 200 bhp) passed through the compressor, and ducted forward through an enormous aluminium air-to-air radiator sitting behind the front grille and in front of an additional oil cooler and the normal water radiator. The inlet air is then ducted to the engine via a long chromed pipe feeding into the standard plenum chamber.

Power for nothing

Cooled inlet air means less thermal stress, better response and economy (thanks to the standard C/R) and a denser charge, therefore "power for nothing." Protection from the possibility of detonation is provided by a Micro Dynamics electronic "engine management" system (also used on the Tickford

Turbo Capri). An electronic spark delay provides one degree of ignition retard per lb of boost over 2 psi, up to the 6 psi reached before the wastegate comes into operation. The system also includes ignition and rev limiter functions. Over 2 psi boost, a pressure switch in the inlet manifold works an additional injector in the inlet pressure pipe to give the necessary on boost enrichment.

Getting acceptable throttle response from a single turbo V6 installation with such long inlet tracts and a cross pipe exhaust has not been easy. In this case the exercise has led to the evolution of a special Rotomaster turbocharger unit using a "Buick trim" compressor housing, matched to an RM60 turbo unit.

It has become well established that the Cologne V6's tortuous siamesed inlet and exhaust passages respond well to forced induction. Outputs are impressive, even if turbo inertia dictates that the sometimes incredible figures achieved on constant full throttle low down in the rev range, are rarely possible on the varying throttle used in road driving. At 3,000 rpm, Janspeed's chassis dynamometer recorded 105 bhp (equivalent to the standard car's maximum power at 5,000 rpm). At 5,000 rpm, 140 bhp is produced at the rear wheels which equates to approximately 200 bhp at the flywheel. No

torque figures are available — a pity, because once on boost, mid range urge was where this unit impressed above all else.

Inevitably such increases in power and torque call the transmission into question. The clutch appears to be well up to the task, but at these outputs the new Ford five speed is operating well beyond its quoted torque capacity. Yet with such a large power hike, taller gearing is vital. There is certainly no higher final drive ratio available, to raise the gearing of the stronger gearboxed four speed cars.

Wisely, Janspeed offer improved braking and fit the well proven AP four pot caliper and disc conversion used by the Group 1 racers. Costs? £2,000 including VAT and fitting for the turbo engine, and £625 inclusive for the brakes.

Strong surge

Janspeed's turbo conversion turns a usefully fast car into a machine that will trounce a Porsche 924 Turbo, Eclat Excel, BMW 635 and Audi Quattro, on acceleration.

Even without a limited slip differential, plenty of grip came with the start line wheelspin. From rest to 30 mph took 2.5 sec. The strong surge forward continued. 60, 80 and 100 mph came up in 6.8, 11.7 and 18.3 sec (standard car 7.9, 13.9 and 23.4). By the time the Janspeed 2.8i was doing 110 mph, the gap had

extended to over eight seconds and we went on to reach 120 mph in 31.7 sec (Esprit Turbo 27.1 sec) within the confines of MIRA's one mile horizontal straights. At the 6,250 rpm rev limit, second, third and fourth gear maxima are 72, 104 and 133 mph — relatively close ratios mean there is a gear to suit all overtaking situations. We were unable to take the car abroad to do a proper maximum speed test, but it would easily dash up to 5,200 rpm in top (134 mph), and under favourable conditions the extra 300 rpm necessary to make this into a 140 mph car would probably not take too long to arrive. Over 110 mph, the blustery weather did push the car around more than one would like (the Capri develops a lot of front lift) and we know from recent wind tunnel development, that a properly designed front and rear spoiler kit (and possibly the extrovert looking RS rear wing, plus front chin spoiler) would transform yaw stability.

Straight line performance is impressive enough, but it is the surge forward in the mid range that is so thrilling — and useful. The standard engine is not renowned for bottom end torque, and first impressions of the turbo engine leave one thinking it dead and relatively unresponsive below 3,000 rpm. Differences in indirect gearing mean that comparisons are only possible between the direct fourth gear of the new car and the 1 to 1 top gear of the old model. Certainly

on constant full throttle the turbo does not lag behind the standard car. From 20 mph onwards it is all gain, and once the legal limit is approached the turbo is an average 4.0 sec quicker over each 20 mph increment.

On the road this translates into a very fast car indeed, without the cumbersome width of the "supercar". Open the throttle much below 3,000 rpm and there was some delay in turbo response. Drop a gear, and the car would surge forward immediately with its very purposeful but muted growl, combined with a whistle from the compressor. Long inclines as on the A3 out of Guildford seemed to have no meaning. It would amble along at 110 mph on a whisker of throttle — uphill. At high cruising speeds engine noise levels were impressively low, but the Janspeed exhaust did produce an irritating boom at idle and 1,500 rpm.

Knowing Capri 2.8i ride and handling tends to be rather variable in quality (the cars respond to careful chassis rigging), Janspeed appear to have been lucky with this one. No handling quirks were apparent — if anything the extra power improved the car. Test track treatment showed that we had the usual balanced throttle understeer, only now it could be countered (so predictably) with power, in 80 or even 90 mph, corners. A spinning inside rear wheel finally limits the amount of

mid corner traction but also makes the car fail-safe releasing excess driving torque. On dry roads at least, the 2.8i is a wonderfully chuckable beast, with none of the XR4i's rather soggy ultimate behaviour. The steering on this example had plenty of feel at all speeds.

Treated as a race car, one senses the small delay before full boost is developed from fully closed to open throttle, but as I have already said, once revving over 3,000 rpm this was of no real consequence on the road. On wet roads, the surge of torque as full

boost is developed is liable to provoke wheelspin in second or third gears but under these circumstances a Capri helps the driver by wanting to run straight, or by simply wheelspinning in mid corner.

Ride quality is more than usually tyre pressure dependent. At 26 psi all round (30 psi used for testing) Janspeed's car had little of the commonly found harshness over coarse surfaces, ridges and potholes, only the worst urban road repairs making the presence of its leaf sprung rigid axle obvious. There was less

1983 model 2.8i Capris have better trim, a five speed gearbox, and redesigned steering wheel

wind noise than usual (though it was still very noticeable) leaving road induced tyre roar as the main high speed cruising noise source.

The braking modifications left a confidence inspiringly firm pedal, and much more powerful slowing from high speeds that standard. They were no fade problems and only a vestige of the braking shimmy/vibration that is so common to the normal Capri 2.8i.

Like standard, starting was immediate from hot or cold, and the idle speed normal. After allowing for the five per cent optimistic mileage recorder, fuel consumption worked out 20.3 mpg. This included some hard road mileage, performance testing, and several laps of Goodwood race circuit, so the interim brim showing 22.3 mpg would probably be more representative.

I can't comment on long term reliability, only that over 534 miles it used no oil, in fact it didn't miss a beat, pink or cough. I couldn't envisage anything but an expertly driven supercar keeping up, and nothing I know of with this much performance (except the even faster Tickford 2.8i Capri) is so easily manageable in town, thanks to its size, power steering, and tolerably good visibility. As I have always said, the big engined Capri — turbocharged or not — has far too much going for it to die just yet.

Left: Purposeful sight: Janspeed's kit mounts the turbocharger on nearside exhaust manifold. Standard Bosch K Jetronic air weighing mechanism is used. Compressed air is ducted forward to intercooler, and thence back to the standard inlet plenum, a layout which only neccessitates holes to be cut in radiator shrouding for piping. Note on boost enrichment injector sited in right angle casting immediately prior to inlet plenum

CAPRI 2.8i TURBO						
Acceleration		**Standing ¼-mile: 15.0 sec 92mph**				
		Standing kilometre: 27.9 sec 117mph				
True mph	Time (sec)	mph	5th	4th	3rd	2nd
30	2.5	10- 30	—	—	7.2	4.4
40	3.9	20- 40	11.5	8.1	6.2	3.7
50	5.2	30- 50	10.3	7.2	5.4	3.0
60	6.8	40- 60	9.6	6.5	4.2	2.8
70	8.8	50- 70	9.0	5.8	4.0	3.6
80	11.7	60- 80	8.4	5.4	4.6	—
90	14.4	70- 90	7.5	5.2	5.3	—
100	18.3	80-100	8.0	6.5	6.7	—
110	23.9	90-110	10.3	8.9	—	—
120	31.7	100-120	15.3	12.5	—	—

CAPRI 2.8i					
Acceleration		**Standing ¼-mile: 16.2 sec, 88 mph**			
		Standing km: 30.0 sec, 108 mph			
True mph	Time (sec)	mph	4th	3rd	2nd
30	2.8	10- 30	9.9	6.2	4.4
40	4.2	20- 40	8.4	5.9	4.0
50	6.0	30- 50	7.9	5.3	3.7
60	7.9	40- 60	8.0	5.1	3.8
70	10.7	50- 70	8.2	5.5	—
80	13.9	60- 80	8.6	6.0	—
90	17.7	70- 90	9.3	7.1	—
100	23.4	80-100	10.6	—	—
110	32.0	90-110	13.8	—	—

CUT-PRICE ASTON ROAD ROCKET

Basically, it's a Capri: but Aston Martin Tickford have reworked it into the fastest four-seater you can buy for less than £15,000. Roger Bell describes and drives this turbocharged slingshot

IF WE'RE to believe Tickford's performance claims, their new Capri Turbo — which goes on sale today — must be the fastest four-seater you can buy for under £15,000. Outside the mega-buck world of bespoke decloning, it must also be one of the most extravagant transformations of an off-the-peg car to go into limited production. At £14,985, it costs £6,332 more than the Capri 2.8i on which it is based.

With a price tag that's only just on the right side of a Porsche 944's, and not that much less than an Audi Quattro's, the Tickford Capri, first shown as a joint Ford-Tickford development exercise at last year's NEC show, is obviously more than a cosmetic special. Aston Martin Tickford have combined modern turbo technology (their own), with traditional coachbuilding skills to produce a car that really does go as well as its looks suggest it should.

Just to recap, the Tickford Capri was the brainchild of Ford of Europe's former supremo, Bob Lutz, and the Chairman of Pace Petroleum and Aston Martin, Victor Gauntlett. Both are car enthusiasts *extraordinaire* with a connoisseur's appreciation of fine machinery. The original idea, set in motion with hardware and development cash from Big

Henry, was that the Tickford Capri would become a listed Ford model. As it happened, the 2.8T was one of the victims of Stuart Turner's flailing axe so in the end AM Tickford went it alone, gained the necessary Type Approval to market the car as a new model, and will now be selling it themselves as an AM Tickford product through selected Ford main dealers.

The aesthetics of the striking body addenda you can judge for yourself. It consists of six bolt-on GRP panels — a grille shroud, deep front air dam, rear valence, two side skirts and a boot-top spoiler. Apart from transforming the car's appearance — it's a stunning head-turner on the road — AM Tickford claim that the body mods also reduce the drag coefficient by 10 per cent (to 0.36) and increase downforce.

With Japanese IHI turbo mounted centrally ahead of the engine (good for cooling) and a large Garret intercooler (which lowers charge temperatures to increase mixture density and decrease thermal loads), the 2.8-litre V6 engine gives a claimed 205 bhp (up from the Capri 2.8i's 150 bhp), and 260lb ft of torque at 3,500 rpm (163lb ft at 4,300 rph). AM Tickford, who developed the engine themselves under the direction of chief development

engineer David Morgan, have gone for mid-range torque rather than top-end power. They didn't want a thirsty screamer that would rev itself to bits prematurely.

Much under-bonnet surgery was needed to accommodate the impressive plumbing and ensure adequate cooling. Surprisingly, nothing has been done to the engine's bottom end (apparently quite strong enough), pistons, cylinder heads or even the compression ratio, which remains a high (for a turbo) 9.2:1. Morgan says that the secret of their foolproof detonation control is highly accurate AFT computerised ignition, sensitive to manifold

Styling changes (heading, and above) are effected by bolting-on six GRP panels. The engine is a tuned 2.8i V6 unit (right) with IHI turbocharger and intercooler

The reworked body (below) is aerodynamically more efficient than standard, with a C_d of 0.36 and greater downforce. Inside, the cabin (above) is lushly furnished

pressure, atmospheric pressure and intake temperature, and Bosch K-Jetronic fuel injection — supplemented by additional electronic injection to ensure an adequate fuel supply during high-boost conditions. Maximum boost is set at 7.5 psi before the wastegate, integrated with the turbo assembly, opens. The installation is a strong pointer, perhaps, to future Aston Martin powerplants, bearing in mind Tickford's dual role as AML's development wing.

To cope with the extra power, the Capri's five-speed manual gearbox has extra lubrication drilling, there's a limited slip diff and the rear drum brakes have been replaced by discs on fully

floating halfshafts. The front MacPherson strut suspension is standard, but the live rear axle has additional A-frame location to prevent lateral deflection of its two single-leaf springs. It was the simplest and most cost-effective arrangement of several that were considered.

The car I drove was the original white show car, allegedly a little tired from development testing even though it had had a new engine only 10,000 miles before, according to a sticker on the speedo. Cabin decor, which smells as rich as it looks, is to coachwork standards with leather upholstery (an extra-cost option) for the supportive Recaro seats, and a polished walnut facia into which the Capri's standard instruments (plus a couple of extras, including a boost gauge) are embedded. There's walnut cappings on the doors, too, as well as carpet and cloth trim. Standard equipment includes electric windows and a sliding steel roof, but you have to pay extra for Wilton carpet, a coach finish respray, electric door mirrors and painted wheels, among other things.

What immediately impressed after instant start-up was the engine's steady idle, muted note and smoothness: mechanical refinement is superior to that of

the normal 2.8i. Although AM Tickford claim strong low-speed torque — twice that of the normal engine at 2,000 rpm, they say — it's not until the rev counter registers 3,000 rpm that turbo thrust really hurls you forward with an impressive kick that's suddenly triggered rather than progressively unleashed. Some drivers will like it that way, others may not.

Tickford claim 0-60 mph acceleration in around six seconds and a top speed of 140 mph — figures that will have to await MIRA verification pending a full road test, coming soon. For what it's worth, I recorded an impressive 60-80 mph fourth gear time of under six seconds from speedo readings, which is quick if anywhere near the truth. Ignition cut-out limits the engine to just under 6,000 rpm according to a rev counter devoid of red paint.

Two chance encounters helped to put the car's formidable performance into perspective. The first was with an Aston Martin V8 (I suspect from the Newport Pagnell works just up the road from AM Tickford's Milton Keynes HQ). We converged from opposite directions at a roundabout and then convoyed together for a couple of miles on a deserted dual carriageway. We were not racing, you understand, just measuring up by pressing on through the gears. Judging by the consistency of the gap between us, the two cars seemed pretty evenly matched. Later on, the driver of what looked like an ordinary 2.8i latched on to my tail on a rural B-road. Out-gunning him was easy, losing him was not, which may or may not prove something about A to B journey times in a superfast car as opposed to a merely quick one.

On 205 section Goodyear NCTs, the Tickford Capri is certainly not lacking in grip. Its roadholding and brakes are terrific. However, I didn't like the feel of the test car's power steering. Turn-in bite was disconcertingly vague when pressing on, calling for much bigger sweeps of the leather-bound thick-rimmed wheel than seemed necessary. Excessive understeer? I think not, but whatever the cause, the result was a lack of directional sharpness — a verdict which puzzled Mr Morgan.

The ride wins no prizes, either. On indifferently surfaced secondaries, the car felt very agitated and wobbly. It also tended to pitch diagonally through fast bends, all of which pointed to a disappointing lack of pedigree poise. It remains to be seen whether these and other shortcomings (like a disturbingly sizzly gearbox) were just quirks of the hard-worked development hack. Hopefully customer cars to be built at a new plant in Bedworth, near Coventry, will not be so flawed. With a one-year, unlimited mileage warranty, AM Tickford are confident they've got their cut-price supercar right

NEWCOMERS

Motor Show specials don't always make the most successful road cars but the Tickford Capri could just be the exception to that rule.

Announced as the show-stopper on the Aston Martin-Tickford stand at last year's NEC Show, the striking looking Capri in fact seemed such a good idea that Ford thought long and hard about taking it under their wing.

When they finally rejected the plan, Tickford – the independently run coach-building arm of AM – decided to go ahead themselves, though Ford will still allow them to sell the car through some selected dealers.

When we tried the car it was the same, white show car that had been on the Birmingham stand 12 months ear-

THE TICKFORD WILL LEAVE A PORSCHE 944 STANDING

lier; it's still the only car in existence but proper production will start soon and Tickford aim to sell 250 cars a year, making it their biggest contract aside from the Jaguar convertible coachbuilding work.

And, as a complete change from previous models of this type, Tickford's Capri will not be a post-registration conversion but a fully Type Approved model in its own right. It costs £14,975 – a price which puts it right into Porsche 944 territory – but for the money the buyers will get an impressively up-rated Capri Injection, with considerable extra performance from a turbocharged engine together with a curious but still quite pleasing mixture of ultra modern body styling add-ons and traditional wood-and-leather interior re-trimming.

It's from the outside that the Tickford car makes its first dramatic impact; there are deep front and rear air dams, linked by side 'skirts' running beneath the doors, a large rear spoiler and a blanked off radiator grille for reduced drag. It's more than a touch boy-

SHOW ON THE ROAD

racerish but stunning nonetheless.

Inside the car, Tickford have called upon their Aston Martin background to devise a walnut veneer housing for the dash, with surrounding leather trim.

But it's the mechanical changes that are likely to excite the Capri enthusiast. Tickford have developed the turbocharged version of the Capri Injection's 2.8 litre V6 themselves and it

Tickford Capri's turbo V6 develops 205 bhp

develops an impressive 205 bhp.

The five-speed transmission has been up-rated to handle the extra power, there's a ZF limited slip differential to keep the back end stable and the braking has been upped to all round discs, ventilated at the front. Suspension has been changed relatively little; the chief modification being a pair of extra locating links on the rear axle to stop it moving sideways under cornering load, a Capri weakness.

If it looks good on paper, it's even better on the road. Sensational in fact. Ours was the solitary, down-on-paper, hacked about example but it still flew like a bird. The engine doesn't feel deceptively quick at first: the Ford V6 isn't known for good bottom end punch. But, into its stride with the turbocharger on full stream – it flies. The mid-range punch that whips it forward from 60 mph to 100 mph plus has to be felt to be believed – in that sort of competition it will leave a Porsche 944 standing.

It handles like a Capri Injection should and that means very well indeed, with the suspension and bodywork modifications arguably adding to absolute limits. Unfortunately we tried the car on a miserably wet day when it needs more than a little respect: tread the throttle too harshly exiting a tight corner and it will go *very* sideways as the turbo power defeats grip.

It's a tremendous performer, then, but underneath the speed and dash, it's still a Capri and its origins as a family coupe do show from time to time. It certainly hasn't the all-round sophistication of a Porsche but there are sure to be 250 enthusiasts a year who will overlook that.

MODEL:	TICKFORD CAPRI
DATE IN UK:	October '83
RANGE:	3-door coupe
ENGINES:	2.8 V6 turbocharged, 205bhp
PERFORMANCE:	145mph
MPG:	n/a
PRICE:	£14,975

MILES
Behind the Wheel
Capri
with a touch of Aston

Ford's down to earth coupé is elevated to the star class

WHEN the going got tough, we came back to the fundamental concept – to make an 8/10 sized Aston Martin Vantage, a civilized muscle car, combining all the down-to-earth advantages of the Ford Capri.

But in the end, the Aston Martin Tickford Capri 2.8T has become a production reality only through the enthusiasm and persistence of the few people directly involved, plus the unwavering financial pledge given by a small Newport Pagnell company that could ill afford such a commitment.

Agreement that the development of the 2.8T might make sense came after a lunchtime meeting between three car nuts, Victor Gauntlett, Bob Lutz (then running Ford of Europe) and the writer. A year ago almost to the day, the running prototype appeared at the 1982 NEC Motor Show. None denied it looked exciting and certainly it attracted a lot of interest. It had the performance to match its looks. Test cars had been lapping Millbrook at around 140 mph, and were managing to reach 60 mph in a fraction over 6 secs. That it did not become an official Ford product was probably due to a combination of management changes and the length of time plus the number of personnel needed for the relevant development programme. Even so, the now defunct RS department in Cologne had a car for a month for evaluation purposes.

Since then there has been much hard bargaining between Ford and Aston Martin Tickford, and further refinement of the mechanical specification and trim, to make it a viable proposition. Meanwhile there has been help from Ford, behind the scene. Most importantly, the 2.8T will be sold through the Ford dealership chain, but with an Aston Martin Tickford warranty. The price including car tax and VAT is £14,985.

A full description of the Show car appeared in *Autocar* (23 October 1982) and since then, there have been relatively few important changes. The engine continues with its single IHI turbocharger mounted in front of the engine, drawing air through the standard Bosch K-Jetronic air weighing mechanism – a position chosen for turbo cooling and to maximize exhaust pulse energy. It is delivered via a huge air-to-air intercooler to the normal inlet plenum. An extra injector in the inlet pipe provides on boost enrichment. Aston Martin engineers would certainly have increased the strength of the engine internals if they had found it necessary, but thanks to the intercooler which is responsible for an inlet air temperature drop of up to 55 deg C no durability problems have been encountered. Production cars run at between 7 and 8 psi and as an additional protection against engine damage at peak cylinder pressures, and a fully computerized AFT ignition system (as used by Ford on the RS 1600i) has been adopted. Using inlet temperatures, manifold vacuum/pressure and rpm as inputs it has been possible to "map" round the likely detonation points. A large capacity radiator and oil cooler are also fitted, and the battery re-sited in the luggage compartment. The sole aim in the minds of AMT engineers has been to increase torque rather than go for top end power. Certainly if the standard engine has a shortcoming, it is its lack of low-to-mid range bite. Normally aspirated, it gives 150 bhp (PS) at 5,700 rpm and 162 lb. ft. torque at 4,200 rpm. For the 2.8T AMT quote 205 bhp at 5,000 – 5,500 rpm, and no less than 260 lb. ft. torque at 3,500 rpm. Full throttle dynamometer figures (relatively unrepresentative of road car behaviour) show that there is over 200 lb. ft. available from 2,000 rpm onwards. The engine meets all current NTA (National Type Approval) emission standards.

Luckily, Ford introduced their five-speed gearbox during the gestation period. Used in conjunction with the normal 3.09 to 1 final drive and 205/60-13 NCT tyres, its indirect fifth gives 25.8 mph per 1,000 rpm, ideal gearing for the car to achieve its 140 mph maximum at 5,400 rpm, which is just within the peak power band. Nominally the gearbox is working some way over its torque capacity in this application, but no failures have been encountered since steps were taken to improve lubrication between the input and output shafts.

Quite surprisingly the standard clutch suffices. The rear axle has the normal pressed steel differential cover replaced by a finned cast alloy part, reputed to lower differential oil temperatures by 15 deg C. and it goes without saying that a limited slip differential is fitted.

The Capri's rear drums are replaced with discs, a development that comes from the CC Racing prepared Group A racing Capris. The front brakes are standard.

Experiments conducted by the writer some years ago indicated that for a given suspension rate no real improvements in stability (and particularly wet weather handling) could be obtained without better sideways location of the rear axle. Acceptable results have been achieved very simply by bracing the spring to axle structure itself. Imagining this as an "H" frame (the axle forming the cross bar) outward pointing rubber bushed links run from brackets alongside the differential to mountings on the springs, thus preventing the "lozenging" of the structure. In turn, sideways movement at the front spring mountings is drastically reduced by the inclusion of "Prescolan" spacers between the spring eye and its mounting box in the chassis.

Springs, dampers and the front suspension geometry remain unchanged, but benefits in handling and more particularly ride have come via careful "rigging". One of the most satisfactory aspects of the new car (apart from its quite un-Capri like levels of noise refinement) is its much improved aerodynamic stability. Key here is the reduction of front lift. It would have been nice to achieve zero front lift forces, but this is not possible with a spoiler design that allows acceptable ramp and kerb clearances.

Various shapes were evaluated in the wind tunnel at MIRA. The final front end bumper-cum-spoiler moulding achieves a lift reduction of 70 per cent. Cutting rear lift to zero was no problem though it required a fairly dramatic looking "shovel" shaped moulding to do it.

For the relatively small numbers involved, all the additional body parts are moulded to a very high standard in glass fibre. In the interests of brake cooling (and looks) the flush fitting wheel trims that appeared on last year's show car have been dispensed with, and in production cars, the rear undertray goes for reasons of accessibility. As a result, drag rises slightly, but at 0.37 remains substantially lower than the standard car which turns in a MIRA measured co-efficient of around 0.39. A nice refinement on production cars will be the addition of a rubber lip seal to

Far left: Dramatic shovel shaped moulding on the tail was needed to cut rear lift to zero. Above, left: Blanked off grille is made possible by collecting enough cooling air from air dam high pressure source

Below: The IHI turbocharger is mounted in front of the engine – a position designed to maximize turbo cooling and exhaust pulse energy. Standard Bosch K-Jetronic air weighing is retained

Opposite page: The 2.8T at speed and at rest. Careful application of aerodynamics has produced substantial improvements on the standard car

Tickford Capri

close the door-to-body gap more effectively, a modification that should do something to reduce the wind noise generated by the break of air flow behind the A pillars.

From the driving seat, one of the most pleasing features is the Capri's traditional and straightforward instrumentation. (We like it, even if the Ford hierachy consider proper instruments dated). On the 2.8T there is a polished walnut overlay and matching walnut inlay on the passengers side facia. The whole facia is retrimmed in leather as is the new more comprehensive centre console. The full leather trim, deep pile carpeting, power mirrors and windows of the NEC Show car are now on the option list, but many (like us) will prefer the basic production model combining the facia treatment mentioned above plus door and rear side panel trim improved to match the standard fitment Recaro seats. All 2.8Ts come with a steel sunshine roof and stero/cassette player.

Brief drives in minimally trimmed development cars over the last couple of years had given me an encouraging insight into the way AMT's turbo installation had evened out the rough patches to which the 2.8i engine is prone – and made it a lot quicker. I wasn't quite prepared for the pleasant surprise provided by the fully developed product. It didn't feel like a Capri at all, but of an altogether more refined and much quieter motor car. Between 1,000 and 5,900 rpm when the rev limiter operates, there are no vibration or boom periods. It lopes along at an indicated 100-110 mph, with the barest of murmurs from under the bonnet. The extra weight, and better trim appear to be an effective cure for the Capri's susceptibility to harshness over rougher motorway surfaces. But for wind noise gradually increasing with speed, you sense

Below: Luxury interior treatment includes walnut overlay dash, full leather trim, deep pile carpet and Recaro seats. Sunroof and stereo radio/cassette player are standard

the car would be as quiet at 100 mph as it is at 80 mph, and very little noisier at 120 mph. Normal conversation is possible at a genuine 100 mph (108 mph indicated).

More refinement comes with a marked improvement in ride quality. Small ridges and broken surfaces are absorbed in a much more compliant manner again adding to the feel of a larger car, and its ability to soak up B-road and back double surfaces more comfortably is obvious. However we occasionally encountered some pitching movement in medium frequency undulations, particularly if the rear was well laden. It was a blustery few days we had the car, arriving in what amounted to a standard 2.8i and driving away the 2.8T highlighted the dramatic improvement in straight line stability that results from the aerodynamic improvements. The car normally runs dead straight, and now only needs the gentlest of guiding hands in stiff cross winds.

It was in just these sort of conditions that all performance testing took place, and on a car running in the heaviest possible specification. The performance figures we achieved must therefore represent the minimum customers can expect.

Using the 100 mph "hands off" banked circuit at Vauxhall's Millbrook proving ground, the car quickly worked its way up to a mean maximum of 137 mph, suggesting that without the slight cornering loads present in this speed bowl the claimed 140 mph would be achievable. Where it matters – say up to 120 mph – it would take a very fast car indeed to make any impression on the 2.8T. As with most turbocharged cars getting it off the line is a delicate balance between virtually no wheelspin and the engine momentarily off boost, or smoking rear tyres with the turbo gaining boost by the instant, and an equally tardy getaway as a result. Judging it right, the car surged off the line to reach 60 mph in 6.7 secs, 100 mph in 18.2 secs, and 120 in 30.8 secs; a considerably more accelerative car than the Porsche 944, Audi Quattro, BMW 635 or TVR Tasmin

350i, and by some considerable margin in every case.

The engine runs smoothly to the rev limiter, but the power curve flattens out noticeably above 5,500 rpm and there was barely any disadvantage in using this lower limit when testing. On the road, its greatest attribute is the slug of torque between 3,000 and 4,500 rpm. We were slightly bemused to discover that between 40–90 mph in third and 50–100 mph in fourth, the Capri proved absolutely comparable in performance with a 911SC, which is actually *lower* geared than the Capri. But as a real demonstration of its mid range urge, we find that in fifth gear it covers the 70–90 and 90–110 spans in 6.6 and 9.5 secs respectively, compared with 10.0 secs in both cases for the 911. The 2.8T takes only 2 secs longer to accelerate from 70–90 in fifth than it does in third!

In the cruise, the problem seems always to be reining it down to vaguely legal speeds. A squeeze of throttle has it galloping away. For overtaking there is always an abundance of acceleration on tap.

Look for immediate response much below 3,000 rpm, and there is a small delay. Turbo inertia is obviously more noticeable in the lower gears, and as one begins to take the strong surge forward higher in the rev range for granted, the engine is bound to feel rather flat at low rpm, even though the figures suggest the 2.8T loses nothing to the standard car on the un-boosted part of the rev range. So much torque could make for an extremely ill balanced car if the chassis and brakes could not cope. Capri 2.8i steering weighting is known to vary considerably in production, and I would have judged this particular example on the light side of ideal. Otherwise 2.8T manners always seemed adequate, and were sometimes delightful. I would not claim it has the ultimate grip of a 944 or Lotus Eclat (they both have more rubber on the road) or their relatively roll free cornering in extremis, but it has enough grip and in the dry conditions encountered, it proved a gentle and progressive handling car.

Experience suggests that on wet roads, drivers will have to exercise discretion with the right foot, because any excess driving torque now goes into pushing the rear end out of line rather than being dissipated in excess wheelspin. On the other hand, the improvement the limited slip differential makes to traction is a revelation. Given a test track, anything from gently understeer to a gloriously long powerslide is available. And where the car differs so obviously from nominally more exotic machinery (with independent rear suspension) is in its reluctance to be provoked into any sort of tail side, by suddenly lifting off in mid-corner, a gain directly attributable to the better rear axle location.

On the road, the brakes provided consistent and powerful retardation, but to make sure, we subjected them to the *Autocar* fade test (10 consecutive 0.5 stops) but this time from 100 mph, rather than the 92 mph reached at the quarter-mile which would have been the normal procedure. Only a very slight rise in pedal pressures occurred, and as if to confirm their subjectively better than standard balance, a 1.0g crash stop was both attainable and repeatable, and at a slightly higher pedal effort than in the normal car, thus forestalling the locking point if braking in panic.

In three days, we covered over 700 mixed (and often very fast) miles, without stress or discomfort – the leather upholstered seats attracted universal praise – and in so doing the 2.8T returned between 23 and 25 mpg, with a worst of 19.0 mph after performance testing. Impressively the overall figure (after correcting for a 4.4 per cent optimistic mileage recorder) turned out to be 21.7 mpg, confirming all AMT claims that the 2.8T provides all the performance one could reasonably ask for at no discernible cost in fuel consumption.

Taking stock, it seemed a bit more than a pretty reasonable blend of qualities – a view shared by those who drove it. I know Ford are not in the business of keeping models going for the sake of it (economies of scale old boy) but for people who like driving – and there are plainly those in the Ford management who *do not* – the Capri still seems to represent a brilliantly straight forward no nonsense high performance motor car. Silly, but I had the notion that the Capri 2.8i could become Ford's Porsche 911: a car that would continue (with odd improvements) until it no longer sold. All the AMT Capri 2.8T did was to convince me that if the will was there, the big engined Capri could continue for years yet.

ACCELERATION

True mph	Time (sec)
30	2.5
40	3.9
50	5.2
60	6.7
70	8.9
80	11.3
90	14.3
100	18.2
110	22.9
120	30.8

Maximum speed: 137*
Overall mpg: 21.7
Standing ¼ mile: 15.1 sec 92 mph
Standing kilometre: 27.8 sec 117 mph

mph	Top	4th	3rd	2nd
10-30	–	–	6.8	4.5
20-40	11.9	8.2	6.2	3.6
30-50	10.2	7.5	5.5	2.9
40-60	10.0	6.4	4.3	3.0
50-70	9.1	5.3	3.8	3.6
60-80	7.2	4.8	4.2	–
70-90	6.6	5.3	4.5	–
80-100	7.5	6.3	7.4	–
90-110	9.5	7.8	–	–
100-120	12.3	11.8	–	–

*see text.

The tide turns

Newly turbocharged, Renault's Fuego faces turbo Colt, Injection Capri and supercharged Lancia in a new-era 120mph coupe clash

That motor sport has an important role to play in the furtherance of road car design and development is without doubt – but equally important, to the manufacturers at least, is the reflected glory of success on the race and rally tracks and the subsequent upswing in sales.

It came as little surprise, therefore, that two major European car makers, both heavily involved in sport (and not without a little success) have recently launched new models in Britain aimed at buyers who would be willing to pay a premium for the kudos of owning a 'competition proved' car.

Renault's timing for the release of their turbo-engined Fuego model had obviously been carefully thought out: it was to be at last October's Motorfair that the car would first be seen by the public, immediately after the last round of the 1983 World Championship which Renault had confidently expected to win with their turbo-powered Formula one cars. That they were pipped at the post is now just history, and testament to the old saying about the best laid plans.

Happily for Lancia's marketing men, their rally team were more conspicuously successful, winning the World Rally Championship in style with a team of supercharged, not turbocharged, cars. Within a matter of days Lancar, Lancia's UK arm, had announced the introduction of two models with this Volumex supercharger system – their well-tried HPE and Coupe models.

Coincidentally, the Renault Fuego Turbo and Lancia HPE Volumex (VX) are direct rivals in the burgeoning coupe market. Both are three-door hatchbacks capable of 120 mph-plus speeds, and they are priced within £200 of each other.

Looking for rivals within this price sector is not a difficult matter: indeed these two models have been pitched into one of the hardest-fought of motoring battlegrounds.

Perhaps the yardstick by which they will both be judged is Ford's evergreen Capri in its 2.8-litre Injection form: a car that has been around in basic form for more years than Ford will care to remember, but which literally had new life breathed into it a couple of years ago by the fitting of a 160 bhp V6 powerplant. Slotting nicely between the two newcomers in terms of price, the Capri was our most obvious choice.

We could have chosen any one of Opel's Manta GT/E, the Honda Prelude EX, or Toyota's Celica ST as our fourth contender, but dismissing them as too cheap for the company (and ruling out the Audi Coupe as too dear) we settled for the Colt Cordia Turbo, with the interesting comparison of two turbos, one supercharged, and one fuel-injected model very much in mind.

Although Americans have enjoyed a Fuego Turbo for a year or so Britain has had to wait: now that it has arrived, however, the delay seems even stranger, as the engine chosen to power the car is only slightly different to the 1565 cc four-cylinder unit found in the R18 Turbo. In the Fuego it is tuned more towards performance than the economy/performance compromise in the 18.

To that end, Renault have lowered the compression ratio to 8.0:1 and altered the turbocharger system to allow an extra 22 per cent of boost pressure which gives an output of 132 bhp at 5500 rpm, a seven bhp advantage over the R18.

In other departments the new model follows the tried and tested Fuego layout: the engine is longitudinally mounted and drives the front wheels through a five-speed gearbox; front suspension is an independent double wishbone and coil spring arrangement with a dead axle and twin trailing arms at the rear. Steering is by rack and pinion and, as on the 2.0 GTX model, the Turbo has power assistance fitted as standard.

Externally the Fuego is similar to its forebears, save for a slightly altered front grille, colour-keyed bumpers, alloy wheels, and indiscreet 'TURBO' signwriting on almost every panel.

The car's drag figure is a quite respectable 0.35, not bad for a body shape that is now more than three years old: at £8700, the turbo is top of Renault's six-model Fuego line-up, and is some £700 more costly than the two-litre GTX.

By contrast to the Fuego, Lancia's HPE Volumex is almost a wolf in sheep's clothing. Aside from a power bulge in the bonnet, front and rear spoilers, and tiny 'Supercharged' lettering hidden away on the sides of the front wings, one would be hard pressed to tell the car apart from its more mundane brother.

But different it is, the supercharger helping to deliver a healthy 135 bhp at 5500 rpm from the familiar four-cylinder 1995 cc twin cam that also powers the HPE 2000IE.

The supercharger works by pressurising the fuel/air mixture drawn from a Weber carburettor, and is driven off the crankshaft via a toothed belt. Thus the mixture is forced into the engine at a much greater rate than normal to provide extra power, whereas the theoretically more efficient turbocharging system harnesses waste exhaust gas to provide the same end result.

However, Lancia – the only manufacturers to employ the system in this country – say a supercharger system's benefits include greater flexibility and maximum engine power at lower rpm, and does not suffer from the turbo's major snag of taking time to spin up to peak rpm and deliver maximum performance.

The VX also has a lowered compression ratio and a heavier clutch, and the five gear speeds have been raised to match the better spread of power. The all-round independent MacPherson strut suspension has been uprated, but otherwise the HPE is much as before.

The car is front-wheel driven, of course, and has power-assisted rack and pinion steering, while the servo-assisted braking system utilises discs all round. Lancia unfortunately don't quote any Cd figures for the HPE, so direct aerodynamic comparisons are impossible to make.

At £8500, the HPE Volumex is £500 more than its 2000IE brother and is also £500 more than the similarly supercharged Coupe.

The Ford Capri has just celebrated its 15th birthday – and there's no sign yet that the car's production life is threatened. With sales still going strongly and more than half a million produced since 1968, why should it?

Undoubtedly the Capri owes its continued existence to Ford's 1981 decision to fit the German V6 2792 cc fuel injected engine from the Granada in favour of the British-built (and less powerful) 3-litre unit, which had to be dropped because of rationalisation within the company. Ford could easily have axed the car then, but with no new sports coupe there to replace it until the Sierra XR4i was ready, they chose to retain it. Now that the XR4 is here the two are being kept in the range, side by side, until sales dictate that the older car should go. But when that will be is anybody's guess - many people prefer the Capri's classic low-slung lines to the bulbous Sierra.

By far the most powerful car in this test, the 2.8i packs a 160 bhp punch at 5700 revs, with 163 lbs ft of torque at 4300. Interestingly the same engine in the XR4 gives 'only' 150 bhp.

If the car shows its age anywhere it is in the drive layout and suspension areas. The Capri is the only rear-wheel-drive car in this test, and the springing couldn't be much simpler: MacPherson struts front and a leaf sprung rear axle, a combination that sounds primitive but that has been honed to perfection by Ford to give a system that is a match for many newer ones. Steering is by rack and pinion, and power assistance is provided. Brakes are servo-assisted ventilated discs and drums.

Surprisingly the Capri can offer a drag factor no better than 0.42, despite its apparently sleek lines – another indication of its age. Top of the three-model Capri range at £8653, the 2.8i is distinguished by seven inch wide tyres on alloy wheels, front and rear spoilers, and Recaro bucket seats.

The fourth car here is from a company that has put its faith very much in turbocharging as a means of improving performance and economy. The Cordia Turbo is one of no less than six turbo models within the Colt range, and sits alongside the

unblown 1600 cc Cordia which sells for £1250 less than the Turbo's price of £8399.

The pair share the same 1597 cc, four-cylinder ohc engine, the Turbo version having a 39 bhp power advantage with an output of 113 bhp at 5500 rpm. Torque is 125 lbs ft at 3500 rpm.

Front-driven, the Cordia Turbo has the unusual 'eight-speed' gearbox – that is it has a normal four-speed unit plus an extra two-position ratio selector for 'Power' or 'Economy' settings. This *does* give eight different ratios, but using them all isn't really feasible.

The all-independent suspension has MacPherson struts front and a trailing link system at the back, while steering is rack and pinion (without power assistance). Brakes are servo-assisted discs and drums. The Cor-

Colt rolls a little under hard cornering but has safe handling. Two gear shifters (below) give eight speeds

dia is, on paper at least, the most aerodynamically efficient car here, with a Cd figure of 0.34.

PERFORMANCE

FORD	●●●●●
RENAULT	●●●●○
COLT	●●●●○
LANCIA	●●●●○

Good marks for a quartet of *very* quick cars. While the Capri stands head and shoulders above the rest in terms of out-and-out power, it must be remembered that all four are capable of speeds in excess of 115 mph, and that three of the four can break the 10 second 0-60 barrier with considerable ease, the fourth just scraping by in 10 seconds dead.

Not only fastest in almost all respects, but also most pleasing in its delivery of power, is the Capri. The smooth V6 revs willingly and responsively at all times, and never sounds unduly harsh or flustered whatever the treatment.

From a standing start the grippy 205 x 13 Goodyear NCTs help the 2.8i off to very impressive acceleration figures indeed: 7.8 seconds to 60 mph and 22.4 to 100. Third gear is

good for 108 mph, while the top speed, achieved in fifth, is a cool 133 mph on the clock.

There's a very even spread of power in the gears, as evidenced by our overtaking-speed times. It is in this department, however, that the Capri loses out slightly over the sling-shot acceleration from 30 to 80 mph that the two turbos provide, but the 2.8i is by no means disgraced.

The gearchange itself is positive and quick, although rather notchy. An irritating buzzing vibration set in the gear lever at high revs, although noise levels generally are good. If driven in a moderate fashion and at legal speeds the engine is never intrusive, although at motorway speeds wind noise is something of a problem. Driven hard and fast the engine is understandably noisier.

Dashboard has plasticky finish but trim is pleasant, save for many 'Turbo' badges

COLT CORDIA TURBO

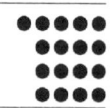

While the Ford's power is always there on tap, ready and willing to be exploited to the full, the Renault Fuego, in common with most turbos, has to be wound up to around 3000 rpm before the boost cuts in with that distinctive whine which rockets the car forward.

The Fuego reaches 60 mph in nine seconds flat, which is certainly impressive for a sub-1600 cc car, turbocharged or not. Its strong suit is, however, that mid-range acceleration punch which makes it easily quickest from 30 to 80 mph, in third gear at

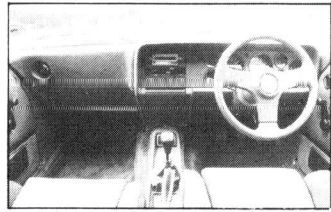
Ford's facia is old fashioned now but is at least clear. Trim is luxurious velour

least. That sort of overtaking power really gives the Turbo an enviable edge in everyday conditions.

Maximum speed is again achieved in fifth, and the car will happily achieve its high of 124 mph without fuss. Accelerating hard in each gear does, however, provide a good deal of unpleasant vibration from the facia, and the engine sounds extremely harsh if made to work that hard.

Under normal conditions the engine is quiet enough, though, but wind noise can be a problem at legal motorway speeds.

The gearchange was rather poor on our test car, but this was more probably due to its youth rather than an inherent fault. It was notchy and all to easy to select fourth instead of second gear.

The Colt Cordia also has that turbo

tion terms there is little to choose between either set of ratios, but if you want to go for the Cordia's top speed of 117 mph you'll need to select Economy. The fastest time we recorded to 60 mph was 9.1 seconds.

The Cordia Turbo's throaty engine note is by no means quiet under acceleration, and above legal speeds it becomes boomy and harsh, accompanied by vibrations from the facia.

The Lancia Volumex provides a surge of power quite unlike that of the turbos. The power is there instantly on tap, and is at its most potent lower down the rev range, as witnessed by the car's fine 30 to 80 mph third-gear acceleration times, which are almost a match for the turbos.

In straight acceleration the Volumex is not so quick, due largely to the raising of the gearing, but with

does – and in a style likely to excite the most timid of drivers. In a nutshell the 2.8i is a thrilling car to drive fast, with levels of grip from the Goodyears that make all dry roads a safe playground for the car.

The ride is certainly on the firm side, but around town is not unpleasantly so. Only on badly made-up country roads can that car's sensitivity to irregularities be a problem. Body roll is minimal and the power steering is simply perfect, the small leather steering wheel needing just 3.2 turns lock-to-lock, and the assistance making for great ease of parking without becoming too light for comfort at speed.

The Capri's natural cornering attitude is one of slight but stable understeer; pushed harder the tail can be made to swing out satisfyingly at will. For the sporting driver it is almost the ideal set up. Only those foolhardy enough to step off the throttle suddenly in a corner can expect any problems – even then, the car is forgiving enough to be easily brought back under control.

But in the wet, beware. A slightly greasy road can turn the 2.8i's tail-happy idiosyncracy into a nasty vice that can catch the unwary.

One blot on the Carpi's copybook is the braking system, which, while not exactly inadequate, does not inspire the greatest of confidence.

The Fuego Turbo also has a pleasingly good ride, perhaps even slightly better than the Capri's, and has a good, neutral feel to it in cornering. The 185/65 HR14 Pirelli P6 tyres help give good levels of grip and allow the Fuego to be cornered spiritedly with no problems.

Unlike the Capri, lifting off in mid-corner merely results in a slight tightening of the otherwise understeering attitude. It is indeed a very safe car at speed. The one bone of contention is the super-light power steering, which makes parking a joy but doesn't allow quite enough feel for the driver at anything other than parking speeds.

The Lancia is fairly sensitive to careless cornering. Lifting off midway will send the tail out sharply, ready to catch those not aware of the trait. Otherwise the HPE handles pleasingly (on identical tyres to the Fuego) and is fairly neutral in attitude, tending towards controllable oversteer.

The ride, too, is not bad, although sharp road bumps tend to jar the driver and passengers. Again, the power steering on this car, although good for parking, is a little too light for high-speed comfort. The all-round disc brakes perform well enough, but are slightly spongy.

Steering is not the Colt Cordia Turbo's strong point, either. It really does need power assistance, for parking is an unpleasant chore, with the 185/70 HR13 Michelin XVS tyres needing a hefty tug on the wheel to move at slow speeds.

Totally controllable handling is a delight to experience. Injected 2.8 engine has pleasant nature and revs freely

FORD CAPRI 2.8i

punch, and it is very nearly as rapid as the Renault in most departments. We found that with the 'Power' ratios selected acceleration from 30 to 80 mph was rapid indeed, but with the higher 'Economy' gears in use forward movement is not so rocket-like.

It is this phenomenon that indicates the likely use of the two-ratio shifter: drivers are likely, once the novelty has worn off, simply to leave it in Economy mode, using Power only when a quick spurt of speed is needed for an overtaking manoeuvre.

In straight standing-start accelera-

60 mph coming up in 10 seconds it is by no means slow for a two-litre, and those extra-long legs give it a comfortable 122 mph top speed.

The penalty of this performance is noise. Under acceleration the harsh-sounding engine note is quite intrusive, and wind noise adds to the cacophony. Even at idling the HPE is not quiet, and when the electric cooling fan cuts in the driver is made aware of it in no uncertain terms.

The car's gearbox is heavy, but positive enough.

HANDLING AND RIDE

FORD	●●●●
RENAULT	●●●
LANCIA	●●●
COLT	●●●

These are all sporty cars, and as such ride can be expected to be on the firm side: not for these 120 mph machines can there be a bump-absorbing floaty feel to things. It is ironic, then, that the oldest car here, the one with the seemingly old fashioned drive and suspension layout, should still provide the best compromise between ride and handling.

Yet that is exactly what the Capri

GROUP TEST: HIGH PERFORMANCE COUPES

Nor is the car's ride exemplary: town driving on uneven roads can mean a lot of jarring in the cabin, but at speed both ride and steering firm up to give a healthy feel.

In cornering there is a little body roll evident, but it takes a good deal of harsh treatment to upset the Michelins. Fairly neutral in balance, understeer gradually and safely builds up, switching suddenly to oversteer if the throttled is closed, snapping the tail out sharply – although this is easy to catch and correct.

ACCOMMODATION

LANCIA	●●●●
RENAULT	●●●
FORD	●●●
COLT	●●●

As all four are two-door coupes (albeit with hatchbacks) space is naturally restricted in absolute terms. But, taking into account the cars' sporty nature, none fares too badly when viewed in a comparative light. Clearly, carrying four passengers and their luggage on a long journey is not really a pleasant proposition for any of these cars, but as weekend tourers for two adults and maybe two children, all fit the bill perfectly.

Although not the most capacious in every respect, the Lancia HPE makes a pretty convincing try at providing enough space for everyone, and has the largest load area by far. It also *feels* the most airy, thanks to largish rear side windows and a huge glass in the tailgate.

The driver fares reasonably well: the seat offers good side and thigh support, although it does not travel far enough rearwards for the tallest; headroom is adequate.

The rear seat passengers are the best off in this car, although by no means able to lounge around in the space. With only two doors, entry to the rear is understandably difficult, and headroom in the rear is barely adequate. The rear seats themselves are comfy, but are shaped to allow only two passengers.

The Lancia has a usefully low rear loading sill and a fairly deep boot, but the sloping rear hatch restricts load space. The split rear seats fold down easily to provide a quite even floor, the rear parcel shelf being formed by two clever flaps attached to the backs of the rear seats.

The Capri's boot has a low sill but is very shallow due mainly to the stowing of the spare wheel beneath. The split rear seats fold easily enough but don't provide a flat floor.

Long-legged drivers will bless the 2.8i's front seats, which move back plenty far enough for them, but the shorter ones may have trouble in getting close enough, and indeed may not even be able to see out properly – the seats are that lowslung in the car's body.

The front seats themselves are admirable. Recaro buckets, they grip one's sides and support the thighs, and are trimmed in a nice velour-like material. In the back it is positively claustrophobic for adults. The tiny tear-shaped rear windows and the high-backed front seats hem people into the cramped space: not pleasant, and not recommended for long journeys with two passengers.

The Fuego Turbo also suffers from high seat-back syndrome. This, coupled with the poor kneeroom and headroom, makes long-distance travel in the rear for adults unpleasantly cramped.

The plush front seats are in a bucket style but do not offer the same degree of comfort as the Capri's. The driving position is fine for most, and an adjustable steering column helps to improve the situation.

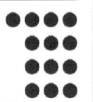

Sensitivity to carelessness is the Lancia's main trait. Treated well it responds with enjoyable and precise handling, though

Load space is a disappointment: the rear sill is unhelpfully high, the wheelarches intrude, the boot floor is raised up, and the split-fold rear seats make the floor uneven. In addition the curving rear screen will restrict the loading of boxy shapes. The parcel shelf is not in fact a shelf at all, but a fabric cover.

A major annoyance when passengers enter the rear of the Colt is that the front seats, once tilted forward, do not return to their original position – the driver has to reset them to his preferred location.

Those in the rear find it comfy enough, with a decent amount of headroom but again insufficient kneeroom, while the driver finds his position fairly good, although if he is tall space could be restricted. The rear sill height is almost as poor as the Renault's but there's quite a good depth to the boot, though it is still shallow. Colt unfortunately do not quote boot volume measurements, but we would put it roughly on a par with the Capri.

In common with the other three cars here, the Cordia has the useful 50/50 split rear seats to aid loading of awkwardly shaped items.

The front seats are quite comfortable and suportive, and include a lumbar support of dubious value.

LIVING WITH THE CARS

FORD	●●●●
RENAULT	●●●●
COLT	●●●
LANCIA	●●

There's no doubting that the Capri truly shows its age in its interior design: it certainly offers less in that department than the other cars here, but we would still rate it highly because of its functional, no-fuss nature and ease of everyday use.

The dashboard, for example, has been unchanged for years and looks curiously old-fashioned and out of place in a 1984 car. Yet it all works admirably well with no confusion.

Plasticky dashboard mars otherwise nice interior, finished in attractive check cloth

LANCIA HPE VOLUMEX

All the instruments one could want in a performance car are there, though admittedly some of the smaller dials are obscured by the neat leather steering wheel. All the controls are well positioned, including those wonderful 'old fashioned' eyeball air vents on either side of the dashboard which provide a powerful jet of air whenever required. Why this system was ever dropped in 'more modern' cars, Ford alone only know.

For extra ventilation a wind-back sunroof is provided as a standard feature. There's also a stereo radio/

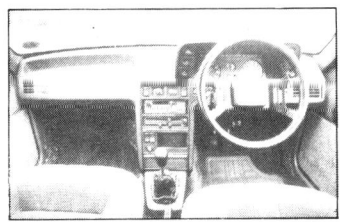
Renault's interior is plush velour with shaped seats. Facia layout is confused

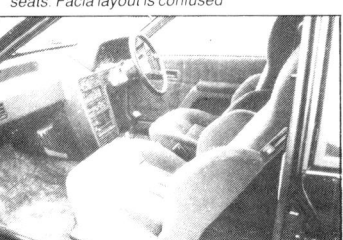

cassette and electric aerial, although on our test car the set performed rather poorly.

By contrast the Fuego Turbo's dashboard is positively chaotic, the dials and guages seemingly situated in a haphazard fashion, although, as with all cars, easy enough to get used to in time. It lights up like a Christmas tree at night, too.

The heating system is powerful but difficult to adjust finely, while ventilation is adequately catered for by separate fan-blown vents at either side of the dashboard.

The Turbo gets a very plush interior treatment, but we wonder how good it will look after a few months' hard treatment. Space for oddments is limited, and the door side pockets are poor and also form a rather inadequate handle for pulling the door shut.

rear wiper which won't wash as well, the manually-operated choke (although starting was never a problem), and those dreadfully loud TURBO badges everywhere which surely must become an embarrassment after a while.

The Colt, too, suffers from Turbomania, designs even appearing on the seat covers to remind occupants! The dashboard is clear enough, if a little plasticky. It is not well illuminated at night, making minor switches hard to find. A radio and separate cassette unit are standard features, as is the glass sunroof, which is opened by a fiddly knurled knob. The sunroof can be completely removed and stowed in the boot.

The heating system is fine, and cool air is available for the face (but only when moving along at speed).

In the end it is noise that is likely to irritate a regular driver most, although it must be said that the VX version is an improvement on its 2000IE cousin, which is very noisy indeed.

COSTS

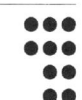

COLT	●●●
RENAULT	●●●
LANCIA	●●
FORD	●●

It is little surprise that our two turbo contenders returned the best average fuel consumptions. Turbocharging has long been held as the ideal way to improve performance without damaging economy too much; fuel injection and supercharging may provide a better, more usable spread of power but they certainly aren't the cheapest at the pumps.

Nor is it a surprise that our fuel returns didn't come anywhere near the quoted Government figures for any of the cars. On paper the Renault should have been best, and it did indeed return the highest peak figure of the four: 26.8 mpg. It was not quite the best on average, the Colt managing 23.7 and the Renault 23.5

The Colt's best figure of 26.1 mpg was returned after a spell of town driving, so given a long enough run and a light right foot economy in the region of the mid-30s should be easily possible. But on the basis of the Government figures, the Renault could be expected to do even better.

The HPE's figures reflect the supercharger's side effect of heavier fuel consumption, although the 22.1 mpg average was not too disappointing given the spirited treatment it received. A motorway run gave 19.3 mpg, while the car's best was 24.3.

Bringing up the rear in the economy stakes is the Capri with a 20.8 mpg average and a range of 19.1 to 23.0, proof positive that if the power is there you tend to use it.

'Hidden extras' in these four cars' pricing are thankfully few, only Renault having a longish list of cost-more options. These include £40 for the provision of the all-important rear seat belts.

Neither can Ford nor Lancia make available desirable extras like electric windows and central locking, and it's worth noting that the two-tone metallic paintwork that our test Capri sported will set you back an extra £193 on top of list price.

Both the Colt and the Ford are in insurance group 7, and we guess that the other pair will be too, although final confirmation has yet to come.

The Colt, Ford, and Lancia all require major servicing at 12,000 miles, plus an oil-change service half way. The Renault alone needs attention at 10,000 and 5000 miles, on the face of it a marginally more expensive proposition. Parts prices are likely to favour the Capri, because of its relative technical simplicity.

Renault is extremely safe in hard cornering, but over-light steering can worry driver. Wide tyres give good grip

RENAULT FUEGO TURBO

Renault's clever remote-controlled door lock opening system (PLIP) is employed in the Turbo, and very useful it is too, allowing drivers laden with shopping to unlock the side doors with a press of the infra-red button, rather than fiddling with keys. Normal locks are also provided just in case the system fails.

This high-tech idea is completely negated, however, by the retention of the Fuego's 'hidden' door catches recessed in the gap between door and frame, which are fiddly and break nails. Neither does the rear hatch

have an outside catch, being released from a knob inside.

Other minor niggles include the Space for oddments is again limited in the front. The rear hatch can either be opened by key or by using the interior catch, but the door has no handle. This means sliding one's fingers in the gap to get a grip, ensuring a handful of grime.

As already mentioned, the Colt's steering is unpleasantly heavy under town conditions.

The HPE's dashboard is neither clear nor modern-looking, with a confused jumble of dials and acres of cheap-looking plastic that seem out of place in an £8500 car. Conversely, the interior trim and headlining is of a very pleasant check cloth material that does look up to scratch.

Electric windows and a sunroof are standard features, as is an awful early-70s style slatted rear window visor which does little but restrict vision. Ventilation is not the HPE's strong point, and the heater is, if anything, *too* effective. The lowest fan setting fills the car with hot air and necessitates continual switching on and off. It seems impossible to direct warm air to the feet, either.

GROUP TEST: FUEGO TURBO, CORDIA TURBO, CAPRI 2.8i, LANCIA HPE VX

COLT CORDIA TURBO

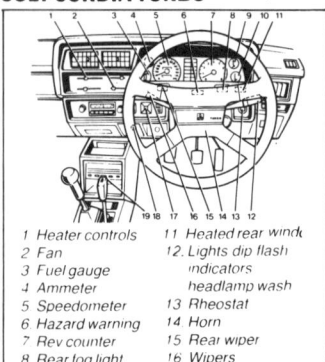

1 Heater controls
2 Fan
3 Fuel gauge
4 Ammeter
5 Speedometer
6 Hazard warning
7 Rev counter
8 Rear fog light
9 Oil pressure
10 Water temperature
11 Heated rear window
12 Lights dip flash indicators headlamp wash
13 Rheostat
14 Horn
15 Rear wiper
16 Wipers
17 Electric mirrors
18 Lighter
19 Gear ratio shifter

FORD CAPRI 2.8i

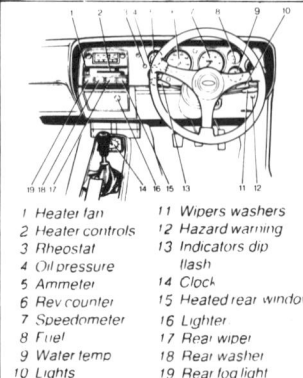

1 Heater fan
2 Heater controls
3 Rheostat
4 Oil pressure
5 Ammeter
6 Rev counter
7 Speedometer
8 Fuel
9 Water temp
10 Lights
11 Wipers washers
12 Hazard warning
13 Indicators dip flash
14 Clock
15 Heated rear window
16 Lighter
17 Rear wiper
18 Rear washer
19 Rear fog light

The Colt offers the longest warranty: three years, unlimited mileage. The others give the more usual 12 months. Rust cover is provided only by Lancia (six years) and Renault (five). Extra mechanical cover is available on the Ford (up to three years, 60,000 miles) for an extra fee.

Dealer spreads are headed, not surprisingly, by Ford with 1200, Renault have 370 (plus 460 service – only points), and bringing up the rear are Colt with 190 and Lancia with a rather thin spread of 130.

VERDICT

FORD	●●●●
RENAULT	●●●●
COLT	●●●
LANCIA	●●●

It is a hard task to split the two coupes at the head of our verdict chart: whether to plump for the old-fashioned but still relevant and attractive Ford powerhouse or the new, efficient, and technologically advanced challenger from France.

It would be tempting to say that the Fuego's attractive lines and brazen exhibitionism make it an obvious choice, but we found the car to be just that little bit too fancy for complete satisfaction, whereas the Capri has a power and roadholding edge that is totally satisfying.

We have our reservations: the 2.8i's facia could be tidied up and its fuel consumption is a definite minus,

LANCIA HPE VX

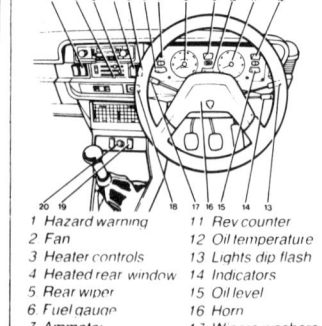

1 Hazard warning
2 Fan
3 Heater controls
4 Heated rear window
5 Rear wiper
6 Fuel gauge
7 Ammeter
8 Speedometer
9 Oil pressure
10 Water temperature
11 Rev counter
12 Oil temperature
13 Lights dip flash
14 Indicators
15 Oil level
16 Horn
17 Wipers washers
18 Clock
19 Rear fog light
20 Lighter

RENAULT FUEGO TURBO

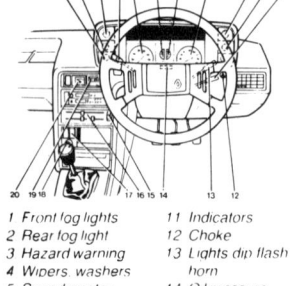

1 Front fog lights
2 Rear fog light
3 Hazard warning
4 Wipers, washers
5 Speedometer
6 Fuel gauge
7 Water temp
8 Rev counter
9 Heated rear window
10 Rear wiper
11 Indicators
12 Choke
13 Lights dip flash horn
14 Oil pressure
15 Fan
16 Heater controls
17 Door locking
18 Lighter
19 Clock
20 Turbo boost

but all in all the car is still conspicuously good value and remains the coupe by which all others will have to be judged.

The Fuego, then, is an honourable second, and will appeal to many with its modern lines, plush interior, and easy-to-handle character. We would heartily recommend it to anyone who finds bigger, heavier sporty cars a handful to park and manoeuvre, and who would rather have a 'tame' performance car than a wild one.

The Colt is a good £300 cheaper than the Fuego, and that, coupled with the excellent warranty offered, will sway many people towards the Japanese turbo.

There's the promise of good fuel economy and reasonable passenger accommodation, although we do have reservations about the Cordia's steering, ride, and noise levels.

Lancia's decision to supercharge the HPE was a good one: performance is bettered and economy only slightly adversely affected. But we wonder whether the Italian firm should not have approached the situation from a modern angle and turbocharged the car to produce a genuine flyer.

That apart, the Volumex system breathes new life into what is a car that is beginning to show its age, yet which still offers a goodly amount of enjoyment and space for its class.

CAR	Colt Cordia Turbo	Ford Capri 2.8i	Lancia HPE Volumex	Renault Fuego Turbo
PRICE	£8399	£8653	£8500	£8700
Other models	1 hatchback	2 hatchbacks	1 hatchback	5 hatchbacks
Price span	£7150-£8399	£5320-£8653	£7975-£8500	£5350-£8700
PERFORMANCE				
Max Speed (mph)	117†/112††	130	122	124
Max in 4th (mph)	—	127	106	110
Max in 3rd (mph)	109/86	108	85	76
Max in 2nd (mph)	71/54	77	57	51
Max in 1st (mph)	38/28	40	37	30
0-30 (sec)	2.9/3.2	2.9	3.7	3.4
0-40 (sec)	4.7/5.2	4.1	5.1	4.8
0-50 (sec)	6.7/6.9	6.0	7.7	6.5
0-60 (sec)	9.1/9.6	7.8	10.0	9.0
0-70 (sec)	11.3/11.6	9.6	13.2	12.0
0-80 (sec)	15.2/15.2	12.9	15.9	15.1
0-90 (sec)	21.2/21.1	15.9	22.0	19.7
0-100 (sec)	27.9/27.0	22.4	29.0	24.7
0-400 metres (sec)	17.2/17.3	16.4	17.6	17.7
Terminal speed (mph)	85/86	92	84	84
30-50 in 3rd/4th/5th (sec)	7.8-4.6/11.4-1-7.4	6.0/6.8/9.0	4.4/6.7/9.7	4.2/8.4/12.6
40-60 in 3rd/4th/5th (sec)	6.4-4.3/14.4-7.3	5.0/6.3/9.4	4.2/5.6/7.9	3.9/6.3/9.2
50-70 in 3rd/4th/5th (sec)	6.2-4.7/12.0-6.8	5.0/7.3/10.0	4.4/6.1/8.5	4.6/7.1/8.8
60-80 in 3rd/4th/5th (sec)	7.7-6.0/10.7-7.5	5.3/7.3/11.0	4.8/6.8/9.0	5.2/7.8/10.3
SPECIFICATIONS				
Cylinders/capacity (cc)	4/1597	V6/2792	4/1995	4/1565
Bore x stroke (mm)	77x86	93x68	84x90	77x84
Valve gear	ohc	ohv	dohc	ohc
Compression ratio	8.5:1	9.2:1	7.5:1	8.0:1
Carburation	Twin choke/turbo	Bosch injection	Twin choke	Inj/turbo
Power/rpm (bhp)	113/5500	160/5700	135/5500	132/5500
Torque/rpm (lbs/ft)	125/3500	163/4300	152/3000	147/3000
Steering	Rack/pin	PA/Rack/pin	PA/Rack/pin	PA/Rack/pin
Turns lock to lock	3.5	3.2	3.1	2.5
Turning circle (ft)	35	35	35	33
Brakes	S/Di/Dr	S/Di/Dr	S/Di/Di	S/Di/Di
Suspension front	I/McP	I/McP	I/McP	I/Wi/C
rear	I/Ta	I/McP	½E	DA/C
COSTS				
Test mpg	21.6-26.1	19.1-23.0	19.3-24.3	21.8-26.8
Govt mpg City/56/75	30.4/46.3/34.9	18.7/38.2/30.1	22.2/39.2/31.0	26.9/49.6/36.7
Tank galls (grade)	11(4)	12.7(4)	11.4(4)	12.5(4)
Major service miles (hours)	12,000(2.4)	12,000(3.0)	12,000(3.5)	10,000(1.5)
Parts costs (fitting hours)				
Front wing	£70.00(1.4)	£66.92(—)	£98.76(3.5)	£60.00(1.8)
Front bumper	£106.00(0.3)	£30.20(0.5)	£91.71(0.6)	£95.50(1.4)
Headlamp unit	£54.75(0.5)	£17.04(0.4)	£65.94(0.4)	£57.50(0.5)
Rear light lens	£33.90(0.6)	£12.50(0.2)	£10.83(0.3)	£22.60(0.3)
Front brake pads/shoes	£33.0(1.0)	£20.26(0.6)	£17.70(0.6)	£10.40(0.8)
Shock absorber	£45.10(0.7)	£47.38(1.0)	£42.41(0.8)	£27.60(0.9)
Windscreen	£54.00(3.5)	£29.11(1.5)	£130.31(7.0)	£80.50(1.2)
Exhaust system	£116.80(1.0)	£156.80(1.1)	£221.90(1.4)	£105.30(1.5)
Clutch unit	£78.73(2.9)	£94.20(2.4)	£96.65(5.6)	£66.50(5.2)
Alternator	£50.00(0.5)	£54.18(0.5)	£168.83(0.7)	£41.80(1.0)
Insurance group	7	7	7*	7*
Warranty	36/UL	12/UL	12/UL	12/UL
Rust warranty	none	none	6 yrs	5 yrs
EQUIPMENT				
Alloy wheels	yes	yes	yes	yes
Automatic choke	yes	yes	yes	no
Five-speed gearbox	no	yes	yes	yes
Central locking system	no	no	no	yes
Electric windows	no	no	yes	yes
Tinted glass	yes	yes	yes	yes
Ammeter	no	yes	yes	no
Petrol cap lock	yes	yes	yes	no
Power steering	no	yes	yes	yes
Adjustable steering column	yes	no	yes	yes
Sound system	s. radio/cassette	s. radio/cassette	none	none
Seat height adjustment	no	no	no	no
Rear seat belts	no	yes	no	£40
Sunroof	yes	yes	no	no
Headlamp wash-wipe	no	no	no	yes
DIMENSIONS				
Front headroom (ins)	33	34	34	33
Front legroom (ins)	34-41	36-42	33-40	34-41
Steering-wheel-seat (ins)	13-20	15-21	15-20	12-20
Rear headroom (ins)	33	31	32	31
Rear kneeroom (ins)	24-32	22-27	26-31	21-29
Length (ins)	168.0	172.0	168.0	172.0
Wheelbase (ins)	96.0	101.0	100.0	96.0
Height (ins)	52.0	53.0	51.0	53.0
Boot Load height (ins)	35.0	28.0	22.0	36.0
Boot depth (ins)	33-55	36-57	36-56	39-60
Overall width (ins)	65.0	67.0	65.0	67.0
Int. width (ins)	53.0	50.0	49.0	55.0
Weight (cwt)	19.1	30.4	22.3	20.8
Boot capacity (cu ft)	—	9/23	11/42	12/28

KEY. Valve gear: ohc, overhead camshaft; ohv, overhead valve; dohc, double overhead camshaft. **Steering:** rack/pin, rack and pinion; PA, power assistance. **Brakes:** Di, discs; Dr, drums; S, servo assistance. **Suspension:** I, independent; C, coil springs; ½E, semi-elliptic springs; Wi, wishbones; McP MacPherson struts; Ta, trailing arm location; DA, dead beam axle. * Denotes estimated insurance grouping. † Economy gear setting. †† 'Power' gear setting.

TVR Tasmin Convertible Ford Capri 2.8i

Power sharing with style. Turning the heads in the Tasmin, cruising with comfort in the Capri

Right: Tasmin Convertible takes on the Capri Injection

IN MECHANICAL terms anyway, the TVR Tasmin convertible and the Ford Capri 2.8i are perfectly comparable, sharing as they do the fuel injected Ford "Cologne" V6 developing 160 bhp and a gutsy 162 lb.ft of torque.

The steel-bodied Ford carries the latest "beetle brow" Capri bodystyle on a revised suspension arrangement that sits it 20 mm closer to the road than the 3-litre Essex engined car it replaced.

Right: Walnut surround and crushed velour trim adds luxury touch to the TVR. Capri (far right) is dated but effective

Weighing 23.4 cwt, the Capri is just over a half hundredweight heavier than the glassfibre bodied TVR which looks sleek and clean in its new shell. Price differential (£13,242 for the TVR, £8,125 for the Capri) reflects the differences in economies of scale between Belgium and Blackpool.

Sonic pattern wide wheels shod with fat Goodyear NCT tyres enhance the Capri's purposeful looks and Ford have thankfully resisted the temptation to go overboard with a special paint job.

The result is something mean looking to please those to whom macho looks are important. Visual appeal of the TVR is more obvious but the wedge shape is not to all tastes.

Right: The Targa top also lives in the narrow but deep TVR boot. Shelf behind rear seats is just that but the Capri has two real seats

Sharing the same powerunit and drivetrain one would expect the performances to be broadly similar, and they are.

Our Autotest maximum of the Capri was 127 mph and for the Convertible 124 mph (the hardtop TVR recorded a maximum of 130 mph). Rest to 60 mph times were equally similar and even over the more significant span of 0 to 100 mph the heavier and probably less aerodynamically effective Capri had the slight edge.

Reasons for this apparent

	TVR Tasmin Convertible	Ford Capri 2.8i
Capacity:	2,792 c.c.	2,792 c.c.
Power/weight ratio:	123 bhp/ton	119 bhp/ton
Maximum speed:	124 mph	123 mph
0-60 mph:	7.8 sec	7.9 sec
0-100 mph:	25.3 sec	23.4 sec
50-70 mph in top:	9.4 sec	8.2 sec
Fuel consumption:	26.2 mpg	25.2 mpg
Insurance group:	7/8	7
Insurance quotation:	£249	£151
Autotest:	27.6.81	20.6.81

anomaly can be many and various including differing exhaust arrangements but both Sam and Nigel found the Capri smoother and the power delivery more effortless. There is the physical impression of having to give the TVR more right foot because of the excessively long throttle pedal travel which incidentally leaves the foot at an awkward cramp-inducing angle at cruising speed.

Gearchange in both cases was the usual slick Ford production although the detente against reverse in the Capri could have been stronger against snatch changes down to second going into the wrong slot.

Handling and ride of both cars was widely different with the Capri emerging as the more refined and relaxed long distance mileeater while the TVR required a higher degree of concentration and effort for rapid progress. The power assisted steering on the Capri was well weighted and transmitted a useful degree of feel. Should the prodigious grip capability of the NCT's be exceeded, easy control by steering and throttle made it a much easier car to drive quickly.

The TVR with its tubular backbone frame gives the impression of being harsher and stiffer but

the ride at higher speeds is good and unlike many sports cars does not deteriorate to buckboard quality over small bumps at slow speeds. Steering is heavy and *very* prone to kickback which can be disconcerting on encounter with mid corner irregularities.

Facia layout of the Capri is beginning to look dated but it remains functional with simple controls and instrument layout. Set in walnut veneer and surrounded by crushed velour, the TVR facia carries something of an image to go with the price tag. The gear lever is now set more forward and falls more easily to hand, the short travel handbrake on top of the high tunnel is less convenient than the Capri's. Seats are supportive but for tall drivers, the fixed neck roll sits uncomfortably low. Controls on the Capri are all well placed and the Recaro seats comfortable if a little narrow across the back causing the firm side rolls to dig into the larger driver's sides.

When the sun shines, the TVR comes into its own. The hood arrangement with its rigid targa type centre section is brilliantly simple and highly effective. With the soft rear section down and side windows raised the open air ride is remarkably free from buffeting and the opinion of both our drivers was the convertible system was the best they had seen. There is a ledge behind the seats but strictly for oddments stowage and the boot — despite losing space to the full sized spare wheel and the Targa top is just adequate for two. Despite modifications to the fuel filler system, our TVR was severely afflicted by a smell of petrol. We were unable to track down the source but the smell was all pervading for the whole time we had the car.

The Capri is, of course very much a four seater, although access to the rear compartment could be tricky for some. The Ghia trim package that goes with the 2.8i includes a sun roof and this together with the very effective facia and eyeball vents enabled a good stream of cool air to be set up. The TVR needed the fresh air flow to the footwells boosting in order to counteract heat generated into the cabin from the engine and gearbox.

In the matter of choice, the price difference must play a significant part and in pure value for money the Capri must win. Performance is so close as to make little difference and as a long distance express, the Ford is an infinitely better proposition. However, the TVR — despite some remaining drawbacks — certainly provides eye-catching exclusivity if you are prepared to pay for it. **SB/NF**

Tickford Capri

Ford with a touch of class

THE Capri 2.8i is to the Ford range what the 911 is to the Porsche range, a rather old-fashioned design that evokes envy, admiration, and pride of ownership that knows no bounds. When Ford of Europe launched the Sierra XR4i on the Targa Florio course last Spring they also offered a 2.8i five-speed to drive over the same course, and we have to say that the raw power and throttle-steering capabilities of the Capri left the biggest impression on us, refined as the Sierra may be. Even in standard form the 2.8i is a machine that gives the keen driver an ear-to-ear smile when he has the chance to open it up . . . so what price a *turbocharged*, 205 bhp conversion?

The story has often been told that Victor Gauntlett of Aston Martin, Bob Lutz (then head of Ford of Europe) and former Lotus driver John Miles hatched the idea of the Tickford Capri over a lunch table. When the project was well down the road, and Tickford had invested a considerable amount of money, Lutz was promoted to Ford of America and the project went onto the back-burner, as they say. Tickford took the courageous decision to continue with the project with the intention of building 250 examples this year in the new Coventry factory which Tickford occupies to finish the Jaguar XJ-S Cabriolet model, and even had to go solo with the expensive and time-consuming business of obtaining Type Approval.

The end product was seen on the Aston Martin Tickford stand at Motorfair and deliveries started at the end of 1983. Inevitably the question must be asked:

THERE is plenty of space ahead of the V6 for the turbocharger, and large-bore copperised pipes take the charged air via an intercooler to the inlet plenum chamber.

"Who in their right mind would pay £14,985 for a Ford Capri — not far off double its original price?" The tag includes much more than an IHI turbo, hiking the power from 160 to 205 bhp . . . a Garrett intercooler for instance, the new AFT digital computerised ignition and electronic fuel management system, restyled body panels, reinforcements to the five-speed gearbox, a limited slip differential, conversion to disc brakes at the rear, and a rear axle locating A-frame.

Inside the car we find electrically operated tinted windows, a manual sunroof, the standard Recaro velour covered seats, a walnut burr fascia trim with leather surrounds, and leather covering for the steering wheel and rear quarter panels; a leather map pocket is installed in front of the passenger.

Does a market exist for 250 examples of the Tickford Capri? Clearly Tickford are convinced that it does, but probably not from Ford's own clientèle. The potential market is comprised of people who are prepared to pay £15,000 for a very quick, sporting car, who would otherwise be looking at the Porsche 944, a BMW 528i, or a Lotus Excel or Esprit — the choice is really very narrow in that sector. To Aston Martin's traditional customers, prepared to spend upwards of £40,000 on the real thing, maybe £15,000 is not so much after all for a second car to be used for journeys into London. . . .

In terms of acceleration and top speed the AMT Capri will out-perform all its potential rivals mentioned above, and by a fair margin. Our definition of a reasonably quick car is one that will reach 60 mph in under 10 sec and 100 mph in under 20 sec. To reach 60 in 6.8 sec and 100 mph in 19.6 sec is quite outstanding, well up in the Porsche 911 SC class, if not up to the latest Carrera, and that sets a yardstick by which the turbocharged Capri may be judged.

Although the turbocharged engine is said to double the torque value at 2,000 rpm there did not seem to be much evidence of this on the road. If you are in too high a gear for the situation there is a yawning wait for something to happen when you floor the throttle, then quite suddenly there is an awakening under the bonnet at 3,300 rpm and an explosive burst of power that goes on to 6,000 rpm, requiring a good deal of mental agility to keep up with the situation! This need not be a criticism since the option is always there to change down and have the power immediately, yet on a wet and perhaps bumpy road the dramatic application of power through the P7 tyres is quite enough to break adhesion — and with a limited slip differential, that can be quite an. adventure.

The ZF differential, with a 50% locking factor, helps to raise the level of adhesion, enabling the Capri to put its power down impressively well. Our best acceleration figures were obtained when the rear wheels could be broken away, causing the tail of the Capri to swing to the left — it did not feel the best way of starting, but on a more grippy surface the acceleration times were slower, and the average of all the times was

slightly slower than the manufacturer's claim. To exchange 60-series Goodyear NCT tyres for 60-series Pirelli P7s, at a cost of £608, sounds doubtful value and it would need a back-to-back test to determine whether the cost is justified. Certainly the Pirellis on the test car complement the revised suspension and give the Tickford Capri phenomenal cornering power, accompanied by a slight twitchiness that worries people unused to Ford's live axle and semi-elliptic leaf spring design, but is easy to live with.

With the limited slip diff the driver has to get used to the mild "pushing" understeer in medium bends, which changes to tuck-in when the throttle is released; also to the need for extra revs when manoeuvring, since the engine has to push against a locking differential. The drive line tends to be harsh, too, with resonance and vibration at certain points under acceleration, but despite these traits we imagine that the Capri would be a handful *without* the ZF differential, and almost impossible to drive effectively in the wet. In the suspension department the springs and dampers have been left standard, though careful tuning and the addition of the rear axle supporting bracket have improved the handling quality without impairing the ride to any great degree; if the ride comfort is slightly harsher than standard, it is likely to be the result of fitting P7s.

Ventilated disc brakes from the racing Capris are fitted at the rear, 10.4 in in diameter and with an integral handbrake system, while the standard ventilated discs are retained at the front. The brakes did feel very secure, with firm pedal pressure and perfectly even retardation at each corner, and the handbrake is surprisingly effective too.

Tuning for performance

Even with 160 bhp available the Capri 2.8i is considered a high performance car, but the addition of a turbocharger takes the Tickford Capri into an altogether higher category. It would be stretching the point a bit to call it a poor man's Porsche Turbo, but the level of performance is on a par with a 911 2.7, for instance, making up with turbo surge what it lacks low down.

The Bosch K-Jetronic injected V6 power unit is very well developed, and no internal changes were needed other than balancing when the IHI turbocharger was mounted in front of the vee, an air-to-air intercooler also being plumbed in. Maximum torque is lifted from 163 lb ft at 4,200 rpm to 260 lb ft at 3,500 rpm, making its contribution to the improvement in performance. The standstill to 60 mph time is slashed from 7.9 sec to 6.8 sec, while the 100 mph figure is reduced from around 25 sec to 19.6 sec. The maximum speed increases from 127 mph to a slightly theoretical 140 mph (which we were not able to check), yet our overall fuel consumption figure of 22.76 mpg is exactly

BOLT ON GRP panels transform the looks of the Capri and make it more stable, though no improvement in drag is recorded. The test car was loaned by Aston Martin (Sales) Ltd in Sloane Street, London.

what the owner of a normally aspirated Capri might expect to return on a regular basis. Something for nothing?

These performance advantages are impressive on paper, even more so on the road. Overtaking distances seem to be halved, making main road journeys faster, safer, and less wearing on the nerves. Motorway driving is more pleasant too, the AMT Capri accelerating much faster through the wall of spray that attends trucks on a rainy day, while the bolt-on appendages have greatly improved stability.

We have not yet mentioned the GRP panels which blank off the usual radiator grille and form an air dam, running along the skirts, and give a revised, more aerodynamic line at the back, topped by a bootlid mounted rear spoiler.

The person who spends £15,000 on a Capri would naturally expect a car which stands out in a crowd, and with all their styling and coachbuilding history Tickford could be relied upon to produce a striking, well balanced style that is visually appealing without being in the least garish. The new panels have virtually eliminated front-end lift and moved back the centre of pressure, making the converted Capri infinitely more stable at high speed.

Criticisms there must be, but only a few. We have mentioned the transmission rumble which lowers the general level of refinement. Maybe there is nothing that Tickford can do about that, but it is something they could be working on. The main beam headlamps are superb . . . but the dipped beam is absolutely pathetic, really making it necessary to halve your speed if a car approaches on a country road. The doors still shut with a clang, rather than a £15,000 thud, and as Capri owners expect the tailgate still gets filthy in the winter time, and needs a handle (interior or exterior) to facilitate closing. As a further development, we would far sooner have a proper rotating control for the lights instead of a hidden third stalk, on the far side of the wipers control, and some lining inside the glove box to avoid the rattling of oddments.

The power steering is nicely weighted, to the point where the driver may not be sure whether it is assisted or not, and Tickford have wisely left this alone. Even so, a great deal of engineering and development has gone into this conversion to justify the price label which, though probably beyond the comprehension of someone who can just about afford a standard Capri, represents good value to those hunting the ultimate. Other than the RS3100 of 10 years ago (an homologation model which hardly set new standards for reliability) the AMT Capri must be the fastest yet offered for road use, improving on power and flexibility. It has been referred to as an eight-tenths size Vantage at a third of the price, and that just about sums it up.

We are left with the thought that the Capri keeps having stays of execution, but at some time in the coming months the chop will come when the line is needed for a new product, and the production level is considered uneconomic. As the specialist manufacturers, including Aston Martin Lagonda Tickford, are now entering a new period of prosperity, could not Ford hand over all the production facilities to ensure the perpetuation of the Capri? — M.L.C.

PERFORMANCE	
Acceleration:	
Speed	Secs
0-30	2.3
0-40	4.1
0-50	5.4
0-60	6.8
0-80	12.1
0-100	19.6
Speed in gears:	
1st	38 mph @ 6,000 rpm
2nd	71 mph @ 6,000 rpm
3rd	100 mph @ 6,000 rpm
4th	129 mph @ 6,000 rpm
5th	140 mph estimated
Fuel consumption:	
22.76 mpg overall	

Ford Capri III

BY FORD'S usual standards, the Capri has now been on sale for a very long time. The original "chassis" and underpan date from 1969, and the smoothed-out Mk II shape from 1974. The current four-headlamp Mk III variety, a lightly facelifted Mk II, has been around for more than six years. Except for the introduction of one outstanding derivative — the 2.8i of 1981 — the Capri has changed very little in recent years, but Ford keep it in production. Last year, more than 22,000 were sold in the UK.

Although the Capri was once assembled in the UK, at Halewood, all Mk IIIs come from Cologne, in West Germany. Because of the large numbers sold over the years (more than 160,000 Mk IIIs so far), there is a lot of choice on the secondhand

market, and the Capri is undoubtedly a best seller in the sporting coupé sector.

What is a Capri III?

All Capris of the current types have the same basic body/chassis unit, suspension and steering, the big differences being in the choice of engines, transmissions, and trim packages. It is a three-door hatchback/coupé, in which there is close-coupled four-seater accommodation, perfectly practical for use by the family on long journeys. As with all such designs, the rear seat can be folded forward to increase the luggage accommodation.

MacPherson strut independent front suspension is used, and a live rear axle located by nothing more complex than semi-elliptic leaf springs, and an anti-roll bar. Rack and pinion

steering is on all models (with power assistance on the V6 versions). All types have front wheel disc brakes with servo assistance (bigger, and more powerful for the larger-engined cars).

The Ford philosophy for the Capri, as with their other ranges, is that the customer can choose between a whole variety of engines, trim specifications, and model types, and that there should be a wide range of extras (for factory or dealer fitment) to back this up.

Engine choice

At first, in 1978, the Capri III was offered with five different engine options. A sixth (the highly fuel-injected 2.8-litre V6) followed in 1981, but by 1983 rationalization had set in, so that the current range includes only

Top: Typical four-headlamp Capri, in this case a 1979 2.0S. Above: 1983 2.8i with 160 bhp is easily distinguished by lowered suspension and special alloy wheels

three different engines.

The smallest Capris (1300/1300L models) had the sturdy, simple, 57 bhp 1.3-litre overhead-valve "Kent" unit, as fitted to many other Fords, ranging from the Fiesta to the Cortina. This was not a popular derivative, however, as the car was underpowered, and it was dropped at the end of 1981.

Next were the 1600s, which used the 1,593 c.c. overhead-cam four-cylinder "Pinto" unit (also found in Cortinas and Granadas).

The 1600L/1600GL/1600LS cars used single carburettor/72 bhp units, and always sold very well indeed, while the 1600S had a dual-choke carb/88 bhp engine.

The 2000/2000S/2000 Ghia models all had the same 1,993 c.c. Pinto engine, in dual-choke Weber/98 bhp tune. This sold well and quite overshadowed the 1600S, for it had much more torque, performed better and was almost as economical.

Most powerful, at first, were the 3000S/3000 Ghia types, which used the massive, heavy, 2,994 c.c. overhead valve "Essex" V6, which had a downdraught dual-choke Weber carb, producing 138 bhp and no less than 174 lb. ft. maximum torque. This was a very satisfying car to drive, as the engine was very flexible, though it was not very fuel-efficient.

The 3-litre cars were phased out early in 1981, to be replaced by the 2.8i, which used the entirely different German "Cologne" V6 still with overhead valves, and sporting Bosch fuel injection (like the hottest Granadas and the Sierra XR4i) 2,792 c.c., this produces no less than 160 bhp, with 162 lb. ft. of torque, and makes the Capri into a really fast road car.

Neither V6 Capri sold in large numbers, but annual UK sales of around 3,000 (actually, 4,629 2.8is were sold in 1983), are very satisfactory for that market sector. The problem is not with the car itself, but with the insurance, maintenance and depreciation costs which go with it.

Transmissions

We will not confuse you with detail, so let's just say that no fewer than three different types of four-speed all-synchromesh, two types of five-speed all-synchromesh, and an automatic transmission option have been available on Capri IIIs over the years. Gearboxes tend to be matched to engines — which is to say that 1600s and 2000s had "German Cortina/Taunus" boxes, while the V6-engined cars had the bigger, "Granada type". The big gearboxes were by no means as sweet in operation as Ford's smaller transmissions have always been, but the synchromesh was most effective.

Five speeds were standardized on the 2.8i for 1983 (XR4i/Granada type), and on the 2000S from March 1983 (Sierra-type), but no five-speed box is available on the 1600LS, not even as an option.

Ford's own-make three-speed automatic transmission was optional on some models — not Ss and 1300s — though rarely specified by customers; it was standard on the 3000 Ghia. The 2.8i has never been offered with automatic transmission.

Above: Graduated side stripe aligning with wraparound bumpers was a feature of Capri S models

Right: Steel wheels and a lower trim level were fitted to the 1600L

Above: Typical Capri interior, of a 1978 3.0S. Note the low seating position

HOW MUCH TO PAY?

Price Range	1300	1600L/LS	1600GL	1600S	2000GL	2000S	2000 Ghia	3000S	3000** Ghia	2.8 Injection
£1,500-£1,600	1978									
£1,700-£1,800		1978	1978							
£1,900-£2,000	1979			1978	1978	1978				
£2,100-£2,200		1979	1979					1978		
£2,300-£2,400	1980			1979	1979	1979	1978			
£2,600-£2,700		1980	1980					1979	1978	
£2,800-£2,900	1981			1980	1980	1980	1979			
£3,200-£3,300		1981*	1981					1980	1979	
£3,400-£3,500				1981	1981	1981	1980			
£3,700-£3,800									1980	
£3,800-£3,900		1982*	1982					1981		
£4,100-£4,200					1982		1981			
£4,200-£4,300		1983*	1983			1982				
£4,400-£4,600					1983	1983			1981	
£5,000-£5,200							1982			1981
£5,300-£5,500							1983			
£5,900-£6,100										1982
£6,700-£6,900										1983

*The 1600LS went on general sale in 1981.
**All 3000 Ghia prices are quoted for automatic transmission models. Automatic transmission was optional on 1600L/LS/GL, 2000GL/Ghia, and on 1978 and 1979 3000 Ghias; values are enhanced by up to £100 for 1983 models.

Ford Capri III

Model cocktails, and popular options

The cheapest Capri was the 1300 "Base" model, but this was dropped in a matter of months. The most sparsely equipped of the normal range were the "L" derivatives, which featured cloth seats, and had only a two-dial facia, but even this type had a three-spoke "sports" type of steering wheel.

Middle-of-the-road Capris were GLs, still only with two-dial facias, but with more equipment, including a radio and more plushy upholstery. The "S" Types were more overtly sporting, with stiffer suspension, alloy wheels, tailgate rubber spoilers, six-dial instrument facias, and the option of figure-hugging Recaro seats.

Finally there were the 2000 Ghia/3000 Ghia types, with even more plush, wooden facia styles, special steering wheels, and other details.

Later, in 1981, came the LS Trim — really, an upgraded L, but with the rear spoiler and the six-dial instrument facia, while the standard of trim was continuously upgraded on all models. In 1983, for instance, the Recaro seats, which had been standardized on 3000s before their demise, were included as standard on the 2000s as well.

The 2.8i has its own unique trim pack, partly from the old "S" which it displaced, and partly from the Ghias, which also disappeared at the same time. It includes Recaro seats and sliding steel sun-roof.

We also ought to mention the "limited edition" Capris sold from time to time — GT4, Tempo, Cameo and Calypso — all of which had more furniture and fittings than a Capri of that mechanical standard would normally enjoy. As with most such cars, Ford had merely upgraded rather down-market types with fittings from the more costly derivatives.

Desirable options on Capri IIIs — only standard on the Ghia in some cases — included the steel tilt or slide sun-roof, remote control drivers' door mirrors, and high-pressure headlamp washers, not to mention the more sophisticated radio/cassettes which the factory could fit. The Recaro seats were for sporty motoring, but certainly not for lounging comfort, fatter wheels and tyres from high-performance types could be fitted to others, and tinted glass was often found (but not standard) on the middle-range Capris.

The 2.8i, fastest and most exclusive of all, is one on its own, for all have the distinctive GKN/Wolfrace wheels, with 7.0in. rims, the optional two-tone paint scheme, and the lowered stance.

Availability and choice

No problems here, for the numbers sold tell their own story, and Ford's UK network of 1,211 UK dealers covers the whole country. Parts are in full and normal supply, since the cars (1600/2000/2.8i, at least) are still on sale, and many components are shared with other models.

In numbers, the least popular was the 1300 model, and frankly we wouldn't recommend it, since the 1600 equivalents are better cars all-round. 2.8is are still quite costly, but amazingly good value for what they offer (0-100 mph

Right: Luggage capacity is greater than might be expected for a sporting car. Not only is the Capri a hatchback, but the rear seats can be folded down individually and the parcels shelf removed to suit varying loads

SPECIFICATION AND PERFORMANCE

Specification:	1300	2000S	3000S	2.8i
Engine size (c.c.)	1,297	1,993	2,994	2,792
Engine layout	ohv 4	ohc 4	ohv V6	ohv V6
Engine power (DIN bhp)	57	98	138	160
Car. length	14ft. 3.3in.			
width	5ft. 6.9in.			
height	4ft. 3in.			
Boot capacity (cu. ft.)	14 cu. ft. (rear seat erect/25 cu. ft.) (seat folded)			
Turning circle (kerbs)	35ft. 0in. approx			
Unladen weight (lb.)	2,154	2,273	2,646	2,620
Max. payload (lb.)	822	841	760	749
Performance summary:				
Tested in Autocar	*10 April 1976	6 Oct 1979	4 March 1978	20 June 1981
Top speed (mph)	86	106	117	127
0-60 mph (sec)	18.8	10.8	8.6	7.9
Overall fuel (mpg)	28.7	25.6	19.5	21.3
Mpg at steady 70 mph	33.1	31.0	23.8	n.a.

* Mk II version with rectangular headlamp nose, but same mechanical specification.

MODELS AVAILABLE

March 1978: Ford Capri Mk III range introduced, slightly modified version of Mk II (1974-early 1978). Main recognition by universal four-headlamp nose style, and all versions with same three-door coupe/hatchback body shell. Different engines, for different derivatives, as follows:

1300/1300L	(57 bhp, 1,297 c.c., 4-cyl)
1600L/GL	(72 bhp, 1,593 c.c., 4-cyl)
1600S	(88 bhp, 1,593 c.c., 4-cyl)
2000GL/S/Ghia	(98 bhp, 1,993 c.c., 4-cyl)
3000S/Ghia	(138 bhp, 2,994 c.c., V6-cyl).

December 1978: 'Base' 1300 dropped; other models continued.
September 1979: 3000 Ghia now with automatic transmission standard, manual transmission only available to special order.
March 1980: 1600S model dropped; other models continued.
December 1980/January 1981: Range rationalized without chassis changes. 1600LS introduced, like 1600L, but better equipment. 3000S and Ghia model dropped. Range now comprised 1300L/1600L/1600LS/1600GL/2000GL/2000S/2000Ghia — seven derivatives.
June 1981: High-performance 2.8i introduced, with special chassis mods, 2,792 c.c. German vee-6, fuel injection, and 160 bhp. Replaced old 3000S, which had been dropped months earlier.
January 1982: 1300L dropped — no 1300 versions now made. Other cars continued.
Autumn 1982: Five-speed gearbox fitted to 2.8i derivative, available at end of year.
March 1983: Range reduced to following: 1600LS, 2000S, 2.8i. Only major mechanical change was standardization of 5-speed gearbox to 2000S as well as 2.8i. These three models continue into 1984.
The following limited editions may be found on offer:
GT4: A 1980 model, based on 1600L, with extra instruments, and decoration.
Tempo: A 1981 model, based on 1300L/1600L.
Cameo: A 1981 model, based on 1300LS/1600LS spec.
Calypso: A 1981 model, based on 1600LS, with two-tone paint, tinted glass, etc.

NUMBERS SOLD

Between 1978 and the end of 1983, a total of 164,876 Capri IIIs were sold in the UK. Individual model-by-model statistics are not available. However, it is known that 9,322 of those cars were the very popular 2.8 Injection model, and it is estimated that about the same number were 3-litres. The least popular was the 1300 (only 1,229 sold in its last full year, 1980) and the most popular were certainly the 1600s, of which perhaps 100,000 have been delivered.

SPARE PRICES

	1600	2000	3000S	2.8i
Engine assembly — bare (exchange)	£467.89	£516.81	£606.46	*£818.19
Short engine (new)	£569.39	£591.08	£686.57	£616.77
Gearbox assembly (exchange)	£113.45	*£305.44	£137.94	*£361.91
Clutch driven plate (new)	£18.84	£21.24	£33.19	£42.21
Clutch, complete (new)	£54.08	£63.68	£99.32	£108.33
Auto trans, less convertor (new)	£446.71	£446.71	£446.71	n.a.
Brake pads — front set (new)	£18.31	£18.31	£18.31	£23.30
Brake shoes — rear set (exchange)	£12.67	£12.95	£16.45	*£41.93
Suspension inserts — front (each)	£41.40	£41.40	£41.40	**£54.49
Suspension dampers — rear (each)	£26.54	£26.54	£26.54	£26.54
Water radiator assembly (exchange)	£50.49	£50.49	£54.60	*£114.71
Alternator (exchange)	£60.05	£60.05	£63.47	£74.55
Starter motor (exchange)	£48.76	£48.76	*£125.14	£105.21
Headlamp unit — each (outer)	£19.60	£19.60	£19.60	£19.60
Taillamp unit — each	£19.26	£19.26	£19.26	£19.26
Front wing panel	£81.58	£81.58	£81.58	£81.58
Front door — skin panel	£38.93	£38.93	£38.93	£38.93
Bumper, front, complete (new)	£60.54	£60.54	£60.54	£60.54
Bumper, rear, complete (new)	£72.76	£72.76	£72.76	£72.76
Windscreen, laminated — tinted	£37.70	£37.70	£37.70	£37.70
Exhaust system—main silencer box only	£34.40	£32.38	£43.14	£42.53
Exhaust system complete	£67.52	£63.42	£149.78	£180.32

*All the above prices include VAT at 15 per cent. * = New ** = Complete strut*

acceleration in 23.4 seconds, and perhaps £5,000 to pay for an early 1981 example — what more could one want?), while the lower-revving 3000s (especially the Ghias) offer nearly the same performance at much lower prices.

The most numerous are the 1600s, but the most satisfying all-round cars are the 2000s, which offer near-110 mph performance with up to 28 mpg, all with a very easy-to-maintain mechanical specification.

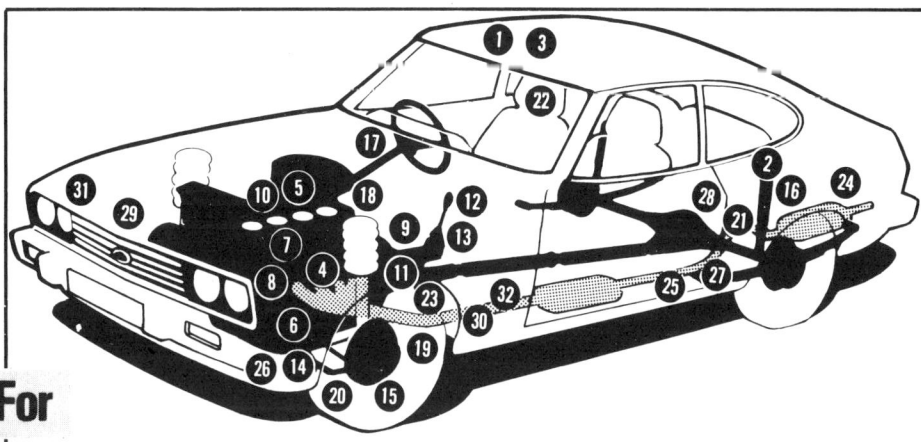

What to Look For

You are almost spoilt for choice, for there is a big selection of Capris on the secondhand market. Prices are fairly consistent across the country, so you should only need to shop around for the particular engine and trim pack that you prefer.

Quite a number of 1600s, and some 2000s, were sold as fleet cars to favoured company staff (1), but they should not have been used as load-carriers. Check up on this, of course, by looking carefully at the stowage area, and the trim panels covering the damper towers and rear wheel arches (2). Because they are really no more than special-bodied Cortinas in many cases, their servicing may have been neglected — especially if they are second or third-hand. Even though servicing is not expensive or onerous, ask to see if there is a service record in the car of your choice (3). The high-performance 3000 and 2.8i models have usually been better loved.

Mechanical

None of the engines, not even the 160 bhp 2.8i unit, are specially tuned for the Capri, so they can be expected to last just as long as they would in a saloon. The rare 1300 used a pushrod Kent engine, a very rugged and reliable unit good for up to 80,000 miles without need for major overhaul, the old-age signs being a smokey exhaust and oil consumption (4). The 1600s and 2000S used standard-tune overhead-camshaft Pinto units, from which the hoary old reputation of camshaft wear has long since been eliminated; the dreaded knocking noise should never be present on a Capri III (5); as with the Kent engine, Pintos last well if properly serviced.

The V6 engines are of entirely different design. The 3-litre Essex is solid, heavy, and long-lived if not habitually over-revved. Signs of distress are oil consumption (6), piston wear (7), and eventually bearing rumble (8). The carburation (by a single downdraught dual-choke Weber) is simple, and should not need adjustment.

The German 2.8 has Bosch fuel injection. Like the 2-litre Pintos, a sticky and un-lubricated throttle cable will feel much more serious than it actually is (9) — two minutes' work with an oil can works wonders. High-speed misfire indicates injection unit problems, which can be expensive (10), but there seem to be no other endemic problems.

As to the transmissions, the quality of change on 1300s and 1600s is up to Ford's accepted standards, and synchromesh should still be good (11). The 2000s sometimes have very sticky changes, due to an exterior linkage needing lubrication (12), and a rather baulky change. The 3-litre and four-speed 2.8i models, too, have rather a slow change, but the box is strong; the latest five-speed boxes are rather more smooth, but there have been worrying rumours of bearing problems, and noisy intermediates, most of which should have been dealt with under warranty (13). The automatic transmission, Ford's own C3 from Bordeaux, has a good reputation, and is well up to its job on all types. It is quite rare, especially on four-cylinder cars, but almost universal on 3-litre V6 models.

If driven hard, a Capri may tend to wear the bushes in the front suspension, or the bushes of the front anti-roll bar (which is part of the geometry) (14). Check for this on the road (wheel wobble, or reaction under braking, is one obvious way to find it), but don't be confused by brake judder which can, and does, occur if the discs get warped due to heavy use (15). Discs can be skimmed, or — better — replaced.

There is little to go wrong to the rear suspension, except that rear dampers (even Bilstein gas-filled types) can go noisy and rattly even without losing their effectiveness (16). Back axles may be slightly noisy at times, but this is not usually any sign of trouble (17). Power-assisted steering, incidentally, is only found on V6 engined models, and occasionally there may be signs of fluid loss in the system (18); our experience confirms that this rarely worsens, and can be kept in check.

On some models alloy wheels are fitted as standard, and the finish on these deteriorates (19) — it is a cosmetic, rather than a structural, problem, which can be restored by elbow grease and refinishing. Tyre wear on the lower-powered versions often exceeds 25,000 miles, but can be down to 10,000/15,000 miles on the V6 cars. Replacement rubber for 2.8is, in particular, is expensive (20). Front pads generally wear out at least twice as often as rear shoes — anything up to 25,000 a set of pads should be normal unless the cars have been flogged.

Exhaust systems are no less vulnerable than on any other Ford, and at two years, or thereabouts (the mileage is not as critical as the age) they tend to start blowing, over the line of the rear axle first of all (21).

Body and trim

Supplies of soft trim for early (1978) and rare, models have already become difficult, so be sure that the equipment is complete (22). Important what-to-look-for areas of wear include the driver's floor carpet (23 — the driving position is such that heels tend to rasp across the pile more than on a more upright saloon), the boot floor covering and damper towers (24), and the scuff pads on the door openings (25).

The oldest Capri III is six years old, and although early cars may be unloved by now, they should not yet be very rusty. Even so, look for evidence of rust at front and rear lower panel welded joints (26 — under bumpers), on the sharp edge of doors (27), and on the sharp styling edge along the sides (28). Corrosion, too, may begin on the sills in front of and behind the wheelarches (29 and 30), for the tuck-under is considerable, and mud-flaps are rarely fitted to these cars. Rust begins to form up under the front wings behind the headlamps (31), and at the rear of the cavity, near the toeboard (32).

General buying points

Dealers we have spoken to confirm that the 1600s are most numerous, that the 2.8is are the best of all, that the "Limited Edition" versions are all good value, but that of the normal range of 2000s are perhaps the pick of the bunch. The 3-litres, they warn, often seem to have been crashed at least once by over-enthusiastic owners, so look for signs of repairs around front chassis legs, and wings and bumpers (33).

We would also add that many modern Fords carry an extended warranty — "Extra Cover" — which is well worth having, as it transfers with ownership, (34). Specially selected secondhand cars, with a 12 month/12,000 mile warranty on major components are sold by Ford dealers under the A1 scheme.

SON OF VANTAGE

Tickford

Developed by Aston Martin Tickford, this dramatic £15,000 turbo-Capri out-accelerates classic Lotus and Porsche rivals. But this mini-supercar needs treating with respect . . .

TAKE A standard Ford Capri 2.8 Injection — by any standards, a lively performer in its own right. Give it a massive performance boost with the aid of modern turbo technology. Dress it up so that its looks match its new-found potential, and so that it slips easily through the air while staying firmly on the ground. Re-upholster the interior using the finest traditional materials. Finally, modify the suspension and brakes to ensure that it handles and stops.

That's the concept behind the Tickford Capri — to create an affordable supercar by developing a freely (and relatively cheaply) available mass-produced car. But why did the small Newport Pagnell-based company — who act as the engineering wing for Aston Martin Lagonda, and who carry out the roof-chop conversion on the XJ-S Cabriolet — choose the Capri on which to base their creation? After all, it's a design fundamentally unchanged since its introduction 15 years ago, still using MacPherson strut front suspension and a leaf-sprung live axle similar to the Mk2 Cortina from which it was derived. Hasn't the Capri had its day?

No, the Capri is perfect for the conversion. The Cologne-built 2.8-litre V6's inherent strength allows it to withstand the mechanical and thermal stresses of turbocharging without internal modification. Rear-wheel drive is essential for good traction and chassis balance with such a high power to weight ratio. And, not least, the Capri remains a stylish coupé in the mould of a down-sized Aston.

At £14,985 (£6,000 more than the 2.8 Injection) the Tickford moves into a different price league, elevated to the ranks of the Lotus Excel 2.2 (£14,735), Porsche 944 (£15,309) and TVR's Tasmin 2+2 2.8 at £14,904. By comparison,

Colt's Starion Turbo and Opel's Monza GSE look positively cheap at £12,499 and £13,801 respectively, while among larger performance saloon offerings, the Rover Vitesse (£15,249) and BMW 528i (£13,895) might be considered rivals on price and performance, if not exclusivity.

One might question what Ford's attitude is towards Tickford producing such a stunning version of the Capri, perhaps reducing the status of their own 2.8 Injection and maybe even anticipating Ford's future plans. In fact, Ford is all for it, to the extent that many Ford main agents feature among the specially appointed Tickford dealers. As a further accolade, the Tickford Capri appears on the front cover of Ford's car sales brochure as a prestigious boost to the more humble models in the Capri range.

The Capri's transformation to stardom takes place at Tickford's new site in Bedworth, near Coventry, where a considerable amount of re-plumbing is needed to house the Japanese IHI turbocharger and Garret intercooler. It's a tight squeeze and there are a few under-bonnet casualties, notably the battery (repositioned in the hatch area), the air-cleaner (repositioned beneath the offside wing) and the engine-driven cooling fan — discarded and replaced by an electric one, in front of the radiator. Surprisingly, few changes are needed to the engine itself — the bottom end, pistons, cylinder head and even the compression ratio remain standard: at 9.2:1 it's very high for a turbo, but the risk of detonation is minimised by cooling the inlet charge and by the AFT digital ignition's precise timing control. Reliability has been confirmed (say Tickford) following extensive testing, including sustained flat-out running for several hours.

In spite of the main objective to

increase mid-speed torque, the turbocharged engine produces no less than 30 per cent more peak power than before — up from 160 bhp at 5,700 rpm to 205 bhp at 5,000 rpm. To put this into perspective, that's nearly as much as a Lotus Esprit Turbo and a good deal more than any of its obvious rivals can manage, including the Rover Vitesse's 190 bhp. If that's impressive, consider that maximum torque is raised by 60 per cent, to a devastating 260 lb ft. This occurs at 3,500 rpm, compared with the 4,300 rpm of the standard engine; at 2,000 rpm Tickford say the torque is doubled!

But building a supercar isn't that simple; the power has to be harnessed and transmitted on to the tarmac. How much of a headache did this give the chassis engineers? Less than might be expected, it seems, because Ford's Special Vehicle Engineering Department have done a pretty good job in the first place. The driveline is virtually unchanged, retaining (surprisingly) the standard 9.5 inch clutch, five-speed gearbox (with modified lubrication) and leaf sprung live axle. A ZF limited slip differential is used in the standard casing, allied to the standard 3.09:1 final drive. Together with the 2.8 Injection's 13 inch alloy wheels and 205/60 Goodyear NCTs, this gives identical gearing of 25.8 mph/1,000 rpm in fifth, or 21.2 mph/1,000 rpm in the direct fourth gear.

The suspension changes are confined to detail fine tuning, and improved rear axle location. To minimise lateral movement in hard cornering (always a problem with leaf sprung live axles) the spring mountings have been modified, and bracing links have been added between the differential casing and the springs themselves, to form an A-frame. The front and rear anti-roll bars and Bilstein gas-filled dampers

are carry-overs from the 2.8 Injection. Normal 2.8 Injection ventilated front discs are retained (with a change of pad material), but solid 10.4 in discs are substituted for the standard car's rear drums.

The changes to the bodywork are less subtle, and there's no mistaking this Capri's purpose. Aston Martin purists might frown at the thought of glass fibre bolt-on body panels, but the mouldings are well formed and blend in well with the car's original lines (there are no sheet metalwork changes behind these panels). Apart from giving the car a new identity, the body changes reduce both lift and drag, giving a claimed Cd figure of 0.37 (a standard Capri 2.8i is about 0.4).

Naturally, the interior gets a bit of the Tickford treatment, including a walnut facia and centre console, leather trimmed dash surround and door cappings, and the inevitable turbo boost gauge mounted on the console, but it's still an essentially functional interior, with most of the really opulent fittings being listed only as very expensive options.

Starting up, the Tickford sounds and idles just like a normal 2.8 Injection — though the exhaust's usually distinctive V6 burble by the turbocharger and the more tortuous exhaust routing associated with it. The engine is tolerably smooth on the move, but some harshness is felt through the gear lever and clutch pedal (it has a cable operated clutch). It doesn't bear comparison with the Rover Vitesse's V8 or the BMW's in-line 6, but it's a fair match for four-cylinder rivals such as the Lotus Excel or Colt Starion. As for what you hear, though (as opposed to what you feel), the Tickford is impressively refined for a sporting high-performer, as our 79 dBA reading at peak revs in second confirms. Around town, the Tickford disguises its potency well, being docile and untemperamental; indeed, it sometimes feels a bit lethargic. Don't be fooled, though: as soon as the turbo starts spinning, it's a different animal, one to be treated with respect.

Out-and-out through the gears acceleration sees the turbo Capri rocketing ahead of any rivals: with such a superior power-to-weight ratio it's hardly surprising. Originally, on a damp surface, it recorded an impressive 6.7 seconds to reach 60 mph, and 18 seconds to 100 mph. Under the circumstances, its traction from a standing start was remarkable, but we weren't satisfied: given better conditions the Capri could do better. We tried again, and so it proved: 6.5 seconds to 60 mph and 17.3 sec to 100 mph.

Prototype cars are rumoured to have cracked 140 mph round Millbrook's high speed bowl during the course of the model's development. Our test car, however, recorded only 134.9 mph at the same site (admittedly in slightly windy conditions) with a best quarter mile leg of 140.5 mph — the speedo, incidentally, hard on the 140 mph stop. The mean maximum corresponds to 5,250 rpm in fifth gear, just beyond the engine's peak

power revs, so perhaps slightly taller gearing is needed for an optimum max. In practical terms, though, the standard Ford gearing is well suited to the turbo's different power characteristics.

So much for the car's ultimate performance, but how successful have Tickford been in the quest for improved mid-range performance? A glance at the fourth- and fifth-gear times tells the story. In fourth gear, the 20-40 mph time of 8.4 seconds is identical to the 2.8 Injection's — hardly surprising as there's negligible boost below 2,000 rpm. Continuing up the speed range, the 40-60 mph time is already a highly respectable 6.0 seconds — the boost gauge reading 7 psi by the time 60 mph (nearly 3,000 rpm) is reached. From here on, the smooth, uninterrupted acceleration is simply breathtaking, all the upper speed range times being covered in about half the time the 2.8 Injection takes — though with the boost gauge on our test car showing 10 psi (maximum boost pressure should be 7.5 psi). The 4.4 second 60-80 mph increment is simply devastating. Consider that a Porsche 911 takes 5.6 seconds to cover the same range, with the advantage of lower gearing in its favour, and you get the message; the Tickford Capri is *quick*.

Of course, it has to stop somewhere, and the first sign of breathlessness comes at around 100 mph in fourth, when the boost gauge starts to descend. At 5,000 rpm (106 mph) it's down to 7 psi, and beyond this, the engine *feels* as though it's past its power peak. There's no tachometer red line for guidance, but a "soft" rev limiter cuts in at 6,000 rpm to minimise abuse by unsympathetic owners. For the standing starts, we found that changing up at 5,750 rpm produced the best results.

That the Tickford has the test-track muscle to match its macho looks is no longer in doubt, but in day-to-day use it's a flawed performer. The problem is that the power is delivered in quantum leaps — it's all or nothing. Very delicate throttle control has to be exercised, especially in the wet. It's also difficult to sustain steady motorway cruising speeds, the car tending to "cycle"

Above right: neat but complicated turbo plumbing places the turbo itself high at the front of the engine bay, with the air cleaner and battery relegated to other areas of the car. Right: comprehensive but reflection-prone standard instrumentation beneath a walnut-clad facia with leather trimmed surrounds. Below: standard and extremely comfortable Capri seats don't exactly lower the tone of the interior, but optional luxury trim and carpeting are available — at a price.

above and below the intended cruising speed. At lower speeds, around town, the combination of pronounced turbo lag, much-reduced output below 3,000 rpm, and a coarse throttle action (when on boost) needs learning. At first, it's all too easy to have insufficient power when it's needed, too much when it isn't . . . From this point of view, it's a challenging car to drive, calling for anticipation and sensitivity. Get it right, and it's satisfying; get it wrong and you're in for jerky progress. One thing is certain, though: all our testers came back smiling . . .

Not unnaturally, there's a tendency to arrive at corners faster than planned — simply through misjudgement, rather than any braking deficiency. When this happens, the car's natural stability and good seat-of-the-pants feel conspire to help you out of trouble, although the light, power-assisted steering is itself uncommunicative. In the dry, the Goodyear NCTs grip well, with the high geared steering and long bonnet helping with accu-

rate placement when cornering. There's a limit to everything, though, and any provocation in the lower gears results in predictable oversteer; with such massive torque available at the rear wheels, the normal, slight bias towards understeer is easily swamped. Given an even, controllable flow of power, there's no doubt that the Capri's cornering attitude could be balanced accurately on the throttle. As it is, the Tickford tends to deliver its power in large uncontrolled doses, with consequentially interesting effects on handling . . .

Fortunately it responds well to correction, avoiding a clumsy series of fishtailing slides, but the fact remains that there are equally powerful cars which are considerably easier to drive close to the limit. The Tickford doesn't have a sophisticated chassis which does all the work for you, but it does provide fun and reward to those who appreciate a challenge.

Subjectively the brakes are hard to fault, with a firm and sensibly weighted pedal action. Time and

PERFORMANCE

WEATHER CONDITIONS
Wind	10 mph
Temperature	37°F/3°C
Barometer	30.0 in Hg
Surface	Dry tarmacadam

MAXIMUM SPEEDS
	mph	kph
Banked circuit	134.9	217.1
Best ½ mile	140.5	226.1
Terminal Speeds:		
at ¼ mile	94	151
at kilometre	119	191
Speeds in gears (at 6,000 rpm):		
1st	38	61
2nd	70	113
3rd	101	163
4th	127	204

ACCELERATION FROM REST
mph	sec	kph	sec
0-30	2.4	0-40	2.1
0-40	3.7	0-60	3.4
0-50	4.9	0-80	4.9
0-60	6.5	0-100	6.9
0-70	8.6	0-120	9.5
0-80	10.8	0-140	12.7
0-90	13.6	0-160	17.0
0-100	17.3	0-180	22.9
0-110	21.6		
0-120	28.2		
Stand'g ¼	15.0	Stand'g km	27.4

ACCELERATION IN TOP
mph	sec	kph	sec
20-40	11.6	40-60	7.3
30-50	10.6	60-80	6.1
40-60	9.4	80-100	5.4
50-70	7.7	100-120	4.0
60-80	6.5	120-140	3.7
70-90	6.2	140-160	4.4
80-100	6.6	160-180	5.8
90-110	8.1		

ACCELERATION IN 4TH
mph	sec	kph	sec
20-40	8.4	40-60	5.2
30-50	7.2	60-80	4.3
40-60	6.0	80-100	3.1
50-70	4.7	100-120	2.7
60-80	4.4	120-140	3.1
70-90	5.0	140-160	3.9
80-100	6.1	160-180	5.6

90-110	7.5
100-120	10.4

FUEL CONSUMPTION
Overall	21.6 mpg
	13.1 litres/100 km
Fuel grade	97 octane
	4 star rating
Tank capacity	13.0 galls
	59 litres
Max range*	312 miles
	502 km
Test distance	1,315 miles
	2,115 km

*Based on estimated 24 mpg touring consumption

NOISE
	dBA	Motor rating*
30 mph	66	12
50 mph	70	16
70 mph	76	24
Maximum†	79	30

*A rating where 1=30 dBA and 100=96 dBA, and where double the number means double the loudness †Peak noise under full-throttle acceleration in 2nd.

SPEEDOMETER (mph)
Speedo								
30	40	50	60	70	80	90	100
True mph								
28	37	46	56	65	75	85	95

Distance recorder: 0.1 per cent fast

WEIGHT
	cwt	kg
Unladen weight*	24.0	1220
Weight as tested	27.7	1408

*with fuel for approx 50 miles

Performance tests carried out by Motor's staff at the Motor Industry Research Association proving ground, Lindley, and Vauxhall Proving Ground, Millbrook.

Test Data: World Copyright reserved. No reproduction in whole or part without written permission.

GENERAL SPECIFICATION

ENGINE
Cylinders	V6
Capacity	2,792cc (170.4 cu in)
Bore/stroke	93.0/68.5mm (3.66/2.70in)
Cooling	Water
Block	Cast iron
Head	Cast iron
Valves	Pushrod ohv
Cam drive	Chain
Compression	9.2:1
Induction	Bosch K/Jetronic fuel injection, plus single point electronic fuel injection on boost; IHI RHB6 turbocharger
Ignition	AFT digital computer
Bearings	4 main
Max power	205 bhp (DIN) at 5,000 rpm
Max torque	260 lb ft (DIN) at 3,500 rpm

TRANSMISSION
Type	5-speed manual
Clutch dia	9.5in
Actuation	Cable

Internal ratios and mph/1,000 rpm
Top	0.82:1	25.8
4th	1.00:1	21.2
3rd	1.26:1	16.8
2nd	1.81:1	11.7
1st	3.36:1	6.3
Rev	3.37:1	
Final drive	3.09:1; ZF limited slip differential	

BODY/CHASSIS
Construction	Unitary, steel, with bolt-on GRP panels
Protection	Cathodic electrocoat; wax injection to cavities; PVC application to wheelarches and lower panels. Underbody sprayed with heavy-duty wax.

SUSPENSION
Front	Independent by MacPherson struts, coil springs; anti-roll bar; gas-filled dampers
Rear	Live axle located and sprung by semi-elliptic leaf springs; additional location by 'A' frame; anti-roll bar; gas-filled dampers

STEERING
Type	Rack and pinion
Assistance	Yes

BRAKES
Front	Ventilated discs, 10.3in dia
Rear	Discs, 10.4in dia
Park	On rear
Servo	Yes
Circuit	Dual, split front/rear
Rear valve	Yes
Adjustment	Automatic

WHEELS/TYRES
Type	Cast alloy, 7J × 13
Tyres	205/60VR13 Goodyear NCT
Pressures	32/32 psi F/R

ELECTRICAL
Battery	12V, 45Ah
Earth	Negative
Generator	Alternator, 45 Amp
Fuses	16
Headlights	
type	Quadruple halogen
dip	110 W total
main	220 W total

---

time again, they hauled the Capri down to 50 mph or so from the 120 mph-plus speeds it was reaching along MIRA's horizontal straights during the acceleration tests, and every time felt as reassuring as the last, with no instability, no fade and no vibration; just the smell of hot lining material to signify that they were being abused beyond any reasonable expectation . . . A minor criticism concerns the handbrake's performance. Its operation on the rear discs feels inferior to the normal Capri drum-brake arrangement, calling for high leverage efforts.

To buyers looking for sophistication, the Tickford's firm and unyielding low speed ride won't be appreciated, though it does smooth out noticeably at speed. The comfortable Recaro seats minimise any discomfort and, indeed, the whole car has a solid rattle-free feel, not always apparent with some specialist low volume cars which are very firmly sprung . . . There are occasions when isolated bumps cause the back of the car to skip laterally, particularly when accelerating.

Fuel consumption will not be too important a priority for most buyers, but it's encouraging to know that the Tickford's amazing performance doesn't incur too high a penalty at the pumps. The overall consumption we recorded was 21.6 mpg, little worse in fact than a normal 2.8i Capri (22.5); it's positively economical when compared with what most slower rivals can manage, though the Porsche 944 (24.8 mpg) is significantly better.

For the remainder, the Tickford inherits most of the Capri's vices and virtues: it's a relaxed high-speed cruiser, marred only by some

wind noise from the window frames. Visibility is about average for a coupé, but the problem of wiper blade lift at speed remains. Despite the bodywork modifications, crosswinds and turbulence from heavy goods vehicles affect it more than one would expect, considering its 24cwt kerb weight.

The instruments and controls are all straightforward Capri, which means that the driving position and major controls are well laid out, but that the old Capri problem of scattered minor controls and reflective instruments persists. The walnut facia and leather trimmed surround add a touch of class, but really there's not much else inside the car that's non-Ford. That's not to imply criticism of the Recaro seats and generally high standard of trim, but this is a £15,000 car and buyers have a right to something special.

At this price, buyers also expect electric windows, a sunroof, good in-car entertainment, etc., and the Tickford does have them. But how they will feel about paying extra (and dearly too) for full leather upholstery — rather than just the facia and console surround — or Wilton carpeting, is another matter.

Let's not nitpick, though: the Tickford is both an exhilarating and challenging car to drive, with enough sheer power to relegate all similarly priced rivals to also-rans in all areas except for sheer maximum speed. It's not just a car to jump into and drive from A to B, but one which begs a driver's full and undivided attention. If you like your cars hairy, and crave for a kind of latter-day Austin-Healey 3000, the Tickford Capri could be just what you're looking for.

Make: Tickford. **Model:** Capri
Maker: Aston Martin Tickford Limited, 58 Tanners Drive, Blakelands North, Milton Keynes MK14 5BW. Tel: Milton Keynes (0908) 614688.
Price: £12,028.10 basic, plus £1,002.34 Car Tax and £1,954.56 VAT equals £14,985.00. Extras fitted to test car: roadwheels painted body colour (£181.96). Price as tested £15,166.96

■ROAD TEST■

Tantalising Tickford

Tickford have added a turbo and many interior and exterior modifications to the Capri 2.8i. NIGEL ROEBUCK discovered the dramatic result under adverse weather conditons.

The weather was lousy for most of the test period, and the car's limited slip diff was appreciated when driving hard in the wet.

I was never much struck by Capris in the early days. In my early twenties a car had to have a racing pedigree to have any appeal, and for a long time I stubbornly put up with the wilfulness and temperament of a succession of Lotus Elans in order to savour the handling and response of what I still consider to be the finest pure sports car ever built.

That little era came to an end when Colin Chapman decided to take his road car company up market. Lotuses were then completely beyond my means (and also, coincidentally, my desires). A variety of vehicles then came and went until, in 1974, I found myself looking hard at a Ford ad of the time, featuring Jackie Stewart and the Capri RS3100.

It was an odd device in many ways, a pure 'homologation special', with up-rated engine, suspension and — in Capri terms, anyway — brakes. It had the original bodyshell, and was introduced at more or less the same time as the Capri II. As a consequence, nobody seemed to want to buy one, and I was able to pick up a new one for a little over £1900.

The car served me well indeed. It was hardly sophisticated, and people taunted me about the huge 'boy racer' wing, but it was quick, handled pretty well and was reliable almost beyond belief. After 65,000 hard miles, I traded it in for a regular 3-litre S, softer and slower, but similarly capable of enduring endless abuse.

That was followed, for a couple of years, by a VW Scirocco GTi which took me back, in lots of ways, to my Cooper S days. A lot of fun, and the ideal short hop car, but a bit tiring in a high rev sort of way for a journey of any length. Last summer, therefore, I sat down with various road test magazines, considered the available gelt, and decided that a Capri 2.8i it had to be. What really swung the issue was the fact that Ford had finally discovered the five-speed gearbox, something for which 'big' Capris had long cried out.

Therefore, last August I took delivery of a new white 2.8i. Early problems with it made me start to believe that even the Germans turn out 'Friday afternoon'

cars, but all is now well, and I love the car.

It is no secret that the Capri's days are numbered, and it did seem to me that the 2.8i was probably the ultimate development of which the now antiquated concept was capable. But not so. A while ago I read about the launch of the Tickford Capri, and one morning in March the Editor asked me how I'd like to write a road test. On a rainy Friday the car was delivered to the office.

A while ago Ford marketed a turbo-charged 2.8i in Germany, but the device

was never made available here. And the Tickford Capri was built originally by Aston Martin Tickford merely as a styling exercise with Ford. Put on display at the Motor Show last year, the car attracted so much interest that it was decided to put it into limited production.

Basically the production story is this: the cars begin life as new standard Capri 2.8is, and are then rebuilt by Tickford (the same company which manufactures turbos for the Honda F1 engines) with Garrett

The increase in torque is most impressive, and the Tickford will out-accelerate almost everything else on the road.

Tickford Capri
A388 WBD

The interior modifications include a walnut burr fascia and Recaro seats.

There is quite a visual difference between the 'before' and 'after' Capri.

intercooler, and also fitted is an AFT digital computerised ignition and electronic fuel management system. Interestingly, Tickford found modifications to be unnecessary for the engine's bottom end, pistons and cylinder heads. Their main objective was to improve power and response in the mid-rev range, a sensible aim for the torque of the standard 2.8i engine is not its strong suit, the only respect indeed in which it is inferior to the old 3-litre.

Turbocharging the 2.8i engine does indeed *transform* its torque, taking it from 162ft/lbs at 4200rpm up to 260ft/lbs at 3500rpm! Power is increased from 160 to 205bhp. And Tickford claim that under most conditions their car's fuel consumption is actually better than that of the standard car, thanks to increased efficiency. This, I may say, I found to be true.

The increased horsepower is helped to the road by means of a limited slip differential, and a modified version of the five-speed gearbox is retained. The brakes, always a bugbear with the big Capris, also come in for major treatment, the rears being converted from drum to disc. The front suspension is left alone, but at the rear there is an 'A' frame better to locate the axle.

More controversial are the styling changes. I do not doubt the Tickford claims that the restyled front and huge rear spoiler materially aid the handling, nor that the body panels substantially improve the drag coefficient. The appearance of them, though, is not to my taste, and I far prefer the rather subtler looks of the standard car. The extra panels are bolted on, and frankly they look it — out of place on a £15,000 car.

Equally I do not care for the walnut fascia, which I thought cumbersome, old-fashioned and out of place in this car. A worthwhile addition, though, is the fitting of electric windows. And the Tickford retains the velour Recaro seats, steel sunroof and stereo radio/cassette

Remarkable increase in torque — with better fuel consumption!

The new up-to-date lines of the Tickford Capri powered by the turbocharged 2.8i engine.

player of the standard car.

It was unfortunate that the weather was lousy for almost the entire week in which the car was in my charge, and I had therefore very little opportunity to drive the car hard on a dry road. When I did, there was good reason to appreciate the limited slip diff out of slow corners, but the overall handling, completely revised rear suspension or not, did not seem greatly different from that of my own car. A little less initial understeer, perhaps. The 7ins alloy wheels and Goodyear NCT tyres are unchanged from standard — save that Tickford require an extra £181.96 of your money to spray the wheels the same colour as the car. Personally, I would willingly shell out that amount of cash to have them put back to plain old alloy colour . . .

On the road the extra power is

immediately impressive, but more remarkable by far is the increase in torque. The whistle of the turbo is barely discernible, but as you hear it things start to happen very quickly indeed, even on quite a light throttle opening. With your right foot no more than a third of the way to the floor, the Tickford Capri will out-accelerate virtually everything else on the road. And you find yourself doing far less gear changing than in the regular 2.8i. Foot lightly down, momentary wait for the boost and you're away.

In the wet this takes a bit of watching. If you should be in the middle of a corner when the turbo chimes in, the tail of the car steps out of line *very* swiftly indeed, and I quickly appreciated that, in Porsche 911 sort of way. The Tickford Capri is not a car in which to chance your arm when there is rain about. In the dry, by contrast, it is resolute and sure-footed.

Fitting the latest Don 600 pads to the front disc brakes has transformed the stopping ability of my own car, and these are standard on the Tickford, which has the added bonus of discs at the rear. For the first time in my life I have now experienced a high-performance Capri which has brakes approximately commensurate with its performance.

The car retails at £14,985, and you can spend a great deal more than that if the mood takes you. None of the optional extras will do anything for the car's performance (with the possible exception of Pirelli P7s), and all are dauntingly pricey. Is it really possible, for example, that anyone has £3262 to spend on a coachfinish respray in pearlescent white?

In 'basic' form, the Tickford Capri comes out at £6000 more than the standard car. Is it worth it? You finish up with more power, *much* more torque,

better fuel consumption (I got 22-24mpg, against 18-20 from my own 2.8i), improved handling and more reassuring brakes. All that I like very much. I am less keen on the bodywork changes — has there ever been a car more calculated to arouse the interest of the constabulary?

As a driving machine, pure and simple, it is a very satisfying car — on a dry road. A driver's car, and one which feels capable of enduring hard use. But the Aston Martin key in the dashboard cannot hide the fact that it remains very much a Capri. It is quieter by far than my own car, but still lacks a certain refinement. I was, in a way, slightly reassured to find that the grunchy clutch cable and gear lever vibration apparently common to all 2.8is are also present in the Tickford car.

I loved driving the car, relished the way it effortlessly swept along. When I got into my own car again, at the end of that week, it seemed like driving with the handbrake on. That great whoosh of power never arrived. Overall, though, it seems to me that £9000 is about right for a Capri. At £15,000, you're getting into Porsche 944 country . . . ∎

TICKFORD CAPRI
£14,985

Specification
Cylinders/capacity	V6/2793cc
Fuel system	Bosch K-Jetronic, plus single point electronic injection on boost
Turbocharger	IHI model RHB6
Power/rpm	205bhp at 5000rpm
Gear ratios	3.36; 1.81; 1.26; 1.1; 0.82; 1.1
Final drive	3.09
Steering	Rack and pinion
Brakes	Discs all round, fully floating half-shafts at rear
Torque/rpm	260lb ft at 3500rpm
Wheels	Alloy 7 x 13
Tyres	Goodyear 205/60 VR 13 NCT
Suspension (F)	McPherson/Bilstein dampers
(R)	Leaf springs

Dimensions
Wheelbase	101 ins
Track (F/R)	53.25/54.5 ins
Length	14ft 7ins
Width	5ft 7ins
Weight	2745lbs

Performance
Max in fifth	140mph
0-60mph	6.1 secs
0-100mph	16.5 secs
60-80mph in fourth (fifth)	4.2 secs (6.3 secs)
70-90mph in fourth (fifth)	4.8 secs (6.1 secs)
80-100mph in fourth (fifth)	6.0 secs (6.5 secs)
Overall fuel consumption	24mpg

THE PRIMITIVE APPEAL OF FORD'S CAPRI

As a value-for-money package, the Ford Capri 2.8i is hard to beat. Short of push-button gadgetry, perhaps, but the Capri has all the motorist needs to buzz around town or roar across the countryside. Bob Cooke reports the test findings overleaf

WHENEVER we compare a group of sports coupés, we almost always come to the same conclusion — the Ford Capri 2.8i offers the best value for money package. The reasons for its relatively low cost may well be the age of its design and the primitive engineering (after all, it is little more than a Mk II Cortina underneath) but, by dint of much tweaking, Ford have endowed the car with levels of refinement well up to modern standards.

Add the sweet-running, flexible Cologne V6 injected engine and you get a car with performance that is also well up to standard. And, ageing as the design may be, the body styling is still strikingly attractive.

In September the price of the Capri 2.8i went up to £9,500 and it took the name "Special". The price rise immediately raised the question in our minds — is the Capri still good value?

The first thing to consider is that the price rise was not an arbitrary one — it accompanied the "Special" extras pack of limited slip differential, revised Recaro seats, new-look alloy wheels and revised interior trim. All this for an extra £172 . . .

Then consider the opposition, probably the most obviously similar in character being the Toyota Celica Supra 2.8i at £11,449 and the Nissan 300 ZX Targa at £14,349. The Japanese cars have added sophisticated equipment like cruise control and power windows.

The Capri might lack the push-button convenience gadgetry, but it has everything the driver needs to get on with the job of driving, whether tootling around town or blasting across country. The Recaros fit perfectly, the steering wheel, gear shift and pedals are all just where they should be and the controls have a firm, no-nonsense feel about them. It's a no-nonsense car.

We worked the Capri 2.8i Special really hard to try to equal the acceleration times of the 2.8i we tested back in June 1981; it was an unfair contest, since the lower ratios of the five-speed gearbox now fitted are higher than the ratios of the original four-speed. The earlier car got to 60 mph in 7.9 seconds, but the Special wouldn't better 8.2. It did, however, achieve higher maximum speeds in those lower gears — 71 mph and 102 mph in second and third, for example, against the earlier car's 66 mph and 99 mph.

The 1-1 fourth ratio is the car's top, with fifth acting as a 25.7 mph per 1,000 rpm overdrive. That fourth is not an ideal top, however, since the best maintainable speed of 126 mph comes up 250 rpm over the power peak crankshaft speed; speed decays in fifth to 123 mph with the crank turning over at 4,800 rpm.

As ever, the engine is impressively flexible; early morning starts are immediate, the automatic choke cuts out smoothly and driveability during the warm-up period is excellent.

The overdrive fifth gear has two very immediate advantages — first it reduces engine noise when running at motorway cruising speeds, and second it leads to a noticeable economy advantage. The Special returned 23.8 mpg while the earlier 2.8i could manage only 21.3.

Our measured consumption included some hectic driving, in particular our punishing performance testing session, suggested that a more restrained driver could easily expect to get better than 26 mpg as a matter of course and a useful range of more than 300 miles.

The Special is also noticeably more quiet than the earlier Capri. It could be better sound insulation, it could be merely the tightening up of production tolerances after years of production. Whatever the reason, the result is pleasing; while there is still pattern noise from the wide tyres running over coarse concrete surfaces, there is a noticeable reduction in the amount of thump as the tyres encounter road joints and ripples. Wind noise is there as well, but never to an obtrusive degree. The engine sounds good during hard acceleration, giving out an enthusiastic growl as it spins up to the rev limiter and emitting a rorty rasp as you change up. Then, once at cruising speed and in fifth gear mechanical noise dies away.

Handling is an important consideration in a sporting car, and Ford have no easy task in making the suspension cope with various load conditions while ensuring an acceptable ride quality, all with a solid rear axle on semi-elliptical leaf springs. The way the rear suspension has been bushed compliantly to the body shows up in the lack of feel, and lack of bump thump, from the rear wheels, when running over a bumpy surface. The stiffness of the springing and damping has the car feeling quite bouncy over such surfaces at moderately slow speeds, but the ride smooths out

Interior lacks gimmicks, but it's purposeful

Capri's mildly muscular looks have timeless charm

Two-tone striping and lettering distinguish this version

FORD CAPRI 2.8i SPECIAL SPECIFICATION

Good access to injected V6

MAXIMUM SPEEDS

Gear		mph	kph	rpm
OD Top (Mean)		124	199	4,800
(Best)		125	201	4,900
4th		126	203	5,950
		127	204	6,000
3rd		102	164	6,100
2nd		71	114	6,100
1st		55	89	6,100

ACCELERATION

FROM REST

True mph	Time (sec)	Speedo mph
30	2.7	33
40	4.3	43
50	6.1	53
60	8.2	64
70	11.0	74
80	14.5	84
90	18.7	95
100	24.7	105
110	32.8	115
120	—	125

Standing ¼-mile: 16.5sec, 86mph
Standing km: 30.7sec, 106mph

IN EACH GEAR

mph	Top	4th	3rd	2nd
10-30	—	9.9	6.8	4.6
20-40	11.6	8.4	6.3	4.3
30-50	10.9	8.0	6.3	4.1
40-60	11.8	8.5	6.4	4.1
50-70	12.9	8.8	6.4	4.7
60-80	14.4	9.2	6.6	—
70-90	16.6	10.3	8.1	—
80-100	19.9	12.6	11.4	—
90-110	—	18.3		

CONSUMPTION

FUEL
Overall mpg: 23.8 (11.9 litres/100km) ? mpl

Autocar formula:	Hard 21.4 mpg
Driving	Average 26.2 mpg
and conditions	Gentle 30.9 mpg

Grade of fuel: Premium, 4-star (98 RM)
Fuel tank: 13 Imp galls (59 litres)
Mileage recorder reads: 4.8 per cent long
Oil: (SAE 20W/50)/negligible

WEIGHT

Kerb: 23.0cwt/2,580lb/1,170kg
(Distribution F/R, 54.6/45.4)
Test: 26.4cwt/2,960lb/1,343kg
Max payload: 749lb/340kg

SPECIFICATION

ENGINE
Longways front, rear-wheel drive.
Head/block cast iron/cast iron.
6 cylinders in 60 deg V, bored block, 4 main bearings. Water cooled, viscous fan.
Bore 93mm (3.7in), **stroke** 68.5mm (2.7in), **capacity** 2,792cc (170 cu in).
Valve gear 2 ohv, 2 valves per cylinder, chain/camshaft drive.

Compression ratio 9.2 to 1.
Breakerless ignition, Bosch K-Jetronic injection.
Max power 160 bhp (PS-DIN) (117.5 kW ISO) at 5,700 rpm. **Max torque** 162 lb ft at 4,200 rpm.

TRANSMISSION

5-speed manual. Single plate diaphragm spring clutch.

Gear	Ratio	mph/1,000 rpm
Top	0.825	25.66
4th	1.00	21.17
3rd	1.26	16.80
2nd	1.81	11.69
1st	2.36	8.97

Final drive: Hypoid bevel, ratio 3.09.

SUSPENSION

Front, independent, MacPherson strut, coil springs, telescopic dampers, anti-roll bar.
Rear, Live axle, half elliptic single leaf springs, telescopic dampers, anti-roll bar.

STEERING

Rack and pinion, power assistance. Steering wheel diameter 14in, 3.3 turns lock to lock.

BRAKES

Dual circuits, split front/rear. Front 10.3in (262mm) dia discs. Rear 9in (229mm) dia drums. Vacuum servo. Handbrake, centre lever acting on rear drums.

WHEELS

Cast alloy, 7in rims. Radial tubeless tyres (Goodyear NCT on test car), size 205 60 VR-13, pressures F28 R28 psi (normal driving).

DIMENSIONS

Wheelbase 101in (2565mm); track, front 53in (1345mm), rear 54.5in (1384mm). Overall length 171.4in (4352mm); width 67in (1702mm); height 51in (1295mm). Turning circle 35ft 1 in (10.7m). Boot capacity 14/25 cu ft.

TEST CONDITIONS

Wind:	8-10mph
Temperature:	18deg C (64deg F)
Barometer:	29.2in Hg (990mbar)
Humidity:	85 per cent
Surface:	damp asphalt and concrete
Test Distance:	1,500 miles

Figures taken at 5,500 miles by our own staff. All Autocar test results are subject to world copyright and may not be reproduced in whole or in part without the Editor's written permission.

WHAT IT COSTS

Prices

Basic	£7,625.42
Special Car Tax	£635.45
VAT	£1,239.13
Total (in GB)	**£9,500.00**
Licence	£90.00
Delivery charge (London) inc VAT	£116.08
Number plates	£15.00
Total on the Road	**£9,721.08**
(exc insurance)	
EXTRAS (inc VAT)	
Black paint	£90.72
Metallic paint	£127.89
2-tone metallic paint	£208.29
Total as tested on the road	**£9,929.37**

WARRANTY

12 months, unlimited mileage

as the speed is increased.

Placed carefully on line and powered through a curve, the Capri understeers moderately all the way through. Sudden unsettling actions such as backing sharply off the throttle in the middle of a fast corner have surprisingly little effect.

Ultimate handling is a delight for rear-drive enthusiasts, since the car is so easily controlled at the limit, the front responding to steering and the rear to throttle action. Stiff anti-roll bar to help neutral steering had the effect of lifting the inside rear wheel when accelerating out of slow corners, but the limited slip differential curbs this problem well.

The Special still exhibits a fair amount of roll — throw the car into a corner and the body heaves over rather ponderously into its cornering attitude. It is not an uncomfortable or unsettling movement, rather more a sort of endearing trait which does nothing to reduce the sheer enjoyment of driving the Capri hard and fast on a winding road.

Behind the wheel the Capri feels as good as it ever did. The seats give good sideways and lumbar support, and the basic adjustments of fore-aft movement and stepless backrest rake are enough to allow most drivers to find a comfortable position in which to drive.

The instrument and switchgear layouts are unchanged — nor do they need changing, being among the most pleasingly straightforward arrangements in existence.

The facia has a large circular speedometer (it overreads by only five per cent, a vast improvement on the 11 per cent overreading of the early test car's instrument) and matching rev counter, the latter not red-lined in any way — an unnecessary detail in view of the rev limiter which is set to cut in at 6,100 rpm. Smaller circular dials around these main instruments are for fuel contents, water temperature, oil pressure and ammeter. Warning lamps are kept to a fuss-free minimum, covering the main functions.

Also in the main instrument binnacle are the stereo radio/cassette player, the heating and ventilation controls and push-button switches for rear wash/wipe, rear fog lamps and heated rear window. The steering column-mounted stalk controls are typical Ford, one on the left for indicators, horn and headlamp dip, a large one on the right for the windscreen wash/wipe (two-speed plus intermittent action)

and a short one on the right for the headlamps.

Still a Capri strong point in comparison with many of its rivals is the excellent heating and ventilation system. The two familiar Ford sliders control an air blending system which gives a good heat output with fine temperature and directional control, plus the outer eyeball vents giving a forceful supply of fresh air quite independent of the main system. The fan — a rather primitive and somewhat noisy two-speed effort — boosts air flow when necessary.

The rear seats are practical in that two adults can be accommodated in the rear, though naturally a little cramped for legroom — particularly if the front seats are set fully to the rear — but headroom is reasonable. Entry to the rear does require a degree of agility.

The rear compartment has hatchback versatility. The moulded plastic luggage cover can be removed and the rear seat backs folded forwards singly or together to give a usefully large luggage space. The normal boot area suffers a little in that a full sized spare wheel is housed in a well pressed into the boot floor, so that the remaining available space is a little shallow.

The long bonnet panel is rather heavy to lift, and has to be propped manually, but the engine is a pleasingly purposeful sight when revealed in the engine bay.

Access to service items is excellent, except for the spark plugs which are a little inaccessible. Main service intervals are at 12,000 miles, with an oil change and inspection at 6,000 miles. There's nothing in the car's make-up that should prove difficult for the averagely competent DIY owner.

When we're talking about value, we should be considering also such aspects as long-term reliability, availability of parts and running and repair costs. The revised Capri 2.8i follows its predecessors and scores well on these points, in our experience.

More modern cars may offer better refinement, and by virtue of all-independent suspension may achieve more readily an acceptable ride and handling compromise. For all their modernity, however, few of the Capri's competitors achieve a better performance-economy compromise. For the money, we still find the Capri very hard to beat. ■

Is the powerful Ford Capri 2.8 Injection Special, a museum piece destined to live out 1985 as a leather-trimmed reminder of the sixties and seventies? We sent **Jeremy Walton** to find out . . .

Nearly two million Capri coupes have been made since Ford launched the car in 1969 to provide a European equivalent to the Mustang's sales record pace in the USA. While the motoring world has been through fuel crisis and recession, this specialist coupe has survived and changed its clothes from phenomenally

successful two door youth as "The Car You Always Promised Yourself," to the present three-door hatchback coupe that still outsells Manta and Scirocco in the UK. Indeed, 1983 saw Capri outsell the entire Rover SD1 lines for a place in the top 20, underlining the fact that this German-made Ford has been kept alive by British patronage, Ford switching to sole Cologne manufacture in October 1976. Now Ford say the Capri — recently pruned down to Laser 1.6/2.0, or two litre S and two injection 2.8 variants — will be

"in production throughout 1985." So what does it offer today?

You can still buy a 1.6 Capri for under £6,000 but even Ford directors discount this option as underpowered with production discontinued in favour of the powerful versions. The well equipped, five speed, Capri 2.8i is still sold at £9,327.79, but the Injection Special assessed here is a solid £9,500.

Extra equipment

The traditional recipe of pushrod V6 — as also used in Granada and Sierra, where it is more honestly rated at 150bhp in identical Bosch K-Jetronic injection trim — is allied to an overdrive Ford five speed and a chunky live rear axle. For the Injection Special Ford engineers selected the optionally available ZF limited slip differential, which works via multiplate clutches set at 25 per cent preload. "We are not far enough down the development road to specify the viscous coupling type of limited slip on a rear drive car," reported a senior engineer from the Special Vehicle Engineering department at Dunton, Essex.

The same group developed both XR2s, XR3i and the Capri injection originally — and now they do have a viscous coupling limited slip differential installed in the production Escort RS Turbo. A world first in front or rear drive, and likely to become increasingly common as four-wheel-drive spreads through BMW and Ford next year.

There was no other money for mechanical development, so the Capri carries on the inevitable Ford recipe of MacPherson front struts and leaf sprung axle, the shock absorbers (Bilstein gas-filled all round) staggered either side of the axle in just the same way as Mustang or original Capri.

Developments on the basic theme over the years, which you can see underneath that still smooth upper panelwork, include the 14mm diameter "bent wire" linkage that doubles as anti-roll bar and picks up on the old axle location mounts underbody. Plus the use of the single rear leaf springs that first appeared on Escort RS2000 in production after an honourable saloon car racing career. You'll find them on the back of the beam axle Escort van today!

Brakes are the mixed bag vented disc at the front and rear drums. The latter date back to the September 1969 Capri 3.0.

Colour coding sets the Injection Special apart from other Capris and only the rear spoiler and bumpers reflect the matt black era
Bottom right: Inside the Capri the story remains the same with large round dials and eyeball vents giving its age away. Leather interior in two-tone grey is tasteful and the Recaro front seats offer the sort of support an oversteering Capri requires

Since ARG persisted in fitting much the same mixture to the 190bhp Vitesse, I suppose Ford are not too vulnerable to criticism on this production point, but there is no doubt that our testers all tended to tread warily on the centre pedal, for front wheel lock-up has been a problem ever since the injection Capri made its debut in 1981.

Externally the wide-wheeled injection Capri displays the same lines that were rated at 0.375 when Capri III appeared in 1978, but with 205/60 Goodyears on seven inch rims (that now look very small in overall 13 inch diameter by today's standards) the rating is 0.42Cd, within a point of Audi quattro coupe.

Changes for Injection Special include the use of seven-spoke RS wheels instead of the spotted ex-Wolfrace design (but not manufacture) found on injection. There is no size advantage over the original, and the tyre specification is the same, with NCTs found on all the seven injection Capris the writer has owned or driven for more than 100 miles.

Staying outside, the injection comes in unique colours with the Special derivatives, "ours" delivered in a plum red with duotone greys within. Inside, the leather trimmed Recaros seem to have been perfumed to underline that real leather is being offered. The same polished hide now adorns sections of the rear seats, gear lever knob and the modified three spoke steering wheel, which has the rim edge slightly sunken below the centre boss.

As on the cheaper Capri 2.8i there is now a four speaker LW/MW/FM radio/cassette player of reasonable stereophonic ability, and that is coupled to an electric aerial. Most sub 30-year-old testers immediately spotted the items Capri cannot offer compared with later hatches: central locking and electric window operation have never been engineered for the oldest model in the Ford range, and seem hardly likely to make their debut now.

However on both 2.8 litre Capris equipment is generous with the ICE standard and joined by an excellent steel tilt and slide sunroof, plus tinted glass, rear seat belts and six-dial instrumentation. The only listed options are metallic or duotone paints on either model.

Acknowledging the widespread use of colour coding, Ford have distinguished the 2.8 Special with this treatment applied to the usually matt black grille, and also to headlamp surrounds. Now the back spoiler and bumpers are the only items to reflect the old matt black fascination . . .

Inside story

The large and unfashionable dials of startling clarity (in themselves, some of the minor ones are shrouded by steering wheel spokes) have changed little since the 1973 modifications were made to the original Capri in preparation for 1974's Capri II. The minor dials tell of oil pressure, water temperature, battery volts and the near 13 gallon fuel tank's contents.

There is also a 140mph speedo and a 7,000rpm tachometer that has no redline marked, just correction dots either side of 6,000rpm. That was the limit we used, the rpm-limiter cutting in just beyond this point.

The seating is generally well stitched — there were two stray threads on the passenger side — and as supportive as the Recaro legend would suggest: but the new Vauxhall GTE's British made equivalents are better all rounders. For you can slip about a little on the seat side panels within the Capri, when the traditional flurry of oversteer grappling with power-assisted rack and pinion is requested by blood-crazed photographers.

The view out is traditional too: restricted! Forward you see the bulging bonnet implying lusty cubic centimetres of propulsion. To the rear you must rely for three-quarter view on a driver's mirror that is adjustable from within and a passenger door mirror that you can only alter externally. Our apologies to the gent in a Vauxhall Cavalier diesel who was overtaking a column of traffic over central road junction markings. We will get you next time, with the aid of intermittent threequarter vision and a lack of the creative imagination one needs to understand that any Vauxhall diesel driver must be desperate enough to overtake *anywhere, anytime!*

The standard of trim fit and finish varies widely within. Release the handbrake and the trim surround tries to escape with it! Yet the rest of the interior features good assembly work and is a straightforward place to concentrate on driving a motor car, rather than playing with electronic gizmos. However, gaining access at night was simplified by the Porsche-style penlite incorporated within the ignition key. A

secondary key is provided to lock the fuel filler cap which, as always, is firmly embossed Capri II . . .

Action

Starting the engine is the usual hassle-free injection experience, but there is some slow speed surge that can annoy you enough in traffic to drop the clutch in order to make smooth progress. In fact our press car was delivered with enormous idling surges in rpm reading and Perry's diagnosed a mixture weak enough to burn a piston . . . No damage was done, but the Capri was a notably reluctant performer compared to others we have enjoyed, the 2,000 miles displayed apparantly insufficient to free off a gearbox with a knife-through-resistant-porridge change quality.

The familiar V6 note emerges from the tortuous twin pipe system that hangs so vulnerably beneath the Capri with a heartiness that promises a generous dollop of performance throughout the rev range. In fact the tall top gear of 25.5mph per 1,000rpm means that the penalty for relaxed 2,745rpm/70mph cruising is the fact that our drivers tended to change down to third when they wanted instant overtaking response. Shades of the hot hatchbacks that can now equal its straightline performance, until 110mph is exceeded.

The power steering is handy for twirling 205 section tyres in tight parking spaces and speaks reliably of the front wheels somewhat erratic path over B-road bumps and cambers.

At the steering wheel rim the messages are of a restlessness over less than flat road contours, but the tugging is never in the twitchy manner of the XR Escorts and Fiestas.

On the road the broad Goodyears and well-sorted suspension provide a good sporting compromise between ride and ultimate cornering capability. Although the axle has only limited travel, making frequent use of the progressive rubber bump stops mounted above it, the ride is not harsh in the manner of some small sports saloons (Escort XR/Peugeot 205 GTI) but is most fairly described as "knobbly" or "sporting seventies." The worst impacts are rounded off, but you can feel the car move about and the driver is always conscious of the surface passing beneath those wide wheels.

Under test track conditions the tail-out oversteer cornering style is safely spectacular. After a few laps you find that slow corners barely demand any braking,

Below: Test track work lets the Capri show off its tail-out style in safe but spectacular fashion

Ford's rumbustuous old 3-litre Capri won a loyal group of followers. When all the world seemed to be down-sizing and striving for increased efficiency from smaller packages – both in terms of body size and mechanical components – the Capri continued to provide its dedicated followers with a much lazier way of travel.

There wasn't much point in continual gear changing; it would lumber along in third and top, the low first and second gears almost redundant. And neither was there very much point in attempting a delicate cornering line. If the Capri hit bumps it would flop about a bit and there wasn't much the driver could do in terms of finesse. Similarly, tightening bends and roundabouts could always be dealt with by a large dollop of power.

The Capri lost some of its distinctly agricultural image with the advent of the German-engined Capri 2.8 Injection. It became a much sharper car (in comparison with the Essex-engined machine) with a genuine attempt made to tie-down the handling courtesy of gas-filled rear dampers and the adoption of that panacea for ill-mannered, under-developed machines – low profile 60 series tyres.

According to the brute-force-and-ignorance school, the car's 2.8 engine was its only let-down: it needed revving and stirring, and the powerband didn't possess the all-encompassing blanket of torque that had become the Essex unit's trade mark.

To be honest, it was a *much* better car. Fully equipped, properly shod, and driven with a degree of concentration it was almost a car of the '80s. Almost, but not quite. Despite the provision of vented discs, the brakes remained completely inadequate and the car still showed the old tractor-heritage in the wet – hopeless understeer and a spinning inside rear wheel – not a combination to savour,

Puss in boots

On the road, complete with Jackie Stewart cap, string-backed driving gloves and KAT Designs' 2.8i Ford Capri turbo. Ian Sadler reports

even if it was, and is, – as Ford test drivers would have it – inherently safe for unenthusiastic drivers.

It is no secret that the 2.8i Capri (and all the other under-powered four cylinder ones) are to be given the Ford Corporate Chop later this year. So what to do with this '60s throwback? One remedy, and a very effective one, is to do what Simon Saunders of KAT Design has done: exploit the good points, improve the driver-pleasure-inputs and give it the kind of gung-ho looks in keeping with the package.

Even though the Capri's interior dimensions are almost ludicrously insufficient, given the overall dimensions; a windscreen rake which isn't much of an improvement on a post-war Austin 16, and a mechanical layout which ought to be in the Science Museum, the big-engined Capri retains a certain macho cachet which is – in the right circumstances – all but irresistible. Sure, a properly driven Ford XR3i or VW GTi will run rings around it in all but straight lines; but that isn't the point.

KAT has produced a Capri-with-knobs-on which should really appeal to the big-and-crude-is-beautiful brigade. The heart of the car is of course a turbocharger; the ubiquitous Turbo Technics installation using a Garrett AiResearch unit with typically effective TT-devised exhaust manifold and large air-to-air intercooler.

On Auto Technique's Luton-based Sun Powertrak rolling road the test car peaked at 179.5bhp at 5500rpm (179.3bhp at 5000rpm), which is no more or less than the expected increase from the standard 150/155bhp (quoted) rating. What the engine really offers is truly mighty low-end response. There is a discernible lag in pick-up, but it is quite unobtrusive in most circumstances, and quite in keeping with the slumbering, fluid, and lazy nature of the car –

a throwback to the days of the Essex engined machine but with a power-hike. In KAT guise the Capri is more than capable of handling it.

The rest of the car is deliberately kept as standard as possible. Luckily this does permit the fitment of competition disc pads. (Even in the pouring rain of our test we appreciated that). Springs and dampers – very effective for a standard manufacturer specification – are left alone, but front suspension and rear axle location is improved, principally with harder bushings; a rear anti-roll bar is added and a limited slip differential is fitted.

Wheels and tyres of the test car comprised beautifully cast Compomotive five spoke split rims with 50 percent aspect ratio 205 section front/rear Goodyear NCTs; a wheel/tyre combination which is exactly right for this car.

Visually, the KAT Capri turns heads. KAT designed panels fit perfectly and integrate cleanly with the Capri's shape (look at a

the handling requires more than the application of a chest-wig to exploit to best effect

KAT Rover or Escort and you will notice that the angles are neatly set for each – the Rover being a much more rounded shape than the chunky aspects of the Capri). It comprises seven mouldings all of hand-laid grp with cut-lines moulded on the formers. The front and rear air dams fit directly over the standard bumper assemblies, so retaining structural strength and utilising standard front/rear lamp clusters. Twin square halogen fog lamps and a single slat grille are trademarks and a feature of all KAT cars. The side-skirts and arches fit clean to the car's steel body without the use of any bonding agents and can be pre-sprayed to body colour and, of course, removed, if desired, prior to resale.

The car's aggressive looks are completed by a red metallic fill-panel adjoining the rear lamp clusters.

The cosmetic pack, painted and fitted, costs £949, or £449 bare, with lamps and wiring for the DIY enthusiast. The deep front air dam (the car is rock-steady at 100+mph) costs £109, as does

Puss in boots

advance) but then it shows the sort of ferocity which will easily break traction in third gear, despite its fat NCT rubberware. Luckily, having an LSD it tends to keep straight and almost gives the impression of clutch slip – best watch the tachometer in such circumstances.

Diabolical weather conditions prevented accurate performance testing, but we would estimate around 6.5 seconds to 60mph. Our best 0-90mph time (before abandoning test runs due to our test track being turned into a lake) was 14.5s – and you can safely lop a couple of seconds off that for a good dry run. We couldn't prevent a degree of wheelspin until well-settled into third gear acceleration.

Harder pad material helps in the braking department, to a degree, but we still suffered

a combination of the turbo coming on-song with the diff locking-up causes oversteer of gargantuan proportions. . .

some fade (in the wet!) after vigorously attacking a number of Milton Keynes roundabouts in rapid succession. For road work the amount of understeer built-in suits the car. Turn-in is on the vague side but never heart-stopping (it caught me out on a couple of occasions when only a brutal clutch-dip proved to be an 11th hour answer to a crossed-arms understeer corner entry) and, providing the throttle is managed with some thought, the car can be tidily neutralised for exits. Slightly de-sensitized power steering is welcome.

But give it too much squirt, and a combination of the turbo coming on-song with the diff locking-up causes oversteer of gargantuan proportions, requiring a degree of mind-over-matter-response to release just *some* throttle and keep steering into the slide. It won't spin, but it could give oncoming road users cardiac arrest.

Alas, with such tidy suspension and willing differential, the braking action spoils the car. It was, at the time of testing, newly built, and that might explain why there was so much braking effort directed to the front wheels. That, and a tendency for the fat 205 section front wheels to float over standing water, made for less-than-serene A and B road progress.

(In addition we were once again maddened by Ford's utterly hopeless, squeaky wiper blades). We would really need to sample the car again on dry roads.

As it is, the KAT Capri is a good-looker with a back-up of power in keeping with its chunky image, along with handling which requires more than the application of a chest-wig to exploit to best effect. Not everybody's brew – and probably not as fast as a well driven front wheel drive hot hatch – but very stylish, and in an old-fashioned way, very enjoyable. ■

● KAT Design can be contacted on Windsor 50210.
Auto Technique (rolling road and tuning) on Luton 414000.

the rear assembly, while side skirts are a very modest £99.50 per pair. The in-fill front grille is £24.50 and the tail panel £22.95. A massive rear spoiler (which works excellently along the King's Road) is £84.50. Although at the time of writing the car hadn't been subjected to a wind tunnel, it all feels as though it works. Such beautification isn't cheap, but the workmanship is first rate and, as previously stated, no bonding or beading is required.

TT's engine conversion costs £1550 while the full handling package including LSD is available for £550. If requested, the interior can be upgraded with leather seats and trim (plus Wilton cloth trimming) for £2295, or any combination to a lesser degree.

On the road this KAT Capri is a real Jekyll and Hyde character, and not recommended for the uninitiated. It has such an easy-going, laid-back nature that it's a simple matter for the driver to be lured into elbow-on-the-window complacency. It will trickle along in the best 3.0 litre Capri tradition, burbling away quietly and raising no offence to the general populace thanks to TT's turbo installation. But push the throttle – a long travel device and not as smooth as it should be for accurate throttle-steer management – and all hell breaks loose. It takes a moment or two to communicate (like the SAAB Turbo, you need to choose overtaking opportunities a little in

TwinTest

FAST FORDS FIGHT IT OUT

**The Capri Injection just won't lie down. It fought off the threat
from its Sierra XR4i stablemate and now it's been treated
to a few more refinements. But which wins the back-to-back
comparison — Capri charisma or Sierra sense?**

IT'S A real problem for the marketing men. They spend thousands of pounds on market research, yet still the buying public's tastes demonstrate an illogical perversity. After all, faced with the choice between a 16-year-old design and a one-year old one, which should you buy? And which *would* you buy?

Ford has just such a problem. When the Sierra was introduced, it was no secret that a sporty version would shortly follow. And when this happened, the corporate plan would allow no place for the Capri. Half a million Capris had been sold in the UK alone since the model's 1968 introduction, and based as it was on a Cortina Mark Two floorpan the design was getting extremely long in the tooth. All right, the V6 2.8-litre version could boast a certain macho muscularity, but once the 2.8-litre three-door Sierra XR4i hit the showrooms who would possibly want to buy a Capri 2.8 Injection?

Quite a lot of people, as it turned out. So much so, in fact, that the Capri has been granted a stay of execution at least until the end of 1985. It's not just the 2.8 that's been reprieved, either: no direct replacement was planned for the smaller-engined Capris, but instead of fading away quietly like Ford hoped, the 1.6-litre model continues to take the lion's share (55 per cent) of total Capri sales, with the two-litre also selling well. And since its introduction in summer 1981 the 2.8 Injection has consistently accounted for around 18 per cent of Capri sales, with 2534 sold in the UK during the first nine months of 1984. Total Capri sales in the UK so far this year are around the 14,000 mark, accounting for 65-70 per cent of production from the Cologne factory.

By the standards of a huge multinational like Ford, these production figures are a drop in the ocean. But you can bet that the Capri still makes money, or else it would have been dropped long ago. Certainly it is not an essential adjunct to Ford's sporting image — the XR2 Fiesta, XR3 Escort and XR4 Sierra see to that — but the tooling costs must have long been amortised and the Capri's major market — the UK — is also the most profitable in Europe.

So the Capri continues, and for 1985 the 2.8 Injection becomes the Injection Special with leather-edging for its Recaro seats, a new leather-covered steering wheel, six-spoke alloy wheels similar to those fitted to the Escort RS Turbo but more deeply dished, and a limited-slip differential — all for £9500.

Meanwhile Ford's other heavyweight hot-rod, the Sierra XR4i, has proved a disappointment. It was originally expected to account for seven per cent of all Sierra sales, but the reality is nearer four per cent, with 4175 sold so far this year. The shortfall is no doubt partly accounted for by 2.8 Capri sales to Ford fans who find the XR4i's looks hard to live with! Certainly the introduction of the XR4i has had no discernible effect on total Capri Injection sales, and there are

sizeable discounts to be had on the £10,324 list price — which for 1985 includes as standard central locking, electric windows, a sliding glass sunroof, and tinted glass. You could probably buy either of these cars for about the same outlay.

So there it is. Capri 2.8 Injection — a rakish coupé with a shallow windscreen and long bonnet, promising a good dose of traditional fun from a potent engine, primitive suspension and fat tyres. Or Sierra XR4i — bang

up to date, much more sophisticated in the suspension department, looking every inch a boy racer's special with its biplane rear spoiler and acres of grey plastic, but powered by the same lusty engine as the Capri. But how do they *really* compare?

PERFORMANCE

Both the XR4i and the Capri Injection share the same 2792 cc "Cologne" V6 engine, the design of which goes

back almost as far as the now-obsolete 3-litre "Essex" engine also used in the Capri until a couple of years ago. It is an iron block, iron head design with pushrod-operated valves and very oversquare bore/stroke dimensions. Both cars use Bosch K-Jetronic fuel injection, and both run on a compression ratio of 9.2:1. Strange then, that Ford quotes different power and torque outputs for each application — 160 bhp (DIN) at 5700 rpm/162 lb ft (DIN) at

4300 rpm for the Capri, and 150 bhp (DIN) at 5700 rpm/160 lb ft (DIN) at 3800 rpm for the Sierra. Ford says the disparity is a result of differences in manifolding, exhaust system and ignition timing.

Power difference or not, both Fords are impressively fast. Thanks partly to its more slippery (0.32 Cd) shape and partly to more favourable gearing, the Sierra overcomes its power deficit to reach a maximum speed of 129.0 mph. This speed is attained in fifth gear and with gearing of 22.5 mph/1000 rpm at just over the 5700 rpm power peak. The Capri, in contrast, reaches its 125.1 mph maximum speed in fourth gear, which at 21.2 mph/1000 rpm is the same as top in our original four-speed road test car. Our maximum speed runs were carried out around the Millbrook bowl were carried out in windy conditions, with the result that the Capri's engine was nudging the rev-limiter on the wind-assisted leg and losing speed into the wind. On a calm day we would expect the Capri to match the 128 mph-plus top speed of the earlier four-speed car.

The Sierra leads the Capri on acceleration, too. Zero to 60 mph takes the XR4i just 7.8 sec, but at 8.4 sec the Capri is not far behind. However, by 100 mph the Sierra has doubled its lead over the Capri, taking 22.9 sec from rest compared with 24.1 sec. The Sierra's shorter gearing must account for its advantage, because at 23.7 cwt it is actually slightly heavier than the 23.0 cwt Capri.

The same factors account for the Sierra's subjectively much punchier feel. Low-speed torque is not the injected Cologne engine's strong point, and it is not flattered by the Capri's long gearing. To make quick progress in the Capri you have to hold on to the lower gears much longer than you do in the XR4i if the engine is not to feel flat after the upchange, and on a fast, winding B-road fifth gear is redundant. But the Sierra, in contrast, has a delightful set of sprinting ratios; there's a gear for every occasion yet the engine does not feel strained even when cruising flat-out.

The fourth and fifth gear acceleration figures tell the story: 30-50 mph in fourth takes the Sierra 6.7 sec and

the Capri 8.0 sec, while 50-70 mph in fifth takes a sprightly 9.1 sec in the XR4i and 10.6 sec in the Capri. But don't let the foregoing make you think the Capri is slow, it isn't. By most standards it is a fast car indeed, but the XR4i is even quicker. Give the Capri a lower back axle ratio, and it would be a different story.

What is common to both cars is the delightful snarl of the V6 at high revs — and for its size, it's a very free-revving engine. It remains smooth right up to the red-line, and its refinement at all speeds is commendable. You are aware of the V6 beat but well-insulated from it, especially in the Sierra.

ECONOMY

Even though the Sierra has the more slippery body shape the Capri just wins the economy contest, no doubt helped by its long fifth gear. Using the figure from our original road test the Sierra returned 22.9 mpg, which is bettered slightly by the Capri's 23.5 mpg overall obtained with a similar mix of driving — including performance testing — to a solo road test. The four-speed Capri Injection we tested in 1981 achieved 22.5 mpg, so the addition of a fifth ratio has made a marginal improvement.

Both cars should be capable of over 25 mpg out of town, which with their identically-sized 13-gallon fuel tanks would give a practical range of well over 300 miles on a tankful of four-star. But you need a lot of patience to squeeze in the last couple of gallons, especially with the Sierra.

TRANSMISSION

Both cars use basically the same gearbox but with different internal ratios. You would think that the quality of the gearchange would be identical, but possibly because the test Sierra had covered a higher mileage than the Capri its gearchange had a looser, slicker feel with less obvious spring biasing. Although the Capri's gearchange felt less rubbery, neither was particularly fast and both had long movements. The action of both was precise enough but neither was really a pleasure to use.

The Capri has longer gearing than the XR4i in all gears, not just the 25.8 mph/1000 rpm fifth. This gives it

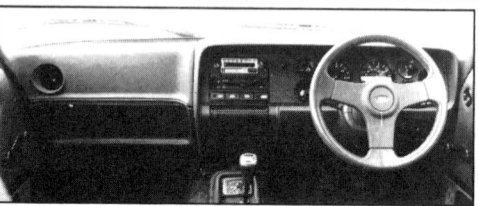

Capri has inviting interior with superb Recaro seats. Leather trim for rear seat passengers, too, but not much room. Traditional-looking dials are prolific but reflection-prone. Dated facia remains attractive, leather-rim wheel is delightful. Seven-spoke alloy wheels and 205-section NCTs give Capri a purposeful look

intermediate maxima of 42, 69 and 95 mph in the first three gears, maximum speed of course being reached in fourth. This compares with the Sierra's more useful maxima of 35, 65, 93 and 116 mph in the first four gears, far better for a sporting car. The curious decision to give the Capri longer gearing is explained by Ford's reluctance to invest in tooling up for a numerically higher final ratio — so near to the end of the Capri's life — when the fifth gear was added. It's a pity, too, as it blunts the performance unnecessarily without giving it a notable advantage in cruising ability over the Sierra.

Both cars have well-cushioned and progressive clutches, but that in the Sierra has an over-long travel and the Capri's suffers from an irritating "twang" from its return spring.

HANDLING

Both cars can be cornered very quickly, taking advantage of the reserves of grip afforded by their fat Goodyear NCTs, but each car goes about it in a very different way. Take the Capri. Although power-assisted, its steering retains feel and is quick and precise yet well weighted. You always know exactly what's happening to the front wheels, which makes mid-corner steering corrections easy to apply. And with the power available it's this ability to be held finely on the limit, balanced by the throttle, that makes the Capri such fun to drive. With taut, responsive handling, on a smooth, dry road the Capri is rapid. Its basically neutral balance turns to power oversteer when the limit is eventually reached, but when

---

FORD CAPRI INJECTION SPECIAL £9500

Make: Ford
Model: Capri Injection Special
Maker: Ford Motor Company Ltd, Eagle Way, Warley, Brentwood, Essex CM13 3BW. Tel: 0277 253000
Price: £7625.42 plus £635.45 Car Tax plus £1239.13 VAT equals £9500.00.
Extras on test car: Two-tone metallic paint £208.29. Total as tested £9708.29

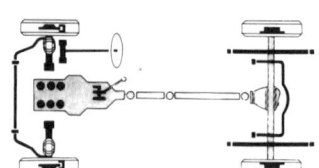

Cylinders	V6		coil springs; anti-roll
Capacity	2792 cc		bar; gas-filled
Bore/stroke	93.0/68.5 mm		dampers
Valves	Pushrod ohv	Rear suspension	Live axle located
Compression	9.2:1		and sprung by
Max power	160 bhp (DIN)		semi-elliptic leaf
	at 5700 rpm		springs; anti-roll
Max torque	162 lb ft (DIN)		bar; gas-filled
	at 4300 rpm		dampers
Gearbox	5-speed, manual	Steering	Rack, power
Mph/1000 rpm	25.8		assisted
Chassis con	Unitary	Brakes	Ventilated
Front suspension	Independent by		disc/drum
	MacPherson struts;	Tyres	205/60 VR13
		Weight	23.0 cwt

FORD SIERRA XR4i £10,323

Make: Ford **Model:** Sierra XR4i
Maker: Ford Motor Company Ltd, Eagle Way, Warley, Brentwood, Essex CM13 3BW. Tel: 0277 253000
Price: £8286.52 plus £690.54 Car Tax plus £1346.56 VAT equals £10,323.62.
Extras on test car: Power-assisted steering £419.76. Total as tested £10,743.38

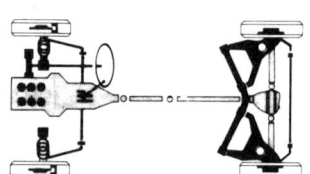

Cylinders	V6		MacPherson struts;
Capacity	2792 cc		coil springs;
Bore/stroke	93.0/68.5 mm		transverse lower
Valves	Pushrod ohv		links; anti-roll bar
Compression	9.2:1	Rear suspension	Independent by
Max power	150 bhp (DIN)		semi-trailing arms;
	at 5700 rpm		coil springs; anti-roll
Max torque	160 lb ft (DIN)		bar; gas-filled
	at 3800 rpm		dampers
Gearbox	5-speed, manual	Steering	Rack
Mph/1000 rpm	22.5	Brakes	Ventilated
Chassis con	Unitary		disc/drum
Front suspension	Independent by	Tyres	195/60 VR 14
		Weight	23.7 cwt

Sierra is light and airy inside but cloth trim is fussily-patterned. Plenty of room in the back, rear seat is asymmetrically-split. Instrument design is 10 years younger than Capri's and it shows — they are clear and reflection-free. Facia is ergonomic but bulky and plasticky. Alloy wheels aren't as stylish as Capri's

this does happen, the breakaway is gentle and progressive.

Throw in a few bumps, and despite the live-axle layout the Capri holds its line. And on wet roads, although the initial low-speed understeer becomes more marked and the tail comes out much more easily under power, the Capri remains easy to control although traction from the NCTs is disappointing despite the limited-slip differential.

You would expect some axle tramp from the Capri under hard acceleration, but such is the quality of the work done on the suspension by Ford's Special Vehicle Engineering Department that there is none. Roll angles, too, are impressively low and a series of S-bends induces no unsettling lurches thanks to firm damping.

If all this sounds too good to be true, there are snags. Driving the Capri fast demands considerable concentration particularly if road conditions are poor — you are aware of every nuance of the road surface, a live axle inevitably has its shortcomings. Here the Sierra scores heavily over its older stablemate: its more supple suspension does a better job of absorbing defects in the road surface, leaving the driver free to concentrate on his line. Our test XR4i, however, was fitted with the optional power-assisted steering, which unfortunately is too light and low geared, robbing the steering of the feel and perceived accuracy of the unassisted set-up. The result of this is that the Sierra has less well-defined limits of grip than the Capri, although on a bumpy bend its adhesion is ulti-

mately better. It, too, will oversteer under power when the limit is reached.

The Sierra may cope better with surface defects but it feels loose and inaccurate when pressed, an impression heightened by the power steering. Turn-in is nevertheless crisp, with less initial understeer than the Capri, but despite having slightly narrower tyres (also NCTs) the XR4i's wet road traction is the worse of the two cars — it, too, could make good use of a limited-slip differential. The Sierra holds the road and handles well, make no mistake, but in the end it's the soggier way it goes about it that means it has to give best to the altogether more sporting Capri. At eight-tenths, the Sierra is the easier to drive quickly; at ten-tenths, the Capri wins.

BRAKES

Advantage Sierra. Its brakes are light, but have good initial bite that is maintained under pressure. Their feel is not masked by the servo, and the only criticism that could be made is that hard use can cause the brakes to rumble.

By contrast, the Capri's brakes are reminiscent of an old-style Volkswagen Golf. On light applications they feel fine, but their lack of bite in a panic stop can be disconcerting even if they do succeed in pulling you up. The problems are compounded by too much bias to the front — it's quite easy to lock the front wheels in the wet.

ACCOMMODATION

Despite its sporting coupé looks, the Sierra has as much room as its more prosaic five-door relatives. There is plenty of headroom front and back, and no shortage of legroom even though the rear seat passengers sit behind bulkier front seats. Oddments space is generous, with a good-sized glovebox, a facia recess, a storage box under the armrest between the front seats, and useful door pockets. And of course the Sierra has a large boot (11.9 cu ft) which can be enlarged further by folding down one or both parts of the asymmetrically-split rear seat.

The Capri cannot compete on space. Headroom, already at a premium in the front, is further reduced by the sliding sunroof and in the rear it is inadequate for many adults. The same goes for rear legroom, although front seat occupants have plenty of space in which to stretch their legs. The fat spare wheel has encroached badly on the modest boot space so that the boot is very shallow but, as in the Sierra, the back seat can be folded flat to increase luggage space. In the Capri, however, the seat back is symmetrically split. There are no door pockets, but the Capri does have a storage box between the front seats like the XR4i, and a usefully-large glovebox with a lid that opens flat — ideal for picnics.

RIDE COMFORT

For a sporting car the Sierra has a very supple ride. There is an underlying firmness at low speeds but surface breaks are well-rounded, never causing jarring. At higher speeds the

ride is fluid and generally well-controlled, although undulations can catch it out and lead to float. It's the XR4i's composure over bumps and excellent suppression of road harshness that helps to make it such a good high-speed cruiser.

The Capri, as you would expect, has a more "sporting" ride — in other words, restless and firm over small bumps although it never jars or crashes. Although sometimes uncomfortable for passengers, the firmness of the ride contributes greatly to the Capri's feeling of tautness and precision. Unfortunately, at higher speeds it doesn't really smooth out if the surface is uneven, and at times it gets very turbulent. The damping remains good, but the Capri would prove the more wearing of the duo on long journeys.

AT THE WHEEL

Both cars have good driving positions, that of the Capri being more sporting with a higher scuttle and a more straight-legged seating position, complementing the long bonnet. The Capri's leather-edged Recaro seats are truly superb, with exactly the right amount of support everywhere. The Sierra's front seats are good, but they are too wide and lack thigh and lateral support compared with the Recaros. By more normal standards, however, they are very comfortable if a little too high — the tilt/height adjuster cannot achieve exactly the right combination of height and tilt.

The leather trim in the Capri extends to the steering wheel, which is small and pleasant to hold, and even the gear-lever knob. The Sierra's steering wheel is plastic-covered and less stylish.

The column stalks are very similar in both cars, with indicator/dip-switch on the left and two stalks — one each for wipers and lights — on the right. Neither car has a flick wipe. The Capri's age shows in its scattered minor controls, contrasting sharply with the Sierra's modern ergonomics that ensure everything is readily to hand.

INSTRUMENTS

The Capri has plenty of instruments; the XR4i should have more, but those it does have are easier to see than those in the Capri. The problem stems from the Capri's now-dated "dial-in-a-hole" design which is reflection-prone and causes the fuel gauge and voltmeter to be obscured by the steering wheel rim. The instruments themselves are neatly presented, but they are too dim at night (the rheostat allows adjustment from dim to very dim) and there is no red-line on the tachometer. The warning lights are scattered all over the place.

The information presented by the Sierra's instruments is altogether easier to assimilate. The main display is attractively illuminated at night, and the row of warning lights gives a clear indication of any malfunction. The XR4i may lack the Capri's voltmeter and oil pressure gauge, but it compensates with a digital clock/calendar/external temperature

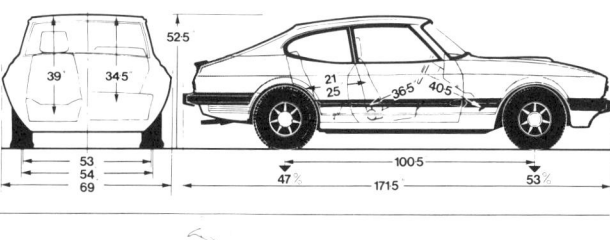

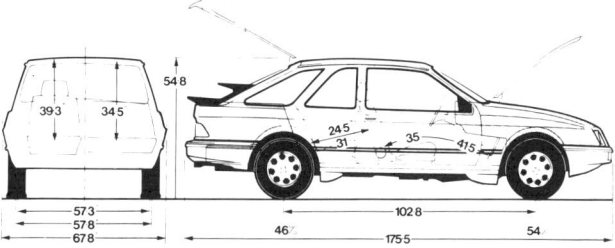

gauge and illuminated vehicle map for bulb failure, door not shut and the like. It also has an analogue clock, as does the Capri.

VISIBILITY

With its shallow windows and thick rear pillars the Capri looks claustrophobic, and it is. The view forward over that long bonnet is fine apart from the obstruction caused by the power bulge, but the steeply raked rear window gives a rather shallow vista and the rear three-quarter view is badly obstructed by headrests and rear pillars. The overall effect is not helped by a sombre grey headlining.

The Sierra has a much more light and airy cabin with deep windows all round. The biplane rear spoiler doesn't get in the way of the view aft as much as you would think, but the extra side pillar (compared with the basic three-door Sierra) does create an unnecessary blind spot. With such a steeply sloping bonnet, it's hard to judge where the front of the car ends.

The XR4i has bigger door mirrors than the Capri, and they are electrically adjustable, and only the driver's side mirror can be adjusted internally in the Capri, which also suffers from wipers that groan if the windscreen is anything other than awash, and which lift at speed. The Sierra also has the more effective headlights on both main and dipped beams.

HEATING AND VENTILATION

Ford's classic Aeroflow cold air ventilation system through eyeball vents, combined with an air-blender heater, lives on in the Capri. The heater itself has a prodigious output and responds quickly to adjustments, but the hot air distribution to the footwells is insufficiently diffuse. The ventilation is very effective with good throughput on ram pressure alone, but when open the vents transmit a lot of wind noise.

The Sierra's system is altogether more modern, with diffused heat distribution and four facia vents. These are heater-linked but a measure of bi-level temperature stratification

can still be achieved provided that the heater isn't on full blast. Although you can't have the torrent of cold air combined with warm feet that you can have in the Capri, the Sierra never gets stuffy and its heater controls are simple to operate.

NOISE

In terms of wind noise, the Capri is showing its age. Above 70 mph this is the dominant sound, as the engine is reasonably restrained and road noise is low. High-speed cruising is wearing in the Capri, but at least there are no rattles or squeaks.

The same cannot be said for the XR4i, for our test car suffered from a number of suspension bonks and trim rattles. But it could be that these were thrown into prominence by the lack of noise from other sources — the engine is muted, road noise is low and the only wind noise appeared to come from the sunroof. The Sierra is much the better motorway cruiser.

FINISH AND EQUIPMENT

Compared with the brash Sierra, the Capri is a model of restrained understatement. Although a bit gloomy, the Capri's interior is well-finished with grey leather and tasteful cloth in abundance. It's the dated facia that lets it down, although it is a nicely-executed example of its type. Outside, the lustrous two-tone metallic paint and handsome wheels give the ageing Capri shape the uplift it needs; the Injection Special is a very attractive car.

The Sierra, on the other hand, tries too hard. If it wasn't for the expanse of grey plastic cladding, which gets to look grubby very quickly, the XR4i could be a good-looking car give or take its biplane wing, but as it is it doesn't quite come off. The interior, too, is overdone with fussy rectangular grid patterns all over the rather ordinary-looking cloth trim and a facia that looks much more complicated than it is. The whole effect is much less inviting than the Capri's interior — and what's more, apart from the red line around the instru-

ment panel and the sporty steering wheel there is little to make you realise you're not in a Sierra 1.6L. But at least it's well-assembled.

Both cars are well equipped, particularly the XR4i now that it has electric windows, central locking, tinted glass and sliding glass sunroof as standard. Both have radio/stereo cassette players, that in the Capri being particularly good, but the Capri's steel sunroof would be better replaced by a glass one to make the cabin a little brighter.

CONCLUSION

In a logical world, the XR4i would have walked all over the Capri. But thankfully the world isn't that logical, and there are a number of ways in which the Capri is better. It's not so much what it does, but the way it does it. The Capri's dated feel ought to count against it, but ironically it is one of the car's attractions. That, and the looks, and the tautness of its handling. But there are drawbacks: the ride is firm, the wind noise is excessive, the accommodation for people and luggage is limited, the gearing is inappropriate, and the brakes are poor.

The Sierra, however, excels where the Capri falls down, without giving too much away where the Capri is good. Under the unhappy looks it is a very good car, but if it to compete with the Capri on out-and-out sporting appeal it needs quicker steering and firmer suspension. Nevertheless it is roomy and practical, and it has the edge on performance.

The Capri's undoubted attractions could wear off after a time while the many irritations came to assume greater importance. Conversely the Sierra's greater completeness as a design would ensure its appeal was lasting. It ought to have the Capri's Recaro seats and leather steering wheel, as well as tauter suspension, but there are plenty of firms willing to carry out such work. Even straight out of the box, however, the Sierra must be the choice — unless you have to have the pure, no-compromise sports coupé. In which case, logic doesn't apply . . .

Comparisons

PERFORMANCE	Capri	Sierra
Max speed, mph	125.1	129.0
Max in 4th	—	116
3rd	95	93
2nd	69	65
1st	42	35
0-60 mph, secs	8.4	7.8
30-50 mph in 4th, secs	8.0	6.7
50-70 mph in top, secs	10.6	9.1
Weight, cwt	23.0	23.7
Turning circle, ft	35.4	34.8
Turns, lock to lock	3.23	3.58
Boot cu. ft.	8.5	11.9

COSTS	Capri	Sierra
Price, inc VAT & Tax, £	9500	10,324
Insurance Group	7	6
Overall mpg	23.5	22.9
Fuel grade	4	4
Tank capacity, gals	13.0	13.2
Service interval, miles	6000	6000
No of dealers	1241	1241
Set brake pads (front) £*	23.30	41.65
Complete clutch £*	118.78	118.78
Complete exhaust £*	212.09	164.02
Front wing panel £*	81.58	52.51
Oil filter £*	5.70	5.70
Starter motor £*	105.21†	105.21†
Windscreen £*	37.12**	35.97**

*inc VAT but not labour charges
**Laminated
†Exchange

STANDARD EQUIPMENT	Capri	Sierra
Adjustable steering		
Air conditioning		
Alloy wheels	●	●
Central door locking		●
Cigar lighter	●	●
Clock	●	●
Cloth trim	●	●
Dipping mirror	●	
Driver seat height adjust		●
Driver seat tilt adjust		●
Electric window lifters		●
Fresh air vents	●	●
Headlamp washers		
Head restraints	●	●
Heated rear window	●	●
Intermit flick wipe	●	●
Laminated screen	●	●
Locker	●	●
Passenger door mirror	●	●
Petrol filler lock	●	●
Power steering	●	
Radio	●	●
Rear central armrest		●
Rear courtesy light		
Rear wash/wipe	●	●
Remote mirror adjust	●	●
Rev counter	●	●
Reverse lights	●	
Seat belts — rear		
Seat recline	●	●
Sliding roof	●	●
Tape player	●	●
Trip computer		
Tinted glass	●	
Vanity mirror	●	●

RATING	Capri	Sierra
Performance	●●●●	●●●●●
Economy	●●●●	●●●●●
Transmission	●●●●	●●●
Handling	●●●●	●●●
Brakes	●●	●●●●
Accom (L)	●●	●●●●●
Accom (P)	●●	●●●●●
Ride	●●●	●●●●
At the wheel	●●●●	●●●●
Visibility	●●	●●●●
Instruments	●●●	●●●●
Heating	●●●	●●●●
Ventilation	●●●	●●●●
Noise	●●●	●●●●
Finish	●●●●	●●●
Equipment	●●●●	●●●●

Excellent ●●●●● Good ●●●●
Average ●●● Poor ●● Bad ●

TOP TEN CAPRIS

Jeremy Walton, Ford enthusiast and author, selects his ideal Capri collection

1) RS2600 GROUP 2 RACER, 1972
Specification: 2995cc V6, Weslake aluminium heads, Kugelfischer injection, 290bhp at 7500rpm. ZF five-speed gearbox. Bodyshell primarily steel with front and rear wheelarch extensions. Cd 0.45, weight 2156lbs
Performance: Max 165mph approx, 0-60mph in 4.6secs, 0-124mph (200kph) in 14.3secs
Value: Not less than £20,000 ready to race
Summary: The most successful racing Capri, including 1-2-3 at Spa and 10-11 at Le Mans, from the most successful year. One example is in Britain, the Kent/Frami car, undergoing restoration in Yorkshire

2) 1600GT, 1969
Specification: In-line four 'Kent' engine, twin-choke carb, 1599cc, 86bhp at 5500rpm. Four-speed gearbox
Performance: Max 100mph, 0-60mph in 13.4secs, 25-27mpg
Value: £1000 for a well-preserved example, £250-£500 for a well-used 'survivor'!
Summary: Since so few 1969 3-litres survive, the one to go for is a 1600GT (rather than the more garish XLR). Kent engine is a tough, reliable performer, lighter weight helps handling. Good rack and pinion steering, non-assisted, possibly better than current assisted set-up. Broadspeed handling kit and 185 tyres worthwhile

3) 3000GXL, POST-AUTUMN 1972
Specification: 'Essex' V6, twin-choke carb, 2994cc, 138bhp, four-speed gearbox
Performance: Max 122mph, 0-60mph in 8.3secs, 0-100mph in 25.1secs, 21-23mpg
Value: Under £1500
Summary: Autumn 1972 saw a quoted 151 changes — but not all are necessarily improvements! Revised dashboard (still there in 1986) and slicker German gearbox were though. The advantage of the GXL model is improved lighting from quad headlamps; deluxe trim pack and steel sunroof bonus fittings

4) CAPRI 3000S 'X-PACK'
Specification: Built to order, but basics included Essex V6 with single down-draught carb (Zakspeed for 200-off run) or triple Webers (in UK), bigger valves, 175bhp at 5000rpm. Mk 3 body with extended glass-fibre wheelarches and front spoiler. Panels still available from RS dealers
Performance: Max 135mph, 0-60mph in 7.5secs, 0-100mph in 21.0secs, 13.5-18mpg
Value: Immaculate, £2500-£3600
Summary: Any Mk 3 Capri can be converted, but the proper 'X-Packs' should include high quality panels to original Zakspeed squared-off pattern, ventilated discs up front; uprated suspension with gas-filled Bilsteins, 7.5 (minimum) x 13 RS four-spoke alloy wheels (not current seven-spokers) and low profile (preferably 205/60) rubber, plus tuned engine with anything from 170bhp to 200bhp plus. Current UK-sourced panels 'have absolutely no problems in fit or finish' according to RS network. Alternative engine mods include a Holley four-barrel or turbo.

5) RS3100, 1973/4
Specification: Special over-sized homologation Essex V6, 3091cc, single twin-choke carb, 148bhp at 5000rpm. Standard Mk I body but with aerodynamic addenda including tail spoiler. Cd 0.37
Performance: Max 125mph, 0-60mph in 7.3secs, 0-100mph in 21.0secs, 20-22mpg
Value: Starts at £1500 to £2000
Summary: UK equivalent of German RS2600, the latter with fuel injection and smoother engine which was probably better, but was unobtainable in the UK, and lhd only. Most sporting production Mk I. Plus points are uprated and lowered (virtually RS2600) suspension with negative camber up front, gas-filled dampers, quad lamps plus improved stability thanks to RS2600 front spoiler and unique rear spoiler. Really a quickly-converted 3.0 Capri. Production estimates vary from 200 to 250. To find a genuine one rather than a converted example is difficult: join Ford AVO Owners Club and seek advice of RS3100 registrar Dennis Sellars

6) CAPRI II GHIA, 1974
Specification: Either 2.0 or 3.0 could be chosen, so 2-litre here for variety's sake. Engine ex-Cortina SOHC in-line four 'Pinto' unit, 1993cc, 98bhp at 5200rpm. Four-speed ex-Cortina gearbox
Performance: Max 108mph, 0-60 in 10.5secs, 26-28mpg
Value: £500 to £750
Summary: Ghia badge and increased trim spec was introduced by Ford on Capri II Ghia. Important as much for model lines it introduced (Ghia and JPS black S) as for hatchback design. Hatch meant more weight and inferior aerodynamics but more convenience, plus better visibility thanks to more glass. Ghia pack included own-brand wheels, much plusher interior in Rialto fabrics, sunroof, vinyl roof and metallic paint. Power steering originally optional, later (October 1975) standard on 3-litre Ghias.

7) FOUR-WHEEL DRIVE, 1969-72
Specification: At least five built for rallycross, 12 for road/police evaluation. All with Essex 3-litre V6 plus Ferguson 4WD (pre-viscous coupling). Road horsepower 128bhp, track 160bhp in 1969 debut rising to 252bhp at 6100rpm with Lucas fuel injection in winter 1970/71. ZF five-speed 'box, but at least one with auto

transmission. Dunlop Maxaret ABS also tried but discarded for competition
Performance: Autocar-calculated max speed at 92mph, 0-60mph unknown, 0-90mph in 7secs
Value: None ever sold, but parts passed along inside rallycross community. Development prototypes will mostly have been destroyed
Summary: These Capris deserve a place in my Capri collection because they pioneered fuel injection, 4WD and anti-lock braking fully ten years before the Audi Quattro. Full-blooded competition examples to be avoided. Not an easy car to drive: get it right and it's perfect, get it wrong and you just wind up with more and more lock and total understeer. A lot of traction though...

8) 2.8i CAPRI
Specification: 2792cc German V6 with Bosch injection yields 160bhp at 5700rpm. Four-speed 'box until Jan 1983, then five-speed standard. Cd 0.39
Performance: Original four-speed car (Autocar): 129mph, 0-60mph in 7.9secs, 0-100 in 23.4secs, 20-23mpg
Value: Early four-speed £3000 or less, five-speed Special with part leather and limited slip diff £4900 to £6000, £8000 for D-reg low-mileage example. Or £11,999 for one of the 1038 Capri 280s...
Summary: The model that saved the Capri from extinction years ago. Low cost suggests summer 1981 launch model, but probably most collectable has to be a 280.

9) ZAKSPEED TURBO, 1981
Specification: 'Silhouette' racer to Group 5 for German National Championship, built by Erich Zakowski's Zakspeed concern. Drew on Ford expertise (wind tunnel and a surprising amount of earlier Capri race hardwear). In-line four had Kent block, KKK or Garrett turbo: most successful with 1427cc (380bhp in 1978 to 460bhp on 1.5 bar boost) in 1981. Getrag five-speed 'box. Alloy tube frame, Capri Mk III outline body in Kevlar. Cd under 0.30. Weight 1738lbs
Performance: Max 168-174mph; 100-200kph (from rolling start) in 9.6secs
Value: £59,000 (1979 prices...)
Summary: Both 1.4- and 1.7-litre Zakspeed Capris were made, but 1.4 finally won Ford driver Klaus Ludwig outright title in 1981. Manfred Winkelhock (1.7) finished third in the same series. Probably the most expensive Ford-associated Capri (apart from prototypes!) and certainly the quickest. At least three babies built, and at least two of the 1.7s. Used crude but effective ground effects with skirts which wore rapidly but survived long enough for blinding opening laps...

10) RS2600, 1971
Specification: German V6, Kugelfischer injection, 2637cc, 150bhp at 5600rpm. Four-speed 'box, standard body with front spoiler and front wheelarch flares, Cd approx 0.40
Performance: Max 126mph, 0-62mph in 7.7secs
Value: One seen for DM equivalent of £5534 in a German mag
Summary: The personal number one, but also the classic road-going Capri. Extreme UK rarity and little likelihood of servicing. Production headed for 4000, much more than Group 2 minimum of 1000. Engine is one of the sweetest around, while modified strut/leaf spring live axle layout was superb. An honourable competition history and a much better road car than any of its contemporaries helps to make it the most collectable of all

LSD TRIPPING

Vandal or visionary? David Mills says he prefers a Capri to a Porsche 911. Is he mad? Perhaps not . .
Photographs by Clickstop Sports Photography

I'M ALWAYS asked "what's the best car you've ever driven?". I used to say "a 911, because of its power, handling and practicality." Then comes the "but surely . . ." response. But surely a Maserati is the best, but surely the Porsche's trailing-throttle cornering . . . Nowadays I have a better answer. "A Ford" I reply. The inquisitor's eyes often glaze over. It's a four letter word to him. He may suddenly see somebody on the other side of the room that he really must say hello to.

Now, if I had it said it was a 2.8-litre, fuel-injected Lotus, with 205/60 NCTs, 160bhp, a limited slip differential, leather trim, low cost servicing and a showroom price of £9,500, you could imagine the difference. Saying "a Ford" is definitely more fun, though, and it's actually true. But for the Lotus appellation, the 2.8 Injection Special Capri fits the specification precisely. OK, its design dates back to when I was a sixth-former, but then the 911 was in the showroom when I was doing my eleven plus. A blasphemous analogy? After a week's reunion, with lots of varied motoring, I don't think so.

The Capri became 'mine' during the photo session. It had been three years since I had sat behind the wheel of a 2.8i Capri, but it felt very familiar. The long bonnet, with its 'power hump' pointed the way. The dashboard still sported unmarked idiot lights all over the shop, the driving position still fitted my average sized frame. But there was that rich anchovy smell of Connolly hide, and its sensuous feel, as the small steering wheel is covered in the stuff.

Blasting off for the "dramatic high-speed oversteer-corner" shot, the exhaust emitted a distinctly sporty brrappp, the speedo registered 60mph in less than 8 seconds, no traffic for miles, and so a touch on the

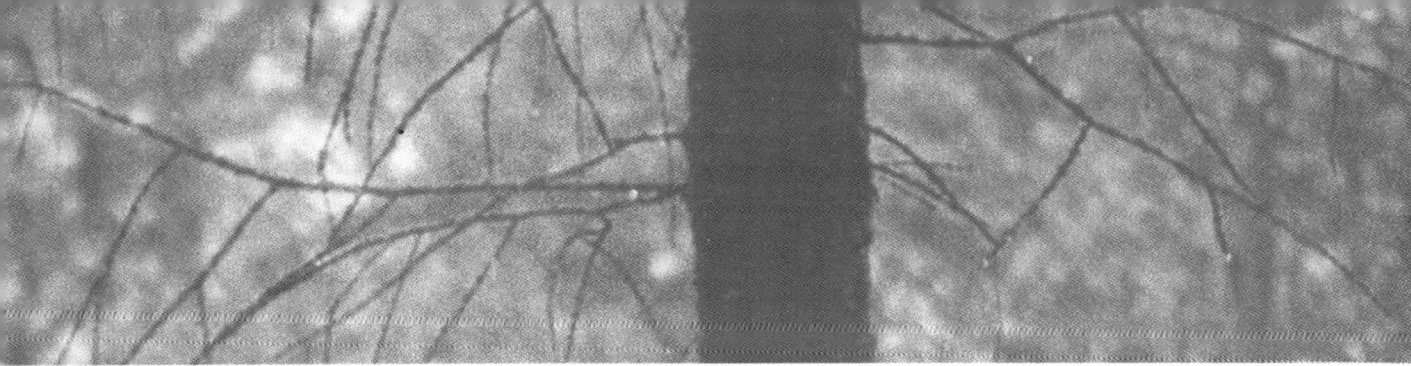

brakes, turn-in for the corner, feel the roll and lateral g build up, gun the throttle and . . . nothing. The initial understeer turned towards neutral, and the photographer wondered what had happened.

Mills had grossly underestimated the Capri's cornering ability. Never mind, turn up the wick. Now all four wheels were sliding. I had to block all that I had learned in my years of high performance road and track driving, and revive Wally Hooligan, that well known wrecker of cars; braking late, turning in very late and hitting the floor to get the back to break away, and even then, the loss of speed enabled it to regain grip and toe the line.

OK, apart from a run-up and the unreal width and safety run-offs of a test track, or a slow, tight corner and unleashing all 160bhp at once, visually spectacular stuff is strictly for a wet or even damp road. Personally, I find actually getting through a corner faster far more attractive anyway. Hooligans should look towards the old 3.0-litre S – slower through the corner, but better for the ego, I suppose.

After the photo session, I thought I'd put the Capri through its paces on a trip from London to Thomas Hardy's Wessex and back in a day – some 300 miles of fun. The M3 motorway gave me a chance to sample its inter-city cruising abilities.

The first thing you notice is the way it takes the bumps. Lively isn't quite the adjective – the low profile tyres obviously transmit more road shock than your average saloon, but Ford's Special Vehicle engineering team have done well to keep much of it from the driver – noticeable but not teeth-chattering.

It's the longer pitch undulations that might annoy a saloon driver; the Injection Special fails to iron out as much force as one might like, but the effect is quickly erased from one's consciousness. The steering is a delight – power assisted, but with plenty of feel and a direct, positive action. With less than three turns lock to lock, it still sets a standard for sports coupés.

The Capri's fifth gear gives a long legged 25.5mph per 1,000rpm, so that 100mph sees less than 4,000rpm on the tacho, offering around 10 per cent better fuel economy than the old four-speed box, yet the Capri is still capable of achieving a maximum top speed of 126mph. 100mph cruising therefore does little to strain the V6, and the only real intrusion on the excellent standard four-speaker stereo radio-cassette comes from wind noise, which is worse than average by current standards, but still quite acceptable.

Averaging 70mph on the motorway should give you a return of around 30mpg, and a comfortable 350-mile range from its 13-gallon fuel tank. Even overall, we returned a surprisingly good 25mpg from

nearly 1,000 miles of enthusiastic driving.

All controls fall easily to hand – horn, flasher/dip and indicators on the left hand stalk, and two for the right hand to operate – lights and two-speed plus intermittent wipers. A facia-mounted switch operates the rear screen wiper. Idiot lights apart, the dash is simple and the large speedo and rev counter are easily visible through the small steering wheel.

Pleasingly quickly, the M3 gave way to the A30 and the undulations of the Salisbury plains. The stretch of old Roman road which leads past the even older Stonehenge and on into Somerset is mostly single carriageway, and the urge from the Cologne V6 enables smooth and comfortable overtaking, though the old Essex V6 offered more torque. Doubling back on the A30, I arrived at the little Dorset village of Pimperne well in time for lunch at the thatched 16th century Anvil Hotel.

Stepping out, I realised just how comfortable the leather-trimmed Recaro seats are. The old S-pack versions didn't offer enough lumbar support, but these do, and keep you snug in the corners with equally good lateral support, as I found out after lunch. I headed out north on the B roads across Cranborne Chase – beautiful hilly countryside threaded with ribbon-like tarmac. Indeed, one of the roads was used as a hill-climb before the war, and so I gunned the Capri. Its cornering ability and tractive force is excellent for a car costing less than £10,000.

Though most of the 'course' was dry, water drained across one particular corner. This is precisely the sort of condition for which the limited slip differential is designed. Torque reaction across the live rear axle tends to make the left wheel lift, an LSD effectively forces that wheel back down, giving even traction when you really turn the power on. A wet, left hand corner accentuates the need for this handy little device. The Capri powered out, gripping well, the nicely geared steering allowing a quick flick of the wrist to correct what little tail slide there was.

All it needs is a little more power, I kept telling myself. Funny, really, because the Capri Injection Special is already on a par with the likes of a Lotus Excel. Well sorted cars often have that effect on the mind – the chassis handles the power so well, the limits feel far off. Turbo units sprang immediately to mind. This lust for power is a terrible thing.

A coffee break in the sun, and a chance to look at the Injection Special as other people see it. The lines are not dated (as they now are on the Mark One Capris). The optional two tone metallic paint job in mineral blue/stratos silver or nimbus grey/stratos

silver adds £208 onto the basic £9,500 price tag, but it does make the Capri look classy, as do the seven-spoke RS alloy wheels and the tinted glass (standard items). The ride home was uneventful and relaxed – some sports cars urge you to drive them hard, but not the Capri.

So what else can you get that is comparable to Ford's finest? For less than £10,000, not a lot. You have to look higher up the price lists. The Alfa GTV6 at £11,300 is perhaps closest in character and performance, then there is the Colt Starion at £12,499. I could buy this Capri *and* a Vauxhall Astra SR for less than the price of a Porsche 944.

It's on the cards, though, that this will be the last Capri. A fine swan song for an excellent marque. I rather think, though, that there may be a stay of execution. I hope so, after all, my party piece won't have the same effect if the Capri passes out of the showrooms.

The Capri's obvious successor as Ford's performance car is the XR4i which at present offers less adrenalin charge than the Injection special. However, a four-wheel-drive version is under development and Ford and Cosworth are engaged in producing a high peformance engine. The potential combination might well make the XR4i a worthy if not glamorous heir to the throne.

ROAD TEST
By MIKE McCARTHY

High speed cruising ability, bags of extras as standard and a place on many collectors' 'wanted' list – the Capri's last fling: the 280.

The last of its kind

The Capri is dead: long live the Capri. One of the world's most popular GTs ceased production on Dec 19, 1986, after a life of 17 years and some 1,886,647 units. It was, at the end, in today's terms an anachronism: front engine, rear-wheel drive, when the hot saloons currently scuttling around this country are invariably small hatchbacks with multiple valves per cylinder (or a turbocharger) and front-wheel drive. The Peugeot 250GTi is fashionable, the Capri isn't. Still, I suspect many will mourn its passing, and the passing in effect of the type of car it represents: a good honest 2+2 with many traditional traits. You can count me among the many . . .

A brief history. Production started in 1968, the range being 1.3, 1.3GT, 1.6 and 1.6GT models: it was launched onto the British market in January 1969. Later that year the 2.0-litre V4, and later still the classic version, the 3.0-litre V6, made their bow, while the luxury 3000E came in 1970. November 1973 saw the charismatic homologation special, the RS3100, appear, rather to the embarrassment of Ford, for a couple of months later came the Mk II models, with sleeker lines and a hatchback: the line-up was similar to before, but the 2.0-litre V4 was replaced by the single ohc 2.0-litre in-line four. Over the next four years various changes were made, the GT models being replaced by the S versions, and the Ghia models topped out the range – and in October 1976 all Capri production was moved to Cologne. The Mk III went on sale in 1978 with minor but appealing styling changes, followed in 1981 by what many regard as the classic Capri: the SVE-developed 2.8i. Towards the end of its run, the range was simplified to the 1600, 2000 and 2.8i models, and the final version of all – and the subject of this farewell road test – is the 280, of which only 1038 have been made. Start collecting now . . .

As implied by the title, it is a special edition of the 2.8i. Thus it features the 2792cc V6 engine with Bosch fuel injection, giving 160bhp at 5700rpm, and 162lb ft of torque at 4200rpm. Mated to this is a five-speed gearbox which feeds power to the live rear axle, suspended on leaf springs, which also incorporated a limited-slip differential. Suspension at the front is by MacPherson struts, and there are anti-roll bars at each end. Braking is by discs at the front and drums at the rear, steering is power-assisted rack and pinion, and 15×7in alloy wheels carry 195/50 Pirellis.

Special features of the 280 include 'Brooklands Green' metallic paint, hide upholstery and Recaro front seats.

Performance is reasonably impressive. Ford claim a maximum of 130mph, and a 0-60mph time of 7.9s: *Autocar* managed 126mph in fourth, and 123mph in fifth (plus an 8.2s time for the 0-60mph dash) in a 2.8i back in 1985. On the understanding that the 2.8i and the 280 are identical mechanically, these figures still stand. It is thus lively rather than a flyer, and some of the little hot hatch-backs could well see it off in a straight line – up to 60mph, at least.

In practice, the 280 is at its best as a motorway cruiser: 70mph is a mere 2700rpm and, in fact, a natural cruising gait is around the 100mph mark. We say this for two reasons: firstly, that the engine is not notably torquey in the lower reaches, and secondly, the gearing feels high – fifth gives 25.7mph/1000rpm – so that you find yourself using the gear lever rather more than you might expect from what is, on paper, a lusty V6 lump. On top of that, in this application, it's not a smooth engine at low revs, and it's only when its rotating fairly rapidly that the vibrations tend to disappear. As consolation – and it is a pleasant consolation – it revs easily, and sounds lovely while doing it. Silent it is not, musical it most definitely is, and this is totally in character with the car's image. One of the pleasures of Capri V6 ownership is simply accelerating hard in the gears and listening for that gruff growl from the exhaust.

The engine vibration at low revs, or when accelerating, may in fact be from the transmission, for it shows itself as a distinct 'zizz' up through the lever. The high ratios too have been mentioned, but those are the only two real criticisms we can make of it. The change itself is chunky and precise, and actually improves with quicker changes. It is matched by a light, progressive clutch which again makes changes clean and easy – much more so than on the 2.8i I tested back in 1985.

The other area where the Capri scores highly with enthusiasts is in its road manners. With a live rear axle and fat Pirellis, it doesn't have the sophisticated habits of more modern machinery with all independent layouts, but by the same token it can be driven with plenty of verve in the good old-fashioned manner. At low cornering speeds it feels quite neutral: as you push it, understeer starts to intrude to a certain degree, but at

The interior may appear dated, but the leather seats are extremely comfortable and the controls ideally placed.

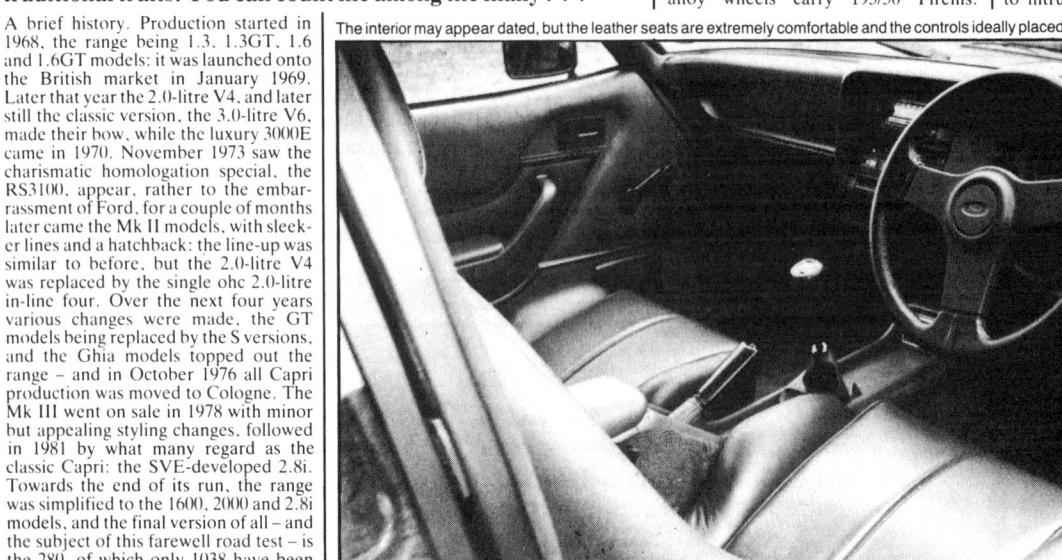

Ford's Capri is now an anachronism, but its lines have held up remarkably well to the tests of time and the whole package still spells fun.

heart the Capri is an oversteer-er, even though the limited-slip diff does its best to stop it. At speed – as on a race track – it is possible to throw the tail out, and then hold it in a progressive slide, but that really is for use in emergency only: far batter to settle the car under braking before a corner, then power through on the throttle. The car squats slightly at the back, the steering sends back all the right impulses, and you flow round with very little roll, the car sitting four-square to the road. There's no front-wheel drive scrabbling for grip, or in-dependent-rear squirreliness, just a sure-footed urge around and away. Bumps, though, can upset the tail slightly, while in the wet more than a modi-cum of caution is called for as grip deteriorates from the excellent dry-road condition to something more easily overcome with a boot full of power. You have been warned . . . The steering is much more weighty than you might

expect from a power-assisted set up, but that to me is a very good thing indeed, since it means more than average feel. Gearing, too, is just about perfect.

Natural driving position

As is the seating position. You tend to sit a bit high, but for shorter drivers the car's extremities are invisible. The Recaro seat, hide-trimmed, is beauti-fully supportive everywhere and without any lumps or bumps to poke into you, while the controls are positioned exactly right: you couldn't find a more natural posture if you tried.

Surrounding you, though, is the one facet of the car that gives its age away: the interior. Not in big things – the seats, steering wheel and gear lever are as up-to-the-minute as you'll get – but in lesser matters. Those eye-ball air vents at the end of the facia, for example, so high-tech in 1969, are now just antediluvian, as are the minor instruments, hidden

down holes in the binnacle where you have to peer around the steering wheel to look at them. Fortunately, the two main dials – the speedo and tacho – are sensibly sized and readable, although their glasses reflect badly. Accommo-dation, too, apart from the front seats, is old-fashioned: the two rear seats are tiny, while the 'boot' is very little larger, being quite shallow. The split rear seat helps in this area, of course, but for a long trip only two travellers can be recommended . . .

Lacking in refinement

Refinement is the other area where old age is creeping in. The Capri is not a quiet car, except when cruising on the motorway: the suspension passes on the sounds of the tyres and the road surface, and road roar is very obstrusive. Wind noise is always there though not exces-sively so, except at very high speed, while the engine and transmission emis-

sions have been mentioned already. This sounds like a catalogue of woes, but in fact it isn't: the Capri isn't bad, just other competitors, more up to date, are better. The ride, too, reflects a relatively unsophisticated suspension and fat tyres, small pot-holes and road works can be distinctly felt at low speeds – say around town – but then the faster you go so matters improve, and in fact quite severe humps can be taken comfortably.

When I tested the 2.8i back in 1985 I asked myself if I could live with a Capri, and the answer was yes. Well, now I am: as reported recently in these pages I am the proud, albeit temporary, posses-sor of the very last Capri, chassis number GG11896. Somehow I *know* I'm going to love it . . . ∎

Ford Capri 280

£11,999

SPECIFICATION

Cylinders/capacity	V6, 2792cc
Bore/Stroke	93 × 58.5mm
Valve gear	OHV, pushrods
Fuel system	Bosch K-Jetronic fuel injection
Power/rpm	160bhp (DIN) at 5700rpm
Torque/rpm	162lb ft (DIN) at 4200rpm
Gear ratios	2:36, 1.81, 1.26, 1.00, 0.825:1
Final drive	3.09:1
Steering	Rack and pinion, power assisted
Brakes	Disk front, drum rear, servo assisted
Wheels	Light alloy, 15 × 7ins
Tyres	195/50VR15
Suspension (F)	Independent by MacPherson struts, coil springs, telescopic dampers, anti-roll bar
Suspension (R)	Live axle, semi-elliptic springs, gas-filled telescopic dampers, anti-roll bar

DIMENSIONS

Length	171.4ins
Wheelbase	101ins
Track (F/R)	53/54.5ins
Width	67ins
Weight	23.0cwt

PERFORMANCE

(Autocar figures)

Maximum	126mph (4th), 124mph (5th)
0-60mph	8.2s
50-70 (4th/5th)	8.8/12.9s
Fuel consumption	18.7/38.2/30.1mpg
(urban/56mph/75mph)	
Test consumption	22.3mpg

The 2.8 injection V6 was first dropped into the Capri in 1981, providing more power (160bhp) than its 3.0-litre predecessor.

ON THE END OF THE LINE

With the limited-edition 280 the Capri has come to the end of its long life. The last one of all is going to Mike McCarthy, but there was a snag — McCarthy had to help build it, which is how he came to find himself in Cologne in December

Once upon a time, many, many years ago — or in days of yore, whichever was the older — you didn't just pop into your local showroom to buy yourself a car. Oh, no. What you did was first choose yourself a chassis, usually by studying one of the weeklies such as *The Autocar* (with the definitive article). Then you found yourself a coachbuilder and chose a body for him to mount on said chassis, at the same time selecting all the exciting little things that went with it (where should the spare be mounted? Partition or not? Bedford cord or leather upholstery? That sort of thing). Having done all that you sat back, often for a not inconsiderable time, while the whole thing was built for you, and when it was ready you (or your chauffeur) collected the car. It was a nice,

relaxed way of doing things, albeit a mite pricy. Nowadays you fill in a form which is stuffed into a computer, a button or two is pressed, and a little while later your car is delivered to your local dealer. Doesn't have quite the same magic, though, does it?

However, last December I did something about as close to the old-fashioned way as you could get. I went along to an assembly line and 'helped' put together my own car. Well, to be honest, it's not exactly 'mine', nor did I actually 'help' in the assembly of it, but at least I was there to see it being screwed, glued, bolted and clipped together. What's more, as you might have gathered by now, I didn't go through all this rigmarole just for any old car.

This wasn't any old car — this was The Last Capri. Well, actually, it

All 280s *come resplendent in*
Brooklands Green (above left)
McCarthy's air *of competence*
(top) is totally false
Our car *was, officially, the last to*
come down the line

wasn't the *very* last Capri down the assembly line, but it *was* the last *numerical* Capri. And it *is* mine for the next six months or so. Well, really, it *was* mine for all of a couple of hours, but then along came a person called a Features Editor and the swine went and took it away from me for a couple of days to take some pictures of it. This story is beginning to sound like Watergate, isn't it?

Let's go back to the beginning. Late last year, when we heard that the Capri was to be halted, it was suggested that one of the last might make suitable transport for an old crock — me — as the utterly famous Editor-at-Large of an old crock magazine, *Classic and Sportscar*. The matter was discussed with the good folks at Ford by Mr Editor Carter, and it was then suggested that I be

loaned The Last Capri for six months. You don't turn down an offer like that, do you? What's more, Ford suggested that it might be a jolly good idea if I were to go across to Cologne and help build it. I thought this was rather brave of them, since my mechanical aptitude is on a par with those three Irishmen needed to change a lightbulb.

Which is how I found myself in Ford's Cologne factory on 19 December last year, along with a couple of other journalists and a BBC TV team who almost seemed to outnumber the Cologne workforce.

"There will be an opportunity to participate in the assembly in a small way," said the Ford spokesman. Like what? "Fitting a headlight assembly," he said. About my level, I thought. "There are the overalls," he

added. The next thing I knew was that I was covered in blue with a Ford badge on the breast pocket. I thought I would blend nicely into the background amidst all the other blue-overalled workers, but theirs had obviously been worked in: mine were pristine. Blend I didn't.

We picked up The Last Capri at the bare-but-painted shell stage, one of a clutch of cars which included Granadas and Fiestas, inching its way along the line. This looks for all the world like a very large, very sluggish snake, inexorably winding its way along the

factory floor, the assembly folk fussing and fiddling and fitting bits and pieces to the cars. With the variety of machinery coming down the line it's not what I would call mind-bogglingly boring, and all the time anyway there's that continual banter you find in such establishments. It's not all high-tech robots, nor is it antiseptic, and I found it friendlier and more relaxed than I expected.

Which is just as well, actually, because when it came my turn to fit the wretched near-side headlamps I made a total dog's dinner of it. First I tried to fit them upside down, which caused the guy who normally does it to start giggling. Then there were all the wires trailing out the back of it, like a disembowelled animal: where they went I couldn't tell. The line ▶

Mechanically *the 280 is identical to the previous 2.8i Special*

Low-profile *P7s on alloy wheels, stripes and badges distinguish 280*

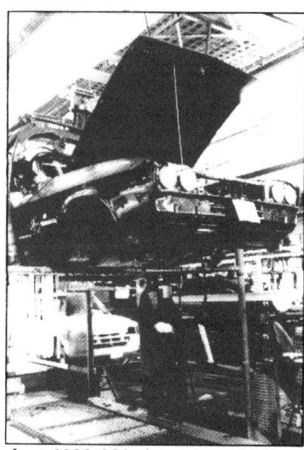

Just 1038 *280s have been built*

Engine and body *mated together*

◄ worker, near hysterics this time, muttered a hugely funny German imprecation (I assume it was funny: all the others laughed), grabbed the unit, poked here, prodded there, slapped it into place, there was a click — and that was it. Four screws had to be tightened. This I tried again — but have you ever tried to tighten up a screw on a moving target? Any pictures you see of me doing anything in this story are strictly posed . . .

At this stage The Last Capri was bereft of any mechanicals and was being fitted with windscreens, windows, door trim and other such bits. We then picked it up on one of its return journeys, where the petrol tank was being attached. Seemed like a good place to have another go at 'assembly'. Except that there were, if anything, even more nuts and bolts, clips and pipes to contend with, so another shot was posed. That's what I mean when I say I didn't actually 'help' to build the car, though I was there. The patience of the assembly workers was marvellous to behold and if any are reading this, sorry I got in the way chaps.

The next major step was the fitment of the mechanicals — engine, transmission and suspension. The cars came down one conveyor belt up there somewhere, the engines on another down below. Now I *know*, with computers and other gadgetry it's impossible for a set of components for, say, a Fiesta, to arrive below a Granada bodyshell, but I was rivetted to the point for a good quarter of an

hour, hoping that once, just *once*, the impossible would happen. Wouldn't Granada running gear in a Fiesta make a sensational Q-car?

Slowly The Last Capri glided along the track. Wheels were fitted, wipers, some petrol put in the tank — and there was the end of the line. A hooter went off, and the line stopped. Actually it was the afternoon tea-break, and The Last Capri had been timed to arrive at just the right time so that production wouldn't be stopped. Doing that is *awfully* expensive . . .

Off the line came The Last Capri, the polishing rags working double-time. There's no rear window in it at the moment, and the little strip on top of the grille is missing: one of the latter is hastily found and clipped in place. The flowers were brought out, plus a whole heap of big Fablon numbers. The Last Capri is driven off the line and ceremoniously parked. The flowers are arranged on the bonnet, and the Fablon numbers lined up in front of it — this causes some confusion, and at one time we had something like 8,164,886, but this is soon rearranged to read the correct figure: 1,886,647. The sum total of Capris.

There's relatively little celebration. The only journalists there are we Brits, sentimental old fools that we are. The Germans join in, though, and all and sundry pose around the car to have their pictures taken, from factory manager to polisher. The TV people want some more shots of it on the line, so back it goes for a moment.

Engine and body *mated together*
The hooter sounds again, and suddenly it's all over. The Last Capri is just another car heading for the dynamometer and the headlamp adjusting bay.

Perhaps the Germans are less sentimental because it isn't actually the *very* last Capri down the line: it does have, however, the highest numerical chassis number, GG11896. Others are following it, but they would arrive at the end at an inconvenient time. Never mind: there is a last official Capri, and this is the one.

It's one of a batch, a limited edition of 1038. The colour is Brooklands Green, a medium metallic which looks horrid in the factory lights but lovely in daylight. It's got Recaro front seats, trimmed in full leather, with contrasting piping. There are 50-series low-profile Pirelli P7s on alloy wheels, a five-speed 'box and a limited slip diff. Contrary to rumours, there is no jacuzzi in the back, but the engine is fuel injected. To finish it off, there is a pair of discreet stripes down the side, and special badges: 280 they say. Ford reckons it'll do 130mph, and accelerate to 60mph in 7.9secs. If you want one, it'll cost you £11,999, and if you want to go faster there's a dealer option of a Turbo Technics blower kit which should do the trick.

It seemed an awful long time between that day in Cologne and the day last week when I picked it up. I parked it — illegally — in pole position outside the office, dead

chuffed. All and sundry came to have a look at it, admire it — and it *is* admirable. I'm going to take her out for a nice day in the country, and pamper her, and look after her. After all, it's not every day I'm given The Last Capri . . .

SPECIFICATION

FORD CAPRI 280

ENGINE
Longways, front, rear-wheel drive. Head/block cast iron/cast iron; 6 cylinders in 60deg V, bored block, 4 main bearings. Water cooled, viscous fan.
Bore 93mm (3.7ins), **stroke** 68.5mm (2.7ins), **capacity** 2792cc (170 cu ins).
Valve gear 2ohv, 2 valves per cylinder, chain camshaft drive. **Compression ratio** 9.2 to 1. Breakerless ignition, Bosch K-Jetronic injection.
Max power 160bhp (PS-DIN) (117.5kW ISO) at 5700rpm. **Max torque** 162lb ft at 4300rpm.

TRANSMISSION
5-speed manual, single plate, diaphragm spring clutch.

Gear	Ratio	mph/1000rpm
Top	0.825	25.66
4th	1.00	21.17
3rd	1.26	16.80
2nd	1.81	11.69
1st	2.36	8.97

Final drive: Hypoid bevel, ratio 3.09.

SUSPENSION
Front, independent, MacPherson struts, coil springs, telescopic dampers, anti-roll bar.
Rear, live axle, semi-elliptic single leaf springs, telescopic dampers, anti-roll bar.

STEERING
Rack and pinion, power assistance. Steering wheel diameter 14ins, 3.3 turns lock-to-lock.

BRAKES
Dual circuits, split front/rear. **Front** 10.3ins (262mm) dia discs. **Rear** 9ins (229mm) dia drums. Vacuum servo. Handbrake, centre lever acting on rear drums.

WHEELS
Aluminium alloy, 7ins rims. 195/50VR15 tyres,

DIMENSIONS, WEIGHTS
Length 171.4s (4352mm)
Width 67ins (1702mm)
Height 51ins (1295mm)
Wheelbase 101ins (2565mm)
Track F/R 53/54.5ins (1345/1384mm)
Weight 2623lb (1190kg)

PERFORMANCE (claimed)

	Manual
Top speed	130mph
0-60mph	7.9secs

FUEL CONSUMPTION
Urban/constant 56mph/constant 75mph 18.7/38.2/30.1mpg

PRICE

Basic	£9631.30
Special Car Tax	£802.61
VAT	£1565.09
Total (in GB)	£11,999.00

EQUIPMENT

Automatic	N/A
Five-speed	●
Power steering	●
Electric windows	N/A
Sunroof	●
Tinted glass	●
Central locking	N/A
Radio/cassette	●

● Standard N/A Not applicable

CLASSIC
PROFILE

THE CAR YOU ALWAYS PROMISED YOURSELF?

Sports car, touring car, muscle car or pose car? More than almost any other car,
the Capri – which has just ceased production – can be all things to all men.
Mike McCarthy, Jeremy Walton and Martin Buckley pay their respects

The Ford Capri was as much a child of its time as the MG TC, the Healey 3000, the Mini-Cooper or the VW Golf GTi today. It represents something quite specific to the seventies, and no car can sum up the GT 2+2 brigade of that decade so accurately. Europe had not seen its like before it arrived, and the chances are it won't see it again.

It was also a unique machine in the Ford family history, a one-off break from their usual line-up of worthy family saloons. There have been Lotus-Cortinas, and today there are Sierra-Cosworths, but they all retained the parent saloon car body: the Capri didn't. And we'll dismiss the Consul Capri instantly: it was an under-powered, rather disastrous styling exercise, no more. The Capris – or the majority of them – had muscle to match their looks.

To put it into context in 1987 is difficult. To some (they usually drive Peugeot 205GTis), it is 'medallion man' personified, to others a rather gruff but solid and rapid fast tourer, to yet more the last expression of the muscle car and sod all the little multi-valved, multi-cammed, turbo-blown tin boxes. Its current image is everything from a show-off's delight to a 'real' sports car. The thing about the Capri, of course, is that it actually *is* all of these things. In Mk1 1.3-litre form it was a poseur's slob-wagon: in RS3100 form – or, indeed in 2.8 injected form – it was a traditional, hairy, fast machine. Its image enveloped all shades of opinion.

It was, of course, born in the heady days of the performance-orientated sixties. Fuel was plentiful, the Yanks were going flat out for more and more power, the sporty image exactly suited the swinging sixties. The idea for the Capri came from across the Atlantic. The Mustang, Lee Iacocca's brainchild, the

'personal' car, aimed at the expanding youth market, had been a wild-fire success. Would not a similar machine, transposed to Britain, do the same?

It was. In the first four-and-a-half years, it sold a million.

Of course there was nothing new in the concept of the GT 2+2 – the MGB GT had been around a few years before the Capri appeared – but where the Capri scored was in the variety of models available, to suit all pockets. And, like the BGT, the Capri used proven mechanicals from production machines dressed up in pretty clothes. But the BGT was trad Brit, the Capri was a touch trans-Atlantic.

Where the MG suffered from a severe lack of cash flow in the development department (even a six- and an eight-cylinder engine didn't do much for sales) Ford made no such mistakes with the Capri. Where improvements could be made, on a proper financial basis of course, they were. It wasn't long before the Capri lost its 'tarted-up two-door Cortina' image and emerged as a potent GT in its own right. A comprehensive racing programme raised its persona, and a succession of bigger and/or more powerful engines ensured a road performance – for those who wanted it – commensurate with its track record, though the purchasing majority tended to stick to the 1.6- and 2-litre versions as an acceptable compromise between show and go. The suspension also came in for steady refinement, so on the road the 1986 Capri is a very different animal to the 1969 version, but they're still sisters under the skin.

The life of the Capri, and all its variants, is documented elsewhere, but it doesn't tell the full story of the soul of the car. It was born in a fairly fun time, but the crises of the mid-seventies buffeted

sales hard: from a peak production of nearly 240,000 in 1970, sales had dropped to just over 100,000 in 1975. Most manufacturers would have lost heart, but even 100,000 cars a year are worth making if they sell, and the smooth re-skin of the Mk II in 1974 gave the car new impetus.

Sales didn't climb, but the slide slowed somewhat, and there was a less frivolous air to the Capri. Mini skirts and flower power ties were out, more sober styles prevailed, and again the Capri caught the mood well. The hatchback helped practicality too, but the boot space was not enormous.

The minor revisions to the Mk III's looks too gave it a more up-market, more executive feel: the more sporting characteristics of the Mk I had evolved with added practicality in the Mk III.

Today, the Capri is no more. I was on the line in the Cologne factory that afternoon in December last year as the 1,886,647th car rolled off the assembly line. There was a brief ceremony to mark the occasion, but the only journalists there were a group from Britain: in its declining years it was sold only in this country. I think we're a sentimental old lot at heart, and the Capri held – and holds – a special place in our hearts.

So just what is the Capri's enduring appeal to us Brits? A form of style, a good solid honesty, a track pedigree, plus the typical Ford attributes of reliability and build quality, all help. We also at times tend to be stubborn, while nostalgia is a national characteristic. I suspect these two last factors made the Capri special. It was stubborn in its refusal to die, and was one of the last of the traditional, front-engined, rear-wheel driven GTs made. The Capri is dead: long live the Capri.

The last of the line, the 280. This was one of a limited edition of 1038 which were finished in 'Brooklands Green'

Above: The Capri Mk II S came in a very smart black and gold colour scheme. Right: A strong feature of the Capri Mk II was the opening rear hatchback

Left; 'The car you always promised yourself' – the Mk I Capri. Getting four kids in the back would have been a squeeze, though. Below; some people did funny things to Capris, so Liam Churchill's Dragster was appropriately a 'funny car'. Bottom; probably the best road Capri was the homologation special RS3100

Above; the road Capri with the most visual impact had to be the Mk III 3.0 with 'X' pack. Those wide flared arches covered fat 205/60 Pirelli P7s, and triple Webers and big valves gave 175bhp and performance to match looks. Left; the incredible 1978 Zakspeed turbo – 460bhp from 1.4 litres ... Below; the works Capris dominated Group 2 racing in 1971 and 1972, but by 1973 (as here at Silverstone) the 'Batmobile' BMWs had appeared

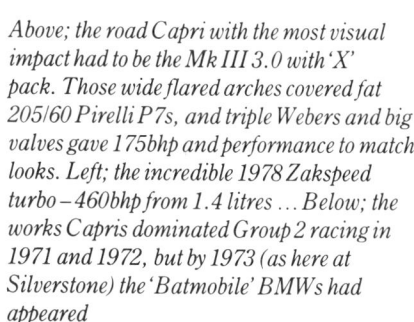

DRIVING IMPRESSIONS

Over the years I've driven a number of Capris, most of them being of the V6 variety. Memories of the early fours are limited to the amount of black vinyl inside – very fashionable that was – and chrome bits all over the facia and instruments. Performance was of the saloon/coupé variety – all right but not wildly exciting, handling ditto. All in all, they were acceptable if nothing more.

As the Capri aged, though, it took on a stronger personality, while the bigger engines gave it the grunt to go with its appearance. I think dynamically the best of the bunch had to be the 3-litre with four-speed 'box: a combination of torque, torque and more torque turned it into a veritable dragster in a straight line, while the gradual increase in tyre width gave it better sticking properties in the corners.

The arrival of the 2.8i introduced refinement into the engine department, but that torque was missing: the five-speed 'box made matters worse, and you tended to row it along on the gear lever.

The last one I drove was one of the last as well, a 280. It's a totally different kettle of fish from the first, brash machines: to call it refined is going too far, for there is considerable roar from the fat Pirellis, wind noise isn't as suppressed as on more modern cars, while the engine – especially on full throttle – gives off a distinctive exhaust bark. This, fortunately, is one of the most pleasant sounds I can think of, so it more than compensates for all the other, less desirable, ructions.

Ride, too, is not a Capri forté: at low speeds, it's as if you're driving over a succession of ripples, although big potholes and road humps are actually absorbed very well. Other complaints are levelled at the interior: those eye-ball vents look positively ancient, while the instruments suffer from reflections off the glass, and the minor ones are hidden from view down deep holes.

But dynamically it is superb. There is none of that frantic front-end scrabble you get with modern front-wheel drive performance cars (not surprisingly), nor some of the tippy-toe skittishness you find with some of the independently sprung machines – BMW, for example. On the other hand there is a live back axle and leaf springs, so road manners are of the good old-fashioned variety: boot it too hard and round comes the tail. In the wet, round comes the tail very rapidly indeed. However, if you like this sort of thing – and, frankly, it is more fun – you'll love it. In fact, a Capri on full throttle in a medium speed corner, controlling the tail on the throttle, has to be one of the pleasures of life.

Compared to those original machines, the fit and trim inside is much more subdued, but far more opulent: the whole car now exudes quality, and is a real pleasure in which to travel.

Just think, a collectable classic which also makes everyday motoring fun. **Mike McCarthy**

BUYER'S SPOT CHECK

The Capri belongs to a previous generation of mass-production Fords and it's a simple car almost to the point of crudity. Every aspect of the evergreen coupé is familiar territory to garages and body-shops up and down the country and most of the problems that develop are simply those of contemporary Escorts, Cortinas and Granadas.

The first thing to consider is the bodywork (1 – see cutaway drawing). In this respect the Capri is no worse off than any other mass-market machine and it just needs to be checked thoroughly and logically. MkI Capris corrode in the same places as later models, but it's becoming quite hard to find one of the original-shape Capris in sound condition.

The front wings go first and should be checked for filler around the headlamps and along the edges nearest the doors. Rust on the outer sills (2) is not always evident so it's important to check the inner structure by pressing firmly on the section covered.

PRODUCTION HISTORY

July 1962-64: Birth and death of II7E Consul Capri coupé. A total of 7573 cars constructed.

Nov/Dec 1964: First drawings of new Capri, coded 'Colt', compiled.

Jun/Nov 1966: Cortina-based 'glassback' prototypes running; £20 million assigned by Ford of Britain to develop 'Colt' (Capri name adopted by November 1967).

October 1967: Body style finalised.

November 1968: Capri production starts at Cologne and at Halewood. Initial UK range: 1300, 1300GT, 1600, 1600GT (using In-line engines). Initial German range: Various from 1300 to 2000 (using Vee engines).

January 1969: European Capri debut at the Brussels Show.

February 1969: UK sales debut. Prices from £890 7s 1d; February 8 – Roger Clark wins 'World of Sport' TV Rallycross in Capri 3000GT 4WD prototype.

March 1969: Capri 2000GT UK sale debut. Priced from £1088; Cologne-entered GT Capris debut on Lyons Charbonnieres Rallye, finishing 4th and 7th. Also this month the Crayford Eliminator (Zodiac six-cylinder power) and Exterminator (5-litre Ford Windsor power) conversions announced, exclusively for Spanish market. 31 made in all.

September 1969: Capri 3000GT UK sales debut. Priced at £1427 12s 8d.

March 1970: 3000E announced for the UK, and 'injection' RS2600 shown at Geneva Motor Show; works Capris contest Safari Rally (Ret'd) and European Championship races; the 2.4-litre Weslake-Ford 2300GTs are 2nd at Monza and Budapest.

April 1970: 275,000 Capris made to date; USA debut (Capri sells over 500,000 units until 1977 Federal death. Name subsequently used by Mercury).

September 1970: RS2600 (first European 'injection' Ford) production begins; UK 1300 and 1600 range updated with more power, brake servos and improved lighting.

April 1971: First European Championship race win – RS2600 at Salzburg. This season sees Capri RS win European, German and Springbok titles; 4WDs take British Castrol TV Rallycross series.

September 1971: First Capri special edition (on 2000GT base).

October 1971: Crayford Convertible, to be called the Caprice, shown at Earls Court – around 30 would be made. UK 3000GT/E receives uprated V6 engine giving 120mph.

June 1972: 3000GT-style power bulge for smaller GTs; two of three Capris entered at Le Mans finish 10th and 11th.

September 1972: Following 3000E demise in July, complete range receives re-vamp: bigger front and rear lamps (quad on new 3000GXL), and modified suspension. Range: 1300L (4cyl, OHV); 1600XL/GT (4cyl, SOHC); 2000GT (V4); 3000GXL/GT (V6).

October 1972: German range (including RS2600) receives equivalent modifications; Racing RS2600s have won European, German, Belgian and Finnish Ice Racing titles, and all but one European Championship round (including a 1-2-3 finish at the Spa 24 hrs).

August 1973: The millionth Capri, an RS2600, is made in Germany.

November 1973: Official end of Capri RS3100 (sold into 1974).

December 1973: Capri two-door production ends.

February 1974: Capri II launch; UK range: 1300L (4 cyl, OHV), 1600L/XL/GT (4 cyl, SOHC), 2000 GT/Ghia (4 cyl, SOHC), 3000GT/Ghia (V6). Prices from £1731 to £3109.

Apr/Aug 1974: Race Cosworth, 24-valve RS3100 debut at Salzburg (Ret'd). First win in August at Zandvoort; Tom Walkinshaw wins UK Championship class in Capri 3-litre (2-dr). (Capri II and III carry on tradition until 1980 with Gordon Spice.)

June 1975: UK receives Capri 'Midnight/JPS' specials. Priced at £2330.

September 1975: All GTs are offered in black (1600, 2000, 3000S); 'XL' re-named 'GL' (1600, 2000); A 1300 available as 'base' or 'L'; Ghias receive internal door mirror adjustment facility; 3000 Ghia gains power steering as standard.

November 1975: Last Works RS3100 outing Kyalami (Ret'd).

October 1976: Halewood Capri production stops after 337,491 units; USA exports fall.

August 1977: USA model production stops after 513,449 units.

March 1978: Capri III debut. Has better aerodynamics, different lighting front and rear, and has longer service intervals. Range: 1300 (4cyl, OHV), 1600L/GL/S (4cyl, SOHC), 2000GL/S (4cyl, SOHC), 3000S/Ghia (V6).

July 1979: Zakspeed 1.4-litre (380bhp) Capri turbo race debut. (No finishes in 1978!) Spice wins Spa 24hrs.

July 1978: Martin brothers (3000S) win Spa 24hrs.

September 1979: Hans Heyer class winner and second overall in German Championship (1.4 turbo).

October 1980: 'GL' gains 5.5ins steel wheels; 'S' gains 6.0ins steel wheels (optional on Ghia).

January 1981: Recaro seats and new trim for standard 'S'.

July 1981: Right-hand drive 2.8 injection released after March 1981 Geneva Motor Show debut. Available with twin-tone paintwork. Priced around £8000. 2.8i is the most powerful of production Capris: 2.8i – 160bhp; RS2600 – 150bhp; RS3100 – 148bhp. UK receives 1.6-litre Calypso and 1.3-litre Cameo special editions.

September 1981: Klaus Ludwig (Zakspeed turbo) is outright German Race Champion.

May 1982: UK receives special edition Capri Cabaret.

October 1982: Aston Martin Tickford Capri 2.8 is previewed. Available from 1983 to 1987 with 200 bhp (IHI turbo equipped).

January 1983: 2.8i receives five-speed gearbox. Soon for 2.0-litre cars also. Special edition Cabaret II offered in 1.6-litre and 2.0-litre specifications.

June 1984: Special edition Laser Capris debut in 1.6-litre and 2.0-litre specifications.

October 1984: 2.8i special edition launched with part leather trim, limited slip differential, RS spoked alloy wheels. Priced at £9500. Only this model and Laser Capris now available in the UK; Six year anti-corrosion warranty offered.

November 1984: Left-hand drive Capri production stops at Cologne.

June 1985: Capri 2.8i production racers finish 1st, 3rd, 4th, 5th and 8th at the Snetterton 24hrs. Also announced this year's BTRDA Rally Championship winner.

May/July 1986: Turbo Technics 200bhp road car available through Ford dealers. Debut at Donington SMMT day (May), Ford confirmation (July).

Jun/Nov 1986: 2.8i models finish 2nd, 3rd and 4th at Snetterton 24hrs. Finish Lombard RAC Rally, 32nd.

December 19 1986: Official last production date. Last of 1038 Capri 280 Specials roll off the line finishing the Capri's 18 year production run of 1,886,647 units.

by carpet inside the car. Capri doors are long and heavy and tend to drop, so see how the doors shut and check the hinge pins for excessive play (3). Have a look for rot on the A-posts that support the doors and, on the doors themselves, check the bottom edge and the normally unseen underside. Bonnets rust on the inside edge and on the MkIII just adjacent to the grille finisher. Rot developing around the MacPherson strut mounts inside the engine compartment (4) seems almost inevitable on most older Fords so it's good to know that the Capri isn't so badly affected in this area, though it's still worth checking.

The tailgate on MkII and MkIII cars often shows signs of rust along the inner bottom edge (5) and the gas dampers that hold the hatch up tend to weaken after a few years; the Capri Owners Club recommend Sierra XR4i replacements.

Only really poor Capris show advanced floorpan rot but don't forget to check the front and rear leaf spring hanger mountings, which can get into a dangerous state on older cars (6).

Restoring Capri bodywork is just as straightforward as it is on any Ford; the front wings are the bolt-on type for a start and none of the other panels present any special problems. All panels are available for the MkIII through Ford and many items for the older cars too, although MkI bits are becoming scarce. The annual Ford autojumble, organised by the Capri Owners Club, brings all kinds of MkI panels to light and at a third of new prices.

Mechanically, Capris are basically very sound. The 3-litre Essex V6 is under-stressed but does have a problem with the hexagonal shaft that drives the oil pump from the distributor skew gears. Cold start-ups – when the oil is thick and the oil pump is thus reluctant to turn – often cause the shaft to fail with subsequent and disastrous loss of oil pressure. Naturally, it is impossible to tell if the oil pump drive is worn when fitted to the engine, but if it shows any discernible wear when the unit is stripped, replace it. The other things to remember are the fibre camshaft timing gears which live under the engine's front cover. These threaten to disintegrate after 30,000 miles or so and it would probably be a good (if expensive) idea to replace them with steel timing gears at about £200 a go. Head gasket problems are not unknown on the 3-litre engine (and sometimes even warped heads) so it might be advisable to do a compression test; look for a figure of 120psi per cylinder on a good unit.

The 2.8-litre injection Cologne V6 effectively cured any problems the 3-litre Essex had, so it's just a question of looking for general signs of wear and tear in the form of excessive tappet noise and smokiness. It's worth mentioning, however, that there were a few early reports of injection system

failure caused by corroded wiring.

The 1600 and 2000 ohc Pinto engines used in many Capris have a well-known problem with camshaft noise (caused by a lack of oil changes) although, if you're lucky, it may just be a case of adjusting the valve clearances. With the cam cover removed, the cam is visible and if it shows wear on the lobes then both the camshaft and cam followers have to be replaced. This isn't a major expense with a mass-production unit like the Pinto and DIY kits for the job are available quite cheaply, although they vary in quality. But whatever happens, get the camshaft replaced as soon as possible if you are using the car, or you will end up forking out for a completely new engine. Otherwise the Pinto has few vices, but look out for excessive blue exhaust smoke (high mileage cars burn a fair bit of oil) and a leaky water pump.

There are no mechanical spares problems for any of the Capris – what you can't get from Ford is readily available from breakers' yards

The Ford variable venturi carburettor fitted to many of these cars is a dead loss; the automatic choke begins to play up after a few thousand miles, making the car hard to start, its idling uneven and early morning acceleration hesitant. Many owners have fitted Webers with manual chokes.

V4 Capris are rare now and not particularly pleasant. Blown head gaskets are the main problem here but otherwise just look for general signs of wear. Much the same applies to the Kent engines, which are very reliable indeed, but watch out for oil seepage from the head joint (a new gasket will be required) and listen for a noisy camshaft and valves.

On all manual gearboxes, look for wear on second gear, a sloppy change quality and noisy bearings (8).

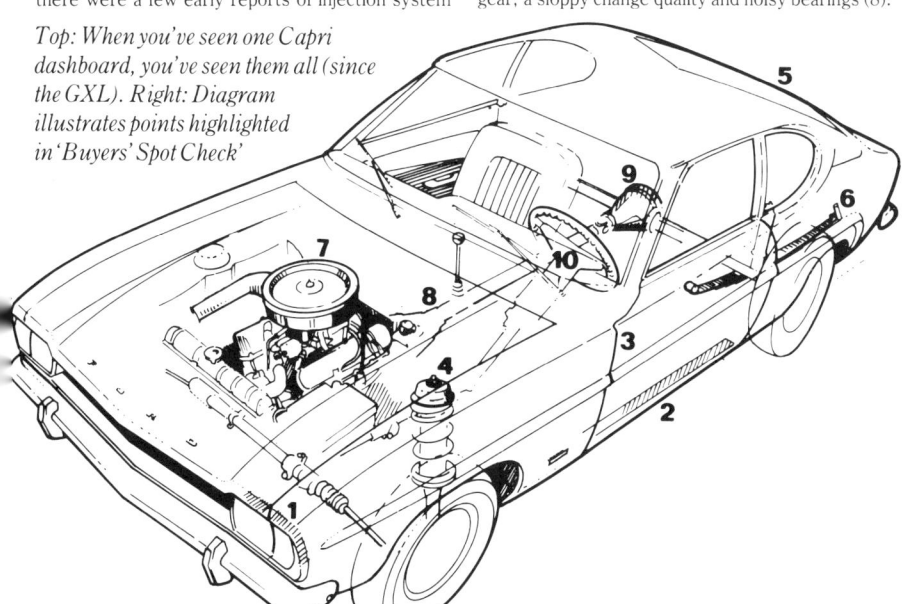

Top: When you've seen one Capri dashboard, you've seen them all (since the GXL). Right: Diagram illustrates points highlighted in 'Buyers' Spot Check'

CLUBS

Capri Owners Club International: Only club catering solely for Capri owners. Monthly magazine, 17 local branches, 2000 members, technical advice, special offers, national meeting at Knebworth on August 8/9. Contact Nigel Powell, Capri Owners Club International, Field House, Redditch, Worcs B98 0AN (tel: 0527 502066).

Ford RS Owners Club: Club for all 'hot' Escort owners plus RS 2600/3100 Capris. Bimonthly magazine, parts discounts, insurance scheme, technical advice service. Contact J. Le Clainche, 80 Reepham, Orton Brimbles, Peterborough PE2 0TT.

Ford AVO Owners Club: For all AVO-built Fords. Formed 1980, approximately 650 members, over 30 RS3100s registered, bimonthly magazine, help finding, spares and accessories. Contact Peter Williams, 67 Rolls Park Avenue, Chingford, London E4.

SPECIALISTS

Rally Equipe, Bolton Street, Bury, Lancashire (tel: 061 761 1178).
SE Specialised Engines, Monorway Industrial Estate, Grays, Essex (tel: 0375 378606).
Burton Performance Centre Ltd, 623/631 Eastern Avenue, Ilford, Essex (tel: 01 554 2281).
Withers of Winsford (RS Parts), Wharton Road, Winsford, Cheshire (tel: 06065 4422).
Brooklyn, Battens Drive, Redditch, Worcestershre (tel: 0527 21212).

There aren't any Capri specialists as such, just a handful of companies selling performance/handling components and providing tuning services. The 1200 UK Ford dealers can supply anything for MKIII Capris and many items for earlier models.

BOOKS

Capri – Development and Competition History by Jeremy Walton (Haynes) £7.95. Very thorough and detailed account of Capri's history on road and track, just revised.
Sporting Fords Volume 3: Capris by Jeremy Walton (MRP Collectors Guide) £8.95. Entertaining look at UK and German Capri developments from earliest designs to 2.8 injection. With competition history and brief buyers' guide.
Capri Muscle Cars (Brooklands Books) £6.50. Usual collection of reprinted articles from various sources, covering wide range of tuned Capris.

ACKNOWLEDGEMENTS

We are grateful to John Hill of the Capri Owners Club International for his help in compiling this feature.

The lever could jump out of gear on the over-run. Test for diff problems by jabbing the throttle on and off while moving in second gear, and then listening for any clonks of protest from the back end (9). In the steering department, simply check for free play at the steering wheel (10), and see if the steering rack bellows are ripped. There are no problems with the front suspension; do the usual bounce test on the dampers and check the wheel bearings by rocking the wheel top to bottom with the car off the ground. A front suspension vibration on the 2.8 means that a disc is warped.

At the back, worn leaf springs sometimes cause the car to sag to one side and the leaves could be cracked in places. On the braking side, judder indicates a warped disc but there are few other problems with the system, although it's worth noting that 3-litre automatics go through pads very quickly.

There are no mechanical spares problems for any of the Capris because what you can't get from Ford is readily available from local breakers' yards.

Capri interiors aren't particularly well-made and the wire frame of the driver's seat could be showing through on tatty cars. Wet carpets in the rear footwells are caused by poor rear door seals which become compressed at the rear corner and allow water in over the sills. Interior trim availability is one of the biggest problems for an older Capri owner because Ford stopped stocking trim for the MkI and MkII long ago.

SPECIFICATION	MKI CAPRI 3000GT	CAPRI 2.8 INJECTION
Engine	V6	V6
Construction	Iron block and heads	Iron block and heads
Bore/stroke	93.7 × 74.2mm	93 × 68.5mm
Capacity	2994cc	2792cc
Valves	Pushrod ohv	Pushrod ohv
Compression ratio	8.9:1	9.2:1
Fuel system	Single, twin choke Weber 40 DFAV carburettor	Bosch K-Jetronic fuel injection
Power	128bhp (DIN) at 5200rpm	150bhp (DIN) at 5700rpm
Torque	173lbs ft (SAE) at 3000rpm	162lbs ft (DIN) at 4300rpm
Transmission	Four-speed manual or three-speed automatic	Four or five-speed manuals
Brakes	9.6ins discs front, 9ins drums rear, with servo	Vented 10.3ins discs front, 9ins drums rear, with servo
Suspension front	MacPherson struts, telescopic dampers, anti-roll bar	MacPherson struts, telescopic dampers, anti-roll bar
Suspension rear	Live axle, semi-elliptic leaf springs, two radius arms, telescopic dampers	Live axle, semi-elliptic leaf springs, anti-roll bar
Steering	Rack and pinion	Rack and pinion
Wheels/tyres	5J × 13ins wheels, 185-13 radial tyres	7J × 13 alloy wheels, 205/60 low-profile tyres
DIMENSIONS		
Length	13ft 11ins	14ft 2.9ins
Width	5ft 4.8ins	5ft 6.9ins
Height	4ft 2.7ins	4ft 3.1ins

OWNER'S VIEW

Costas Constantinou is your average Ford Capri owner, as Richard Sutton found out

The trouble with Ford Capris is that, when it comes to interviewing their typical owners in the hope they will have fascinating tales of Capri love and hate to tell, they invariably have nothing to say. Because Ford Capris are as cheap and easy to run as All Bran with prunes, and as predictable as salmonella from service station sausages.

In fact, an *Owner's View* of any Ford Capri would be a veritable lullaby if it wasn't for the V6-engined versions. For the V6 Capri rapidly developed into a real cult car in this country, and particularly among the suburban sprawls of North London. Here the night-time Capri boys have been keeping the police on their toes for nigh on a decade. And there is no man better to recall such halcyon days as one Costas Constantinou of Palmers Green N13 – Capri performance guru, instigator of North London street racing as once was, and owner of the fastest Capris south of Cockfosters.

Costas, or 'Cos' to his friends and the Constabulary, has owned "definitely going on for 40 Capris" to date and that little lot includes no less than 10 desirable RS3100s. In fact, he's owned more RS3100s than anyone else. Of course, he's not really the ideal person to talk to about the costs of servicing or the rate of brake pad wear on your average Capri, but he can say a thing or two about making your Capri more spritely ...

Mr Constantinou speaks in an unfamiliar jargon to we advocators of the lost age of romantic motoring. He talks of "Stage 1,2,3 and 4 engine conversions" and of "the hottest cams you can get". He respects the Holley carburettor, the single leaf spring and the ventilated disc brake as if they were esteemed members of the family. He worships Horsepower, and swears by the wizardry of Nitrous Oxide.

Quite simply, Cos Constantinou is a Ford Capri '~ase' whose enthusiasm stems from the V6 '~sophy of unrivalled performance, fun and / the money.

"What else is there?" he pleads with me, only too eager to learn of a cure to his Dagenham disorder ... I proposed the American alternative. What with all that power and axle tramp he'd surely feel at home.

"Nope – I don't like left-hand drives", came the blunt reply. I suggested Opel Mantas, Toyota Celicas, Vauxhall Firenzas.

"Now you've insulted me!" he choked. "They've only got four cylinders. Those extra two pots make all the difference ..."

Costa's 24-hour preoccupation with owning the fastest Capri in the district is nothing new. He bought his first Capri – a 3000GXL – when he was 17 years old, the same month he passed his driving test. Insurance "wangled" on his father's policy, he

Cos has owned "definitely going on for 40 Capris" to date, including 10 of the desirable RS3100s

was soon out-running all his mates, and before he knew it the North Circular Road performance race was on.

The GXL was replaced after a year with a 3000E, but the E's luxuries (steel sunroof, cloth upholstery, blah) soon lost their appeal as an RS3100 became financially possible. It took 10 months of 'doing up' nine GXLs before Cos got his first 3.1. With it he "was a wild man".

Now Costa's tales of Friday night road racing along the fabled Pinkham's Way against Escorts with V6s in and Kawasaki 1300s (among other things)

unfortunately won't impress those *C&S* readers who think 'car lengths' are statistics used for gauging 'garagability'.

"I always made sure," recalled a nostalgic Cos, "that I could beat anyone by 15 to 20 car lengths. Only once did I lose by 'a half' with one of my RSs, but I took the next day off work, spent £430 on performance parts from Burtons, and beat the xxxxx that night." And I don't think that Cos's recollections of Saturday cruising and racing from Chelsea to Heathrow will rouse much enthusiasm among our Morris 8 readership either. Suffice to say that Costas Constantinou's Capris got faster, and faster, and faster, and that the North London Capri-owning fraternity grew at a proportional pace. Cos:

"The trouble was, that I soon got to the stage, when the RS3.1s weren't feeling fast any more, even with the Stage 4 engine. Then I heard about a guy with a 5-litre Ford Windsor V8 in his Capri, so I had to buy it." That "ridiculous" machine was soon sold to Cos's chip shop-owning partner and mechanicing mate Peter Panayiotou though, when Cos heard about another V8-engined Capri with a 5.7-litre Boss Mustang engine in. Built by Superspeed at a cost of £15,000 in the mid seventies for an Arab Prince, it had to be the ultimate roadable Capri.

"It got to the stage when Pete and I used to sit in the chip shop worrying about the 5.7. We knew it was out there somewhere. You see, we had our customers to think of (they all had Capris) – we had a reputation to keep up."

Needless to say, the 380bhp Boss Mustang Capri was found and bought – "£3900 for a Mk1 Capri! Can you imagine that?" – and its engine was developed further to boost its output to well over 450bhp, before a nitous oxide kit was bolted on, adding another 280bhp, according to the instructions ...

"It was the fastest thing on the road – just incredible", boasts Cos, who is now firmly convinced that V8-powered Capris are the only Capris to have. And having been out in the 5.7 car on the day I visited the Constantinou household, I'm inclined to agree ...

I left Palmers Green that day amazed and refreshed from meeting such an enthusiast, and one who has motoring in no perspective at all. But Costas isn't that blinded by Capris, although he's never really owned anything else. Even Capris are not without fault. He said to me over a civilised breakfast of scrambled egg and jam:

"You know Richard, the trouble with the V6s is, that they just can't take the stick ..."